A BRIEF HISTORY OF THE WESTERN WORLD

*the text of this book is printed
on 100% recycled paper*

EVERYDAY HANDBOOKS

A BRIEF HISTORY

OF THE

WESTERN WORLD

Second Edition

STEWART C. EASTON

BARNES & NOBLE BOOKS

A DIVISION OF HARPER & ROW, PUBLISHERS

New York, Evanston, San Francisco, London

Manufactured in the United States of America

to Elena

without whose help and encouragement
this book could not have been written

TABLE OF CONTENTS

MAPS

A BRIEF HISTORY OF THE WESTERN WORLD

INTRODUCTION—WHAT IS THE "WESTERN WORLD"?

Western civilization, to which most readers of this book probably belong, is the creation of the men and women who succeeded to the inheritance of the Greeks and Romans in the fifth century A.D. But no civilization is an entirely new creation; all are dependent upon the achievement of their forebears, and many pioneers of a new civilization are the actual physical descendants of the last representatives of the civilization that they supplanted. Much of the Greek heritage was in turn inherited by the Romans, and the Greeks themselves were one of the most gifted peoples of the Roman Empire. Similarly, some of the Teutonic barbarians who came into the possession of former Roman lands from the fourth century onward, desired nothing better than to maintain as much as they could of the advanced institutions of Rome, while keeping their old tribal allegiances and the manners to which they were accustomed. Nevertheless, comparatively little survived from Roman times. The Teutonic element predominated in all the Western countries, and the new civilization which we call "Western" is a distinctive achievement—the work of the peoples the Romans called barbarian, grafted upon a base provided by the "classical civilization" of the Greeks and Romans.

In Eastern Europe, less of the Greco-Roman heritage was lost. The civilization that we call Byzantine, from Byzantium, the old name of its capital, Constantinople, used Roman law and much of the Roman governmental administrative system; and the people, oddly enough, called themselves Romans, even though they were in fact Greek. Some scholars and historians regard Byzantine civilization as separate from "Western civilization." In this book, however, we prefer to treat Byzantium as one of the successor states of Rome, and its own successor, Russia, as a part also of Western civilization. The book, therefore, treats in a broad sense the history of Europe and of the American continent. It regards Western civilization as, to a large degree, a single civilization, in which many component parts may be distinguished.

1

Greece and Rome were themselves not original civilizations. The Greeks were closely affiliated with the much older Aegean civilization based on Crete, and Crete itself took much from Egypt. Moreover, one extremely important aspect of Western civilization, its dominant religion, was inherited from an Asian people, the Hebrews; and the Hebrews themselves emerged from a Mesopotamian background, by which they were greatly influenced—as they also were by the ancient Persians who ruled the land of Israel for two centuries. We shall therefore deal with the ancient Egyptians, Mesopotamians, Persians, and other peoples of Western Asia in the early part of this book; but we shall not consider in detail the later history of these peoples, nor the history of India and the Far East. Interesting and important as this history is, it must of necessity be excluded from this book. We shall confine ourselves here to a discussion of non-Western peoples only when their history impinges on that of the West, as, for instance, when the early Muslims conquered Spain and North Africa and threatened Constantinople. We shall again deal with Asia and Africa when, in modern times, Western civilization began to expand into these areas, imposing upon them many Western institutions and inventions, and, to some degree, the Western sense of values. Today the rest of the world is in the process of accepting and transforming very much that it has received, willingly or unwillingly, from the West.

Thus, the book becomes, as its title states, a brief history of the Western world. On this history we have tried to be as comprehensive as possible, having regard to limitations of space. The book is intended primarily for the general reader and can be read as a whole in a few days. It is hoped that it will serve to fill in the gaps in historical knowledge from which we all suffer and that it may prove a lasting work of reference for those who want to know the essential facts of Western history in their context and in relation to other historical events that accompanied them.

CHAPTER I

PREHISTORY

It is the custom of historians to distinguish history from what came before history, largely on the basis of whether or not we possess written records in a language which we have been able to decipher. Even so, the distinction is rather an arbitrary one. The ancient peoples of Central America, for example, are usually classed in the West as prehistoric, even though in fact both the Mayas and Aztecs had a written language which is now deciphered, and historians are usually content to leave their history to the anthropologists, one of whose specialties is the study of early cultures. By convention, which we admit to be arbitrary, we consider prehistory as the preliterate stage of man, and very little attention will be given to it in this book.

Man is now generally believed to have roamed the earth for hundreds of thousands of years. But only in the last fifty thousand or so has the type of human being whom we know today been in existence, and from such men have we descended. The other types of man, known as *anthropoi,* with some prefix (protoanthropoi, paleoanthropoi, and so on), became extinct, possibly destroyed by the representatives or ancestors of the more advanced human type whom we please to call *Homo sapiens* ("man of intelligence").

THE EARLIEST MEN

We know very little indeed about the first beings whom we can call really human. We are, indeed, wholly dependent for our knowledge on random finds of their fossilized skeletons and of tools which are discovered in the same deposits and are therefore presumed to have been used by these men. Archaeologists have acquired some experience in guessing where it is best to look for these fossils, and the attention of many of the most distinguished among them has recently been devoted to Africa, until a few years ago a little-explored continent. Several of the African finds may prove to be older than

3

the most important fossils of Asia, *Pithecanthropus erectus* (Java Man, found in 1891) and *Sinanthropus pekinensis* (Peking Man, found in 1929). Both of these fossil men are believed to date from about 500,000 B.C. But there is at present no known method of dating exactly any fossils as ancient as these. The method of dating by calculating the radioactive carbon content of the bones, a modern technique which is fairly accurate for comparatively recent material, fails altogether for such distant periods in the past.

Several hundred thousand years later Neanderthal Man and his relatives the Neanderthaloids took possession of much of the known earth, and lived on it until perhaps as recently as 100,000 B.C. or even later. He was then replaced by the first *Homo sapiens* of whose existence we can be quite certain—others are claimed on various grounds and with various degrees of probability for much earlier epochs— the type of man, called Cro-Magnon, whose skeletons in all essential respects are similar to our own. The cultural achievements of Cro-Magnon men are so striking that culture periods have been assigned to their work, which included the magnificent cave paintings of Lascaux in southern France, Altamira in northern Spain, and other places. All the peoples hitherto mentioned used some form of tools, except perhaps Java Man, of whom too little is still known, and fire was probably used as early as Peking Man. The movements of glaciers, with the consequent changes of climate, may be assumed to have kept most of these men wandering from place to place in search of the wild plants and animals on which they subsisted. Sometimes they lived in caves, and sometimes on the surface of the earth. These people are therefore classified as "food gatherers." It was the transition from food gathering to food growing that makes the first, and without doubt still the greatest, cultural change in the history of mankind, since it made all subsequent history possible. In a very real sense the nomad food gatherer has no history. Life proceeds in much the same way from day to day. There is little leisure, for such men have to win their subsistence every day anew; they are dependent on the presence of plants and game in their immediate environment, and over this they have no control. If the plants are consumed and the animals move away, they are compelled to follow them or find new ones. Primitive man, therefore, had not yet begun to shape his own destiny. This was made possible only when he discovered he could *control* the growth of plants and could domesticate animals and use them either for work or for food. Then at last he could settle down in one place, and make use, controlled use, of what he had been provided with by nature.

THE NEOLITHIC REVOLUTION

Historians and anthropologists recognize the existence of a period called the Mesolithic, sandwiched between the Paleolithic (Old Stone Age—so called because the men used only stone tools) and the Neolithic, when the agricultural revolution of which we have been speaking took place. During this intermediate period the stone tools were greatly improved and the first animals, especially the dog, were domesticated. But it was not until about 5000 B.C., or perhaps a millennium or so earlier, that somewhere in western Asia a great genius and human benefactor discovered that if a seed was planted in the ground by conscious intelligence, then a plant would grow where the seed had been planted. Although we are ignorant as to how this news was spread, we may safely assume that other peoples learned about the discovery or remade it for themselves. The discovery created a veritable revolution, usually called the Neolithic Revolution, and before very many years had passed we find the first beginnings of established villages, whose inhabitants lived a settled life, cultivating their fields from year to year and staying in the same place, usually one much favored by nature, with an easily accessible source of water and a fertile soil.

The farmer and husbandman do not have to work every day in the year. There are periods when all they can do is wait for the seeds to ripen. Then they and their families can turn to other pursuits and employ their inventive and artistic talents to provide for themselves small luxuries impossible before. Thus, pottery arose in the early centuries of the Neolithic Revolution and before very long men had learned to beat copper and use it for some of their implements and utensils. This was a considerable achievement, but much greater was the invention of bronze, an alloy of tin and copper which does not of course appear in nature. We can only speculate on how it was ever discovered that tin ore contained a useful metal since, unlike copper, it does not present the appearance of a metal. Moreover, the metallurgical technique of smelting had to be invented before bronze could be produced.

The advances of the Neolithic Revolution did not spread to western Europe until long after they were in use in western Asia. Nor did they, as far as is known, spread to the New World, which had its own separate "Neolithic Revolution," cultivated plants having been dated as early as 2500 B.C. by the radioactive carbon method. The European peoples developed their stone techniques, however, to such an·extent that they were able to erect huge monuments of stone for religious purposes without the use of any metal implements. Such outdoor "temples" as Carnac in France and Stonehenge in England are remarkable examples of the "megalithic" (Great Stone) culture of these countries. Meanwhile, the island of Crete in the Mediterranean became the center of a culture based on bronze at least as early as 3000 B.C., as we shall see in a later chapter.

Almost nothing is known for certain of the manner of life and the beliefs of early preliterate peoples. It is possible at the most to make inferences from the existence of such monuments as Stonehenge and Carnac, and from the contents of paleolithic and neolithic graves. It seems clear that the stone temples were in some manner connected with sun-worship, even though we have no actual knowledge of the cult. It is less certain that the burial of corpses in unnatural positions and the presence of valuable tools and ornaments in the graves imply any belief in immortality, as has sometimes been urged. Undoubtedly there was some ritual connected with the dead, but there is no real reason to suppose that the dead man was expected to use the possessions in the hereafter. Most of such inferences have been derived from our knowledge of present day so-called primitive and preliterate men, whose ceremonial and religious practices are indeed, as we can discover from questioning them, based upon such beliefs. But the historian is not justified in projecting this knowledge back into the remote past without emphasizing that we do not know anything for certain except the material facts that have been uncovered by archeologists.

We are therefore brought once again to the point where this chapter began, with the statement that preliterate man had no history. History is the *recorded* statement of events. We know what the Egyptians believed because they have recorded it in their writings, but we can tell little of even the life, and nothing of the beliefs, of the artistic Cro-Magnon men, who created the cave paintings—though it is clear that some religious beliefs were involved. All information on the ceremonial practices of more ancient peoples is entirely conjectural. History proper, therefore, begins with the written records of the peoples of western Asia and the Egyptians, to whose achievements the next chapter will be devoted.

CHAPTER II

THE EARLIEST CIVILIZATIONS

The Neolithic Revolution probably occurred in Egypt during the sixth millennium B.C., but most of the very early history of Egypt is still shrouded in obscurity. Part of the valley of the Nile River, on whose waters Egypt has always been dependent for prosperity, was gradually cultivated during the following millenniums. But planned irrigation was not known until the union of Upper and Lower Egypt, and the beginning of the so-called dynastic period. The people lived in oval mud huts, and in later years also in houses made of mud bricks. Some of Egypt's finest pottery was made in predynastic times, though without the use of the potter's wheel. Toward the end of the period Egypt entered the Copper Age and developed a fairly extensive export trade, making use of the Nile as the highway of commerce. Many different tribes inhabited the country, but gradually local chieftains extended their rule over wider areas, laying the basis for the unification of Upper and Lower Egypt under a single monarch, which was the great achievement of the earliest dynasties.

EGYPT

The Old Kingdom. Egyptian history, properly so called, begins with what has come to be termed the First Dynasty, although there is much uncertainty as to exactly when the First Dynasty reigned and whether or not it really was the first family of monarchs to rule over the country. Modern scholars are inclined to push the First Dynasty further back into the past than tradition has placed it. Tradition itself stems from the work of a late Egyptian priest who calculated the number of dynasties on the basis of the information available to him, which was in fact less than is now available to us. The Egyptians were a people not inclined to be interested in the details of the historical past for reasons that will appear; and though they kept records of the deeds of the various Pharaohs, albeit unsystematically, they do not appear to have cared greatly which particular Pharaohs were responsible for which particular deeds. To them the deeds were performed by the divine monarchy, and thus indirectly by the upper gods themselves, who worked through all the monarchs equally. These beliefs have presented often insuperable difficulties to all later historians.

About 3000 B.C., Upper (that is southern) and Lower Egypt were united by a monarch whom the Greeks called Menes, who reigned over the whole country from his Lower Egyptian capital of Memphis. It has been found impossible to equate this Menes for certain with any particular Egyptian monarch who appears in the king lists. Let us therefore just call him Menes (though he may have been A-ha, Narmer, or another). The deed of unification itself was of crucial importance for Egypt, since the centralized monarchy became for the Egyptians the ideal form of government, to which men looked back in later times when the country was divided or ruled by alien conquerors and which they always wished to restore. Indeed, it was considered not only the ideal but a perfect form of government, the only one desired by the gods for Egypt; and it came to be believed that the Pharaoh himself was a god, administering the land of Egypt by divine right, owner of the entire land, subject to no restraints save those entailed by his divine responsibility. The upper gods, whom he would rejoin after death, made disclosures to him through his heart, and what he spoke and decreed had behind it all the authority of his divine mentors.

Thus began what is called the Old Kingdom, a period of some eight hundred years during which six dynasties occupied the throne, and the land was in general prosperous, and Egypt the undoubted leader of the world in all civilized arts. All the characteristic forms of Egyptian art were developed in these years, especially during the great Fourth Dynasty (the Pyramid Age). From the Third Dynasty onward these huge monumental tombs were built by each Pharaoh to house his mortal remains; even though they were extremely costly, they served the purpose of employing the labor of the people during the period when the Nile was flooded, as well as glorifying the god who sat on the Egyptian throne. A complex theology was developed around the god Ptah who had created the earth by the might of his word; and hieroglyphic (picture) writing was brought to a peak of perfection, together with hieratic (a cursive form of hieroglyphic). Even the common writing of the people, the demotic, came into use. The land of Egypt was free from invaders, and the Nile was harnessed to man's use by the organizing genius of the

Pharaohs and their servants; and the servants themselves were buried close to the Pharaoh in death, so that they might partake of his immortality and continue to serve him in the hereafter.

The long reign of Pepi II of the Sixth Dynasty brought this "golden age" of Egyptian history to an end. The centralized monarchy began to lose its grip on the *nomes* or provinces of Egypt, and governors began to arrogate to themselves the powers of the monarch in their areas. The borders of Egypt were evidently left insufficiently guarded; and we hear of foreigners penetrating unbidden into the land. A strange revolution, Egyptian style, occurred. The Pharaohs from the Seventh through the Eleventh Dynasties ruled effectively only a small part of their realm. They changed their capital to Heracleopolis, in the center of their country, the north and south having thrown off their allegiance. The land, in the words of a prophet and courtier, "spins like a potter's wheel"; the great lady had now only a plank to sleep on, the laundry woman took possession of her mistress's bedchamber. No one seemed to be happy about the change, as far as can be ascertained from the records. *Ma'at*, the divine order of the universe, had disappeared from the land. The order, which had been believed as unchanging as the constant procession of the seasons, had gone, and only chaos took its place. The feeble Pharaohs in Heracleopolis even doubted their own divinity. They had been unable to repel the invaders; and though foreigners do not seem to have actually ruled over any substantial areas in Egypt, there can be little doubt that the extensive organization, especially the management of the Nile, that had been the work of the centralized monarchy and justified its absolutism, fell into disrepair, and the entire land and people suffered from it. Poets and minstrels looked at the great pyramids and marvelled that their ancestors had been able to build them, but they no longer comprehended their purpose. The Old Kingdom had passed into history, a golden age that would never be restored, though always looked back to with awe and wonder by the peoples who succeeded to its inheritance.

The Middle Kingdom. Late in the Eleventh Dynasty a prince from Thebes in Upper Egypt launched a program of reunification by conquest, and by about 2000 B.C. his successor, Amenenhat I, ruled Upper and Lower Egypt. Thus began the age of full Egyptian maturity, the period known as the Middle Kingdom. The kingdom was united once more, Ma'at had been restored to the land, and the evil memory of chaos and anarchy had been obliterated. But many changes had taken place. Prosperity returned, but it is doubtful if the authority of the Pharaoh was as great as before. Nobles had ruled their nomes during the Intermediate Period from 2200 to 2000 B.C.; hence they were of more importance in the land than they had been in the Old Kingdom. Most significantly the Pharaohs themselves, though still regarded as gods and given divine honors by the people, made a serious effort to establish social justice in the land. (Only one seems to have attempted a pyramid.) The majesty of the Old Kingdom Pharaohs was less stressed in royal statues; now they were depicted as compassionate, even suffering, men. The shepherd's crook becomes a favorite symbol among the hieroglyphs describing the Pharaoh's names and titles. A great necropolis at Abydos housed the earthly remains of great numbers of the Pharaoh's subjects, of high or low degree. It is significant that the nobles sought lavish burials for themselves and that into their coffins were placed texts hitherto preserved for their royal master, texts that had been intended to help the dead Pharaoh in his journey in the afterworld. The ordinary man did not aspire to such dignities until the New Kingdom, but the Middle Kingdom already marked the beginning of what the American Egyptologist James Breasted has called the "democratization of the hereafter."

In the minor arts and crafts, especially jewelry, the Egyptians always excelled; but the work of the Middle Kingdom is in many respects the best that Egypt ever produced. Even though during the imperial period of the New Kingdom there was a greater demand for such goods and thus a far greater supply, and the resulting products were more elaborate and more richly ornamented, the design and workmanship of the Middle Kingdom were not surpassed. Indeed, so great was the artistic conservatism of ancient Egypt that it was common for the New Kingdom merely to use the Middle Kingdom styles and elaborate them to conform to contemporary taste for luxury.

The rulers of the Middle Kingdom belonged to only one dynasty, the Twelfth, which survived for some two hundred years, and then appears to have collapsed about 1800 B.C. for reasons which are as yet not fully known. As at the end of the Old Kingdom, it seems likely that the centralized government lost its grip. The frontiers were insufficiently guarded, and infiltration of foreigners over the Egyptian borders once more became possible. This time the result was a series of invasions by people the Egyptians merely called foreigners (*hikau khasut*), a word which has been corrupted into Hyksos (at one time incorrectly called the Shepherd Kings). They brought with them the light war chariot, perfected by the Hittites and thereafter used by the Egyptians in their own wars. The Hyksos never ruled effectively the whole of Upper and Lower Egypt, but their leaders were powerful enough to win the title of Pharaoh for themselves. Ruling, as in the Old Kingdom, from the Delta, they were able to compel an acknowledgment at least of their suzerainty even from the princes of Thebes in Upper Egypt. From the Thirteenth to the Seventeenth Dynasty the Pharaohs belonged to the Hyksos. Then once more a prince of Thebes (Ahmose I) threw off the foreign yoke and began the great Eighteenth Dynasty which ushered in the period known as the New Kingdom (1580 B.C.).

The New Kingdom. The Pharaohs of the new dynasty, for the first time in Egyptian history, were greatly concerned with military security. The Hyksos had retired only into Syria and Palestine and continued to present a threat to Egypt. Ahmose and his successors made several campaigns into Syria which met with success. But it was not before nearly a century had passed that the Egyptians became true imperialists in our sense of the word. Indeed, there is evidence to show that there was considerable difference of opinion among the royal princes and Pharaohs as to the advisability of planned expansion. Queen Hatshepsut (1486–1468 B.C.), was an exponent of the anti-imperialist viewpoint, preferring to utilize the resources of her country in peaceful expansion of trade, combined with the building of temples, public buildings, palaces, and obelisks. Hatshepsut's stepson and nephew Thutmose III, who was for some years coruler with her, obviously nursed other ambitions, which he had to suppress during her lifetime. As soon as she died he entered upon a career of conquest in western Asia which won Syria for him as far as the river Euphrates.

Although his successors enjoyed the fruits of his work and for a time maintained and exploited the empire, they added little to it. As early as the reign of Akhenaton (Amenhotep IV) (1377–1360 B.C.), there were grumblings from the provincial governors that they lacked adequate reinforcements and this unwarlike monarch was indeed far more interested in accomplishing his religious revolution than in keeping his frontiers intact. From his reign onward the empire was on the defensive, and in spite of some ephemeral military successes, it never recovered the position it had held in the time of Thutmose

III. Rameses II (1301–1234 B.C.) of the Nineteenth Dynasty signed a treaty with the Hittites in Syria and Asia Minor, which he represented as a victory; it was the first written treaty known to history. But in fact Rameses conceded much, retaining only a part of Palestine and leaving all the northern territories of Thutmose to his enemies. Rameses III (1195–1164 B.C.) repelled a dangerous invasion by the "peoples of the sea" and recovered a part of Palestine lost by his immediate predecessors. But by his death there was little of the empire left, and the throne of Egypt soon fell to foreigners and leaders of mercenary armies. Indeed, only for brief periods thereafter was there a native Egyptian on the throne. Assyria under Esarhaddon conquered the country about 670 B.C., and held it for a few years until expelled by Greek mercenaries. The Persians under Cambyses conquered it again in 525 B.C. and held it, at least nominally, until it fell without a struggle into the hands of Alexander the Great in 330 B.C. Alexander's leading general, Ptolemy I, Soter, captured the throne, and his successors sat upon it until Cleopatra, the last of the line, was defeated by Octavianus Caesar, who as the emperor Augustus incorporated Egypt within the Roman Empire.

Results of the Conquests. The conquests of Thutmose III and the establishment of an Egyptian empire had many important consequences. The power and prestige of the Pharaoh were greatly enhanced. He was once again the all-powerful god who owned the land of Egypt as his personal estate, the supreme fount of power and justice, in comparison with whom all other men, Egyptians and foreigners alike, were but puny mortals incapable of resisting him or questioning his will. Egyptian art of the period always therefore depicts the Pharaoh as of gigantic size and his enemies as feeble creatures, doomed to be slaughtered by the invincible royal arms. The monarch himself owed his victories to the imperial god of Thebes, Amon-Re, whose priesthood became powerful in proportion to his victories and successes. A great deal of the land of Egypt, as well as much foreign spoil, was donated by the Pharaoh to Amon-Re and was of course administered by the priesthood as its own.

The isolation of Egypt was broken, once and for all, by the conquests. Captives and booty flowed into the country, and these captives were put to work by the conquerors as slaves. The result was the depression of the economic status of the free-born Egyptian, while the nobles profited. In other words the Egyptian empire is a classic case of the rich growing richer while the poor grew poorer.

A result of this appears to have been the increasing preoccupation of all classes, but especially the poor who could ill afford it, with the hereafter. They were anxious to have the burial ceremonies that alone could ensure that it would be a blessed one and not one subject to the same disabilities as the earthly life they no longer enjoyed. The priests of Osiris, the popular religion, to be distinguished from the state religion of Amon-Re, supplied the needs of the people, who bought charms and spells to ward off the dangers of the beyond and to supply the proper answers to give to the judges of the afterworld. The *Book of the Dead* is primarily a collection of such charms and spells. This tendency continued throughout the whole period of the decline of the empire, so that Herodotus, the Greek historian, anthropologist, and traveler, was able to report that the Egyptians were the "most religious" of all peoples he had encountered.

The Religious Revolution of Akhenaton. One effort was made, which proved to be a transitory one, to take away the power that the priests had won during the expansion. The Pharaoh Amenhotep IV of the Eighteenth Dynasty claimed that he had received an inspiration from the divine sources open to him to the effect that the only true god was the Aton, the sun-disk. He therefore changed his name to Akhenaton ("he who is serviceable to the Aton") and built a new capital for the worship of the new god. But the Pharaoh was apparently unable to persuade any but his courtiers to follow him to the new city. He had arrayed against him all the forces of conservatism, the priesthood of Amon-Re, and no doubt the vast majority of the people who were uninterested in his innovations. Moreover, only Akhenaton himself had access to the Aton—the courtiers and people were expected to worship the Aton through him. Thus, though he still had enough power at his disposal to compel the temporary abandonment of the worship of Amon-Re and blot out his name from his statues and temples, his successors soon returned to the old worship, and the true converts must have been few indeed. Though the Aton worship was a monotheism of a kind, and was long hailed as such by historians who wished to see in it an anticipation of Hebrew monotheism, it should not be overlooked that hymns in the reigns of his predecessors show that Amon-Re was likewise beginning to be regarded as the god of the whole earth. Perhaps the most important result of the "religious revolution" of Akhenaton consists in the impulse toward naturalism in art, which no doubt stemmed from the Pharaoh's delight in nature and in the sun as the power behind nature. This naturalism never wholly disappeared from Egyptian art.

Decline of Egyptian Civilization. The visitor to Egypt cannot fail to be impressed by the monumental works of the New Kingdom, the great temples and palaces at Thebes, Luxor, and elsewhere, paid for by the imperial conquests, and he is likely to be impressed also by the great tombs of the nobles as well as of the Pharaohs. But by the Twentieth Dynasty economic conditions forbade the creation of any more such monuments, and there are even records of tomb-robbers who redistributed the wealth long locked up within the tombs and prevented from circulating. In the last years of Egyptian independence, as during the rule by foreigners, there was a constant tendency to look back to the past for inspiration. Many of the late Pharaohs meticulously copied the inscriptions of their ancestors, and antiquarians elaborated texts and art forms from the remote past. There is no escaping the fact that long before the end all creativity had left the civilization. But in its day it had been great and powerful. It left relatively little to other civilizations as a heritage. Its writing was adapted by the Phoenicians and other Canaanite peoples to form our alphabet. Its mathematical discoveries and practical knowledge of surveying were inherited by the Greeks. But almost none of its thought was taken over. Nevertheless, the civilization endured for more than two thousand years without substantial change and without major revolutions. If stability is a virtue, as we may well think in our rapidly changing days, the Egyptians achieved it beyond any other people in history. Only the Chinese could put forward a similar claim, but even the Chinese have been plagued by revolutions from which the Egyptians were spared.

MESOPOTAMIA

The Sumerian City-States. The Fertile Crescent is a term now conventionally used to cover the river valleys of the Tigris and the Euphrates and the fertile areas of Syria and Palestine. The entire crescent is bounded on the south by the Arabian desert. In the eastern sector of the crescent is the land known as Mesopotamia, roughly comprising the river valleys of the parallel great rivers, the Tigris and the Euphrates. To this area the Neolithic Revolution came early, and there are evidences of small cities (or large villages) dating back into the fifth millennium B.C. These cities appear to have been independent entities, self-governing and largely self-

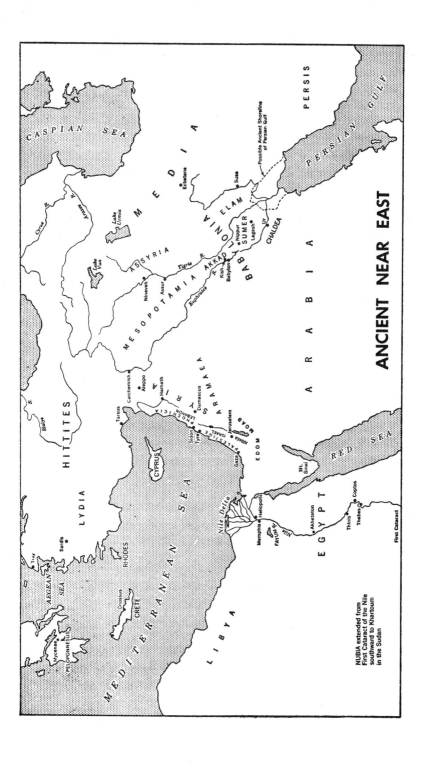

ANCIENT NEAR EAST

NUBIA extended from
First Cataract of the Nile
southward to Khartoum
in the Sudan

supporting. They were inhabited by a people who described themselves only as "the black-headed people," known to historians as Sumerians. The land in which they dwelt is usually called Sumer.

The origin of the Sumerians is unknown. They are generally believed to have penetrated to Mesopotamia from further east, but of the background of their remarkable cultural achievements we are totally ignorant. When they emerged into the light of history they already possessed a developed language and the cuneiform writing made with a stylus on clay, which was then baked to form a permanent record. The Sumerian religion and mythology were to become the basis for the religion and mythology of all the other peoples who lived in Mesopotamia until the Persian conquest. Though modified by these peoples, the Sumerian creation story, the myth of the Great Flood, the interest in divination to discover the will of the gods, the relations of the people with their gods, and the Sumerian law codes are all recognizably similar, whether the land was peopled by Babylonians, Assyrians, or late Chaldeans.

The earliest form of political organization to be found among the Sumerians is the temple community. In these communities all the land was theoretically owned by the god of the city, whose representative on earth was the *ensi,* or steward of the gods. In the larger communities there was no doubt also a professional priesthood, but it was the ensi whose task it was to discover the will of the gods and put it into effect. The ensi was thus in reality a priest-king, subordinate to no man on earth but held responsible by the city god for the welfare of his domain. The god, it was believed, manifested his wishes by various natural signs and by dreams which the ensi and his priesthood were expected to interpret. When more than one such temple community came under a single ruler, the latter became a *lugal* or king, with subordinate ensis under him. The true city-state into which the temple community developed was therefore usually under the rule of a lugal.

Early in the second half of the third millennium B.C. an Akkadian-speaking (Semitic) ruler named Sargon of Agade conquered the Sumerian city-states from the north, and established a short-lived Akkadian empire which extended into Syria to the west and Elam to the east. But his successors could not maintain the empire, though its existence had the effect of largely supplanting the ancient Sumerian language with Akkadian. Soon most of the city-states had recovered their virtual independence under the nominal suzerainty of a barbarian people called the Guti. It was during this period that all the city-states developed their separate but similar law codes which were later to be consolidated by the great Amorite ruler, Hammurabi, into the code that bears his name.

The Old Babylonian Empire. The Amorites were a desert Semitic people who conquered the whole of Mesopotamia about 2000 B.C. and consolidated the various city-states into what is known as the Old Babylonian Empire, ruled from the capital of Babylon. Hammurabi (*fl.* 1800 B.C.) was the sixth Amorite king. As part of his policy of unifying the administration of his empire, he promulgated his famous code, the first of the ancient law codes to become known to the West, though it was by no means the first of the Mesopotamian codes and in some respects, indeed, not as advanced as some of the earlier codes of the Sumerian city-states now known to us. The Hammurabi Code is a combination of primitive tribal practices and a number of enlightened provisions. The former have given the code the reputation of being based simply on the principle of an eye for an eye and a tooth for a tooth, carried to what moderns would regard as absurd extremes. But it is sometimes overlooked that the code also attempted to modify this principle and to replace the punishments hallowed by antiquity with fines and money compensation paid to the family of the aggrieved parties. Above all, it set the state up as the defender of the peace and the judge of quarrels which might lead to public disorder. It attempted to mitigate the lot of the man called out for military service and arranged for the proper performance of his obligations during his absence on campaign. It regulated the procedures for divorce and confirmed the interest of the state in the sanctity of commercial contracts. In short, it was an enlightened effort to put order and regularity into the affairs of the empire, and especially to bring all the divergent practices and laws of the old city-states into harmony with one another. It may have been an exaggeration when Hammurabi in the epilogue to his code claimed to be defending the cause of the widow and the orphan and ensuring that the strong could not oppress the weak. But at least it was a start in the right direction, and we know from the royal correspondence that Hammurabi took a personal interest in seeing to the enforcement of his code. He thereby succeeded in assuming, at least for his lifetime, a jurisdiction superior to all those local authorities who might have preferred to administer the customary laws of their areas.

The Assyrian Empire. Soon after Hammurabi's death the unified Babylonian Empire fell into the hands of another barbarian people, the Kassites, who added little to Babylonian civilization. For many centuries thereafter Mesopotamia ceased to be the center of Near Eastern civilization, this position falling to the Hittites of Asia Minor, who will be dealt with separately later. Only with the rise of the Assyrians to power and the extension of their empire over Mesopotamia, Palestine, and briefly over Egypt, in the first half of the first millennium B.C., did the peoples of the Tigris and Euphrates valleys again assume the leadership in the Near East. The Assyrians were a relatively small people from northern Mesopotamia who apparently decided to put an end to their state of chronic insecurity by specializing in militarism and establishing undisputed leadership themselves. Under a number of able rulers they built an army which was more than a match for their divided enemies. Nineveh became a great and rich capital, supported by the labor and resources of all the neighboring peoples. The written records purloined from subject peoples were preserved in the library of Nineveh, which remained undiscovered until the nineteenth century and have since provided us with the great bulk of our historical information about this period. The Assyrians organized their vast empire by methods which have been the model for all later imperialists. They built strategic roads to take messages from the monarchs to their outlying provinces; they visited immediate and brutal punishment upon all rebels; in order to keep sedition at a minimum they did not hesitate to exchange whole populations—including the population of the ten northern tribes of Israel. But in the end the Assyrians proved to have too few resources and too little manpower of their own to maintain their empire. When a coalition was organized against them by a Babylonian prince, and the coalition was willing to absorb the inevitable losses sustained by fighting against a technically superior army, the Assyrians were doomed. Late in the seventh century B.C. Nineveh fell to the coalition and soon afterward all Assyrian resistance collapsed. The coalition took exemplary vengeance on its oppressors, and the Assyrians disappeared as a people—a classic example of the dangers of militarism which has been celebrated by, among others, the Hebrews, who were their victims.

The New Babylonian or Chaldean Empire. The Assyrian Empire was partitioned, a revived Babylonian state inheriting the richest sectors. A much smaller but very prosperous empire, usually known as the New Babylonian, or Chaldean, Empire, was founded by Nebuchadnezzar, king of Babylon, who among other deeds deported the southern tribes of Israel to his capital, with incalculable consequences for the religious future of mankind. The kings of Nebuchadnezzar's line bequeathed little to posterity save a revived interest in astrology and, as a by-product, a considerable body of mathematical and astronomical lore, in addition to a rebuilt capital, which contained the "hanging gardens," one of the wonders of the ancient world. In 538 B.C. the city fell to a semibarbarian Indo-European people, the Persians, and their leader Cyrus. Cyrus also conquered all Asia Minor, and he and his successors won Palestine and Egypt.

Cultural Achievements of Mesopotamia. Before dealing with the new empire whose center was outside the Tigris and the Euphrates valleys, let us consider the specific achievements of the various civilizations of Mesopotamia. The unique achievement of writing must almost certainly be granted to the Sumerians. In addition they invented a positional mathematical system with special symbols, based on the number 60, which was in most respects superior to the system of using letters as numbers favored by the Greeks and Romans. The Sumerians or their successors divided the circle into 360 degrees, a system we inherited from them and still use today. The later Babylonians made extensive charts of the heavens and accumulated numerous observations of the stars which were inherited by the Greeks, who, with their aid, elaborated a theoretical astronomy. The most important religious perception of the Mesopotamian peoples was the idea that the deeds of men are of interest to the gods. The Mesopotamian gods were arbitrary, treating human beings as slaves who owed obedience to them but who were not worthy to be taken into their confidence. However, this same perception of a personal deity when developed by the Hebrews provided a possibility for a system of ethics based upon obedience to the commandments of God. It may be added that the weakness of Babylonian religion, from our point of view, lies in the fact that the presence of numerous gods made it impossible for even the most fervent of believers to know which god he had offended and what indeed was expected of him.

He might even be caught in the middle of a quarrel between competing gods who made different demands on him. Thus he could derive no consistent system of ethics from his religion.

Finally, the Babylonian law codes provided a model for the Hebrews and other later peoples and thus passed into the tradition of Western civilization. More important, however, than the details of the codes is the notion that law should be written and made known to all and should be administered by the judges in accordance with stated principles. This was a very different procedure from the Egyptian, under which the monarch was expected by the use of his divine power to "know" the right, and therefore administered a justice which we can only call personal. It follows that in Egypt there was no need for a written law code, and none, as far as is known, ever existed among the ancient Egyptians.

THE PERSIAN EMPIRE

The Persian Empire, stretching from the Aegean to the Indus, was the first of the great world empires to have any marked influence on Western civilization. Cyrus (550–530 b.c.), the Persian hero and conqueror, founder of the empire, was not himself a direct inheritor of the Assyrians. The Medes, a people that lived to the west of Persia, had formed part of the winning coalition and inherited the eastern section of the empire. Thereafter they extended their territories eastward and came at once into contact with the Persians. After some desultory warfare Cyrus the Persian won for himself the Median throne. Thereafter the two peoples appear to have amalgamated and in time to have become indistinguishable from one another. But the drive toward empire was supplied by Cyrus and his Persians, who also provided the new kingdom with its official religion, which will be considered later.

Cyrus died young, and though his son Cambyses conquered Egypt, it was Darius I, not a direct descendant of Cyrus, who fully organized the empire. He divided it into provinces under governors, or satraps. Each satrap was provided with two officials who were responsible not to the satrap but to the monarch and who were expected to keep the king informed, in particular, of any matters in which the satrap exceeded his authority. Darius also sent out inspectors, known as the "eyes and ears of the king," to oversee the provincial administration. For the security of the state Darius organized an elite force of ten thousand men known as the "Immortals" and a royal bodyguard, which because of an excellent system of roads, could be used to put down rebellions in the remote districts of the empire. The king could also command the services of local levies, as was done by Xerxes when he had to organize a major army for the proposed conquest of Greece. But these troops, being drawn from all parts of the empire and most of them unable to speak Persian, required considerable training before they could be used in battle. Hence the Persians preferred not to expand beyond their boundaries except on such extraordinary occasions as the expedition to Greece. The Greek territory of Thrace, however, was conquered by Darius and was incorporated within the empire as a satrapy.

The Persian Empire was probably the most humane, and one of the best governed, of ancient empires. The Great King, as the ruler was called, was primarily interested in receiving his taxes from the outlying provinces and interfered little with their local customs and religion. Although the Persians had a religion of their own, acknowledging a supreme god, Ahura-Mazda, as the lord of the universe, they did not as a rule interfere with the religion of their subjects. Marduk, the god of Babylon, was still revered by the Babylonians; and the Persian king supported the priesthood of Marduk, no doubt as a stabilizing influence in the empire. The king himself accepted the position traditional in Mesopotamia as the chief representative of the god on earth.

The religion of the Persians themselves, however, was far different, both in its theology and ethics, from that of their Mesopotamian subjects. This religion is usually called Zoroastrianism, after the name of a prophet of whom little is known, but who was probably a contemporary of Cyrus. The basis of the religion is clearly much older than this, however, since the Zend-Avesta, the holy book of the religion makes reference to very ancient times when an earlier prophet, apparently also named Zoroaster, brought agriculture to the Persians. According to Zoroastrian developed teaching there were two great gods of almost equal power in the universe, the god of light, Ahura-Mazda, and the god of darkness, Ahriman. The earth was a field of struggle between these two powers, and both gods strove for the possession of man's soul. Man could choose to ally himself with either light or darkness, good or evil. Both gods had their attendant hosts; the good man after death would be borne upward by the good angels for an afterlife of bliss, while the devils would take possession of the soul of the malefactor and bear him away to perdition. Thus, Zoroastrian ethics offered man a reward for good deeds on earth in the afterlife, and threatened him with punishment for evil deeds. This was the first religion of antiquity that we know to have consistently provided man with the expectation of reward or punishment after death in compensation for his deeds on earth. Although the belief was apparently held by some in Egypt (in the Middle Kingdom), in later times this system of compensation became confused with belief in the efficacy of charms and spells to ward off the perils of the afterlife, and proper religious observance took the place of ethical deeds as the means for attaining happiness in the hereafter. The Mesopotamian peoples never came to believe in anything more substantial about the afterlife than that men continued a shadowy existence in a kind of intermediate condition between life and death—a belief which corresponds to the Hebrew notion of Sheol, the only idea of an afterlife accepted by the Hebrews and Jews until after their sojourn in Babylon, where they perhaps became acquainted with the teachings of Zoroastrianism.

THE HITTITES

Little was known until very recent times about the Hittites (or, more correctly, Hattians), to whom reference has already been made as inheritors of much of the Egyptian empire in western Asia. Now that the Hittite cuneiform and some of the Hittite hieroglyphic inscriptions have been deciphered, much more information is available. From linguistic evidence it appears that they were an Indo-European and not a Semitic people. They descended upon Asia Minor and northern Syria from the north near the beginning of the second millennium B.C. By 1600 B.C. the Hittite king Mursilis I had built an empire, based on a confederation of former city-states and rivaling in size and power that of the contemporary empires of Egypt and Babylonia. This same king, in fact, captured Babylon itself, but he was unable to retain it. Toward the end of the sixteenth century B.C. the Hittite crown became hereditary and the monarch for the first time in the ancient world, as far as we know, allowed himself to be judged, and in certain cases deposed, by his own nobles. The council of nobles by accepting the king legitimized his authority. The Hittite monarch was neither himself considered divine, as in Egypt, nor the chosen representative of the gods on earth, as in Mesopotamia. In other words, the Hittite monarchy was a secular one. In the same reign as part of what we may call a court reform the laws of the separate states were codified and became binding on the whole empire.

After the death of Telipinus, the founder of the constitutional monarchy, the empire was forced to contract through the pressure of various migratory peoples, possibly including the Hyksos who have already been noted as conquerors of Egypt. The Mitannians to the east proved especially dangerous but were soundly defeated by the Hittite monarch, the greatest of all Hittite kings, Suppiluliumas I (1375–1335 B.C.), who extended the empire deep into Syria at the expense of the Egyptians and allied himself by marriage with several of his neighbors. The widowed queen of Egypt attempted to win one of the sons of Suppiluliumas as her husband, with the offer to seat him on the throne of Egypt—evidence as to the extent of Hittite prestige at this period. But the scheme was foiled by Egyptian courtiers. Not until Rameses II became Pharaoh of Egypt did the Egyptian monarchs attempt to recover their lost empire in Syria. But in the Battle of Kadesh Rameses was heavily defeated by the Hittite Muwatallis (1306–1282 B.C.), and only with difficulty was he able to extricate himself from the trap into which he had been drawn by his more competent and less reckless enemy. Thereafter, the Egyptians agreed to a sensible treaty, the earliest treaty of whose terms we have the full record, which endured for seventy years. The daughter of the Hittite monarch became the chief queen of Rameses.

But the empire which had been built up over several centuries suddenly collapsed at the end of the thirteenth century B.C., its capital was burned, and the confederation of city-states that had preceded the empire now also replaced it. This was apparently a part of the general disintegration of that period, a disintegration which saw the destruction of the Minoan empire of Crete by invaders from over the sea, and the bare survival of the Egyptian monarchy under Rameses III, after victories over men he called "the peoples of the sea."

The Hittites in older books of history are credited almost exclusively with the development of iron, and they used to be remembered for little else. In fact, the Hittites did develop iron, of which they had a virtual monopoly, though the invention itself may not have been theirs. But iron remained in very short supply (as it was in the time of the Greek *Iliad*), and was more expensive than either gold or silver. It was guarded as a monopoly, and the Hittite rulers refused to send even samples to the Egyptian monarchs who requested them. It is probable that the people that made the most extensive early use of iron, especially for weapons, were the same "peoples of the sea" who may have put an end to the Hittite empire. The Dorians certainly used it for the conquest of Greece and possibly of Crete. Also it has been recently discovered that the Dorian Spartans were skilled in the metallurgy of steel, and much of their military success may have been due to the excellent material of their weapons. The military instrument which the Hittites did indeed develop beyond their contemporaries was the light war chariot. To this may be attributed most of their victories. Not until the Assyrians was this type of chariot again to be put to such effective use in warfare.

The Hittites can be credited with little in the cultural field. Most of their gods were borrowed from others, and their art and architecture were derivative and unoriginal. But they had a well-developed political sense and were skilled in diplomacy; and as much as we know of their empire suggests that it was well administered and generally acceptable to the foreign peoples they ruled. Their law codes reflect some enlightenment and humanity, more clearly indeed than any developed by their contemporaries. The recent discoveries of Hittite history do not add much to our knowledge of the heritage of Western civilization; but they have filled in many important gaps in our knowledge of the second millennium B.C., and have breathed some life into the bare Biblical mentions of the Hittites. Surely the most famous of all Hittites until recently was that Uriah whose wife, Bathsheba, King David coveted and was willing to commit virtual murder to win. (II Samuel 11:1–27.)

COMMERCIAL PEOPLES OF WESTERN ASIA

The Lydians. The Lydians, like the Hittites a non-Semitic people, inhabited the western part of Asia Minor from some time probably in the second millennium B.C., and they may have inherited a part of the Hittite empire after its destruction. Lydia was a commercial state and is credited with the first coinage of money, made from electrum, a mixture of gold and silver found in one of the Lydian rivers. It was a secure and prosperous kingdom at the end of the eighth century B.C. Thereafter it expanded both to east and west, for a brief period ruling all Asia Minor to the Halys River. Croesus, the last and most powerful Lydian king, was a synonym for wealth among the Greeks. He also became a byword among them when he suddenly fell from power, a terrible example of how one may "call no man happy until his end has also been seen." For Croesus' wealthy capital of Sardis was captured and he himself made prisoner by Cyrus in 543 B.C. Cyrus took possession of all his territories, including the prosperous and cultured coastal cities in Asia Minor inhabited by Greeks, whom the Lydians had permitted full autonomy as long as they paid taxes. The Persians soon changed this policy, and embroiled themselves with the mainland Greeks across the Aegean, thus paving the way for the disastrous expedition of Xerxes which forever set limits on the Persian expansion to the west.

The Aramaeans. There remain the two commercial civilizations of the Aramaeans and the Phoenicians. These two peoples lived not by conquest but by peaceful trade and survived the conquerors who nominally incorporated them into their domains. The Aramaean people were probably descended from nomad desert tribes who eventually settled down in Syria, with their capital at Damascus. The Aramaean state provided a buffer between the Assyrians and the Israelites; and as long as it survived northern Israel was safe. But the conquering Assyrians conquered Damascus in 732 B.C., and soon afterward northern Israel suffered the same fate. Nevertheless, the Aramaeans survived the rule of Assyria and became the greatest land traders of western Asia, in the process developing the cuneiform alphabet used by the Chaldeans in their empire. The Aramaean language (Aramaic) became the most common language of western Asia, spreading far outside its country of origin. Jesus Christ spoke Aramaic, and the earliest versions of some of the New Testament documents are written in that language.

The Phoenicians. The Phoenicians settled in the coastal cities of Palestine and especially in the great ports of Tyre and Sidon. Having almost no hinterland, they took to the sea and for centuries were the leading sea traders of Europe and western Asia, succeeding to the inheritance of Minoan Crete. Their navies were powerful, and the seafaring city of Carthage in North Africa was one of their colonies. Some of them enlisted in the navies of Persia and provided most of the ships required by the Persian king, on several occasions having to fight on behalf of their employer against the Greeks. Others took service with the later Egyptian Pharaohs. The Phoenicians developed Tyrian purple, a dye produced by a shellfish of which they had for a long time a monopoly. Not until the conquest of Tyre by Alexander the Great, a conquest that had to be repeated by one of his successors, did Phoenician commerce decline, and even then Carthage carried on the maritime tradition of the mother country until she too was destroyed by the Romans.

The Phoenicians played an important part in the development of the Greek alphabet, although it is now known that other Canaanite peoples and the Cretans also had their share in it. The Phoenician alphabet, which was spread throughout most of western Asia and was adapted to their own use by the Greeks, has as its parent Egyptian hieroglyphic, which was not developed by the Egyptians themselves as far as the alphabet, though they did progress so far as to make the separate pictures represent syllables. The Phoenicians, of course, were also in close contact with the Hebrews, and it was the Phoenician Hiram, king of Tyre, who provided Solomon with the cedars necessary for the building of his temple, taking impressed Israelite labor in return. The Hebrews themselves, whose work might geographically be included in this chapter, will however be left for a separate chapter, in view of their incalculable importance for the history of Western civilization.

CHAPTER III

THE HEBREW CIVILIZATION
AND RELIGION

It is not generally recognized that the Hebrews virtually created the art of writing history. Previous peoples had written annals, but these were little but records of the deeds of the kings and often enough falsified to suit the royal purposes. The Hebrews, however, had the belief that history was meaningful, that no event took place without some purpose in it. The fact that they regarded this purpose as a part of God's purposes toward man, and particularly toward the Hebrews, his chosen people, in no way detracts from this achievement. All historians must select from the abundance of material at their disposal those particular events which they regard as significant.

The Hebrews did not regard the reigns of successful monarchs as necessarily important; on the contrary, it was often the least successful monarchs whose lives demonstrated a lesson which they considered important. Thus Ahab, king of Israel, who was far from being a successful monarch, has far more space devoted to him in the Old Testament than has his father Omri, who reigned long and successfully. This latter monarch, however, did "that which was evil in the sight of the Lord"; and his success, therefore, was contrary to what the Hebrews believed should have been the case. Ahab, who was no less evil than his father, came to a bad end, and therefore his premature demise could be made to point a moral. We ourselves in this age may or may not believe that Ahab's unfortunate end was due to his wickedness; but few historians would go so far as to suggest his wickedness as the sole, or even the most important, cause for this end. We are inclined to look for material causes, such as, for example, the poor training of Ahab's army, or the superior training and armament of the armies which he had to meet in battle. In like manner, when the Hebrews in the Seventy-eighth Psalm provided a brief history of the people since the Exodus from

Egypt, all the events were described from the point of view of God's pleasure or displeasure in the deeds of his people.

The Hebrew method, however out of accord with modern historical canons, was to have a great future. As recently as the seventeenth century Bishop Bossuet wrote a universal history for the benefit of the French monarch Louis XIV, in which he hardly deviated at all from the method of the ancient Hebrews. Throughout the Middle Ages Hebrew history was considered by Christians as the divinely inspired history of people they were inclined to regard as their own ancestors. All literate Christians in the Middle Ages were thoroughly familiar with the most obscure passages in Biblical history, even though they might know little of the history of their own time or that of the Greeks or Romans who preceded them. Whatever the defects of the Hebrew method, their history was at least meaningful, and they regarded no events as the result of pure chance. Nothing could be further from a Hebrew or an early Christian or medieval mind than to regard history simply as "a tale told by an idiot, signifying nothing."

For much of the period covered by Old Testament history we have few other sources available. Nevertheless, such of the history contained in it as we have been able to check conforms remarkably well to the records which we have secured from inscriptions and documents of contemporary peoples. Yet there are so many gaps that much must still be taken on the sole word of the Hebrew chroniclers. What follows, therefore, will be an account of Hebrew history as it was recorded by the Hebrews themselves in the Old Testament, though we shall make occasional references to passages in this history which are either confirmed or denied by the records of other peoples.

THE PATRIARCHS

Hebrew history, properly so called, begins with Abraham. Abraham, we are told, came from Ur of the Chaldees, which account suggests, probably perfectly correctly, that his ancestors came from Mesopotamia. Abraham was instructed by God to go to the land of Canaan and settle his family there. This he did, and for a long time he enjoyed much prosperity, though to his great sorrow he had only one child, who was the son of a bondwoman. Late in life, however, by divine dispensation his wife, who was already far advanced in age, gave birth to a son whom Abraham called Isaac. As a test of his faith God commanded Abraham to sacrifice Isaac. This Abraham was willing to do, but at the last moment God stayed his hand and thus preserved the life of his only legitimate son. This event was naturally regarded as extremely significant by the Hebrew chronicler, since the child Isaac had been born by a divine dispensation, and by a divine dispensation also he had been allowed to survive and grow to manhood. Thus Abraham, the ancestor of the whole Hebrew people, according to the Old Testament, had had his faith severely tested, and the entire people of Israel, the chosen people of God, would never have come into being had not God refused to accept the proffered sacrifice.

Isaac in due course grew up and had two children, Esau and Jacob. But divine favor rested upon Jacob rather than upon his elder brother, and he received the major portion of his father's inheritance. When Jacob was an old man a famine fell upon the land of Israel (Israel is another name for Jacob), and Jacob and his sons were compelled to go to Egypt, where there was plenty of grain. This grain had been stored at the suggestion of one of Jacob's sons, Joseph, who had been sold into bondage in Egypt by his jealous brothers when he was a very young man. Joseph now welcomed Jacob and his brothers, and the entire family settled down in Egypt and enjoyed the favor of the Pharaoh who had made Joseph his grand vizier.

Many generations passed, and a "Pharaoh arose who knew not Joseph." This new Pharaoh enslaved the Israelites and made them work on his great monuments. The oppressed Israelites found a leader in the person of Moses, a Hebrew who had been brought up in the Pharaoh's palace but who remembered his Hebrew ancestry. With great difficulty Moses was able to persuade the Pharaoh to let the Israelites return to the land of Canaan. Nevertheless, many of the Israelites were evidently far from dissatisfied in the land of Egypt, and it fell to Moses to organize them into a fighting force united in the worship of God. The "wanderings in the wilderness" occupied about forty years, and the people were not permitted to enter the land of Canaan until after Moses' death. During the sojourn in the wilderness Moses received directly from God tablets of stone on which were engraved God's Ten Commandments to His chosen people.

THE CONQUEST AND SETTLEMENT OF CANAAN

The land of Canaan was far from uninhabited when the band of Israelites invaded it. Some of the existing tribes were most certainly closely related to the Hebrews, and it is probable that some joined with them in subduing the entire country. Much of the country was indeed conquered, but to the west of the lands occupied by the Twelve Tribes (supposedly descended from the sons of Jacob) were the people known as the Philistines and to the northwest, the Phoenicians. The Philistines, in particular, gave great trouble to the Israelites, and various Hebrew heroes, especially the famous Samson, gained their reputations by destroying Philistine enemies. For the early centuries the Israelites were ruled by judges, who had both political and religious duties to perform. The last of these was the great prophet Samuel, whom the people petitioned for a king. Samuel was hesitant, but God finally allowed him to choose a king named Saul, who, however, was disobedient to God; he and his sons were killed in battle by the Philistines.

Meanwhile, Samuel, realizing that God would not allow Saul's sons to succeed him, asked him what was to be done. God then instructed Samuel to choose a stripling, named David, of the tribe of Judah, and David won his spurs by killing a Philistine giant, Goliath. For a time Saul was favorable to David and made him his armor-bearer, but soon he became jealous of him. To escape Saul's wrath, David was forced to go into exile, where he engaged in separate guerrilla warfare with the Philistines and continued to add to his reputation. When Saul died in battle David was proclaimed king and ruled for forty years in his new capital of Jerusalem. This was the height of the Hebrew kingdom. David was succeeded by Solomon, who overextended his resources both in building a temple and in trying to live like an Oriental monarch. One of the unfortunate policies that Solomon adopted in order to build his temple was to compel northern Israelites to perform unpaid labor for Hiram, king of Tyre. The result was that at the death of Solomon in 933 B.C. the northern tribes of Israel had a real grievance against the central monarchy in Jerusalem, and a rebellion was set on foot by Jeroboam (an Ephraimite and servant of Solomon), who, with Egyptian help, staged a secession and became the first king of Israel. The southern kingdom of Judah was never able to recover the ten tribes of northern Israel. Thereafter, the monarchies of Judah and Israel, as the northern kingdom was called, were separated.

DIVISION OF THE KINGDOM OF ISRAEL—THE EXILE AND RETURN

The northern kingdom was both richer and more dangerously exposed than the southern kingdom, which was poor and mountainous but far more easily defended from the north; and at this time most of the danger came from the north. The Aramaean kingdom of Syria was constantly dangerous, but of course even more dangerous were the Assyrians, who ultimately conquered the northern kingdom and deported much of the population, sending in other peoples from different parts of their territories. In 721 B.C., when Sargon, king of Assyria, captured Samaria, the history of the northern kingdom came to an end. Judah was more successful against the Assyrians. The Bible recounts the story of how the Assyrian host was stricken by plague and was unable to take the city of Jerusalem. The Assyrian records, however, tell a different story. It is true that the Assyrians did not capture Jerusalem, but the Assyrians claim that the kings of Judah paid them tribute. If this is true, then it would appear that the kings of Judah bought off the Assyrians, either at the time of the siege of Jerusalem, or later. Judah, indeed, was able to sit out the Assyrian rule, but the last kings entered into an unfortunate alliance with Egypt against the Chaldean Empire which succeeded the Assyrians. When Egypt proved "a broken reed," the Chaldeans took Jerusalem and deported many of Judah's leaders to Babylon.

In Babylon the priests and prophets who were in exile kept the people together and indeed purified their worship of God, since it was their view that Jerusalem had fallen because of the disobedience of the people to God's commands. When Cyrus captured Babylon, he allowed the Jews, as they may now be called, to return to Jerusalem, where they built a temple. Under Persian rule the Jews were granted substantial autonomy. But when Alexander the Great conquered all Palestine (in 332 B.C.) and the land was later ruled by his successors, the Greek rulers tried to make the Jews conform to many of their practices, regarding with distaste the Jewish belief in one god whose representation was never to be shown on earth. The Hellenizing policy of Antiochus Epiphanes met with considerable resistance from Jewish religious leaders, resulting in the revolt of the Maccabees in 168 B.C. The revolt ultimately proving successful, the Jews were permitted to live under their own form of government until the Roman Pompey conquered the entire Near East. Thereafter the Jews were ruled by a "client" of the Romans in the person of the Herod family. But this family was permitted ever less power, and the province of Judea became fully subject to the Romans. The Romans, however, recognizing the devotion of the Jewish people to their religion, did not insist that they should worship the Roman emperor. Nevertheless, there were many efforts on the part of the Jews to escape the Roman dominion altogether, culminating in a great revolt in 68 A.D. In spite of a stubborn defense Jerusalem fell to the arms of the Roman general Titus, son of the emperor, in 70 A.D. This was the end of Israelite independence and unity as a people until the foundation of the present state of Israel in 1948.

THE CONTRIBUTION OF HEBREW RELIGION
TO WESTERN CIVILIZATION

The Hebrews are usually credited with being the first to worship one god. Though it is true that the Hebrews were the most consistent monotheists in the ancient world, this in itself would not be such a great achievement. Many other religions, including the Egyptian religion, tended toward regarding one particular god as the lord of the universe. What is different about the Hebrew religion is the nature of the Hebrew god. At the beginning of Hebrew history, it would appear that the Hebrews were not informed that their god was the god of the whole universe, and in the earlier books of the Bible some recognition was given to the tribal gods of other nations. But in due course there can be no doubt that the Hebrews came to believe in one God as the sole true God of the universe, the creator of heaven and earth. This concept is at its most striking in the book of the prophet Isaiah. The Hebrew God was unique in that He *cared* about His people and whether they were wicked or righteous, and He punished and rewarded them according to their deeds. We have already noted that the many gods of the Mesopotamian peoples sometimes competed among themselves for the worship of the people and did not inform their worshipers what they required from them. The Hebrew God, on the contrary, gave His people the Ten Commandments, instructing them what they should not do; and throughout Hebrew history God revealed more of His will through His prophets. Thus it was possible to arrive at the concept of sin, as disobedience to God's commands, a concept not to be found among either the Greeks or the Mesopotamians, whose gods gave them no such clear commands.

The notion of sin as disobedience presented no difficulty. The difficulty arose only when attention was given to the question of punishment, which naturally accompanies the idea of sin. In the Ten Commandments it is explained that the sins of the father are to be visited upon the children. During the Exile the prophet Ezekiel took serious exception to this notion and propounded the contradictory thought that "when the wicked man turns away from his wickedness and does that which is lawful and right he shall save his soul alive." In other words, as Ezekiel explains, if a wicked man sees the light and turns from his evil ways he will be saved, whereas if he persists in his wickedness he will be damned. A righteous father may have a wicked son and vice versa, but each must suffer for his own sins. A further difficult question arose through the fact that until relatively late in their history the Jews did not believe in an afterlife of rewards and punishments. This meant that a wicked man would have to be punished in this life. Nevertheless, it was clear to all thinking men that wicked men are not always punished in this life, but sometimes flourish "like green bay trees." This, as the Seventy-third Psalm suggests, was a problem too great for the thinkers of Israel to solve. The Psalmist retreats into the sanctuary and perceives the latter end of the wicked. But there is no indication of what this latter end consists, nor where it is accomplished. Nor does the long book of Job, entirely devoted to the problem of why a righteous man suffers, offer any clearer solution, since God Himself, who appears at the end, in effect tells Job that His ways are past understanding.

Difficulties also arose when the history of the people of Israel was considered. Several Biblical stories suggest that the evil deeds of the king would be visited upon the entire people. When the kings, as sometimes happened, took to idolatry, often to satisfy their foreign wives, the people of Israel might expect to have punishment inflicted upon them. The question then arose as to why peoples, such as the Assyrians, who were evidently much more wicked in all respects than the Jews, should escape punishment and enjoy long periods of prosperity. Of course, if one waited long enough, the wicked people would probably receive their just deserts, but the waiting period was a severe test of faith. Although many answers are given in the course of the Old Testament to this problem, perhaps the most lasting answer was that the Jews alone had been the recipients of God's promises and therefore much more was expected of them than of the heathen who had never been informed directly of God's existence. There is, however, one book of the Bible (Jonah), which suggests that even the Assyrians were on one occasion informed of God's anger toward them and repented. Because God loved the Jews, they were chastened for their own good.

There is also the thought that the Jews were a special kind of scapegoat for the sins of all the rest of the world. This notion of vicarious suffering is implicit in some of the great prophecies of Isaiah, who pictures the people of Israel as God's Servant upon whom God has laid the "iniquity of us all." Christians, it may be said, have regarded these prophecies concerning the Servant as applicable solely to Jesus Christ, although it is not at all clear from the prophecies themselves that the picture of the suffering Servant was ever intended to apply to a particular person. Lastly, the late prophets told of a final return to Jerusalem, where there would be a great ingathering of the exiles. The people of Israel, now purified by suffering and their souls refined by the long period of testing, would dwell in Jerusalem, an example to the rest of the world. They would again be ruled by God's chosen servant. Believing these prophecies, the Jews who returned to Jerusalem after exile in Babylon were far more intent than before on keeping all the rituals and observances demanded by the Law, and the orthodox Jews continue to believe in this prophecy of the final Restoration. Zionism (which believes in the "ingathering of all Jews into one state," preferably in Palestine) is an outcome of this belief.

Hebrew monotheism was taken over by Islam in the same uncompromising form as it had been evolved by the Jews. Christians likewise accept the Hebrew God as God the Father in their religion. But since Jesus Christ was believed to be the Son of God and the Holy Spirit was sent (according to Catholic but not to Greek Orthodox thought) from the Father and the Son, Christianity holds that there is a Trinity, one God, but three Persons. Nevertheless the Hebrew concept of God in its essentials is that of almost all Christians; a loving, kind father who cares for His children, is just yet merciful, and has given men the opportunity to win salvation in the hereafter. The Old Testament of the Jews remains an essential part of the Christian Bible and is regarded as in no way less inspired than the New Testament, the specifically Christian scriptures. All Western civilization has been nourished by the Bible. Once it had been translated into the vernacular languages, it remained until very recently the most familiar of all books. Indeed, the translations have played a great part in shaping the Western languages, especially the English and German.

The Hebrews contributed little else to Western civilization. Their art was negligible, and their history unimportant in the history of the world. They were independent only for a few centuries, and cut no great figure among the empires contemporary with them. It was an extraordinary destiny that their religion and history should have become the heritage of the West, and that the Jewish people themselves should have survived as a people to this day, still unified by their religion. Perhaps the most important lesson that can be drawn from this destiny is that there is an enduring quality of great thoughts, great ideas, and great literature that is denied to all other achievements of men. It is for this reason that the Hebrews have been granted in this book a chapter to themselves.

CHAPTER IV

THE CIVILIZATION OF THE
ANCIENT GREEKS

The civilization of the Greeks begins properly with the island of Crete in the Mediterranean Sea, even though the mainland Greeks were not descended from the Cretans. We shall therefore first give attention to the Cretan civilization, sometimes known as Aegean civilization, since it was diffused throughout the Aegean islands and coastal lands.

CRETAN CIVILIZATION, PRECURSOR OF GREECE

Today the island of Crete is part of the Greek state, as it has been for centuries. But Cretan civilization long antedates the civilization of the mainland. As early as 3000 B.C. the Cretans were traders, and since at that time the Egyptians were not much interested in venturing beyond the delta of the Nile, the Cretans enjoyed most of their carrying trade. It was a Bronze Age civilization, and, indeed, the Cretans were leaders in bronze metallurgy. Over the course of not much less than two thousand years the Cretans expanded commercially into the Aegean, and offshoots of Cretan civilization appear to have colonized much of the coastal area of Asia Minor.

There were ups and downs in the prosperity of the island empire, and in the middle of the second millennium B.C. it appears to have reached the height of its prosperity. By that time barbarians were invading the mainland of Greece, and they adapted much from the Cretans. The latter, however, were content to enjoy their virtual commercial monopoly and made no attempt to conquer the mainland. On the contrary, they did not even take good care of their own defense. The mainland cities adopted a different policy and were far more warlike than the Cretans. Thus it was the former barbarians from the north who eventually took the initiative and attacked Crete itself about 1400 B.C. For the last two hundred years of Cretan civilization the former masters were controlled by relative barbarians from the mainland. About 1200 B.C. a new wave of barbarians, the Dorians, conquered Crete and destroyed the remnants of the civilization. The island of Crete has never been of great importance in Western civilization since that day.

Even today there is still very little known about Cretan civilization. Until very recently it was not possible to understand the Cretan script, and all our knowledge was based upon archeological investigations, especially those of Sir Arthur Evans beginning in the late nineteenth century. Cretan (or Minoan after the name of a great monarch Minos) art has been very extensively studied and classified into various "Minoan" periods. The archeological remains have revealed a good deal about the ordinary life of the Cretans, their interest in such sports as bull-leaping and their excellent houses with plumbing which is in many ways superior to any known in the Western world until almost the nineteenth century. But we know little about either their beliefs or the structure of their government. We do now know that their language was an early form of Greek, and it has become clear that the later Greeks learned much from them, probably through the medium of the Achaeans, the earliest invaders from the north, who ruled Mycenae in southern Greece and subjected Crete to their rule about 1400 B.C.

THE SETTLEMENT OF THE GREEK MAINLAND

During the course of the second half of the second millennium B.C. numerous invaders settled in Greece. These are known by the names of their leading tribes, the Ionians, the Aeolians, and the Dorians. The Ionians settled primarily in the east of Greece and penetrated across the Aegean into western Asia. The Aeolians were concentrated more in the north, and in the northern islands of the Aegean, as well as in northwestern Asia Minor. The Dorians penetrated into the Peloponnesus, where their leading city was Sparta, and, as we have seen, into Crete. The Dorians also made some settlements on the southern Aegean islands and in southern Asia Minor.

For a long period little is known about the Greeks who were now living on the mainland. The two great poems of Homer, the *Iliad* and the *Odyssey* purport to tell of a war carried out by the Greek states against Troy, on the mainland of Asia Minor. The poems, however, probably contained more information about conditions in Greece around 800 B.C., when Homer probably lived, than about the period, say 1200 B.C., when the Trojan War was supposed to have been fought. In fact, the Trojan War may well have been an expedition sent by the Achaeans against the Cretan-dominated city of Troy. It may be significant that the leader of the Greek host was Agamemnon, king of the chief Achaean city of Mycenae. The war may have been concerned, not with the abduction of Helen but with the more prosaic matter of breaking the Cretan monopoly of northern Asian trade. We do know, however, that at least as early as 1000 B.C. the Greeks were sending expeditions, forming colonies in Italy and even further west, and trading with them. These expeditions may well have been a consequence of the overpopulation of Greece, which at no time was rich in natural resources and much of whose land was mountainous and barren. Sparta and the leading Ionian city of Athens played little part in the colonization movement, having too much to do nearer home, since both were possessed of extensive hinterlands.

THE SPARTAN STATE

The invaders as a rule were led by military aristocracies. This fact is reflected in the kind of cities they built, which congregated around a military strong point, known as an *acropolis*. In times of war the agricultural population which lived outside the acropolis and ministered to the needs of the aristocracy, would come into the acropolis for protection. The Dorians were probably the most militarily-minded and most effective, in a military sense, of all the Greek invaders. The city-state of Sparta was from early times interested in expanding its territory, especially to the west where other Dorians, called Messenians, were in possession. Nevertheless, at the beginning of the eighth century B.C. Sparta was at least as culturally developed as the other city-states (*poleis,* plural of *polis*) of Greece. Then the Spartans engaged in two serious wars with the Messenians, in which they were very nearly defeated. However, after the defection from the Messenians of another powerful city, Argos, the Spartans were able to win. Instead of making a reasonable peace treaty which would have left substantial autonomy to the Messenians, they preferred to enslave the entire Messenian population. Since the Messenian population was greater than that of the Spartans themselves, it was necessary for the Spartans to set up a system which would enable them to keep firm control of their late enemies. This they did by specializing in the profession of arms and compelling all their free male citizens to engage in military training for almost all their lives. Each Spartan citizen had to look after a number of *helots* or state serfs. From the work of these men they could supply their share of the sustenance required by the military. Even the Spartan wives were trained, since in time of war they would have to look after the helots themselves.

Nevertheless, it may be understood that the Spartans were not usually interested in expanding further. Though they were militaristic by training, essentially their job was to keep the helots from revolting. They could not afford to lose many men in foreign warfare, since the helots would almost certainly revolt if there was any relaxation of their supervision. The Spartan army was greatly dreaded by the rest of the Greeks, and had a reputation for invincibility, a reputation which was sustained until the end of the fifth century B.C. and later. But the Spartans were not an enterprising people, nor did they have time to engage in the cultural pursuits beloved by the Athenians. They also made no experiments in government, being ruled by an oligarchy of *ephors* elected by a restricted franchise, and by two kings who held their position by heredity, but who rarely had much power of their own unless the Spartan state was engaged in warfare—in which case the kings had the right to command the army.

THE ATHENIAN STATE

Early Political Evolution. The Athenian polis included the whole peninsula of Attica, a substantial hinterland, which for a long time occupied all Athenian energies. At some remote time in the past there had been kings in Athens, but by the time that she emerged into the full light of history the kings had already been replaced by an aristocratic council known as the Areopagus, composed exclusively of the leaders of the large landowning families. There was much discontent with the rule of the Areopagus, both among the middle classes and among the poor peasants. The latter had fallen into debt since it was almost impossible to make a living from their small holdings and to pay at the same time a substantial share of their income to the landowners. Although the country was not really suitable for the growing of wheat, wheat nevertheless was their principal export, and in the seventh century B.C. Athens itself was little more than a village, with a very small middle class engaged in the transport of the wheat. There were several peasant revolts against the landowners, and all the resources of the state were used to put them down. In 621 B.C. an aristocrat named Draco codified the existing severe laws of Athens and thereby earned a personal reputation for harshness. These laws did not, however, solve the social problem, even though they ensured a fair trial for peasants accused of homicide and other crimes. Peasants continued to be enslaved for debt, and frequently they were sold outside the country.

About 594 B.C. the aristocrats at last realized that the social conditions in the country were such that some reforms would have to be granted. They therefore agreed to allow an aristocrat, who had extensive commercial interests also, to become the chief *archon* of the state, with a mandate to put into effect any reforms that he felt to be necessary. This man was Solon, one of the famous wise men of Greece. His reforms were well-calculated to solve the problems. First of all he forbade the export of wheat. This measure ultimately had the effect of making Athens an importing country, living on largely imported food and exporting manufactures in exchange (compare Britain and Japan in our own times). Solon decreed that each man should teach his son a trade, and he encouraged the immigration into Athens of skilled craftsmen from other areas, offering them full citizenship. Thus Athens for the first time became a center of industry to which peasants could go when they lost their land through incurring debt. Solon also forbade enslavement for debt. In the political sphere Solon set up a Council of 400 (chosen by lot from the propertied classes) and decreased the power of the Areopagus. The new Council managed the main business of the state, while an Assembly made up of persons with some property became the central authority of the state to which the Council was responsible. Solon also instituted an extensive reform of the law courts.

Since wheat was no longer to be exported, the landowners and peasants were encouraged to produce vines and olives, which were far more suited for the soil of Attica. It was expected that wine and olive oil would be exported in the future through the port of Athens and that a new industry would arise to employ the Athenian craftsmen in the form of decorated pottery to hold the wine and oil. However, it was not an easy task to turn the land over to vines and olives, and it is probable that for some time there was little improvement in rural conditions. Indeed, it took an absolute ruler, Pisistratus, to make the reforms of Solon really effective.

Pisistratus was a very gifted politician and statesman who by shrewd manipulation of the new Assembly was able to attain absolute power based on the support of the middle classes and the peasants who had been organized into parties. Once he was in secure control of the state, he used his power to compel the landowners to support his economic and agricultural policy, on pain of dispossession. Indeed, many of Pisistratus' enemies among the Athenian aristocracy went into exile, and their lands were given to the peasants. Pisistratus inaugurated a large building program for Athens, built a fleet, and raised the prestige, as well as the trade, of the city to a new high. By the time of his death Athens was already the leading power in Greece, not in any way inferior to Sparta except perhaps in military preparedness.

The Establishment of Democratic Institutions. On the death of Pisistratus his two sons, Hippias and Hipparchus, assumed power. But the citizens of Athens were no longer prepared to put up with a tyranny. When Hipparchus was murdered, Hippias began, indeed, to act like a true tyrant, as his father had never presumed to do. At this moment, when the Athenian citizens were thoroughly disgusted with Hippias, the exiled nobles who had been living near Sparta decided that the time was now ripe to take control of Athens for themselves. Aided by a Spartan army, they returned and took possession of Athens, but they were unable to agree among themselves as to which among the various noble families should rule. At this juncture Cleisthenes, a noble of the Alcmaeonid family, decided to become a democrat and espouse the cause of popular government against the aristocracy to which he himself belonged. Winning by this means the support of the majority of the people, he was entrusted with full powers to revise the constitution and institute popular government. Though the government that he established was not yet fully democratic, it was a substantial step in that direction. Under the constitution of Cleisthenes there were three major bodies in the state: a Board of Generals (*strategoi*) elected annually by the ten tribes, one to each tribe; a Council of 500 (*boule*) which served for a single year and whose members were chosen by lot from the whole citizenry; and a sovereign Assembly (*ecclesia*), which soon came to comprise the whole citizenry. The Assembly made all major decisions, including which, if any, of the generals, was to hold command in the event of war; the primary job of the Council was to prepare legislation for the Assembly; while the Board of Generals acted as the executive of the state, carrying out the wishes of the

Assembly. Athens thus, in effect, became a direct democracy. To guard against the possibility of a new tyrant a curious system known as *ostracism* was introduced soon after the time of Cleisthenes, under which once a year all the citizens could vote on whether any of their number should be sent into honorable exile for ten years.

In the years following the work of Cleisthenes, the Areopagus lost almost all the remainder of its power and various difficulties in the constitution were ironed out so that by the time of the ascendancy of the great Athenian statesman, Pericles, the democracy was in full working order. Pericles was first elected to the position of strategos in 460 B.C., and was re-elected every year for almost thirty years. During this time he was the unquestioned leader of the state, although he was himself an aristocrat. This was the great period of Athenian democracy, and of Athens' greatest prosperity.

THE PERSIAN WARS

Soon after the democracy had been established in Athens the Greek people as a whole had to undergo their most severe test. In revenge for assistance given by the Athenians and one or two other of the Greek peoples to a revolt against the Persian monarch in Ionia, across the Aegean Sea, Darius, the "Great King" of Persia, sent a naval expedition to punish the offenders. The brunt of the attack fell upon Athens. Darius, it seems, expected to be aided by the dissident antidemocratic party of Hippias, but although the latter was apparently willing to play traitor, it was unable to give him much assistance. The tactics adopted by the Persians were not well suited to the conditions, and the army which landed near Marathon in 490 B.C. was severely defeated by the Athenians, aided by the Plataeans, but without much support from any other of the Greeks. During the battle the Persians could not decide whether to use their superior navy to take Athens directly or to aid their land troops which were being beaten. This indecision meant the defeat of the entire expedition. The navy was unable to take the Piraeus, the port of Athens, and returned to Persia.

Darius bequeathed the chastisement of the Greeks to his son Xerxes, who spent the next ten years in preparing a huge if motley army which was expected to overwhelm the Greeks. In the meanwhile, however, the great Athenian leader Themistocles, well aware of the impending expedition, had persuaded the Athenians to use all their surplus money to build a fleet. But Themistocles did not have at his disposal from the citizenry of Athens a really worthwhile army. He therefore attempted to persuade the Spartans of the great danger that all the Greeks were in from the aggressive intentions of the Persians. The Spartans, however, were very jealous of the Athenians and had different notions on the strategy that ought to be employed against the Persians. Indeed, they went so far as to suggest that Greece north of the Peloponnesus was indefensible, and that a wall should be constructed to the north of the peninsula beyond which the Persians would not be able to march. Nothing had been settled when the Persian army in 480 b.c. crossed the Hellespont and proceeded into Greece from the north, receiving the submission of almost all the Greeks in their path. Too late the Spartans sent the flower of their army to stop the Persians but were overwhelmed at the Battle of Thermopylae, after a traitor had betrayed to the Persians the path over the mountains by which the Spartan soldiers could be taken in the rear. The Spartans were killed to the last man, winning undying fame, but not holding up the Persians for any significant period of time.

Athens was now wide open to the invaders. By winning a great naval battle at Salamis, the Athenians prevented the Persian fleet from invading the Peloponnese. But Athens itself was captured and its citizens took refuge on the island of Salamis, just outside the Athenian harbor. The next year, for the first and almost the only time in Greek history, all the Greeks who had not submitted to the Persians joined together, and under Spartan leadership they defeated the Persians at the decisive Battle of Plataea (479 b.c.). The Athenians performed their part of the bargain by again defeating the Persians on sea at the Battle of Mycale. This proved to be the end of the Persian threat until almost a century later. In the late fifth century Persia had her revenge by subsidizing and assisting the Spartans to win the Peloponnesian War, and throughout much of the fourth century it was Persian intrigues and money that kept most of the Greek states in constant enmity with one another.

After the victory the Athenians felt it to be so important to keep the Persians out of the Aegean Sea that they formed a league of the various Aegean islands and themselves, together with a few other mainland cities that agreed to join. The League, called the Confederation of Delos, had a common treasury which was maintained on the island of Delos, and each state was assessed a certain amount of either money or ships for the common cause. Although the Persians had been soundly defeated in another naval battle and there was by 460 B.C. very little apparent danger from them, Pericles insisted on keeping the League in operation, and refused to allow the city-states which wished to do so to secede. Thus the Confederation became in effect an Athenian empire. At the suggestion of one of the islands the treasury was moved to Athens, and Pericles thereafter used the money as he wished. During the next twenty years he pursued a policy of attempting to isolate Sparta and Corinth, the leading commercial city of the Peloponnese, while at the same time rebuilding Athens. Indeed, it is to the misappropriations of Pericles that we owe such wonderful buildings as the Parthenon. In defense of Pericles, it may be said that the Athenians had suffered very greatly from the common enemy and the city needed to be rebuilt after the Persian depredations. Nevertheless, the islands were not consulted on the manner in which their money was spent, and though the Athenians provided the navy in accordance with the provisions of the treaty, there was a considerable surplus of money, and Athens did, as the cities asserted, use the Confederation as its own instrument. Several of the cities of the League, indeed, complained that their freedom was being taken away, since they were not allowed to leave the League. Pericles also insisted on setting up a democratic form of government in many cities to replace the former oligarchies which he did not trust to be loyal to Athens.

THE PELOPONNESIAN WAR

The policy of Pericles succeeded in arousing the fear of both Sparta and Corinth, who might expect in the event of a war to be aided by dissident cities of the League who wished to escape from the domination of Athens. In 431 B.C., the league that had been organized by Sparta launched a preventive war, known to history as the Peloponnesian War, one of the most destructive wars of the ancient world. In general, it may be said that the Spartans and their allies were successful by land, while the Athenians were successful by sea. But after the death of Pericles about a year after the beginning of the war, the leadership in Athens fell into the hands of less moderate statesmen. Although for a time a peace was patched up under the influence of a conservative Athenian statesman, the war-party, evidently supported by the mass of the people, soon renewed the war. In 415 B.C., under the leadership of Alcibiades, a brilliant but erratic genius, a great expedition which ought to have succeeded was launched against Syracuse, a colony of Corinth. But the enemies of Alcibiades, though unable to prevent the launching of the expedition, were strong enough to force his recall before he had won any successes in Sicily. This left the command in the hands of a general who had from the first disapproved of the expedition. He wasted time and took no decisive action, while Alcibiades, who had refused to come home to stand trial for a supposed impiety he had committed, went to Sparta and divulged the strategic secrets of Athens. The Spartans sent out an effective general named Gylippus, who destroyed the entire Athenian expedition.

The Athenians were so shocked by their defeat that they abolished the democracy for a period of about a year. The new government, however, was unpopular and did not achieve much. In despair the Athenians recalled Alcibiades and gave him the command. Though he won several victories he soon fell from favor, accused this time of intriguing with the Persians for his own profit. The Persians, in fact, regarded Alcibiades as their most dangerous enemy, but dealt with him as well as with his Spartan opponent, the able admiral Lysander (son of a helot woman) in their attempts to accomplish the defeat of Athens by means of well-placed bribes. It was Lysander whom the Persians really favored, and he who won the crucial battle of Aegospotami in 404 B.C., after Alcibiades had once more been driven into exile. The victory enabled him to cut off the Athenian grain supply and compelled the surrender of the city. Sparta, ever mindful of the fact that Athens had played a noble part in defeating the Persians a century before, refused to accept the advice of her allies that the city should be destroyed and contented herself with dismantling its defences. Nevertheless, Athens was not able in the following century to recover the leadership in Greece which she lost through the Peloponnesian War.

THE FOURTH CENTURY—RISE OF PHILIP OF MACEDON

By the end of the war Sparta was the acknowledged head of Greece. But though for a while she tried to play the part of an imperialist, she soon lost Persian aid, which was then for a time given to Thebes, previously a relatively unimportant city. Thebes, indeed, had lost all title to respect in Greece by collaborating with the Persians during the Persian Wars. Now however, she developed a new military tactic, and under the leadership of two great generals established herself temporarily as the leading power in Greece. By defeating the Spartans in open warfare she freed the helots, thereby reducing Sparta forever to the rank of a second- or third-rate power. But away in the north from 359 B.C. onward, a new power was rising in Greece. This was Macedon, ruled by a shrewd and crafty semibarbarian named Philip. Philip perceived very clearly that if he could keep the Greeks disunited he could pick them off one by one.

Thebes never did come to realize the dangerous nature of Philip, nor the threat that he presented to Greece. The Athenians were divided in their opinions, one party thinking it best to collaborate and "appease" Philip; the other, led by Demosthenes, believing that the only safe policy was to stop Philip before he became too strong. Philip himself did his best to win support in both cities, spending lavishly of the gold which he had won in northeastern Greece, while at the same time building himself a small but strong and effective army, with new military formations hitherto unknown in Greece. Though Demosthenes was able to persuade the Athenians to send an expedition to Olynthus, which Philip was threatening, the expedition was too small and arrived too late to be of any great assistance. Philip, after capturing Olynthus, destroyed it utterly, thereby providing an example to the rest of the Greeks which he hoped would prove salutary.

Philip's barbarity incensed Demosthenes but cowed most of the Athenian statesmen. Indeed, a writer of speeches named Isocrates even urged Philip to unite the Greeks and engage in a great expedition against Persia. Philip in fact intended to make such an expedition, but the means by which he proposed to unite Greece were not calculated to please any Athenian democrats. In fact Philip's diplomacy paid off handsomely. Although he was not himself regarded as a Greek by the other Greeks, who thought they could use him for their own ends, he was made head of a Greek religious league and invited to chastise some Greek cities which had been accused of sacrilege. Philip, nothing loath, came down into Greece, and suddenly confronted Thebes, which realized at last that there was nothing to hinder him if he wished to turn upon Thebes itself. Demosthenes hastily organized an alliance between Athens and Thebes, but it was too late. Philip defeated the united armies at the battle of Chaeronea in 338 B.C., and thereafter was the undisputed leader of Greece.

Philip, however, had not forgotten his intention of invading Persia. He wished to be supported by the Greeks so that the attack would appear to be a Greek expedition as a revenge for the fifth century invasion by Xerxes, even though it was headed by a Macedonian. The Greeks had no objection to making him their formal leader, though they had no intention of supplying him with any forces. It was, after all, possible that he would meet his death in Asia! Philip returned to his country to prepare for the expedition, but was shortly thereafter murdered. At once all the Greek cities revolted. However, Philip was succeeded not by a nonentity like most of his ancestors, but by Alexander the Great. As soon as his hands were free, Alexander descended upon the rebellious Greeks and destroyed the city of Thebes. Athens, fearing the same fate, submitted abjectly, even going so far as to congratulate Alexander on his destruction of Thebes. Alexander's terms were mild, though he insisted that Demosthenes should be sent into exile. But he was so much more interested in his expedition to Persia than he was in the affairs of Greece that he left a military governor in Greece and immediately embarked on the Persian expedition. Like his father, he was made head of the expedition by the Greeks. But most of the latter postponed any serious military support until it could be seen whether Alexander was likely to be successful.

ALEXANDER THE GREAT

The extraordinary campaigns of Alexander need not detain us long here. It is sufficient to say that his first victory in Asia Minor over the Persian satrap, aided by Greek mercenaries in Persian employ, was the really decisive one of his victories. He nearly lost the battle, but by the exercise of skillful diplomacy on the Greek mercenaries, coupled with severe threats, he was able to divide the forces arrayed against him and win it. He then proceeded to Egypt, which he took from Persia with scarcely a battle, since the Egyptians had no use for the Persians and no loyalty to them, while the Persian armies were too small to resist him. More difficult was the conquest of the Phoenician city of Tyre, which Alexander took after a long siege. But he had not yet come to grips with the Great King, Darius III. In 333 b.c. and again in 331 he succeeded in defeating Darius, and in 330 Darius was murdered by his own subjects. Thereafter Alexander himself became the Great King, marrying one of Darius' daughters. In 327 b.c. Alexander began an expedition which took him as far as India. But after defeating the Indians and learning

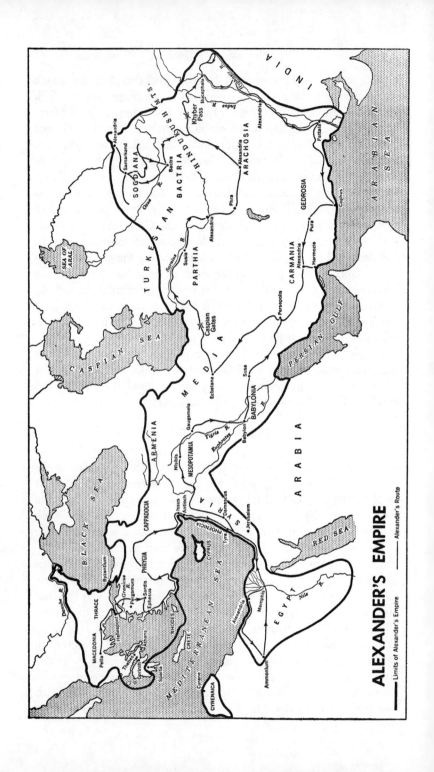

ALEXANDER'S EMPIRE

—— Limits of Alexander's Empire   —— Alexander's Route

to counter the elephants brought against them by the Indian leader, his troops mutinied and refused to go further. Alexander then descended the Indus River and returned home via the desert, suffering great hardships on the way. Soon after returning to Babylon, one of the old Persian capitals, he died at the early age of thirty-three. He had never lost a battle, and his campaigns had changed the course of history in a decisive manner.

The entire Near East was now opened to immigration from the greatly overpopulated mainland of Greece. Immigrants swarmed into the area, altogether changing the character of the rather static civilization they encountered. The culture became a mixture of Greek and Oriental, the Greeks supplying most of the drive and initiative. But the governments of the new states into which the empire was divided were despotic in the Oriental manner.

Since Alexander died without designating a successor—his last wife, Roxane, gave birth shortly afterward to an heir—his generals disputed the succession between them. None was able to make good his claim to the whole, with the result that Egypt and a part of Palestine fell to Ptolemy, who became Pharaoh of Egypt in his own right, whereas the bulk of Alexander's Asiatic possessions fell in the end to a general named Seleucus. A small kingdom in northwestern Asia Minor centered around the city of Pergamum became an independent and prosperous state, while Macedonia and Greece fell to another general named Antigonus. Thus the leaders of Asia were now Greeks, and the Greek immigrants on the whole became a privileged class throughout Alexander's possessions.

Alexander himself, however, had possessed many ideas that were far from common in his time. Educated by Aristotle, the greatest living Greek philosopher, he had absorbed Aristotle's taste for science, which he apparently shared, and he went beyond his master in his notion of the equality of the different peoples of mankind. At quite an early stage in his career he decided that Persians should be given leading positions in his army, thereby incurring much resentment from his Macedonian elite troops. Nevertheless, Alexander persisted and suppressed the discontent, and the policy was continued after his death, even though probably considerably modified from Alexander's own ideas. Believing with Aristotle that the polis was the ideal form of political organization and that the democracy as practiced in Athens was one worthy of imitation in his new empire, he founded a considerable number of new city-states, which he endowed with institutions similar to those of the Athenians. Evidently he did not stop to consider that the Athenian institutions were suitable only for a free people, with a free power of decision in vital matters. Such vital matters, it is needless to say, were not entrusted to the assemblies and councils by the Hellenistic kings who succeeded him. The new monarchy therefore was more Oriental than Greek; but the culture of the Greeks was widely regarded in Asia as superior, and leading Persians took to it with great enthusiasm. The energetic and commercially-minded Greeks created an economic transformation in the Persian realms. In fact Hellenistic society was a strongly commercial one, aided by the great accumulation of riches, which had hitherto been prevented from circulating, taken by Alexander from the Persian monarch. In many respects the Hellenistic civilization resembled our own commercial civilization, with somewhat the same incentives. But the Greeks had little in the way of religion to offer their Oriental subjects, and, for the most part, it was the Oriental religions that conquered this part of the world rather than anything imported from Greece.

CULTURAL ACHIEVEMENTS OF THE GREEKS

General Characteristics. It is now time to turn to the intellectual and artistic achievements of the Greeks. Important as the Greek experiments in self-government were to the world, it is their contributions to thought that constitute their greatest title to fame. For the first time, with the Greeks, the human being emancipated his thinking from the bonds imposed by accepted tradition and, at least in his thought, separated himself from the world about him, observed it objectively, and formulated concepts about it. This achievement, of course, was passed on to their successors, so that we do not ordinarily recognize that conceptual thinking really had a beginning and was not something that was born full-grown with the first man who walked upright on the earth. For this achievement the Greek language was the most perfect vehicle yet devised by human beings, as in some respects it still is. Whenever science needs a new word, it is to the Greek language that even today it automatically turns. It is no idle remark when we say that "the Greeks had a word for it." If they did not possess it, there was no difficulty in creating a suitable new word in a language so fully inflected, with so many tenses, and with such a multitude of prefixes that any possible shade of meaning can be achieved by merely making new combinations—as we continue to do today in our own languages by using the Greek forms.

The Greeks were the first people who possessed an insatiable curiosity about everything in heaven or on earth. The answers they propounded on physical questions are no longer accepted today, for they did not possess a very great knowledge of physical phenomena, and they quickly jumped to conclusions. It was rare for a Greek to be disciplined in thought, or, indeed, in any other way, save in his art, which we call classical. In short he was intelligent without being intellectual; not for the Greek the hard, disciplined type of thought we call scientific. He speculated, wondered, questioned, and invented ingenious answers which pleased him and satisfied his aesthetic sense, in preference to setting himself industriously to the task of finding the correct answer based on a firm knowledge and authentic information. Aristotle, the teacher of Alexander, was the first Greek thinker who seriously tried to be "scientific" in our sense of the word, and even he had his limitations which have prevented modern scientists from giving him his due as the great pioneer to whom they are in far deeper debt than they usually realize.

Greek Science and Philosophy. When the first Greeks (in the colonies of Ionia and southern Italy) began to ask questions about the universe they jumped to the immediate conclusion that every thing visible must be made of, or derived from, one underlying substance. They were not sure whether this substance was a material one (like water, air, or fire) or whether it was immaterial, but they were already far from the stage of explaining it in terms of gods. In the fifth century B.C. Leucippus and Democritus hit on the idea of atoms, which they pictured as not unlike the modern concept of molecules; but of course they had no idea of how to go about verifying their guess. Only in recent centuries has the idea been revived, but our atom (literally, "the unsplittable thing") is clearly unlike their notion of it. Some of the same Greek thinkers founded the science of geometry, forever associated with the name Euclid, a Hellenistic compiler of theorems, most of which were devised by others (for example, the so-called Pythagorean theorem attributed to a much earlier Greek from southern Italy). The Egyptians and Mesopotamians, of course, had been familiar with practical geometry and surveying; but it was left to the Greeks, using the data of experience provided by the Egyptians, to abstract the universal theorems applicable to *all* examples of a phenomenon.

Greek thought reached its apogee in the work of the big three of ancient philosophy, Socrates, Plato, and Aristotle. Socrates never wrote a line, and we know of his work only from Plato and Xenophon, his pupils. It is clear that he was primarily interested in the study of man, and in what we call ethics—what is the nature of the good and how man may pursue it. He invented what Plato called the dialectical (Greek *dialektikē*) method, the method of questioning and answering, for the purpose of revealing how much knowledge a man really has and how much of his supposed knowledge consists of generally accepted beliefs passed down to him by his forefathers and by his society. His purpose was to discover for himself a way of acting that would be in accordance with the best thought of which he was capable, irrespective of the received opinions of society. When he was seventy years old, in 399 B.C., Socrates was brought to trial on charges that he was an atheist (or made new gods) and corrupted the youth, a charge which it was difficult to refute, although to most of us he appears to have been one of the most religious and high-minded of men. He was condemned to death and executed, since his defense was, in essence, *"nolo contendere"*— he admitted most of what was urged against him but denied that it added up to the crimes of which he was charged.

At the death of Socrates Plato was a young man in his twenties who was, incidentally, permanently embittered against the democratic form of government because of what the Athenian democracy, newly restored after the Peloponnesian War, had done to his teacher. Plato was a man of much wider interests than Socrates, and he can be regarded as the first man to merit the name of philosopher (some philosophers, even today, think of him as the greatest). One of his primary interests was answering the questions implicit in the work of Socrates. If a man can indeed discover the good from examining his own self and does not have to rely on revealed religion or on any other outside source, where does he obtain that knowledge? How can it be thought to be within him, ready to be brought out into the open by dialectic? The answer Plato gave was that a man must be born with it, he must have innate knowledge of "the good"—and if of the good then why not everything else? So he comes to propound the notion that the soul has existed in the spiritual world before being clothed in the body for his earthly life, and that this soul has experienced in perfection all Ideas, all abstractions. Thus when man acquires an Idea it is a form of "recognition," recognition of the earthly copy as the inferior counterpart of the perfect heavenly Idea. The Idea of beauty, for example, is innate in man as the result of his prenatal experience. When he sees a beautiful thing on earth he knows that it is beautiful because his soul compares it unconsciously with the heavenly archetype of beauty. Similarly for all abstractions. Justice on earth is imperfect, but the self-conscious man can examine himself through the dialectic and achieve an ever more perfect Idea of justice, because the true ideal is within his soul. Hence the constant search of Plato for the ideal form of the state which, in his view, must be an embodiment of justice. This is the heart of his great work *The Republic*. Though the medievals called the Platonic philosophy realism (because Plato held that Ideas were real), we think of it as the forerunner of all our "idealist" philosophies which culminated in the work of Hegel in the early nineteenth century. Idealist philosophies are now out of fashion in our materialistic age, but they have been very influential throughout the course of history.

Aristotle gave his answer to the Platonic problem in less uncompromising terms. For him both the abstraction and the concrete object were equally real, but he did not find it necessary to postulate pre-existence. He held that man derives his idea of beauty by abstracting it from innumerable beautiful things, since the power of abstraction happens to be a quality that he possesses by nature. Aristotle's interests were wider even than those of Plato. A biologist before everything else, he was inclined to see all earthly phenomena in terms of growing and becoming. Man possesses infinite potentialities and it is his task to develop as many of these as he can in his lifetime. The search for happiness is the center of Aristotle's ethics, but this happiness must consist in "self-realization," as we should call it. He thus regards pleasure and wealth as at best means to an end, which may indeed contribute not at all to the development of his potentialities, and thus become even evil. Aristotle was the first to attempt a classification of living beings by genus and species, and in his many logical works he put forward a method by which descriptions could be made which would include all the essentials of a phenomenon. He also gave the first systematic account of the laws involved in reasoning. The sum total of his work is prodigious, and without doubt he must be considered as the founder of what we now call science.

The thinkers in the following age, which we call Hellenistic, to be distinguished from the classical Hellenic period which closed with the death of Aristotle in 322 B.C., were all inclined to be more specialized than those we have thus far considered. This was especially true in Alexandria, which was made into a center of learning by the Ptolemaic dynasty. None of these men approached Aristotle in the breadth of his interests and learning. Astronomers, who were able to use the observations accumulated over many centuries in Babylonia, made great advances. Hipparchus discovered the precession of the equinoxes, Aristarchus propounded the hypothesis that the earth moved around the sun—which created so many scientific difficulties that it won few converts. Archimedes discovered the principle of specific gravity and formulated many mathematical laws. Euclid, as already noted, enunciated new geometrical theorems. For nearly three centuries Alexandria attracted scholars and scientific writers, as well as doctors, who followed in the traditions of the classical Greek doctor, Hippocrates of Cos, and scholarly editors who edited the greater works of the Hellenic period and preserved them for posterity.

Other Hellenistic thinkers considered the great problems of man's relation to the gods and to the universe and to those problems of ethics which had already been considered in Hellenic times. The Stoic philosophy (founded by Zeno in the late fourth century B.C.) formulated the notion of the absolute equality of man, owing to the presence of the spark of Divine Reason in each, and held that man was able to overcome all the ills that beset him in the world, by developing an inner fortitude and not relying upon any divine help or interference. The Epicurean philosophy (founded by Epicurus in the third century B.C.), seeking the same goal of *ataraxia,* a state of being "unshaken by the world," believed that it would best be found by limiting one's desires, since desiring much leads to unhappiness and inner turmoil. By enjoying simple pleasures, and above all by disbelieving in the interest of the gods in earthly matters and so freeing himself from irrational fear, man could win happiness for himself. The Pyrrhonists or Skeptics believed that man was incapable of knowing anything for certain at all. Thus the wheel had come full circle from Plato; and it will be apparent that almost all the problems man still considers today were already recognized as such by the Greeks, who gave their interested attention to them—even if the answers they formulated may not be acceptable to us, still less the last word to be said on the subject.

Greek Religion. Greek religion has always presented great difficulties, not only to scholars but to many modern men and women
who have wondered how such an intelligent people could be
willing to accept such often apparently childish notions. Everyone
is familiar with the fact that the Greeks apparently believed in
gods much like themselves, possessed of divine power, but without
attributes that most of us think of as divine. The great poems of
Homer, who was regarded with reverence by all subsequent Greeks,
make it clear enough what kind of beings the gods were. Then
there are the wonderful Greek myths, thousands of them, most of
which do not appear to ascribe any moral qualities to their gods.
Even the Greek tragedians, especially Euripides, do not appear
to regard the gods very highly. Without going in detail into these
problems, it should only be said here that the Greek religion unquestionably evolved, and that it is very doubtful if many people
by the fifth century B.C. believed in gods who lived on Mount
Olympus and behaved like the gods in Homer. Certainly no trace of
such belief can be found in the works of the great philosophers.

But it would seem that the Greeks did believe very seriously
indeed in a divine element in the world, which they revered under
many forms, particularly evidenced in the rituals of the great
festivals. But unlike believers in monotheistic religions, they attached no great importance to mere *belief*—no Greek would have
felt his religion should include a *creed*—nor were the gods *prayed*
to and expected to assist the individual. Moreover, beneath the forms
of religious observance, and underlying even many of the myths,
is the thought, already to be found in Homer, that the life of man
is predestined and that there is a limit to what can be accomplished
by him on earth. Man by evaluating himself too highly and becoming proud, draws upon himself the anger of the gods for his
presumption and brings on his own destruction. This theme under-
lies the two great histories of Herodotus (where it is a Persian
monarch who is presumptuous) and Thucydides (where it is the
Athenians), and much of the earlier Greek tragedy. This tragedy,
it should be remembered, is not *literature* in our sense. It was
performed at the Dionysiac festival, and belongs to the religious
observance of the festival. Hence the usually exalted themes and
the heroes who are, at least until Euripides, something more than
ordinary mortals, and have to endure destinies that do not fall to the
lot of common man.

Greek Art. Greek art is likewise religious in the Hellenic period. Here man builds temples to the gods, usually the tutelary gods of his city. The Pan-Athenaic procession is depicted in the friezes of the Parthenon on the Acropolis at Athens, a religious procession in honor of Athena, as the temple itself was built to house the goddess. The architects, laborers, and everyone connected with the building worked for the same daily wage, while building for the city and its goddess. Only in the Hellenistic period, when, owing to the highly competitive life in a strange world, the individual man had to learn self-reliance or suffer defeat in the competion, do we find art itself becoming in any degree commercialized. The great kings, nobles, and merchants became patrons of art, and the Greek craftsmen satisfied the demand. Gradually Greek art became less idealistic, though never as realistic as among the Romans. While in the Hellenic period the artist tried to portray the universal man in his ideal form, the Hellenistic artist sometimes came close to portraying him as he was. Speed and movement also are characteristic of Hellenistic scupture, whereas the Hellenic artist strove to catch the moment of eternity in stone.

This brief summary of Greek achievements cannot hope to do more than indicate the realms in which the Greeks excelled and the incalculable debt we, their successors, owe to them for blazing the path we have followed. There is very little indeed in the Western world that does not rest upon a Greek foundation— perhaps only our religions, which we owe more to the Orient than to Greece. In due time later Greeks were even to add much to Christian theology. If the Romans, whom we are to consider in the next chapter, gave more to our government than the Greeks (who could not govern themselves well and thus were compelled to submit to Rome), in Athens and Sparta we nevertheless possess at least the type of the two extremes of society, called by Henri Bergson the "open" society (one capable of internal change and development through its existing institutions), and the "closed" society (one with a rigid constitutional framework that can be changed only by revolution). This struggle, it need hardly be mentioned, has not yet been concluded, even twenty-four centuries after the Peloponnesian War.

CHAPTER V

ROMAN CIVILIZATION

Roman history falls naturally into two parts. The city of Rome became an independent republic in 509 B.C. and remained a republic until the old self-governing institutions were replaced by one-man rule after the Battle of Actium in 31 B.C. Thereafter Rome and the empire it had by now acquired were ruled by a single man, holding initially the title of *princeps* (first citizen), and later the title of *imperator* (emperor) or *dominus* (lord). This one-man rule lasted from 31 B.C. to A.D. 476, when a barbarian chieftain deposed the last emperor—although, in fact, the emperors had lost their real power many decades before. The era of one-man rule is often called the "Roman Empire," to be distinguished from the Roman Republic. But this distinction is somewhat misleading, since most of the empire was acquired during the period of the republic. The distinction between Republic and Empire is therefore a distinction between the different kinds of government, and the word *empire* in this connection should not be confused with our modern use of the term in the territorial sense.

Prior to the establishment of the Republic there had been kings in Rome, traditionally from the founding of Rome by Romulus in 753 B.C. The famous story of this founding should not, however, be taken too seriously, since it is certain that a city existed on the site of Rome long before 753. The Italians who inhabited the Italian peninsula probably descended into Italy at about the same time as the various barbarian peoples entered Greece, during the second millennium B.C. Even before these invasions there is evidence of prehistoric cultures in Italy, but we need not concern ourselves with these in this book. The native kings of Rome were certainly replaced toward the end of the seventh century B.C. when an Etruscan named Tarquinius Priscus added Rome to his territories. The Etruscans were at that time in control of most of Italy north of Rome. By capturing Rome they reached their furthest point of expansion to the south, and Rome became one of their capitals.

The Etruscans appear to have come from Asia Minor about 900 B.C. They brought a distinctive culture of their own and bequeathed to the Romans such practices as divination by the observation of the flight of birds and of other natural phenomena; the Romans continued throughout the history of both the Republic and the Empire to rely much upon the information as to lucky and unlucky days given by the augurs. It was also the Etruscans who probably reunited the small villages around Rome into one great city. But the Etruscans were never popular in Rome, and the rule by Etruscan kings was such that the Romans detested the title of king forever afterward. Although the traditional sixth king of Rome, Servius Tullius, was regarded much more favorably by the later Romans, it is possible that even he was an Etruscan, or ruled with Etruscan consent. The Roman nobles rebelled against the seventh king of Rome, Tarquinius the Proud (Superbus), and succeeded in setting up their own institutions after they had expelled him from the city. The famous story of the Rape of Lucrece (by a son of Tarquinius) concerns the incident which led to the Etruscan expulsion.

POLITICAL INSTITUTIONS OF EARLY ROME

When the Romans took over their own government Roman society was rigidly stratified, being composed of the upper classes known as *patricians,* and the lower classes collectively known as the *plebs* (or *plebeians*). These two groups formed two virtually separate societies, and intermarriage was not permitted between them. It is indeed quite possible that the plebeians were sorry to see the expulsion of the Etruscans, since it is likely that the Etruscan monarch was less oppressive toward them than the native patricians. However this may be, it is certain that before twenty years of the Republic had elapsed the plebeians were in full revolt against the patricians. Since it was they who had to provide the bulk of the manpower in the continuous wars, both against the Etruscans who wished to recapture the city and against other tribes in the area with whom the Romans were at enmity, they naturally began to demand more rights for themselves. The patricians monopolized all the high offices of state, which they administered in accordance with their own class interests. They also exercised the power of life and death over the plebeians and, as in Greece, enslaved the peasants and sold them when they fell into debt. About 594 B.C. the plebeians took advantage of the one opportunity they had to force concessions from the patricians. Called out to go on the annual campaign, they decided to go on strike instead. The patricians at once came to terms and permitted the plebeians to elect an official of their own to be designated a *tribune,* who was granted the power of vetoing any act committed by a magistrate, as long as he was present in person to exercise the veto. The plebeians were soon granted an assembly of their own (*Council of the Plebs*) which could pass laws binding on the plebs. There were now two legislative bodies in the state, the Senate, which was composed of the heads of the patrician families, who held their position only by birth, and the new plebeian assembly. In addition there was another Assembly, whose special task it was to elect the two senior magistrates, called consuls, who exercised separately all the previous powers of the kings and in war alternated their commands, and to authorize declarations of war by the state. This Assembly was made up of all men who were enrolled in the Roman army. But the vote in the Assembly was weighted according to the equipment which a man brought with him on campaign. Thus the rich men, who at that time were mostly patricians, were able to dominate the Assembly, and the poor man had virtually no vote.

About 460 B.C. the Council of the Plebs was enlarged to take in all Roman citizens, whether patricians or plebeians. But the Senate continued to have a veto on legislation. Thus there was both an aristocratic legislature, the Senate, and a potentially democratic legislature, the Council of the Tribes (the new enlarged assembly which had arisen from the Council of the Plebs). At this time the consuls exercised almost unlimited authority in the state, since there were no written laws. They were inhibited only by the veto of the tribunes, then two in number, later increased to ten. An agitation therefore arose for written laws, and a commission was sent to Greece to study the laws of Solon to see whether they might be applicable to Rome. But the plebeians were not to obtain their codified laws without a struggle. It is probable that a formal second secession of the plebs took place about 449 B.C., which was followed by the issuing of the Twelve Tables, the fundamental laws of Rome. These laws were severe enough, and may perhaps well be compared with the Constitution of Draco in Athens of more than a hundred and fifty years before. But at least they were written laws, and in later years statutes passed by the assemblies greatly modified their severity.

The plebeians followed up their success in obtaining the laws with a second victory the following year. The Senate agreed that the Assembly of the Tribes could make laws which would come into effect if the Senate did not veto them. Although the Senate indeed did try to veto many important laws, the Assembly continued to pass them until such time as the Senate decided it had had enough. Then it gave way, and thus the democratization began to move rather more rapidly. A few years after the promulgation of the Twelve Tables intermarriage was permitted between plebeians and patricians, thus, to some degree, breaking down the social barrier. This degree, however, should not be exaggerated, since the poor peasants and artisans would hardly be likely to be welcomed into senatorial houses. The class whom the legislation did affect was the small group of merchants and richer farmers who were not patrician by birth but who had acquired often as much, and sometimes more, wealth than the senators. The senators themselves were not permitted to engage in trading and had to live exclusively from their lands.

But the patricians objected very strongly to the notion that any plebeian was fit to be a consul, which was regarded as a position not only of power but of much social prestige. When the Assembly of Tribes began to put pressure upon the Senate to admit plebeians to the consulship, the Senate preferred to abolish the consulship altogether, and for almost eighty years there were no consuls in Rome. Finally in 367 B.C. the Senate gave way and decided to allow the plebeians to become consuls. But this still did not mean that any plebeians would be made consuls by the military Assembly which elected them. This difficulty was overcome by forcing the Senate to accept a law that one of the consuls must be a plebeian. Thereafter the senators and their friends chose plebeians who were, as a rule, conservative and some of whom had become allied by marriage with them. During the next hundred years the senators fought a skillful rear-guard action; but the Assembly of Tribes, now led by the plebeian tribunes, continued to force reforms through until at last in 287 B.C. the Senate, after a third secession of the plebs, agreed to abolish its own veto power. Thereafter, formal democracy reigned in Rome, and the popular Assembly of Tribes passed all the legislation.

The Senate, however, was far from powerless. In fact the senatorial oligarchy, except on rare occasions, continued to rule Rome. By this time the plebeian tribunes sat in the Senate and took part in its debates. Indeed, it was only in the Senate that policies were debated at all. The Assembly of Tribes could only vote Yes or No, having no information beyond what the consuls or tribunes pleased to give them. The ordinary citizens were therefore in a difficult position and could not formulate policy for themselves. The Senate also continued to control the treasury and foreign policy, although the military Assembly was democratized in 242 B.C. All the important officials of the state sat in the Senate, and there was usually no one left to give any leadership to the people. This situation continued until the popular revolution of the brothers Gracchi, which will be discussed in a later part of this chapter.

THE EXPANSION OF ROME TO 133 B.C.

Consolidation of Italy. It has been said with some justice that the Romans, like the British, acquired their empire in a fit of absence of mind. In fact the expansion of the city-state of Rome was at least as much due to propitious circumstances as to any aggressive tendency on the part of the Romans. At the beginning of the Republic they were compelled to fight against the Etruscans. When they themselves tried to take over the cities that had formerly been dominated by the Etruscans, they were regarded as no better than the Etruscans themselves. After a time they were able by shrewd diplomacy and by granting certain rights to their allies to form a Latin League which was usually, but not always, loyal to Rome. This league consisted of a considerable number of territories to the immediate south of Rome. If the Etruscans and the Latin League had joined together to fight the Romans they would certainly have put an end to Rome. But this never happened. When the Gauls, a Celtic tribe from the north, took all of Rome except the Capitol, the Latin cities did not rise against them. At other times the Etruscans joined with some of the enemies of Rome but not with all. Thus the Romans were never left without allies, and since there was little to sack in Rome, there was nothing much to be gained by conquering her. The Samnites for nearly a hundred years fought against Rome, but in the end they were defeated. By 290 B.C., the Romans were in control of the former Etruria and all Italy down to the Greek cities in the south. Rome had signed treaties with all the conquered territiories, giving them some rights. All had agreed to allow Rome to be their protector and were thus not permitted to exercise foreign policies of their own, but in other respects they were entirely free to do as they wished. In 290 B.C., therefore, Italy was virtually a confederation of semiautonomous states under the general jurisdiction and control of Rome.

Wars with Pyrrhus. One of the difficulties of undertaking the foreign policy of allies was that Rome automatically became responsible for the settlement of quarrels between these allies and neighboring states, in which quarrels Rome herself had no special interest. A Greek city-state in southern Italy was already under her protection, and unquestionably used it for the purpose of gaining advantages over her neighbors. When this involved the state in war with other Greek states, she naturally called upon Rome for assistance. The largest of the Greek city-states, Tarentum, thereupon appealed to the king of Epirus across the Adriatic in Greece. Pyrrhus, the king of Epirus, invaded Italy and won several victories which were very costly to him (hence the term Pyrrhic victory). Rome might have made peace with Pyrrhus after these battles had not the Carthaginians, the great commercial people of the area, offered Rome an alliance. This brought the powerful Carthaginian fleet into the war against Pyrrhus, who then was compelled to retreat and defend himself against the new attack. Rome was thereby enabled to recover the ground she had lost in Italy, and Pyrrhus was finally defeated in 275 B.C. by the combined efforts of Rome and Carthage. As a result of the wars the Greek city-states in southern Italy were forced into the confederation led by Rome, and accepted virtually the same terms as her other allies.

The Punic Wars. Carthage and Rome were not natural allies. Though Rome herself did not have any trading interests abroad, the Greek states whom she had now undertaken to protect were commercial rivals. One of these states soon picked a quarrel with Carthage, who was the overlord of Sicily, and the Romans were forced into the resulting war. Thus began the first Punic (from the Latin word *Poenus* for Carthaginian) War, which lasted for more than twenty years, while the Romans were building a fleet capable of defeating the Carthaginians. The war was not unlike the early phases of the Peloponnesian War, in that a land power was pitted against a sea power. The Greeks, who could have given the Roman assistance in the naval warfare, were reluctant to do so. The Roman consuls, brought up as land warriors from their childhood, but by constitutional precedent holding office only for a single one-year term during their lifetime, were unable to learn the arts of naval warfare in such a short time. More Romans were lost at sea by shipwreck than were killed by the Carthaginians. In due course, nevertheless, the Romans were able to build an effective fleet and to defeat the enemy. The war came to an end in 241 B.C. with the cession of the island of Sicily to the Romans.

But the Carthaginians were unwilling to regard the contest with the Romans as settled. A leader of genius named Hannibal trained a land army with which he invaded Italy in 218 B.C. The Romans, ill-led, and often locally outnumbered, were unable to defeat Hannibal in battle. Passing through Spain and Gaul with a large army which included elephants, he crossed the Alps and devastated northern Italy, bypassing Rome, but taking over the most valuable allied territory of Campania and ruining it. Hannibal after his first failure to take Rome, which most historians, both modern and ancient, believe he could have captured, never had such an opportunity again. While he was in Campania the Romans had a breathing space during which Quintus Fabius Maximus, as dictator (an office supposedly held for six months only, during which he was in sole command of the Roman armies) was able to keep the Carthaginian armies from uniting and perhaps subjugating all Italy. Hannibal's army, meanwhile, was disintegrating and Hannibal himself had difficulty in keeping it disciplined. The Romans, on the other hand, were determined to expel the invader. In the end, under the leadership of a Roman general of genius, Scipio Africanus, they organized a new and disciplined army and sent it to Africa to attack Hannibal's own homeland. The Carthaginians, unprepared for this move, summoned Hannibal back at once, and he was compelled to leave Italy to defend Carthage. Back in Africa he was defeated decisively at the Battle of Zama in 202 B.C., and the war came to an end a year later. The great Carthaginian general then went to Macedonia to try to arouse resistance to the Romans in that country.

Wars with Macedonia and the Near East. The Romans in defeating Carthage and taking over several of the former Carthaginian possessions, had undertaken at the same time certain important responsibilities, one of which was to see that the Adriatic Sea was kept free for commerce. When a group of pirates threatened this commerce, the Romans as a matter of course were called in to suppress them. As long as pirates were able to threaten this sea, the Romans felt that the only course was to take for themselves a bridgehead on the Greek side of the Adriatic. This brought them into conflict with the rulers of Greece.

Since we last considered the Greek cities of the mainland, Macedonia had maintained a general jurisdiction over the whole country, although many different areas possessed virtual autonomy. Leagues of city-states had grown up, as in the Hellenic period, but the northern and the southern leagues were in constant conflict with one another, and with Macedonia. Already before the end of the Punic Wars, Rome had had to fight against Macedonia, but the war had ended with a peace satisfactory to the Romans. Meanwhile, King Philip V of Macedonia, though willing to be at peace with Rome, was trying to expand his domain elsewhere. This brought requests to Rome from both the Aetolian League of Greece and other small states in Greece and the Near East. Philip had as an ally the Seleucid monarch Antiochus III the Great, who was engaged in expanding his own empire at the expense of the Egyptian Ptolemies. The Romans therefore sent an ultimatum to Philip to stop his aggressions, and when this was rejected they entered the war against him and quickly won the support of both leagues in Greece (198 B.C.), which were anxious to lessen the power of their Macedonian overlord. The war was soon settled in favor of the Romans, and the Roman consul Flamininus in a magnificent gesture proclaimed the complete independence of all Greeks who had previously been subject to Macedonia.

Though Philip had learned his lesson Antiochus had not. The Romans were soon at war with him when he attempted to conquer Thrace on the Greek mainland, on the pretext that it had been part of the earlier Seleucid domains. Once more Roman arms were successful and Antiochus was utterly defeated. In the course of the war the Aetolian League of northern Greece had joined Antiochus, and its members were now reduced to the status of Roman subject allies. Philip of Macedonia had remained loyal to the Romans during the war, but was disgruntled by the peace, which was wholly in

Rome's favor. After Rome had fought another brief war with Philip's successor, Perseus, the Macedonian kingdom was destroyed and the territory divided into four self-governing republics under Roman protection.

In comparison with earlier wars this last war with Macedonia was much closer to a real war of aggression. The wealthier classes in Rome were finding that the possession of an empire gave fine opportunities both for war leaders and for bankers to make considerable profits. From this time on it may be considered that the Romans were not so much drawn into wars as anxious to engage in them for profit. Following the defeat of Perseus in 172 B.C., the Romans began to interfere in Spain. The pacification of Macedonia proved to be impossible under the system just inaugurated by the Romans, and Rome finally annexed the country and made it into a province in 148 B.C. Another rebellion broke out in central Greece almost immediately afterwards and the Romans took severe vengeance, destroying Corinth, the richest city in Greece, and winning enormous booty thereby (146 B.C.). In the same year Carthage, which had given very little offence to Rome since the Second Punic War but nevertheless continued to be feared by Rome, was likewise destroyed.

Finally the ancient and prosperous kingdom of Pergamum in northwestern Asia Minor was bequeathed by its king to Rome in 133 B.C. The old ruler had no successor to inherit his domain, and it seemed better to give the territory to Rome freely rather than to have it conquered in due course.

The Provincial System. Brief mention should be made of the system by which Rome governed the new territories that she conquered. At first Rome preferred to keep allies, if reliable, on the thrones of the territories she conquered. But such men were rare, and usually did not remain reliable, from a Roman point of view. The almost invariable result was that sooner or later the territory was annexed and became a province, under direct Roman control.

Provinces were ruled by Roman governors, either proconsuls or propraetors, according to their importance. These men received their appointments the year after they had held office as consuls or praetors, holding them, as a rule, for not more than two years. They were provided with a small army, but not with a civil service. Thus taxes could be collected only by private enterprise, with the governor supplying the necessary compulsion. This private enterprise was permitted by law to keep a small percentage of the tax money in exchange for its services, the percentage being regulated by a charter, issued by the Romans when the province was annexed. The trouble with this system was that no proper check could be kept on the capitalists who collected the taxes except by the governor, who only in rare cases performed his duty. Usually he himself was bribed by the capitalists to wink at their depredations, and although there were special courts at Rome set up to try cases of corruption, it was difficult to secure convictions from the senators who manned the courts, since they themselves might hope at some time in their lives to take advantage of the system when they too became provincial governors. Because senators were not permitted to engage in business directly and were never paid for their public services, it was not surprising that many of them looked forward to their years as provincial governors to recoup the very considerable expenses they had incurred by holding office, including the huge sums they had been compelled to expend to win elections.

Consequences of the Expansion. A few results of the conquests should be noted. The devastations of Hannibal in Italy had driven many of the old small peasant proprietors from their land, and the land itself was grievously laid waste. When the Romans again took over this territory, much capital was needed to reclaim it and bring it again under cultivation. Such funds were not available to the former peasant proprietors. Only rich senators and bankers had the kind of capital needed. The greater part of southern Italy therefore was divided into large estates called *latifundia,* worked by slave labor, which was readily available since prisoners of war were usually enslaved. Even when the land had not been devastated by the enemy, the ordinary conscript soldier too often found when he returned from a long campaign that his land had been taken over by some member of the upper classes whom he was in no position to expel. His only recourse was to join the Roman urban proletariat and use his vote, which he still possessed, to try to win back his land. Meanwhile, it was very difficult for him to make any kind of living in Rome, which was not an industrial city, and where work was scarce. The Roman proletarian problem, indeed, was never solved; republican politicians and emperors alike were compelled to buy the good will or votes of the proletariat by ever increasing grain subsidies and free entertainment.

Lastly mention should also be made of the increasing wealth of the Roman middle classes during the last period of the Republic. The expansion of Rome presented many opportunities for enrichment. Capitalists could make money from tax farming and land speculation; lawyers suffered from no lack of clients. Generals, and even common soldiers, were able to lay their hands on much booty during successful campaigns, such as those in Greece and Macedonia. Though they kept some of the money, much more fell into the hands of men experienced in its management. When campaigns were profitable, it was natural for generals to see to it that some wars were fought during their period of command; thus competition for lucrative commands increased, and would-be commanders were willing to invest their capital in election campaigns by which they could rise to the higher official ranks and thus win these commands.

The stage was thus set for the efforts at reform made by the brothers Gracchi. The Senate and the middle classes, aside from a few men of moral principle, were no doubt well enough satisfied with the existing system. But it was the poor citizens who commanded the majority of votes in the Tribal Assembly. What they needed was a leader who could channel their inchoate grievances into a program of social and economic reform. This leadership was now offered by the Gracchi.

FROM THE GRACCHAN REVOLUTION TO THE FALL OF THE REPUBLIC

The Failure of the Gracchi Brothers. Tiberius Gracchus was elected tribune in 133 B.C. on a program of land redistribution calculated to appeal above all to the dispossessed farmers, many of whom were now living in Rome or were willing to come to Rome for the voting. But any tribune who braved the opposition of the Senate was necessarily in a difficult position. He himself could hold office only for a single year, and any legislation he proposed could be vetoed by any of his colleagues. Since there were now ten tribunes, it was not too difficult for his opponents to persuade or bribe one of them to interpose his veto. Furthermore, the tribune and his Tribal Assembly did not control the funds, which remained safely in the senatorial treasury.

Tiberius succeeded in overcoming these obstacles for a few months, but the effort cost him his life. A tribune named Octavius duly cast his veto, whereupon Tiberius called the Assembly and had him deposed and replaced by another man more favorable to his program. A land-reform law, limiting the size of holdings, was then passed, but it had of course been passed illegally. By an unusual coincidence, as noted earlier, the king of Pergamum died in 133 B.C., leaving his whole kingdom, with its treasury, to the Roman people. Both Tiberius and the Senate accepted the bequest, but Tiberius had the greater right to be considered as the representative of the Roman people, and the Senate acquiesced. The money was then used to put the land reform into operation. What caused Tiberius' downfall was his decision to stand illegally for re-election. Rather than face an indefinite period of popular rule, under the leadership of a tribune, the Senate took the law into its own hands, and murdered Tiberius on election day. It took no further steps to prevent the land redistribution, demonstrating thereby that it was not the reform itself so much as popular government to which it objected.

The land reform did not by any means solve the problems of the Roman proletariat. There was simply not enough land available in Italy to be divided among all the would-be farmers. Moreover, some of the men who had acquired the land promptly sold it back again to its original owners, thus defeating the purpose of the measure. During the course of the next ten years it seems that a law was passed allowing the tribunes to succeed themselves, for when Gaius Gracchus, the younger brother of Tiberius, was elected tribune in his turn in 123 B.C. it was expected that he would be able to be re-elected to office for as long as he held the good opinion of the people.

Gaius Gracchus, however, inaugurated a much more ambitious program than his brother, and this time his senatorial opposition adopted tactics quite different from those of 133. A senatorial tool was elected tribune at the same time as Gaius Gracchus, and proceeded, with no intention of putting his own laws into effect, to outbid him rather than veto his bills. This was possible because Gaius Gracchus was fairly conservative in the measures he suggested, and not all of them were popular with the people. Especially unpopular was his proposal to confer Roman citizenship on the

Italians who did not yet possess it. The poor of Rome did not wish to share their privileges with the Italians, preferring to retain the position of superiority in Rome to which their citizenship entitled them. Thus Gaius' program ran into opposition, and when he stood for re-election in 122 B.C. his senatorial opponent received more votes than he, though both were elected. When he stood again in 121 B.C., he was actually defeated. This provided the senatorial party with the chance for which it had been waiting. Gracchus, knowing that he was in danger, enrolled a personal bodyguard, a game at which two could play. The consul of the year was a well-known Roman gangster, elected with senatorial help because of the role that was expected of him. Gang warfare broke out in Rome, and the Senate declared martial law, calling upon the consul to take all measures to preserve the peace. Thus fortified, he took active steps against Gracchus and his followers. In the ensuing purge of the popular party Gracchus lost his life.

By this action, the senatorial party had declared its own bankruptcy. Rather than submit to popular government and the loss of its privileged position, it had preferred to take to the sword. Thereafter it was never again supreme in the country, for the future lay with the soldiers of fortune who could depend upon an army. The rest of the history of the Roman Republic consists of little but the competition between the various military leaders for control of the state.

Marius and the Jugurthine War. The first contender was a common soldier of some military ability who used the office of consul to make himself supreme in the state. Marius, however, had no political ability whatever, and the period of his ascendancy was marked by extreme demagogic measures introduced and put into effect by his political henchmen. Marius obtained his chance in 107 B.C. when a war in Africa with a prince named Jugurtha went consistently against the Romans, in spite of changes in the consulship and, thus, in the command of the army. It was widely bruited that the commanders were being bought off by Jugurtha, who had indeed said in his youth that Rome was a place where everything was for sale. Marius, who was the equivalent of a colonel in the Roman army and second in command to the consul, was able to instigate among his political allies enough trouble in Rome to obtain permission to return to stand for the office of consul. He was elected without difficulty and returned to Africa as commander. In order to win the war he carried out a thoroughgoing reform of the army.

The Roman army up to this time was a conscript force, but since the founding of the Republic no man had been allowed to serve in the army unless he possessed a minimum of property. What Marius did was to put the army on a volunteer basis. This does not look like an exceptional kind of reform, but its results were momentous. The volunteers who were enrolled were taken primarily from the landless and often penniless lower classes in Rome and were whipped into shape as soldiers by Marius, who had a considerable talent as a drill sergeant. But funds for their pay were scarce and naturally were not to be relied upon, since the Senate had to vote them. Marius therefore began the policy for paying for his troops out of the booty won in warfare. This meant that the soldier's pay was dependent on the success of his arms and that he would not be too willing to serve under an incompetent general who could not win victories for him. Thus the armies of the last century of the Republic became almost the personal property of their generals.

Marius put a fairly speedy end to the war in Africa, largely owing to the diplomatic abilities of his own second in command, one Cornelius Sulla, who managed to capture Jugurtha. Marius was soon called home to deal with a serious threat from invading German tribes, known as the Cimbri and Teutones. Since Rome was in very great danger from these barbarians, Marius was allowed to be re-elected consul and to use his newly organized army to defeat the Germans. Although it took him some considerable time, during which he was elected consul six times, he was able to settle the threat in the end. For his sixth consulship he needed the support of a popular party, since the war in Italy was virtually over. He obtained this through the maneuvers of two demagogues who distributed bribes wholesale for his election and proceeded to plunder the city for the purpose of making a profit out of their rule. However, when conditions in Rome became so bad that the Senate called upon Marius to restore law and order and declared martial law once more, Marius obeyed and disavowed his henchmen. His usefulness to both the people and the Senate now being over, he went into exile in Africa.

The Social War. Meanwhile, the Italians who had been promised enfranchisement by Gaius Gracchus had been becoming increasingly restive. Several Roman officials had in the course of the first decade of the first century B.C. taken up the Italian cause. But this cause continued to be unpopular with the people and nothing was done. In 90 B.C. a war broke out with the Italian allies, and the Senate was forced to recall Marius and to allow him to enroll non-Italian troops, which were slowly able to make headway. Before the war was over the rights the Italians had demanded were granted. Marius himself did not gain much glory from the war, most of which went to his more successful lieutenant of African days, Sulla. When the war ended a new and potentially lucrative command in the East opened up, for which Marius and Sulla were rivals.

The Ascendancy of Sulla. The Assembly, still dominated by the popular party, had no use for the aristocrat Sulla. It therefore appointed Marius, in spite of the fact that he was now sixty-seven years old, to the command, while the Senate appointed Sulla. The Senate had handled such matters in the past, but in the existing circumstances no one could say which of the two parties was really entitled to appoint the leader. Both enrolled armies, but Sulla, with a better reputation at the time than Marius, had a considerably superior army at his command. But he was at first unable to join it, and for a while was a fugitive in Rome before he could escape to join his army. Once he had done so he turned the army against Rome, and Marius was again forced into exile. Sulla went off to the East with his army, where he succeeded in defeating Mithridates VI, king of Pontus, an inveterate enemy of Rome, who had been expanding his kingdom at the expense of the Romans, and had recently massacred all the Italians in his dominions.

As soon as Sulla was out of Italy, Marius returned. But after being elected to his seventh consulship he died within one month. Though the popular party was able to control Rome during Sulla's absence it was clear that unless it could enroll an army equal to that of Sulla, as soon as the latter returned, it could expect nothing but punishment and vengeance from him. In due course Sulla did return, carried out a purge of the popular party, and had himself elected dictator for an unlimited period. Since Sulla was not interested in overthrowing the state and ruling indefinitely himself, and since he belonged to the senatorial class, he decided to throw his weight on the side of the senatorial oligarchy and take away power from the popular Assembly. But the constitution that he dictated worked only for the two years more that he lived.

The First Triumvirate. Soon after Sulla's death the Senate infringed his constitution by appointing a young soldier who had won his spurs under Sulla to a long-term command in Spain, where a rebellion was in progress. While this young man, Pompey, was settling the Spanish troubles, a slave war broke out in Italy which required the attention of the Senate. It appointed another capable soldier named Crassus, who was later to be well known as a banker and capitalist, to the command in Italy. When both these minor wars were settled at the same time, Pompey and Crassus joined together to demand that they be elected consuls, although they had neither of them gone through all the offices required before they could become consuls under the Sullan constitution. The Senate being in no position to refuse, Pompey and Crassus at once restored the legislative power to the Assembly, without any serious opposition. Soon afterward Pompey was given a long-term command by the Assembly, first in the Mediterranean to clear up some pirates who were threatening the food supply of Rome, and then in the East. Pompey, indeed, was an extremely capable soldier and administrator, but the work to be done in the East occupied him for many years, since he finally undertook to organize into an efficient provincial system the entire Near East that had come under Roman control. During the period when he was away all the politicians in Rome were aware of what his return would mean for them and that no force in Rome could possibly stand against him if he wished to become the first one-man ruler of Rome. During these years Cicero held the consulship for one year and suppressed the famous conspiracy of Cataline, against whom he delivered some of his most famous orations. But in due course Pompey settled the problems confronting him in the East and returned to Rome with his army.

Pompey, to the surprise of most Romans, disbanded his army as soon as he set foot in Italy, relying upon his personal prestige to obtain from the Senate what he wanted, which was the ratification of all his acts in the East and pensions for his soldiers. But since he no longer held any office of state in Rome, he needed some political support. This he did not possess at the time, even though he had behaved with perfect legality and propriety in disbanding his army. With more courage than good sense the Senate, led by a disgruntled general who had been superseded by Pompey, refused to grant him his moderate requests, in spite of the enormous booty that he supplied to the senatorial treasury. It was therefore necessary for him to look around for some means of persuading the Senate. The only means available was his army, which, though disbanded, was perfectly capable of springing to arms again for the sake of its pensions. Political support was offered to him by the man who was next in line to become a consul, Julius Caesar, and by Crassus, who had financed Caesar in his earlier years and was naturally interested in seeing that his protégé had the means to pay his debts. Thus Pompey was forced into the arms of Caesar and Crassus, and when the Senate again refused his demands, Caesar, now consul, was able to make use of Pompey's troops to compel the Senate to acquiesce. This informal and irregular alliance between Pompey, with the largest army in the empire, Caesar, a rising soldier who had just come from a successful campaign in Spain, and Crassus, a former general but now the richest man in Rome, was known as the First Triumvirate (60 B.C.).

Caesar, having invested so much in his career, and with no real love lost between him and Pompey, wished for a command similar to that Pompey had held, by which he might hope to win a similar reputation and power. The Senate was disinclined to grant much of a command following his year as consul, but again Pompey's troops supplied it with a good reason for agreeing to his requests. Caesar was appointed to a long-term command in Gaul, where at the moment there were minor disturbances, but not such as to lead Pompey to believe that Caesar would be able to make very much capital out of them. He could not have been more mistaken. Caesar soon embarked on the conquest of the whole of Gaul, while Pompey was left as a private citizen. He still nominally commanded the Roman navy and some paper armies, but he rapidly lost his position of supremacy to the able and ambitious Caesar. During the ten years of the Triumvirate Caesar's power constantly increased as he trained loyal officers and legions, while Pompey, although he was occasionally called upon by the Senate to restore order in Rome, gained little in prestige or military experience. Meanwhile, Crassus, desiring to repeat the military exploits of his youth, and no doubt jealous of his colleagues, suddenly asked for a command in the East against the Parthians. On this being granted,

he set out for the East, but was led into a trap by the Parthians. The
Romans suffered a stunning defeat at Carrhae in 53 B.C., and Crassus
himself was killed. Thus the stage was set for a final struggle
between Pompey and Caesar.

Julius Caesar and the Civil War. During the years of the
Triumvirate, Pompey had been gradually inclining toward the
senatorial side, and his jealousy of Caesar had been increasing. The
Senate demanded that Caesar should return to give an accounting
of his deeds in Gaul and possibly to stand trial for some of them.
It also commanded him to leave his army as soon as he returned
to Italy. Caesar, however, not wishing to suffer the same fate as
Pompey a few years before, after a few abortive negotiations with
Pompey and the Senate, entered Italy with his army and marched
straight on Rome. Pompey, calling for his troops, was unable to
recruit an adequate army in the time available and went to Greece,
where he was better known and had more support than in the West.
Caesar pursued him there; and Pompey, in spite of a numerical
superiority of troops, was defeated at the Battle of Pharsalus in 48
B.C. and fled to Egypt, where he was murdered. Caesar pursued him
to Egypt, where he met the Egyptian queen, Cleopatra, by whom
he had a son. Thereafter Caesar mopped up the remains of the
senatorial supporters in further battles in North Africa and Spain.
At last, in 46 B.C., he returned to Rome, where he was undisputed
master. He assumed the title of dictator, like Sulla before him, but
was unable to decide on exactly the form that the new state was to
take. Caesar, therefore, did not really found the Roman Empire,
although he made it possible for his great-nephew, Octavian, to
become the first *princeps* of Rome.

During the next two years, which were all that remained of
Caesar's life, he did a prodigious work in trying to reform the
provincial system and to make some reforms in Italy. But he did
not have the time or, apparently, the political ability to regularize
his position and to carry out the reform of the Senate and the assemblies which had clearly been demonstrated to be necessary.
In 44 B.C. on the Ides (fifteenth) of March, he was murdered by
some of his dissident officers and senatorial opponents.

The Second Triumvirate. The conspirators who had murdered
Caesar had no idea of just what they wanted to do afterward. Although they controlled Rome, they appeared to feel that their only
quarrel was with Caesar himself and did not therefore put an end

to the consul Marcus Antonius, who was in their power, in spite of the fact that he was a well-known supporter of Caesar. Caesar's official second-in-command, a man named Lepidus, was fortunate in that he was able to join his army, but the army was not likely to be loyal to him, since he possessed few qualifications for his position. Meanwhile Caesar's great-nephew, Gaius Octavianus, a young man with little military experience, who had been named as Caesar's personal heir, and adopted and given the name of Caesar in the dictator's will, was busy exploiting his new name and position. He was successful in winning over much of Caesar's army by paying the donatives promised to the soldiers under Caesar's will, a task neglected by Antony and Lepidus. With the aid of this army Octavian entered Rome, and was entrusted with the command against Antony, who was engaged in fighting an army led by one of Caesar's murderers in the north. Helped by the two consuls, Octavian succeeded in defeating Antony, who escaped across the Alps. Then he returned to Rome in triumph, expecting at least the thanks of the Senate.

But the Senate proceeded to make the same mistake that it had made before with Pompey. Under the leadership of the aging Cicero, it treated Octavian in an offhand manner and refused him the consulship on the (correct) technical grounds that he was not qualified for it. Nevertheless it was a serious blunder, for Octavian at once entered into an agreement with Antony and Lepidus, known as the Second Triumvirate. This combination possessed all the military forces in the state that were not in the hands of the murderers of Caesar, who had been busily engaged in raising an army in Greece. Once the triumvirs had defeated this army at the battle of Philippi in 42 B.C., Rome was at their feet. They carried out further proscriptions of the senatorial class, and each of the triumvirs used force to dispose of his enemies. Cicero fell to the vengeance of Antony, against whom he had directed some of the most eloquent orations in his life, known as the *Philippics* (after the orations of Demosthenes against Philip of Macedon). Antony was then granted by his colleagues an extended command in the East, to avenge the battle of Carrhae against the Parthians, while Octavian was permitted to rule in Italy. Lepidus, who had been accepted as triumvir only because he happened at the time to command a small army, was shunted aside and thereafter became of little account.

The next years were spent by both Octavian and Antony in exploiting their respective positions for the purpose of winning supreme power in the state. Antony began his famous liaison with Cleopatra and to some degree neglected his duties in the East, while trying to build himself a loyal personal following. Octavian cleared the Mediterranean of pirates and gave his attention to many pressing political tasks, including the creation of a strong political party that supported him. The history of Pompey and Caesar did not repeat itself. Octavian did not neglect the tasks that fell to him, and he was, in his way, at least as energetic as Antony. The triumvirate was renewed regularly, but all the time that Antony was in the East, Octavian was busy drawing unfavorable attention in Rome to his rival's activities. The Romans regarded the Egyptians and other Orientals as far inferior to themselves, and Octavian lost no opportunity of suggesting that if Antony were to defeat him, Rome might well be ruled from the East, and the traditional institutions be overthrown in favor of an Oriental despotism. In 33 B.C. the triumvirate was not renewed, and it was evident that Antony was at last prepared to make his bid for power in Rome and to dispossess his rival.

Octavian, however, was very well prepared for him, and had at his disposal a first-class general named Agrippa. The final contest was a naval one, which Octavian won without any difficulty (Battle of Actium, 31 B.C.). Shortly afterward both Antony and Cleopatra committed suicide, leaving Octavian the undisputed master of the Roman Empire, without any visible competitor on the horizon.

THE PRINCIPATE

The Reign of Augustus. When he returned, Octavian was granted by the Senate the title of *pater patriae,* the "father of his country." From this time onward he adopted the title of Augustus, by which name he is usually known. For the last few years Augustus had been settling one by one the major problems in Italy and that part of the empire under his control. He was now faced with the necessity of legitimizing his position once and for all. The course of action that he chose was well calculated to please the Roman people, who were very conservative and attached to their old institutions. Whereas Julius Caesar had packed the Senate with provincials and soldiers, altering its aristocratic composition considerably, and incurring the enmity of the old senators in the process, Augustus decided that he would, as he termed it, "restore the Republic." This of course he did not do. What he did was restore the old forms of the Republic and carve out for himself a special position which had no precedent in the past. He called himself *princeps* or "first citizen." This title, however, gave him no power. The powers he needed were complete control over the army and over legislation. He, therefore, without becoming actually proconsul, assumed for himself, or had conferred on him, the *power* of a proconsul (*proconsulare imperium*), and he assumed the civil power of a republican tribune, again without becoming tribune himself (*tribunicia potestas*). When he decided later in his life that he wished to reform the religion, he became also *pontifex maximus* or chief priest. Sometimes during his reign Augustus also undertook the duties and the official title of consul, but at other times he caused the men whom he wished to hold office to be elected. It goes without saying that no one in the reign of Augustus was ever elected contrary to his expressed wishes. But the elections were nevertheless formally carried out. All the principes or emperors after Augustus were granted the proconsular and tribunician powers, and many of the emperors insured the succession of their sons or other nominees by granting them these powers before their own deaths. Augustus treated the Senate with great respect and used it as his legislature. But since the only method of entering the Senate was by holding office, and Augustus' approval was necessary to hold office, the Senate soon became a stronghold of his supporters.

The proconsular power enjoyed by Augustus gave him supreme command of all Roman armies. But he rarely exercised this command himself. He reorganized the system of provinces and divided them into three categories. Those provinces which did not have any frontiers on the outskirts of the Roman Empire and facing the barbarians, he entrusted to the Senate, and their governors were officially appointed by the Senate, as in the time of the Republic. The outer provinces, with boundaries bordering on the barbarian lands, Augustus entrusted to his own nominees who were responsible to him alone. Such governors could retain their commands indefinitely, as long as they continued to hold the confidence of the emperor. Egypt alone, being the chief granary of Rome, was entrusted to a member of the middle class (equestrian order) with the title of *prefect*. Augustus himself was a Pharaoh in Egypt. The new governors of all types of provinces were now paid adequate salaries, and to be corrupt was now both less necessary and far more dangerous, since the governor could be brought to justice without difficulty by the emperor.

Augustus ruled Rome for forty-five years after the Battle of Actium, and he made some headway in solving almost all the problems bequeathed to him by the Republic. Though his greatest achievement was certainly the re-establishment of a stable and accepted government after more than a century of near-anarchy, second to it was the reform of the provincial administration. From these reforms stemmed all the others. For example, tax collectors were now made aware that they had a master in Rome, as were the old tax-farming corporations, and private armies were abolished. The numerous city-states which dotted the Roman Empire were left undisturbed, and their self-governing institutions confirmed. Only the unemployment problem in Rome remained intractable. Toward the end of Augustus' life his legions in Germany were so seriously defeated that he decided to keep the Rhine as the imperial frontier and abandoned the effort to reach the Elbe. The greatest difficulty for such an empire as his, was what to do about the succession. Augustus himself lived so long that even his grandsons died before him. He himself was therefore obliged to choose his stepson, with whom he had maintained rather poor relations during his reign, as his successor. This man, who ruled under the name of Tiberius, was granted Augustus' two chief powers before the latter died. Tiberius therefore was able to succeed to the position of princeps without opposition.

The problem of succession was to persist throughout the entire Roman Empire. The empire was not one that could be ruled by an incompetent, and if the hereditary principle were used, there was nothing to prevent the rule from falling into the hands of a man totally unfitted to hold it. On the other hand, if any ruler passed over his son and chose someone else to occupy the position, this son, in view of the hereditary principle accepted in most other countries at the time, would be likely to be seriously disgruntled by the choice of his father and perhaps rebel against the designated successor. When Tiberius himself died, he also had no sons, but the hereditary principle was observed since Tiberius had designated no successor himself. The incompetent madman who then ascended the throne nearly destroyed the whole imperial system while it was yet in its infancy.

The Julian Line. Tiberius was a very expert soldier and under-stood the provinces. Thus the provincial administration under his rule was even better than it had been under Augustus. But Tiberius was himself very unpopular in Rome since he had none of the easy graces of his predecessor and had been indeed studiously snubbed by Augustus until it was clear that he would have to be his succes-sor. During the reign of Tiberius the praetorian guard, the only body of troops in Rome, already gave indications of how important it would be in determining the imperial succession. The prefect of the praetorian guard in the reign of Tiberius, a man named Sejanus, conspired against his master at a time when Tiberius had retired to the beautiful island of Capri in order to escape from his unpopular-ity in Rome. Information was supplied to the exiled princeps about this conspiracy, and a letter from him was sufficient to cause the fall of the prefect. Thereafter Tiberius lived in fear of assassination and began the notorious system of using informers (*delatores*) who were paid for information (or misinformation) on plots that were being hatched against the ruler. Probably it was fear of informers that led Pontius Pilate to agree to the crucifixion of Jesus Christ in the Roman province of Judaea in the reign of Tiberius, as described in the next chapter. Tiberius died in A.D. 37, perhaps murdered, as was rumored at the time, leaving a reputation for implacable tyranny, which was almost certainly unjustified—though it is probably true that his rule was based less on consent than that of Augustus, and he relied heavily on the treason law (*maiestas*), under which he punished his many enemies.

The great-nephew of Tiberius, adopted as his grandson, and usu-ally known by his nickname of Caligula rather than his formal name of Gaius, was a hopeless incompetent, highly extravagant, and cer-tainly was insane before he died. He had little hesitation in executing his enemies; indeed, at one time he is said to have wished that the people of Rome might have only one head among them so that it might be cut off at one blow. The provincial government, however, which had been established so effectively by Augustus and Tiberius, was little affected by the feeble rule at home, though Caligula set up a number of client-kings in the provinces and thus weakened the defense against the barbarians. He also created many difficulties for the Jews in Palestine and nearly provoked them to rebellion. It was his crazy intention to set up a statue of himself in the Holy of Holies in the Temple, but he was murdered before he could put his plan into operation. He was succeeded by his uncle, a middle-aged historian, Claudius, who was chosen by the praetorian guard and accepted by the Senate.

In spite of being completely under the domination of successive wives, Claudius proved himself to be an excellent administrator and greatly improved the provincial system during his reign. He may also be credited with the founding of the Roman imperial civil service, a very necessary innovation since the old republican system of tax farming was still largely in operation. The new imperial bureaucrats, often chosen from former slaves of Greek ancestry, undertook much of the difficult clerical work which had to be performed now that the emperor had so many tasks. Claudius virtually inaugurated a cabinet system under which his secretaries were responsible for the various departments of states. He also began the conquest of England, which Julius Caesar himself had not been able to carry out, although he had been the first Roman soldier to engage in hostilities with Britain. Claudius' two wives, Messalina and Agrippina (the Younger), played a considerable part in affairs of state. Messalina had her favorites, whom she persuaded Claudius to employ, while Agrippina spent most of her period of marriage to Claudius in trying to ensure the succession for her own son (by a former marriage) named Nero. In this she proved successful, since Claudius in fact disinherited his own son, Britannicus, before his death. Soon after Nero's succession, Britannicus, needless to say, was murdered.

Nero was the last of the Julian line to sit on the throne. During the first five years of Nero's rule, he was content to leave the administration of the realm to his former tutor, the Stoic philosopher Seneca, and to Burrus, the praetorian prefect. For these five years Rome was ruled well, and Nero did not as yet show those marks of an unbalanced nature which were to appear so conspicuously later. Nero's interests then lay in such affairs as chariot races and acting on the public stage. The tremendous shows he put on in Rome endeared him to the populace but quickly emptied the treasury. When a fire broke out in Rome, Nero was accused of having started it, probably because he enjoyed the fire and sang verses from Homer to the accompaniment of his lyre while it was raging. It was for this fire that the Christians were blamed, and as a result of it many Christians met their deaths in the arena. In the later years of his reign Nero became a capricious tyrant, using his autocratic power to execute those who criticized him, without any form of trial, or, at best, sending them his instructions to commit suicide. His tutor Seneca died in response to just such a request. In the last years of his reign there were several rebellions against him until at last one was successful, and Nero was compelled to commit suicide.

FROM PRINCIPATE TO EMPIRE

The Year of the Four Emperors. This event ushered in the so-called Year of the Four Emperors. Nero being childless and having made no provision whatever for his succession, some of the provincial governors, who commanded armies loyal to their own persons, decided that they would seek the throne for themselves. Galba, commander of the Spanish legions, reached Rome first and had himself proclaimed emperor. This was not to the taste of the praetorian guards, who had Galba assassinated and elevated their own prefect, Otho, to the throne. But meanwhile the German legions were on the march to Rome under their own leader, Vitellius, who marched on Rome with his legions from Germany and put an end to Otho. However, a more substantial leader was already on the way to Rome. One of the commanders in the East, Titus Flavius Vespasianus, proclaimed himself emperor at Alexandria and marched in a rather leisurely manner to Rome, many troops from other provinces joining him on the way. Rome was captured in spite of the defense offered by the Vitellians, and Vitellius himself was killed. Vespasian was able to have himself accepted by the Senate and the people, and founded the Flavian dynasty.

The Flavian Dynasty. Vespasian was an Italian of rural plebeian stock. He was a fairly effective emperor, and at his death he left his throne to his eldest son Titus, who succeeded without any opposition. When Titus died after a very brief reign, he was succeeded by Domitian, who proved himself quite a good soldier and in many ways improved the provincial administration. But he was personally autocratic and capricious and excited many revolts. He revived the worst excesses from the reigns of Tiberius and Nero by encouraging informers and demanded that he should be called *dominus* (lord) and *deus* (god). This was the first time that any Roman emperor save the unbalanced Caligula and Nero had claimed divinity in his own lifetime. Previously the emperors had been deified after death if the Senate authorized such deification. The Senate, in particular, resented the pretensions of a man of such a low-born family and was, in general, behind most of the revolts against him. He was murdered in a palace revolution in A.D. 96. During his reign his general Agricola succeeded in completing the conquest of Britain, and many small annexations were made in Germany, thus extending gradually the boundaries of the empire.

The "Good Emperors." At the unexpected murder of Domitian, no general was ready to proclaim himself emperor, and the right to nominate a successor fell to the Senate, which chose one of its most respected members, a man named Nerva, as emperor. Nerva's most valuable act during his reign was to adopt a Spaniard named Trajan, the most effective general in the imperial armies, as his successor. Being childless, Nerva actually went through a form of ceremony of adoption of Trajan as his son, thus combining the principles of heredity and nomination. Trajan was a well-balanced man and he was almost certainly the best emperor since Augustus. But he engaged in a military campaign of dubious value for the empire and annexed the province of Dacia (Rumania), to the north of the river Danube, a territory which could be defended only with great difficulty. Trajan himself, like Nerva, had no son, and thus chose a man who was noted as a first-class administrator to succeed him. This was Hadrian, whose administrative talents were now to be put at the service of the empire.

During the reign of Hadrian (117–138) Roman civilization reached its height. But the empire was now clearly an autocracy, and the notion that the emperor was merely the first citizen was tacitly abandoned. Hadrian, an indefatigable bureaucrat himself, reorganized the administration of the empire in such a manner that all phases of Roman life were under his direct control. Imperial tax collectors had now almost completely replaced the old tax farmers; and the municipalities in the provinces, which for the first century of the Empire had been virtually self-governing under their own elected magistrates, now had to submit to the presence of imperial bureaucrats who saw to it that taxes were paid and the administration was efficient. The Senate, which had had much to do during the first century of the Empire, was always treated with great respect by the "Good Emperors," but it lost what power it had left during the period. The old senatorial provinces were now subordinated to imperial control in the interests of efficiency, although the senators still had nominal control and had certain tasks remaining to them. The army's pay was increased and much of it was recruited locally, losing thereby in mobility, but making this still voluntary service

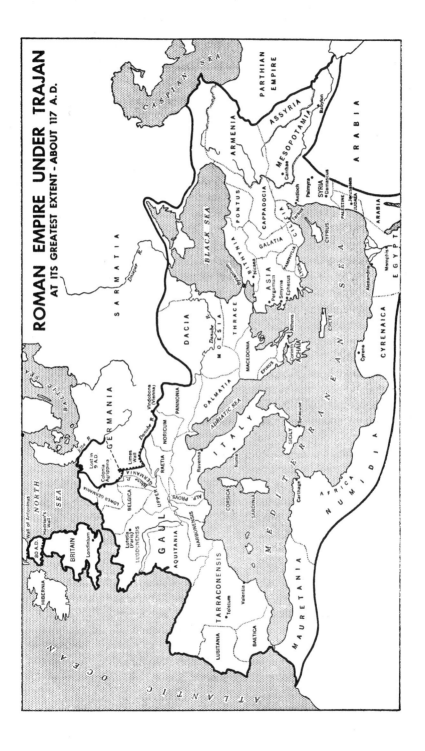

ROMAN EMPIRE UNDER TRAJAN
AT ITS GREATEST EXTENT - ABOUT 117 A.D.

PARTHIAN EMPIRE

CASPIAN SEA

ARMENIA

ASSYRIA

MESOPOTAMIA

Carrhae

Babylon

PONTUS

CAPPADOCIA

SYRIA

Palmyra

Damascus

ARABIA

A R A B I A

SARMATIA

Dniester R.

BLACK SEA

BITHYNIA

GALATIA

Nicaea

ASIA

CILICIA

Antioch

PALESTINE

Jerusalem

JUDEA

CYPRUS

Tarsus

Pergamum

Smyrna

Ephesus

DACIA

Danube R.

THRACE

MOESIA

MACEDONIA

EPIRUS

Athens

Corinth

ACHAIA

CRETE

Cyrene

CYRENAICA

M E D I T E R R A N E A N   S E A

EGYPT

Memphis

Alexandria

GERMANIA

Vindobona (Vienna)

Danube R.

PANNONIA

NORICUM

DALMATIA

ADRIATIC SEA

I T A L Y

Ravenna

Rome

SICILY

Syracuse

Carthage

AFRICA

NUMIDIA

Lost in 9 A.D.

Colonia Agrippina

Limes Wall

RAETIA

ALP. PROVS.

Elbe R.

Weser R.

Rhine R.

BELGICA

LOWER GERMANIA

UPPER GERMANIA

Wall of Antoninus

Hadrian's Wall

80 A.D.

BRITAIN

Londinium

HIBERNIA

NORTH SEA

BALTIC SEA

G A U L

Lutetia (Paris)

LUGDUNENSIS

AQUITANIA

NARBONENSIS

CORSICA

SARDINIA

TARRACONENSIS

Toletum

Valentia

LUSITANIA

BAETICA

MAURETANIA

A T L A N T I C   O C E A N

one of some profit to its members. Roman citizenship was greatly extended, and at least the upper classes in all the municipalities of the empire were likely to be composed entirely of citizens. The emperor no longer used the Senate for legislation, a task which had been entrusted to it by the first emperors. Hadrian became accustomed to issuing edicts which had all the force of law, sometimes without troubling to consult the Senate at all. The law courts, which had not been greatly changed from the time of Sulla in the last century of the Republic, likewise fell under imperial control. The praetors, who were the chief judges in Rome, no longer had any worthwhile initiative left to them. The principles of law under which cases were to be tried, which in previous times had been announced by the praetors at the beginning of their terms of office, were now announced by the emperor and expected to be used until a subsequent emperor changed them. This reform, also, was in the interest of efficiency, especially since Hadrian took the advice of the most skilled lawyers in his realm before announcing his legal policy. Lastly, it may be said that during the reign of Hadrian and of his successor, Antoninus Pius, almost the entire empire was at peace, and there was little danger from barbarians. The frontiers were as strongly fortified as was possible in that epoch, and the trained troops had little difficulty in repelling such border raids as were made occasionally by the barbarians.

The reign of Antoninus Pius need not detain us long. He was the inheritor of a functioning system and few problems arose in his reign. This situation was to change with the reign of Marcus Aurelius, who was forced to spend much of his life, contrary to his inclination (for he was a philosopher and a scholar, known especially for his Stoic *Meditations*), fighting against invasions by the barbarian Marcomanni. From this time onward the empire was almost never free from danger from enroaching tribes, most of which wished only for living space within it, and had no intention whatever of attempting to destroy it. When Marcus Aurelius died in 180, he left an empire which was no longer so secure as in the past. It was unfortunate that Marcus, who had himself, like his immediate predecessor, been chosen for the succession when already a mature man, should have had a son. To this utterly incompetent son, Commodus, he bequeathed the empire. With Commodus begins the real decline of the Roman Empire, though it was to survive for several centuries yet. This decline will be the subject of the next chapter.

CULTURAL AND POLITICAL ACHIEVEMENTS OF THE ROMANS

Roman Law. The greatest achievement of the Romans lies in the fields of law and government. The culture of all the lands of the empire east of Italy remained Greek, and to the Greeks the Romans never appeared as anything but cultured barbarians who had subdued them by military might and taken over their government—an attitude not unlike that of the Poles, Czechoslovaks, and East Germans toward the present-day Soviet Union. Their lives, however, were changed little by the Roman occupation until they began to be ground down by severe taxation from the third century onward. Until then the municipalities continued in most respects to be self-governing. They elected their own magistrates, and the units of the Roman army which protected them were usually stationed outside the city and caused them little trouble. To the northern and western territories of the empire, on the contrary, the Romans brought civilization. Gaul and Spain became thoroughly Romanized, Britain to a lesser extent. The ancient Celtic culture in these countries became overlaid by Roman culture, with an admixture of Greek that the Italians themselves had taken over from their eastern possessions. Even the languages of modern France and Spain are largely derived from the Latin tongue of the Romans. The governmental system of Italy was in the main transferred to these western territories; again there were prosperous municipalities with a considerable degree of self-government, and above these municipalities was the Roman imperial administration which made few demands on them, save for the taxes which were assessed on the whole empire.

Roman law was the greatest unifying influence in the empire. For the first time the human mind set itself to work on the principles of equity and tried to make law conform to what the greatest jurists thought best, rather than merely to codify the disparate customs of a great number of peoples with widely varying ethnic backgrounds. At first, under the Republic, Roman law applied only to the relatively few citizens (*jus civile*); then, as time went on and the Romans brought other peoples into their empire, a different kind of law was used to determine cases between Romans and foreigners (*jus gentium*). As the empire expanded and foreigners continued to become citizens, the older Roman civil codes fell into disuse, and it was the *jus gentium* that was extended rather than the *jus civile*. In the imperial period the *jus gentium* became the law of the whole empire, applying to citizens and noncitizens alike.

This law was always being improved by the application by Roman jurists of intensive thought to what was truly equitable. The Stoics, with their notion of "natural law" and the equality of man, made a considerable contribution to this thought. Most law is concerned with civil matters, especially the enforcement of contracts; criminal law, which the ordinary layman is accustomed to think of as "the law," actually forms a very small part of the body of law. There are many legal cases where both parties have some justice on their side. What principle is then to be used? Suppose, for example, that a man buys a property in good faith from another and resells it, only to find that the original vendor did not possess a clear title to it. The true owner then sues the last purchaser for the return of the property. Should he be compelled to restore it without being indemnified by the man from whom he bought it? The general principle as stated by the Romans which has passed into the law of the Western world, is *caveat emptor*—"Let the buyer beware." It is up to him to discover whether the man from whom he bought has a clear title and the right to dispose of it.

Under the Republic the city praetor, an official who might have no knowledge of the law, judged all cases. In 242 B.C. a foreign praetor was appointed to deal with cases involving noncitizens. Both these men might be nothing but soldiers on the way up the ladder of office, and expecting in due course to become consuls and proconsuls, military men for whom the praetorship was but a steppingstone to high military command. Obviously they needed assistance, and it became the custom for them to draw up the list of the principles under which they proposed to judge, based on past precedents. After consultation with professional jurists (*juris prudentes* —men skilled in the law, hence our word *jurisprudence*), they then issued their *edict,* by which they agreed to be bound in their year of office; and in the handling of individual cases under the edict, they constantly took advice from the professionals. At the command of the emperor Hadrian a "perpetual edict" was issued, based on previous precedents and on the best thought of which the jurists were capable. Thereafter only statute law, especially later edicts of the emperor and the Senate, modified the perpetual edict. Even so, as ever new cases were decided, new precedents for judgment were created. In the later years of the Empire, the laws were frequently collected and codified, and new decrees were issued by the emperor, whose will now "had the force of law," to take care of new situations. The process culminated in the great codification known as the *corpus juris civilis* of the Byzantine emperor Justinian in the sixth century. Thus for many centuries the law continued to grow; and when the code of Justinian was rediscovered and modified in the Middle Ages to fit the new conditions, Roman law remained the basis for the national law of all the Latin countries, and of many others, for example, Holland, which came under their influence.

Roman Cultural Achievements. For the rest, there is a very respectable body of Latin literature, much of it based, like Vergil's epic *Aeneid,* on Greek originals. However, the Romans developed several new forms, for example, satire and letters. But there was little original Roman thought, save in the specialized field of the law. The Romans, being an essentially practical people, were little interested in speculation. Their art likewise is a development of the Greek originals, tending more to decoration and massiveness, as well as to realism, than the work of their predecessors. They were extremely competent engineers, and the great Roman roads developed in Italy during the Republic, and elsewhere during the Empire, though their prime purpose was strategic, served as the means for communication between the center at Rome and the periphery of the empire and as highways for commerce. The Romans were especially skillful in building aqueducts, which carried water for long distances to areas short of rainfall.

The Latin language is spare and sinewy, not easily expressing the nuances popular with the Greeks. But it is also extremely precise, and abstract words are easily created in it, far more easily than in the more mobile and flexible Greek. Thus the languages, such as French, which are based on Latin, are even today far more precise than the Teutonic tongues, based on German, which is more suitable than Latin for the expression of feeling and of vague, rather than precise concepts. English, of course, owes its richness to the combination of Latin and Teutonic elements.

Pax Romana. The greatest achievement of the Romans was without doubt the *Pax Romana,* the Roman peace, which was maintained in the inner provinces of the empire, right up to the fifth century. The Romans put an end to the internecine struggles between the small independent city-states of the Greek mainland, and to the larger-scale wars of the Hellenistic kings. The constant struggles for the succession to the throne made little impact on the life of the ordinary provincial, who gave his allegiance without question to the winner and who was, as a rule, supremely uninterested in what particular man sat on the throne, so long as he did not disturb the provincial administration. During this period of internal peace, Europe, as a whole, became civilized and learned to live for the first time under a stable and settled regime. Without doubt the Roman government was expensive, and taxes at no time were light. But until the third century the burden was bearable, and a great deal was given by the Romans in exchange. The ordinary man throughout his lifetime never heard the tramp of marching feet, and he could expect to live out his days without dread of violence. Thus he learned to devote himself to the tasks of peace, and in the process at least the upper and middle classes became thoroughly civilized. Rome was regarded as the Eternal City, and the Empire as the most natural form of government, destined like its capital, to endure forever. It would have taken a bold prophet to foresee that the barbarians who were already pressing on the boundaries of the empire by the end of the second century, would one day succeed to its inheritance and that the order and stability provided by it would pass into history, to be replaced in the West by a full thousand years of semianarchy and local rule which we call the Middle Ages—and that not again in the history of Western man, at least to the twentieth century, would another empire arise which would provide order and reasonably good government to so many.

CHAPTER VI

CHRISTIANITY AND THE END OF THE WESTERN EMPIRE

In the early days of the Roman Empire there arose the new religion and ecclesiastical organization which were destined to succeed in large measure to its heritage. Many decades before the fall of the Empire in the West in A.D. 476, the emperor himself had moved his court from Rome, leaving its bishop, the leading official in the Christian Church, clothed with imperial authority as the virtual ruler of the city. It was the bishop of Rome who negotiated with the barbarian leaders for the safety of the Roman people during the invasions, and it was a later bishop, now called a pope (Gregory I), who a century later kept some Italian lands north of Rome out of the hands of the encroaching Lombards. These formed the nucleus of the later States of the Church. Although Gregory and his successors for a century and a half continued to acknowledge the formal suzerainty of the Byzantine emperor, for practical purposes they were sovereign in these domains.

The Catholic Church inherited the organization of the later Roman Empire, with its absolute lord, the pope, at its head, and its officials (at least in theory) appointed by and responsible to him and subject to his discipline. The canon law of the Church is solidly based on Roman law and procedure; the language of the Church to this day remains Latin, the language of the Romans. The concept of Christendom, the area in which Christianity is (or should be) the universal religion, is Roman in origin—its bounds, until Christianity expanded with new conquests and discoveries, coterminous with those of the old Empire.

Yet Christianity was in its origin a Hellenistic religion, arising out of the Near East, and it spread only slowly into the Roman lands of the West. Its earliest converts were Jews and Orientals, soon followed by Greeks. But the religion had great difficulty in making headway among the influential Romans, who were inclined to regard it as fit only for slaves, since it was the slaves, the poorer classes, and women who supplied the earliest converts. Moreover, Christianity believed in a Messiah who had been put to death by the Romans and had triumphed by sacrifice and renunciation, rather than by the kind of victory understood by the down-to-earth Romans. The soldiers of the Roman legions for two centuries preferred the competing Oriental religion of Mithraism, an offshoot of Zoroastrianism, which accepted only men as converts. But slowly, in part as the result of sporadic, sometimes severe persecutions, Christianity made headway until the Roman emperor Constantine, battling for his throne with a competitor, is said to have bargained with the Christian God that he would tolerate the new religion if he were granted the victory. He won the battle, granted toleration under the so-called Edict of Milan (A.D. 313), and before the end of his life he himself had become a Christian. Thereafter, only one of the Roman emperors, Julian (called the Apostate), adopted any other religion than Christianity. By the end of the fourth century, an emperor had proclaimed Christianity as the established and sole permitted religion of the Empire.

THE RISE OF CHRISTIANITY

The Mission of Jesus Christ. Christianity begins with the mission of Jesus Christ in Palestine. His work was performed among the Jews, who were expecting a Messiah to establish his kingdom in Jerusalem, as prophesied by Ezekiel. But only a few Jews accepted Christ in his lifetime as the Messiah. The leaders of organized Jewry accused him of trying to make himself a king. Since Tiberius was on the throne it was impossible for Pontius Pilate, the Roman procurator of Judaea, to ignore such a charge, and after much hesitation and protesting that he personally did not believe Christ to be guilty, he delivered him to be crucified, confirming the death sentence for blasphemy which the Jews lacked the authority to carry out without his consent.

In his lifetime Christ had taught a gospel of love, with only two positive commandments: to love God and one's neighbor—in which were comprised "all the Law and the prophets." He had attacked above all the hypocrisy of many of the Jewish groups, especially the Pharisees, who were content to keep the prescribed observances of their religion, but lacked charity. In some of his more profound teachings Christ had spoken of himself as the Son of God and taught without hesitation of the future life that awaited those who believed him and kept his commandments. It is therefore clear enough why so many Jews regarded him as a false Messiah, especially after his shameful death; how the party of the Sadducees, who adopted a policy of collaboration with the Roman conquerors, came to believe that his popularity and the demonstrations for him by the lower classes would endanger the whole Jewish people; and how the Pharisees, the party of strict orthodoxy, could believe that he was destroying the very basis of their religion. When the two parties, for different reasons, combined to demand his execution, and when the sentence was now duly carried out (traditionally A.D. 33, perhaps earlier), almost all, including even some of the more lukewarm among his own followers, agreed that he could not have been the awaited Messiah.

The Founding of the Christian Church. But his more faithful disciples continued to believe in spite of what had happened. When some visited his tomb on the third day after his death and found the body gone, they remembered that in speaking of his death, he had said that after three days he would rise again and they proclaimed his resurrection. When the resurrected Christ then appeared to many, the disciples no longer doubted; and, after receiving the inspiration of the Holy Spirit, as also promised by Christ, they went forth to proclaim the gospel of salvation. Though the orthodox Jews tried to hinder the movement, it spread rapidly, the Romans paying little attention to the matter, which they regarded as a religious quarrel among the always contentious Jews. The missionary journeys, especially in Asia Minor and Greece, of St. Paul, a late convert from Pharisaism, were particularly successful, in part because of the eloquence and enthusiasm of Paul himself, but perhaps in even larger measure as a result of his remarkable capacity for organization. Everywhere he went he founded small Christian communities which were self-sustaining after his departure, though his advice and assistance were always at their disposal. He wrote many letters (the Biblical Epistles), expounding Christian theology as he understood it and giving practical instructions. When Paul was finally arrested in Palestine, and was about to be treated as a malefactor, he claimed his rights as a Roman citizen, still something of a rarity at that early period of the Empire, and appealed to the emperor himself. But when he arrived in Rome, about A.D. 60, the case was quickly forgotten and Paul was apparently never tried. Instead he devoted himself to the church in Rome, to which came in due course many others of the leading disciples, presumably including St. Peter, who according to tradition was the first bishop of Rome.

The Church and the Roman Empire. The attention of official Rome was first drawn to the Christians during the reign of Nero. We learn from the later Roman historian Tacitus that the Christians were regarded as haters of mankind, although we can only guess at the reason for such an accusation. We know that they lived quietly and had the simplest of rituals, in particular, the commemoration of the Last Supper of Christ on earth. But the official religion of Rome was emperor worship, which the Christians, like the Jews, regarded as idolatry. Whereas the Jews by this time were well known in Rome, and several leading Jews had been close to the imperial court, the Christians were virtually unknown, and it was easy to cast suspicion on them as being both treasonable in that they refused to worship the emperor and guilty of unnameable secret practices. At all events, when a scapegoat was required to blame for the great fire of Rome, it was the Christians who were accused. Many of them were executed, including, according to tradition, both Peter and Paul (A.D. 65). Thereafter the laws against Christians remained in force, but by the time of the "Good Emperors," little notice was taken of them. A famous correspondence is extant between the emperor Trajan and Pliny, governor of Bithynia, in which the latter inquired how he should treat them. Trajan replied sensibly that if the Christians were properly accused and tried for the disloyalty to the state implied by their belief, they should be punished if they refused to recant, but that Pliny was not to take any initiative against them. In general, until the third century, little action was taken by Roman emperors against the Christians; but there are many cases of local mob violence of which Christians were the victims, and occasionally local Roman officials allowed the violence to run its course and afterward prosecuted the Christians as responsible for it.

By the beginning of the third century the Christian Church was well organized; and though loyal to the imperial state in ordinary matters, its members owed their primary loyalty to the Church. By this time it had its own professional clergy who ministered to the needs of their congregations and was rapidly becoming a state within a state, and thus potentially dangerous to the Empire. Several of the numerous short-lived emperors who ruled during the third century took official action against the Christians and tried to suppress the Church, using the method of the loyalty-oath to ferret out secret

Christians. No convinced Christian would take the oath and acknowledge the divinity of the emperor. Thus many individuals suffered for their beliefs and died as martyrs. Their constancy at all times, however, had the effect of increasing the number of believers. The average Roman, who had no religion but worship of the state in the person of the emperor, was rather naturally impressed by the evidence that others believed in redemption and a blessed hereafter enough to be willing to sacrifice their lives rather than deny their faith. The most serious attempt by the Romans to suppress the Church did not occur until a few years before the conversion of Constantine. The official action taken by Diocletian against the Christians was a part of that emperor's general political and religious policy, which will be dealt with later in the chapter.

Little need be said here of the beliefs of early Christianity. Most of its theology had been formulated by St. Paul, especially in his letters to the churches that he founded, and no doubt largely in response to questions asked by the new converts. Various later theologians who had wrestled with the problems were also acknowledged as having spoken with authority and under inspiration. Some of the teachings of these men, who were collectively known as Fathers of the Church, became incorporated into Catholic dogma.

The central belief of Christianity was that Jesus Christ, the Son of God, had been incarnated as a man, had suffered death by crucifixion, and had been resurrected. Thereafter he ascended into heaven, where he sat on the right hand of the Father. Salvation is possible for all men who believe in Christ as the Son of God; according to Paul this belief should show itself in a radical change of the inner being, which will enable the believer thereafter to do good. Salvation, according to Paul, is therefore by faith and good works— "Show me your faith by your works." Since salvation was not withheld from anyone who became a true Christian, Christianity had a universal appeal that was missing in all other religions of the day; and when the general tolerance, good order, and excellent communications of the Roman Empire are also taken into account, little else needs to be offered as a reason for its rapid spread. Later on, when all the resources of the state were at the disposal of the Church, the conversion of Roman Europe into Christendom was completed. The barbarians on the fringes of the empire were converted by missionaries from either the Western or the Eastern Empire and when they entered into the Roman inheritance none of these groups were still pagans with the exception of the Franks—whose leader, Clovis, soon allowed himself to be converted for good political reasons, as will be discussed later.

THE BEGINNING OF THE TOTALITARIAN EMPIRE— DIOCLETIAN AND CONSTANTINE

When Commodus inherited the Roman throne in A.D. 180 the process had already begun by which the Empire was to become an undisguised military despotism. Already in the Year of the Four Emperors, as Tacitus observes, "the secret was revealed that emperors could be made elsewhere than at Rome." But the "Good Emperors" had acceded to their thrones without military opposition; and though they were careful to keep the army satisfied, all classes in Rome had accepted them, and the Empire during their reigns had undoubtedly rested on general consent. But when Commodus began to exhibit signs of being as capricious and extravagant a tyrant as Nero and lost the support of much of his army and the upper classes by concluding a humiliating peace with the Germans, it was not long before he was murdered. Soon afterward another civil war broke out between army commanders battling for the throne. When Septimius Severus succeeded in defeating his competitors and established himself securely as emperor in 193, he recognized the logic of his position and set himself to restore discipline and loyalty to the armies and to keep them thoroughly satisfied, whatever the cost to the other classes in the state. From this time onward all the emperors ruled as military despots, and an army career became the steppingstone to all other offices in the state, including the throne itself. Nevertheless, the military reforms of Severus which included the recruiting of the Roman armies, not excepting their officers, from the provinces where they served, had the effect of creating relatively immobile armies, ill-suited to reinforce the dangerous sectors of the empire where barbarian encroachments were to be expected. These armies, moreover, in time came to consume the substance of the peasants in the outer provinces of the empire to such an extent that the peasants preferred to join rather than feed the army.

These effects were not, however, immediately noticeable. They became visible early in the third century when the succession principle again broke down, and for the better part of the century one military man after another, backed by his own army, usurped the throne. These so-called "barrack emperors" were almost all murdered. The provinces were ravaged by civil war, and sometimes barbarians roamed at will over the outer ones. Parts of the empire threw off the allegiance of Rome altogether and were only with difficulty restored by later emperors. Not until an Illyrian general named Diocletian assumed the throne in A.D. 284 did this period of anarchy come to an end.

Diocletian was an extremely able man who perceived clearly the only way in which the empire could be restored, even though this perception led to the conclusion that the military despotism would have to be more firmly established than ever. He reformed the army by admitting foreigners from outside the empire, men who would owe everything to, and therefore might be expected to remain loyal to, the emperors who paid them; for these men the army represented a professional career voluntarily undertaken and provided them with an entry into a civilization they admired. To obtain the necessary pay for his armies, Diocletian imposed what can only be described as a totalitarian system upon the civilians throughout the empire. The policy was continued and thoroughly systematized by Constantine. Small farmers were forbidden to leave their land; urban workers and their sons after them were compelled to follow their particular trades. Men of the middle classes (*curiales*) were made to undertake the full burden of paying for the public expenses of their own municipalities and were later compelled to collect the taxes and themselves make up all deficiencies in the quota imposed upon them. The eagle eye of the imperial officials was always upon them. Diocletian attempted to soften the impact of his program by price controls and similar measures, and for a time the burden of heavy taxation did not too severely damage the classes affected by it. But the formerly prosperous middle class was gradually squeezed dry and destroyed. Only the privileged army officers, imperial bureaucrats, and large landowners profited by the system. (The landowners were often strong enough to escape the tax collectors, and the others were granted immunity from taxation.) Diocletian also tried to strengthen respect for the rulers by introducing an elaborate Oriental ritual and insisting more strongly than had been done in the past on the formality of emperor worship. It was this policy which brought him into conflict with the Christians, and in pursuit of these aims he instituted the most prolonged series of efforts in imperial history to destroy Christianity.

To solve the problems of the succession and the administration of the empire, which was too much for one man, Diocletian devised a system under which there were two emperors (Augusti) and two heirs apparent (Caesars). After twenty years the former were expected to abdicate and leave the rule to their chosen heirs. Diocletian himself was strong enough to compel his own coemperor to abdicate with him, but the system thereafter never worked. Though later emperors never abdicated, the system of the Augusti and Caesars was formally maintained throughout the rest of the Empire. Soon the civil wars over the succession broke out again. In the struggle Constantine was able to defeat his competitors and ultimately to establish his undisputed rule as the sole emperor in A.D. 324. He completed the military reforms of Diocletian, and it was under him that German mercenaries became the crack troops of the empire and the backbone of his armies, the provincial troops being degraded to the position of local militia. Thus, in effect, Constantine ruled his empire by means of foreign mercenaries, whose wages and subsistence were paid by the Roman citizens. But the army did for a long time perform its proper function of maintaining the boundaries of the empire and keeping the barbarians beyond them. The empire itself was therefore preserved, though the price paid by the citizens was high. In due time the less prosperous and more agricultural West became little but an imposing edifice still protected by its foreign armies but decaying rapidly from within.

Perhaps the most significant act of Constantine, apart from his conversion to Christianity, mentioned already, was the founding of a new city on the Bosporus on the site of the old Greek colony of Byzantium, which he made his capital. This city of Constantinople, called after him, was destined to be the greatest city of Europe for a millennium, and the capital of the Eastern Roman (in reality, Greek) Empire, the most prosperous and substantial of the successor states of Rome, which took a new lease on life when severed from the decaying West.

For the remainder of the fourth century the empire continued to be ruled by one emperor, but each of these emperors (Augusti) chose one or more Caesars to administer the West and protect it from the various barbarian infiltrations that began to grow serious during the century. However, in reality East and West were drawing apart, and only exceptionally energetic rulers, such as Julian the Apostate and Theodosius the Great, ever fully controlled the whole empire. When the barbarian invasions began in earnest in the fifth century, Constantinople soon occupied itself with defending the East, leaving the West to its fate. The separate sectors now became formally divided and the Western emperor Honorius departed for Ravenna, leaving Rome for the pope to administer as best he could.

THE BARBARIAN INVASIONS AND THE NEW KINGDOMS OF THE WEST

We have several times alluded to the so-called barbarian invasions, known to the Germans as the "wanderings of the peoples." The latter, indeed, seems to be the more appropriate term, since there were scarcely any planned invasions until the fifth century. At all times the island of civilization represented by the Roman Empire had been subjected to periodic invasions by German tribes in search of living space in the underpopulated empire. In the fifth century the movement became too strong for Rome to resist any longer. The frontiers were defended to a very large degree by people of the same race as the invaders. They could not be expected to resist indefinitely for the sake of their pay, especially when they were no longer officered by Romans who believed in and were prepared to defend their empire and when the emperors themselves lacked energy and fortitude.

This situation was much worse in the West than in the East. The eastern frontiers of the empire bordered on the lands of the Parthians, Persians, and others who were far from being barbarians, and were not impelled by the same desire for new territories as the Germanic tribes. The Eastern Romans were therefore not subjected to such severe pressures from the east; the danger to them came from the north and west. In addition, the Eastern Empire was more worth defending. In spite of the high taxes, there was still some prosperity, and the middle class was still fairly strong. Commerce and industry were far better developed in the cities of the East, and sea communications were less disrupted than the land communications of the West. Above all, Constantinople was a center of industry and almost impregnable from attack. What the Eastern emperors therefore had to do was to try to defend their shorter frontiers by means of their superior armies and to keep those armies in good fighting shape. In this they were on the whole successful. They quickly lost the province of Dacia north of the Danube that had been added to the empire by Trajan and were compelled to allow barbarians to settle on the southern side of the river; but they were able to turn back the actual armies that threatened Constantinople, even though an emperor (Valens) was killed in battle in 376, and some of the outer territories were frequently ravaged by barbarian peoples.

Attila's Asiatic Huns were in large part responsible for the pressure by the Germanic peoples, the West Goths (Visigoths), East Goths (Ostrogoths), Vandals, Franks, Burgundians, and others. By the end of the fourth century the Huns had invaded the Danube Valley, driving the Germanic tribes before them. The Ostrogoths were penned into a territory north of the Black Sea, but the Visigoths pressed against the Byzantine territories, some of their leaders gaining military experience in the Byzantine armies. One such leader, Alaric the Visigoth, rebelled against the Byzantines after the death of the emperor Theodosius I, who had employed him. Thereafter he was expelled from the Byzantine territories by the Eastern armies led by the Vandal Stilicho; but he could not be prevented from invading Italy. Alaric, after suffering a further defeat from Stilicho in Italy, marched on Rome, which he sacked in 410, Stilicho having in the meantime been assassinated. Soon afterward Alaric died in southern Italy, and the immediate threat was over. Meanwhile the Vandals and other peoples overran Gaul, and Britain was evacuated by the Roman troops, leaving the country unable to defend itself effectively from Celtic marauders and German tribes from the Continent. The Vandals and Visigoths fought over Spain, which ultimately fell to the Visigoths, a permanent Visigothic kingdom being established there in 419. The Vandals crossed over to Africa under their leader Gaeseric, and a permanent Vandal kingdom was established there in 435.

Shortly afterward the Western Empire, still being fought over by the various barbarian groups, was compelled to defend itself against a purposeful invasion by the Huns, under the leadership of Attila. The Roman armies under Aetius, the last of the great Roman generals, allied with the Visigoths, defeated Attila in 451 at the so-called battle of Chalons (actually fought near Troyes) and halted his march westward. The following year Attila invaded Italy, but was probably bought off by the pope when he reached Rome. He died shortly afterward and the Hunnish host disintegrated. Rome, however, had to submit to a sack by the Vandals from Africa in 455, and this time Pope Leo I was unable to do more than ensure the lives of the citizens provided they did not resist. In 454 Aetius was murdered by Emperor Valentinian III, who was himself murdered the following year by some of Aetius' guards.

Thereafter the Western emperors, who had hitherto continued to wield a little power and authority from their capital of Ravenna, were nothing but puppets set up and maintained by barbarian generals. In 476 a Herulian named Odovacar (Odoacer) put an end to the nominal rule of the last emperor, Romulus Augustulus, and was recognized by the Eastern Emperor Zeno as *patricius,* a name for the barbarian military representative of the emperor; this event marked the "Fall of Rome." In theory thereafter the Eastern emperor was the sole ruler of the Empire, but in fact the Western Empire was no more, and Odovacar was an independent king of Italy. A few years later Clovis and his Franks subdued Gaul and established a Frankish kingdom there (the Merovingian kingdom). In 488 Theodoric, leader of the Ostrogoths, whose people had succeeded in escaping from their confinement after the death of Attila, was permitted or encouraged by the Byzantine emperor to invade Italy, where he put an end to the rule of Odovacar, and established an independent Ostrogothic kingdom of Italy (493). He ruled Italy for over thirty years.

Thus by the end of the fifth century there was a Vandal kingdom in Africa, a Visigothic kingdom in Spain, a Frankish kingdom in Gaul, and an Ostrogothic kingdom in Italy, while the Angles, Saxons, and Jutes were gradually penetrating Britain and establishing small Germanic kingdoms there. The former Roman Empire in the West was therefore thoroughly partitioned, leaving the Byzantines with most of the eastern territories, which they proceeded to consolidate into an empire that persisted for a further thousand years. The later fortunes of the Eastern Roman or Byzantine Empire will be considered in the next chapter, leaving the subsequent history of the West to Chapter VIII.

CHAPTER VII

THE SUCCESSOR STATES OF THE ROMAN EMPIRE

For sixty years after the Fall of Rome the Byzantine Empire was fully occupied with consolidating its own position. It had survived the Germanic assaults, but its troubles with other invaders, both civilized and uncivilized, were to persist throughout all Byzantine history until at last it fell to the Turks.

THE BYZANTINE EMPIRE

The Reconquest of Italy. To the east of the Byzantine frontiers a new power was rising steadily, a revived Persian empire under the Sassanid dynasty which had succeeded to the Parthian monarchy of the early Roman Empire. This empire reached the height of its culture in the late fourth century, but had been compelled to wage a long series of wars with the Romans on its western frontiers. Treaties were frequently made between the two powers, but both sides kept them indifferently. When Justinian I came to the Byzantine throne in 525 he determined to settle the Persian question once and for all by negotiations, even though it cost him money. He needed to have his hands free to pursue the reconquest of the West, which was his prime objective; and his country was still not free from barbarian invasions from the north, especially from the Asiatic Avars, Huns, and Slavs, who were beginning to raid across the Danube. A peace was duly concluded in 533, under which Justinian agreed to pay tribute to the Persian monarch; and though the latter soon broke it, and the war was renewed, a further peace was made in 562 on similar terms.

Meanwhile Justinian fortified his frontiers against the barbarians, building numerous forts, and set himself wholeheartedly to reunite the old Empire under his rule. Africa was quickly taken from the now enfeebled Vandal monarchs by Justinian's general Belisarius, and the conquest of Sicily soon followed. In a murderous war with the Ostrogoths lasting nineteen years (535–554), Belisarius, later succeeded by Narses, reconquered Italy, destroying the Ostrogothic kingdom. Southeastern Spain was taken from the Visgoths in 554. But this was the limit of Justinian's expansion. He was hard put to it to defend his own capital against the Huns and Slavs, who raided far into Greece and late in his reign had to be driven off from Constantinople by Belisarius.

The reconquest was, quite certainly, from the point of view of Byzantine interests, ill-conceived. The new empire could not be defended with the resources available to Constantinople. Justinian, who fancied himself as a Roman emperor, though he was a Macedonian Greek, did not perceive that the empire he and his successors could maintain and administer effectively must be in Eastern Europe and Asia Minor. Italy was invaded by the Lombards three years after his death, leaving only southern Italy and the exarchate of Ravenna in the northeast to his successors. In 616 the Byzantine possessions in Spain were recovered by the Visigoths, and north Africa fell almost without a struggle to the Muslim invaders in 699. However the Byzantines were able to retain southern Italy for a considerable period, and they won recognition of their suzerainty over Rome—largely an empty honor, since Rome made its own terms with the Lombards and later, in the eighth century, called in the Franks as protectors, when the Byzantines proved unable and unwilling to defend it against the encroaching Lombards.

Church and State in Constantinople. The reign of Justinian also marked the beginning of serious differences on doctrine and Church organization with the papacy in Rome. Justinian was himself deeply interested in theological questions, and had no hesitation in dictating to the popes, who had to confine themselves to verbal protests. The chief Church official in Constantinople, the patriarch, was appointed by the emperor and could be dismissed by him. Although on certain occasions in Byzantine history the patriarch stood up to his imperial master, he could not long sustain his position without imperial support. Thus the Church in Constantinople had all the power of the state behind it, while the popes in Rome were usually able to act more independently. The emperors thus constantly came into conflict with the pope, who claimed jurisdiction over the patriarch. In the eighth century a controversy broke out between the Byzantine emperor Leo III and the pope concerning the use of icons or images in church worship, the emperor taking the position that the icons were an aid only to superstition while the pope claimed that they heightened religious feeling. When Leo and his successors forbade the use of images and ordered them to be broken, the pope was powerless to do more than protest; but the Iconoclastic Controversy embittered relations between Rome and Constantinople for a century, and undoubtedly contributed to the desire of the popes to be protected by the Franks rather than by the Byzantine emperors, who were in their own view little better than heretics. The controversy was at last settled in favor of the papal position in the ninth century. But only twenty-four years later a further schism developed between the two Churches, and a Church council dominated by the Byzantines anathematized the pope and rejected papal supremacy (867). Though this quarrel too was patched up, Greek national feeling became involved, and the pretensions of Rome became ever more abhorrent to the Byzantines. Finally in 1054 the split became permanent, ostensibly on a question of doctrine—though the competing interests of pope and patriarch in southern Italy, which had just been conquered by the Normans, were perhaps more important at the time. The Orthodox and Roman branches of the Church have diverged on doctrine ever since.

The Persian Wars of Heraclius. It was not long before the calamitous effects of Justinian's foreign policy became visible. The Persians had grown stronger, while Justinian added little strength to his resources by winning back part of the old Empire. He was unable to make much use of any of his western provinces for the defense of his eastern territories; and the burden of the tribute paid to Persia was one that his successors did not care to tolerate. The wars with Persia were resumed in 572, and though Byzantine arms were at first successful, it was at the expense of the northern frontiers. During the next decade great numbers of Slavs poured into Greece and settled permanently in the Balkan Peninsula, while the Avars captured the Danubian forts and raided up to the gates of Constantinople. When Heraclius became emperor in 610 he was faced with dangerous Avar armies from the north and an expanding Persia. In the first decade of his reign the Persians took all Asia Minor and reached Chalcedon opposite Constantinople across the Bosporus, shearing off Egypt also from the Empire. In 619 the Avars reached Constantinople on the land side. All then appeared to be lost, and Heraclius had to be dissuaded by his energetic patriarch from abandoning his city and embarking for

Africa. But the danger passed. Heraclius with his best troops set out from Constantinople by sea and took the Persians in the rear, while Patriarch Sergius defended Constantinople from the Avars. The Persian army was utterly defeated at Nineveh in 627, and soon afterwards a peace was concluded.

But the cost had been high. Though the well-organized and administered Byzantine Empire had been able to recruit and pay new armies, the provinces had been ground down by taxation to maintain them, and both Persians and Greeks had been worn down by the long and murderous war. So when a fresh new power arrived on the scene, neither Constantinople nor Persia was able to stand against it. Indeed, many of the peoples in the empire welcomed the Muslims as liberators. The Byzantines lost many of their fairest provinces forever, and the Persian Empire was destroyed and ruled thereafter by the Muslims. The great conquests of Islam will be dealt with in the last part of this chapter.

It was not long before the Muslims also captured Asia Minor, the most valuable of the provinces of Constantinople. In many different campaigns they strove to capture the impregnable city. But the Greek fleet was always too much for them, especially after it had learned to use "Greek fire." In time the Muslim menace receded, and some of the Asiatic provinces lost to Islam were reconquered by the energetic Isaurian dynasty founded by Leo III (717–741).

Byzantine Political and Cultural Achievements. The Byzantine Empire showed in its long history a remarkable power of survival. Although the throne was often occupied by utterly incompetent rulers, and political assassination was common, sometimes resulting in destructive, if brief, civil wars between competitors for the throne, the administrative service was so efficiently organized that it could function effectively even when the throne was occupied by men (and women) of neither ability or character. Though the administration itself was often scandalously corrupt, the empire never went bankrupt. Taxes were always collected, the bureaucracy and the armies were paid, and the peasants never sank to the poverty and misery experienced in the contemporary West. Though the boundaries of the empire frequently expanded and contracted with the fortunes of war, its rump could and did always support itself and had enough strength to fight back and retake a considerable portion of what it had lost when the tide of war was against it. Thus the Greeks, having inherited much of the Roman system of administration and law, showed that they could rule and administer an empire which survived even longer than that of their former masters.

The upper and middle classes of the empire enjoyed a high standard of living, unmatched in the West until very recent times. Trade and industry prospered. The emperor lived in Oriental luxury and maintained an Oriental ceremonial which emphasized the immense distance between himself and his subjects—a ceremonial that impressed even while it excited the verbal derision of Western ambassadors from countries that were still little removed from barbarism. This ritual, like that introduced by Diocletian, was for political purposes. It served the same purposes among the Byzantines as among the later Romans; but it had now borrowed so much from the East that it was hardly to be distinguished from the splendor of an Oriental court, and the daily life of a Byzantine monarch was as marked by a prescribed protocol as that of an ancient Egyptian Pharaoh.

Probably the chief intellectual interest of the Byzantines and Greeks for many centuries was theological speculation, which at times permeated even the lower urban classes. There were endless disputes over the difficult questions concerned with the Christian Trinity—the relation of each Person to the others, the nature of Christ and how it was to be distinguished from that of God the Father, and similar matters incapable of definitive solution. The emperor and his patriarch, with the aid of Church councils, defined dogmas; but always there were dissident groups that could not accept the "orthodox" ("right opinion") solution and thus became heretics ("choosers"). These heretics were persecuted and sometimes expelled from the empire, and on occasion took their religious beliefs to other parts of the world, where they proselytized among the native peoples (for example, they founded the Nestorian Church in China).

There was much excellent literary scholarship in the empire, but on the whole little new creative work, nothing in any way to be compared in originality and depth with the work of the fifth and fourth centuries B.C. Byzantine art, however, though not always to the taste of the West, was profoundly religious and in many respects quite original, especially its mosaics and icons (when they were allowed); the craftsmanship of Constantinople was often superb and quite beyond comparison with anything in the West until at least the High Middle Ages. Byzantine law was a development of Roman law, frequently codified again after the great *Corpus* of Justinian and sometimes humanized under Christian influence. This was especially true of the *Ecloga* of Leo III, perhaps the most humane law code that had been drawn up in history until that time—though it did not prevent the Byzantine rulers from inflicting the most barbarous atrocities upon their political enemies and on prisoners of war when such deeds appeared to be justified by their political purposes.

Influence of Byzantine Empire on Eastern Europe. The Byzantine Empire was for centuries the only civilized European power. It therefore exercised an incalculable influence on those barbarian peoples who came into contact with it. All the Slavic peoples came under its influence, even though in the case of those Slavs (for example, the Bohemians) who were absorbed into the Roman Church, the influence may have been short-lived. The Bulgars, Serbs, and Russians, together with the Greeks and some peoples of Western Asia who did not convert to Islam, all became members of the Orthodox Church, owing not even nominal allegiance to Rome after the eleventh century. This influence was, indeed, from the beginning of great importance. As early as the reign of Constantine I the Council of Nicaea (325), presided over by the emperor, decided that the correct interpretation of the relation between the Father and the Son should be that propounded by St. Athanasius, which maintained the full divinity of Christ—as distinct from that held by Bishop Arius, which regarded Christ as inferior to the Father. This, however, did not settle the controversy since several emperors thereafter supported the doctrine of Arius. Byzantine missionaries during the period naturally preached Arianism to their converts—especially Bishop Ulfilas, whose work lay among the Germanic tribes who afterward took over the Roman West. Thus the Goths, Vandals, Lombards, and others were, from the Roman Catholic point of view, heretics when they invaded the Roman territories; and the papacy had the greatest difficulty converting them to the orthodox Catholic beliefs. In later centuries the Byzantines continued to preach their own form of Christianity, which was still doubtfully orthodox in the eyes of the pope. The most important single mission was probably that in the ninth century of Cyril and Methodius, who devised a Slavonic alphabet, making possible the use of a Slavonic liturgy for church services. Though the Slavs as far west as Bohemia and Moravia were converted as a result of their work, the German bishops and the popes who supported them were too powerful to allow this penetration from Constantinople to become permanent. But territories to the east for the most part came within the Byzantine religious, and consequently cultural and political, sphere of influence.

Above all, Russia came under Byzantine influence, not only in religion, but in government—a heritage whose consequences are still with us today. The regime of the tsars was closer to that of Constantinople than it was to any Western autocracy. When Constantinople fell to the Turks in 1453 the grand duke of Moscow, soon to proclaim himself Tsar of all the Russias, called his capital the "third Rome" and symbolized the title by marrying the niece of the last emperor of Constantinople. He also proclaimed the patriarch of Moscow as the chief official of the Orthodox Church. Barbarian as Russia still was in essence, in comparison with the regime the tsar claimed to have inherited, the form of Byzantine rule, itself inherited from the later Roman Empire, was retained in Moscow until the Revolution of 1917. Even under Stalin a family likeness to Byzantine absolutism could still be discerned, in spite of the Marxian intellectual framework which had become the official philosophy and justification for his state.

THE BARBARIAN KINGDOMS OF THE WEST

Germanic Dominance. It should not be thought that with the barbarian conquest of the Roman Empire in the West all Roman civilization was thereupon destroyed. In fact this civilization had been so firmly implanted in almost all the Western countries that it survived for a long time with relatively little change. But the economic and social conditions of the successor states prevented any renewal of the impulses provided by the Romans, and gradually Germanic influences prevailed—even though the more assimilated territories of the former empire retained permanently much that was Roman as a substratum beneath their own national cultures. Italy, the heartland of the empire, was never subjected to Germanic influences as fully as were the other territories; the part of the country ruled by the Roman Church remained essentially Roman and Italian; and southern Italy retained much of its Greek, as well as its Italian, heritage. Southern Italy and Rome were never subjugated by the Lombards, and the Ostrogothic kingdom of Italy lasted for too short a time to have much enduring influence on Italian culture.

It should also be recognized as a fact of prime importance that the barbarian rulers who inherited the empire did not intend to destroy it and that in many regions their peoples formed only a small percentage of its inhabitants. Though retaining their characteristic Germanic tribal institutions and customs, they proposed to use that part of the Roman heritage that was useful to them, especially the services of the literate and cultured Roman clergy. Only rarely did they consciously attempt to destroy or supersede what they found in the territories they conquered. Nevertheless, the old Roman culture gradually was submerged, since it had no means of renewing itself. Germanic customs began to prevail even in the Church, and Church officials appointed by the Germanic rulers often behaved like Germanic chieftains rather than Christian priests. German methods of land tenure also began to take precedence over Roman laws of inheritance. By the age of Charlemagne little that was authentically Roman was left in his empire. Western civilization had become in all essentials a new type of civilization, descended from the Greek and Roman, but recognizably distinct from them. The so-called Middle Ages are therefore the first stage of our own civilization, not an intermediate period between "ancient" and "modern," as they were regarded when they received the conventional name by which they are still known.

Italy. The Ostrogothic kingdom in Italy which lasted from the death of Odovacar, the Herulian, in 493, to the conquest of Justinian, was a brief interlude of often excellent government provided by the Ostrogothic king Theodoric and his Roman advisers. Rome, though depopulated over the last century and now a relatively small city, was still able to support itself and to serve as a capital for a predominantly agricultural Italy. Italy itself, shorn of its empire, knew an economic recovery and was able to provide fully for its own subsistence. The pope maintained correct relations with the heretical Arian Ostrogothic king but welcomed the arrival of the legions of the orthodox Justinian when he reconquered the country. After the Lombard invasion in 568 the papacy was compelled to assert itself as an independent secular power, ruling its own territories whose boundaries the various Lombard dukes respected. Gradually the Lombards were converted to Catholic Christianity, but in the eighth century they became more united under a monarch who claimed, and was sometimes able to assert, his suzerainty over the Lombard nobles. During this period successive monarchs seriously threatened the integrity of the papal territories, necessitating appeals by the pope for outside aid, as described in the next chapter.

Spain. The Visigothic kingdom of Spain was at its most powerful during the fifth century. After its partial conquest by Justinian it was never able to recover its full strength. It fell without prolonged resistance to the Muslim invasions in the early part of the eighth century; and with the exception of some small areas in the northwest it became a Muslim State, ruled by the caliph of Cordova.

Britain and Ireland. Britain had been less Romanized than the nearer provinces of the Roman Empire. Before the end of the fifth century, Angles, Saxons, and Jutes had already begun to take over the country from the Romanized Celts, whom they drove westward into Wales. These Germanic invaders then proceeded to found their own kingdoms in England, which were usually rather weak and often warred among themselves. In the ninth century England first became united under a single monarch when the country was compelled to defend itself against invasions by the Danes, as will be discussed briefly in the next chapter.

Though there had been some conversion of the English to Christianity before the fall of the Empire, there was little ecclesiastical organization in the country. Ireland, on the other hand, was converted and organized in the fifth century by St. Patrick, soon after the departure of the Roman legions from Britain, and Irish influence was strong in Britain in the succeeding centuries. Irish Christianity itself was largely cut off from Rome during this period and developed in its own way, more mystical and less dogmatic than Rome, and free from the Roman type of ecclesiastical organization. At the turn of the seventh century Pope Gregory I (590–604) sent a churchman named Augustine to Britain with instructions to organize the English Church according to Roman principles. This he and his assistants did with marked success, working out of their headquarters at Canterbury. In due course this Romanized Church came into conflict with Irish Christianity in the north, and for a time there was serious competition between the two. This was eventually settled at the Synod of Whitby in 664, the Irish accepting defeat when they were unable to overcome the argument put forward by their opponents that Christ himself through St. Peter had founded the Roman

Church, and that the popes thereafter had held their office in un-broken succession from St. Peter.

Gaul. When the Franks entered Gaul they were still pagan, and had not, like the other Germanic barbarians, been converted to a heretical form of Christianity. They were therefore potential sup-porters of the papacy if only they could be converted to Roman Catholic Christianity; and they might be expected to give it much-needed aid against the Arians. One of their leaders, Clovis, showed himself amenable to persuasion. Determined to make himself master of the country and to subject all the other Frankish princes to his rule, he allowed his wife to convert him to Christianity, and thus gained the support of the Roman clergy in Gaul, which was of great assistance to him in his designs. He and his sons who succeeded to his inheritance were able to conquer the whole country and estab-lished several kingdoms, the most important of which were Neustria (a Gallo-Roman territory), and Austrasia (mainly Germanic). These kingdoms were ruled over by his house, called the Merovingians from Meroveus the father of Clovis. Sometimes two or more king-doms were united under one rule, but usually there were at least two separate kings, since it was the Germanic custom to divide an inheritance among all the sons, and the Frankish kings regarded Gaul as their personal estate.

For a period the country, which had been one of the most civil-ized territories of the empire, remained partly Roman in culture, and the peoples who had survived from Roman times were permitted to retain their law and customs. But gradually it became Germanized and German customs predominated. The Merovingian rulers quar-reled incessantly among themselves and with the great lords of their realm, and few of them died in their beds. Several of the earlier monarchs were effective rulers. But after the death, about 638, of Dagobert I, who had ruled both kingdoms and tried to centralize the monarchy in his own hands, his successors in both kingdoms fell under the domination of their own chief ministers, usually known as "mayors of the palace." These officials gradually took power into their hands, leaving the Merovingian titular kings to receive royal honors, but with little of importance to do. Eventually these *rois fainéants* ("do-nothing kings") were superseded by the mayors of the house of Pepin, the penultimate of whom, Charles Martel, united the whole Merovingian kingdom under his effective rule and defeated the Muslims, thus opening the way to his son

Pepin the Short to become king himself in 751. On taking the throne, Pepin sent his Merovingian puppet to a monastery to end his days.

THE CIVILIZATION OF ISLAM

Early Progress in Arabia. Arabia before Mahomet (the name is also spelled Mohammed and Muhammad) had been a land of no importance in world affairs. A section of the north had been a Roman province, but the south had been inhabited only by Bedouin tribes. There were a few cities in the peninsula in places where there was an adequate water supply. All the cities had their caravan traders, and merchants who made their living exporting the few specialties of Arabia, mostly luxuries, and importing consumer goods in exchange. The leading city was Mecca, already a holy city since it housed a sacred object, a meteorite known as the Ka'aba stone. The peoples of Arabia were fiercely independent, owing loyalty at most to their family and their tribe; they were pagans in their religion, though some were well aware of the teachings of Judaism, and others had had some contact with Christianity.

Mahomet was born in Mecca, and was for many years a substantial trader. In middle life he began to have visions, in which it was revealed to him that there was only one God (Allah), and that he himself must be his prophet. When he began to preach this strict monotheism he aroused much opposition, especially from his own clan, the Kuraish, of which he was a junior member. Mahomet therefore decided to leave for Yathrib, an inland city to the north of Mecca. From the date of this so-called Flight from Mecca (the Hegira), A.D. 622, the Muslim era is dated. To Yathrib with Mahomet went the small group of believers he had converted in his home city, and there the new religion of Islam (Arabic for "submission") grew rapidly, to such an extent that the city as a whole was converted and became the first Commonwealth of Islam. After some indecisive fighting between Mecca and Yathrib, whose name was now changed to Medina ("the city of the Prophet"), Mahomet and his followers were able to threaten Mecca and the Prophet's own powerful clan. In 630 the Kuraish accepted the religion, and in subsequent years the entire peninsula was converted.

Beliefs and Practices of Islam. Islam is a revealed religion, stemming from the revelations to Mahomet which are collected in the Koran. These revelations are supplemented by "sayings" (*hadith*) of Mahomet, and throughout history they have been extensively interpreted by doctors of Islam. According to these teachings there is one God, and Mahomet was chosen to reveal him—the last of a line of prophets, including Jesus Christ and Moses, who gave partial revelations. With Mahomet the revelation was complete. It is the task of Muslims (the word means "surrender to God") to convert the entire world; but there is no necessity to insist on the adoption of Islam by other peoples who had received the partial revelations, written them down, and taught them to their converts (the "Peoples of the Book"). Pagans, on the other hand, had to be forcibly converted if they would not accept Islam voluntarily. Mahomet taught of a Paradise for the faithful and a place of punishment (Gehenna) for the wicked. The Muslim who died in battle for his religion would go straight to Paradise. A holy war (*jehad*) could be proclaimed by Muslims against the heathen or infidels who endangered their religion, and it was the duty of all Muslims to support and fight in such a war.

There were many laws concerning ritual cleanliness, based in large measure upon those of the Jews, who had likewise been a desert people when their laws were proclaimed; a whole month (*Ramadan*) was set aside for fasting between sunrise and sundown, and images were forbidden, as in the Ten Commandments. The Muslims were enjoined to repeat five daily prayers and to make a pilgrimage to Mecca at least once during their lifetime. They had to give alms to the poor and in general aid all their brothers of Islam. The good Muslim should never touch strong drink. Clearly these rules could only with difficulty be kept in a civilized urban society. There have therefore frequently been reform movements in Islam, in which reformers have urged the return to the strict teachings of the Prophet. One of the most recent was the *Wahabi* reform, adopted and strongly supported by Ibn Saud, whose son sits now on the throne of Saudi Arabia.

Expansion of Islam. Before the death of Mahomet in 632 the Arabs had already begun to expand far down the Arabian peninsula, but the expansion to the north began only with the reign of Abu Bekr, the father-in-law of Mahomet, who succeeded him as *caliph*, or vicegerent of the Prophet. The ruler of Islam therefore had both religious and political functions. It was not as yet decided who was to rule the new Islamic commonwealth, nor whether the title should be hereditary. The first caliphs were chosen by the community from among the leading companions of the Prophet, but there were many proponents of the idea of the hereditary succession. Mahomet had left no son, but his daughter Fatima was married to Ali, who was also Mahomet's cousin. Though Ali had to submit to the rule of Omar and Othman as well as to that of Abu Bekr, he was able to assume the title and rule from 656 to 661. When he was murdered and his son Hussein, who had revolted against the reigning caliph, was killed in battle in 680, the first great schism in Islam occurred which has remained unhealed to this day. The Shi'ites, mainly in Persia, claim that the succession of the Prophet passed through Ali and Hussein and have refused to recognize any other line of descent. The caliphs from among the competing families who actually held the throne were, in the Shi'ite view, all usurpers, whereas the majority of Muslims (Sunnites) held that the actual succession was legitimate.

The Arabs early found a great military leader in the person of Khalid ("the sword of Allah"), who during the caliphate of Omar (634-644) conquered Syria from the Byzantines. At the same time Persia was attacked by other Arab armies and decisively defeated in 641. Egypt capitulated in 642. Thereafter, there was a lull in the conquests while the Byzantines attempted to recover their lost provinces and the new Arabic domains were gradually becoming accustomed to their new masters. With the end of the civil war over the succession, the dynasty of the Ommeyad family secured its position and ruled from Damascus. Moawiya, the founder of the dynasty, continued the conquests, making the first great attack on Constantinople (669). North Africa was captured during his reign, and the Muslim domains in the East were extended to India, Afghanistan, and Turkestan. Further civil wars broke out in the Arab homelands, and the eastern conquests were several times lost and retaken. But at the beginning of the eighth century, the conquest of North Africa was completed, and the Berbers, who had resisted Islam stoutly, accepted the new religion. The Arabs and Berbers then conquered Spain under the leadership of Tarik, during the caliphate of Walid I (705-715). All resistance save in the northern sectors was at an end by 713, and in 732 southern France was invaded by the Spanish Muslim governor, Abdurrahman. The Muslims (usually called Saracens by the Westerners) were, however, defeated at Tours by the Franks and Lombards under Charles Martel, and thereafter they were gradually expelled from southern France by the Franks. Meanwhile major attacks on Constantinople by land and sea were repulsed by the Byzantine emperor Leo III.

From 744 to 750 there was a severe struggle over the succession, followed by prolonged civil war. This brought to an end the Ommeyad dynasty of Damascus, the caliphate fell into the hands of the Abbasid family, and the capital was transferred shortly afterward to the newly built city of Bagdad. However, an Ommeyad escaped the general destruction of his family and became the Ommeyad caliph of Cordova in Spain, which never recognized the authority or legitimacy of the Abbasids. The Abbasid caliphate was securely based on Persia, the most civilized part of the Muslim empire, and for the next century was to reach its greatest cultural and intellectual fame under the caliphs Harun al Rashid and al-Mamun. Thereafter the Bagdad caliphate fell into decay, losing Egypt and North Africa to an independent caliphate in the tenth century. In the last centuries of the Bagdad caliphate, the Abbasids fell under the control of the Seljuk Turks. In 1258 the city of Bagdad was captured and sacked by the Mongols, and the dynasty came to an end.

The Achievements of Muslim Civilization. The Muslims, on the whole, were as humane as any conquerors up to that time, and their government did not greatly differ from any other Oriental despotism. Their administration varied according to the countries they ruled, but Islam always remained the national religion of each state, and the caliph's first task was to maintain it. The ethics of Islam were expected to be those of the ruler. Pagans had to be converted, as already noted. Members of other religions were tolerated and permitted to retain their church organization, but they were always regarded as second-class citizens and subjected to special taxation, in theory because they did not accept the obligations of a Muslim. Nevertheless, they could become in all respects equal with the Muslims if they converted to Islam, since Islam always remained a brotherhood of believers, the successor of the original Commonwealth of Islam founded by the Prophet.

Though the Arabs provided the initial leadership for the Muslim expansion and all the early rulers of the empire were Arabs, having little original culture of their own, they soon absorbed that of the peoples whom they conquered, and with whom they mingled. Thus the Abbasid empire of Bagdad was at all times far more Persian than Arabic. What the Arabs provided was their marvelously flexible and in many respects subtle language, which, being the language of the Koran, had to be learned by all good Muslims. (It was, indeed, forbidden to translate the revelations of Mahomet into any other language.) But few of the great Muslim thinkers were Arabs, and the leading names in Muslim science are Persian.

Muslim civilization preserved far more than it destroyed. Exiles from Constantinople who settled in Syria early provided them with Greek philosophy and science. Having a literature of their own, the Arabs were little interested in Greek poetry and literature. But they had neither science nor philosophy, and they were eager learners. The very word for philosophy did not exist in the Arabic language until they Arabicized the Greek word. Aristotle was for the Arabs the "master of those who know," as he was for the medieval West; several important Muslim philosophers, including the Persian physician Avicenna, and the Spaniard Averroës, had a marked influence on medieval Scholasticism. The latter's commentaries on Aristotle, indeed, were far better known in the West than they were in his own country. Many of Aristotle's works first became known in the West in Arabic translations, which were finally discovered when the Christians captured Toledo in the late eleventh century.

But it was in science that the Muslims excelled. The Hellenistic scientists were well known to them, and they themselves carried on original work in astronomy, optics, and various branches of mathematics, especially trigonometry and algebra—the very word for which, like many other words beginning in *al* (for example, *alcove* and *alchemy*) is Arabic. Omar Khayyam, the Persian poet, was more famed in his own country as a master of algebra. The work of the Muslims in alchemy, carried on for many centuries, laid many of the foundations of modern chemistry. The so-called Arabic numerals, though almost certainly not invented by the Arabs, were greatly developed by them. They are probably Hindu in origin, and from the Hindus also it is likely that the Arabs took the zero.

As a trading and later sea-faring people the Arabs developed the Greek invention of the astrolabe which in skilled hands could determine latitude and longitude, as long as the stars could be observed, and the mariner's compass, which may have come from China. Many Arabs were skilled navigators and geographers. The various Muslim people also excelled in craftsmanship, especially the inlay work known as damascene. Their art, though it did not, of course, represent the human form, developed the beautiful geometrical figures known as arabesques, and Persian carpets from that day to this are noted for their intricate geometrical designs. The graceful forms of Muslim architecture, with its domes and minarets, and its horse-shoe arches, are widely known; and the building that many think the most beautiful in the world, the Taj Mahal, was built by a later Muslim conqueror of India, using the traditional Muslim style. By the tenth century the prestige of learned works written in the Arabic language was greater even than that of the Greeks, and many early medieval students of science won their reputations in their own country by bringing back titbits of Arabic lore that they had dis-covered on their travels. Although medieval scientists in most fields ultimately improved upon their work, in medicine they never did equal the Muslims, and Muslim, especially Syrian, doctors were much sought after by those Westerners who could afford their services.

It is customary to credit the Muslims with being the medium by which much Greek and Oriental learning was made available to the West, and it is for this reason that their work is touched upon in this book. It is also widely recognized that much might have been lost if the Muslims had not preserved it. But it should also be realized that Muslim civilization from the latter part of the eighth to the tenth century was the leading civilization in the West, and much more creative and original in almost all respects than the Byzantine. It was a considerable culture in its own right and far from being deriva-tive, though, like others, it rested on the achievements of its prede-cessors. It is also worth remembering that when the Western crusaders launched their attack on the Near East at the end of the tenth century, it was the Muslim civilization that they found there which absorbed the crusaders and not vice versa. It was not until at least the next century that the West began to forge ahead. By that time Muslim civilization in the Near East was already in decline, and Spain had been reconquered by the Christians. Though the Turks were to inherit much from their coreligionists who preceded them, their civilization was distinct and lies outside the scope of this book.

CHAPTER VIII

EARLY MEDIEVAL EUROPE TO THE END OF THE TENTH CENTURY

The next three chapters will be devoted to the period conventioi: ally called the Middle Ages. Although there is something to be said for the concept of the Middle Ages as a cultural unity, to be distinguished from the early modern and modern ages that followed it, it should not be thought that there was no development during the period. But the pace of change between the eighth and fourteenth centuries was slower than that between the fourteenth and the twentieth centuries; if it appears to increase as it nears the present day, this, as will be shown in later chapters of this book, is probably due more than anything else to the advance of science and technology in the modern period, and to the social and political consequences of this advance. During the period covered by the next three chapters, there was little technological progress and relatively little social change. But there was constant political change as the various European states began to take on their modern form. Much of the material of these chapters is therefore necessarily concerned with the political events of the period, and especially with the struggle between the two institutions with universalist pretensions, the Catholic Church and the Holy Roman Empire, and with the eventual failure of the efforts of both to establish their supremacy. Thus the national states, the creation of the Middle Ages, were left to fulfill the tasks of Western civilization during the succeeding centuries to the present time.

THE CAROLINGIAN EMPIRE

The Donation of Pepin. When Pepin the Short became king of the Franks in 751 his realm comprised almost all of present-day France and those parts of present-day Germany that had been Christianized. But many of the outlying areas were ruled by nobles who enjoyed a virtual autonomy, acknowledging the formal suzerainty of the Frankish king only as long as he did not attempt to make his rights effective. The pagans to the north, however, were in the process of being converted by Christian missionaries, many of them of English or Irish origin. When they accepted Christianity they naturally came under the rulership of the Franks. It was therefore to the interest of the Frankish monarchy to support the missionary movement and to make use of the clergy for the purpose of consolidating its rule. Pepin and his successor, Charlemagne, therefore consistently tried to keep the Frankish and foreign clerics under their control, and while co-operating with the papacy which sponsored the missionaries, had no intention of allowing the popes to take clerical appointments out of their hands. For their part, the popes of that epoch were mainly interested in seeing Europe Christianized, and, beholden as they were to the Frankish monarchs, did not wish to antagonize them as long as the clerical appointees of the monarchs were reasonably well-suited to their position. Since both Pepin and Charlemagne were anxious to have effective clergymen in key positions in their state, as they had to perform so many administrative tasks in addition to their tasks in the Church, on the whole the system worked well and with relatively little friction as long as the monarch left theological questions to the papacy.

The papacy was in considerable danger from the Lombards in the eighth century. Although the Lombards had now ceased to be Arians and become Catholic Christians, a number of Lombard monarchs coveted the rulership of Rome, which was still under the nominal suzerainty of the Byzantine emperor. They had already engaged in hostilities with the Byzantine exarch at Ravenna and captured some of his territories. Rome, which likewise came within the exarch's jurisdiction, was only one of such territories which they proposed to add to their domain. Rome was already threatened at the time Pepin sent to Pope Zacharias to ask him in effect whether he had papal approval for abolishing the last remnants of Merovingian rule and assuming the crown himself. By agreeing to the step, and calling upon Archbishop Boniface, the leading Christian missionary, to crown him, the pope had already put Pepin in his debt. Only three years later, a new pope, Stephen II, was endangered by the encroaching Lombards. He thereupon visited Pepin, crowned him again with his own hands, and obtained the promise of his protection, having meanwhile failed to obtain any effective support from the Byzantine emperor. Pepin fought two campaigns against the Lombards and compelled their king to relinquish the territories in Italy claimed by the pope. He then made a formal deed of gift of the territories to the pope, and had his emissaries deposit the keys of the city of Rome on the tomb of St. Peter. The pope in return recognized Pepin as *patricius* of Italy. The Byzantine emperor protested but was powerless to intervene. Thus the papacy became possessed of a swath of territory reaching right across Italy from Rome northwest to the Adriatic (Donation of Pepin, 756).

The Reign of Charlemagne. When Pepin died, his two sons, Charles and Carloman, fell heirs to his kingdom. But the brothers quarreled with one another, and serious civil war might well have broken out had not Carloman died early. A new Lombard king, Desiderius, thought the time had come to win back his territories which he had never fully yielded to the pope. By supporting Carloman's young children he hoped to be able to keep the Frankish kingdom divided and prevent Charles from intervening in Italy. But Charles was quickly able to consolidate Carloman's share of Pepin's estate under his own rule, and in response to another appeal from the papacy crossed the Alps into Italy. This time he put a final end to the independent Lombard kingdom and assumed the Lombard crown himself (774). The pope was allowed at last to assume control of the territories allotted to him by Pepin, though Charles retained a general suzerainty over them and accepted some responsibility for their administration.

During the course of his reign Charles reduced the semiautonomous princes in his domains to the status of subjects and placed his sons as rulers over some of the former dukedoms. He waged a long and merciless war against the Saxons, whom he compelled to adopt Christianity, and defeated the Avars in central Europe, incorporating their territories into his growing empire. They likewise became Christians. The only loss of importance that Charles sustained was the defeat of his rear guard by the Basques after an expedition into Spain against the Saracens which had failed of its major objective. Thereafter, he was able to establish a *march* or frontier zone in Spain, which served to keep the Saracens from making any headway in his own kingdom.

Charles made full use of the services of the clergy and the nobles in his realm, giving them numerous administrative tasks to perform. He set up marches in all his frontiers under *margraves,* or counts of the march. He was strong enough to keep these men disciplined and loyal to him, in part through a system similar to that of the ancient Persian Empire, by which he sent out inspectors (one lay, one clerical), known as the *missi dominici,* who reported to him on how the various provinces were being administered. All Charles's officials, with the exception of his permanent secretariat in his capital of Aachen, were granted lands to provide them with means of subsistence. These, indeed, were their only source of income outside the proceeds of the courts of justice in which they were permitted to share. The Church officials were no exception to this rule. The higher clergy lived from the proceeds of their bishoprics, and were in all essential respects nobles, although they might not be noble by birth. As a rule, since they had so many duties to perform for the monarch, they left the actual religious tasks of their dioceses to their subordinates.

Charles kept a close watch on all the activities that went on in his empire. He issued numerous royal ordinances, called *capitularies,* and in his lifetime they were obeyed. But the success of the system depended on the supervision exercised by the monarch. If this were relaxed, as it was after Charles's death, it was not at all difficult for the counts to throw off their allegiance to the central monarchy and continue to exercise their various local functions as before, but without supervision. Thus they tended to become independent princes, their power based securely on their possession of the land, which now no one was strong enough to take from them. The Carolingian system was therefore one that held within it the seeds of its own decay. Unlike the Roman imperial system it was not based on an army and bureaucracy under central control and able to compel the provincial authorities to obey them. The Carolingian army was a militia supplied by the nobles and based on the universal obligation of free men to serve in it, under the direction of local magnates. If the latter could not be compelled by the monarch to bring their troops to battle, then the obligation lapsed. Thus arose the feudal system under which the feudal monarch enjoyed theoretical rights which he was seldom able to enforce, and local authorities assumed the real tasks of rulership, possessing as they did a real power but one limited by the extent of the lands over which they exercised effective control and jurisdiction.

Relations between Charlemagne and the papacy were, on the whole, good throughout the reign. The monarch treated the pope as a valuable collaborator but did not admit his right to dictate in any way to him or to the Frankish clergy. On several occasions Charles took the initiative in deciding even theological questions. For example, he took a different view of the Iconoclastic Controversy with Constantinople from that of the papacy and did not hesitate to have the German clergy proclaim his own view. When a doctrinal heresy arose during his reign, it was Charles who summoned a synod and dictated its decisions, with which the pope perforce had to agree. When a new pope was elected toward the end of the eighth century, Charles addressed to him a letter of admonition as to how he was to behave in order to set a good example to Christendom. When the same pope, Leo III, was accused of various malpractices by his enemies in Rome, he fled to Charles's court, and the monarch had him restored to his office, after he had taken an oath that he was not guilty of the charges. A few days later, on Christmas Day, 800, the pope crowned Charles emperor of the Romans in the church of St. Peter's.

Einhard, Charles's biographer, states that the monarch was displeased by this act, although it has seemed to many scholars that he could not have been unaware that it was intended. It had the unfortunate and predictable result that it embroiled him with the Byzantine emperor, who alone was entitled to be called emperor of the Romans—even though actually he was in effective control of little that could be called Roman. Charles, after waging war with the emperor, finally had his title acknowledged in exchange for the return of some of his conquests, including Venice. It is possible that Charles and his advisers foresaw that in later times it would be thought that his successors needed to be crowned by the pope before they were regarded as legitimate emperors. At all events, before his death he had his sole surviving son, Louis, crowned without the assistance of the papacy, presumably hoping to dispel the precedent. But since this son later insisted on being crowned by the pope and accepted the papal terms for the ceremony, nothing was achieved. In fact the German monarchs did come to believe that the coronation was necessary before they would be regarded as true emperors; and all who could, took the required pilgrimage to Rome.

The reigns of Charles and his immediate successors were marked by an educational revival that is commonly called the Carolingian Renaissance. Charles brought scholars from all over Europe, especially from England, to teach at his palace school at Aachen, and he ordered schools to be set up by all bishops in their dioceses. Alcuin of York organized the palace school and taught there; his pupils spread out over the empire to continue the work. There was certainly a revival of literacy after the long Merovingian decline of both literacy and learning, and a new script, the Carolingian minuscule, was developed in Carolingian monasteries. Some creative work in literature was done, notably in the century following Charles's death. But it was in no sense a great age of literature, either in Latin or in the vernacular; and only a small elite class of intellectuals resulted from the efforts. However, the organization of education had at least been begun, and what Charles had founded never again died out completely, even in the renewed barbarian invasions that followed the breakup of his empire. In time the Middle Ages were to build again on the Carolingian foundations and begin the long and continuous growth of Western culture.

The Successors of Charlemagne. Louis, called the Pious (814–840), proved to be an indifferent ruler, and had great trouble throughout his reign with his three sons, among whom he soon divided the empire, with the exception of Italy which was given to a subking. When he married again and had a fourth son, Charles (the Bald), the empress insisted on a suitable share for him. Though one son, Pepin, died before his father, there had already been acrimony over the share of Charles, and it continued after Louis' death in 840. The eldest son, Lothair, the emperor, soon found his surviving brothers allied against him, and in 843 he was compelled to agree to a division of the realm (Treaty of Verdun, 843) under which Louis (Ludwig the German) held roughly the eastern portion (Germany), and Charles the western portion (France), with Lothair keeping a so-called "middle kingdom" and an overlordship over Italy. This middle kingdom, later called Lotharingia (Lorraine), has been a bone of contention between France and Germany down into modern times. When Lothair died before his brothers, his domains were once more divided among his surviving sons. When two of these sons died before their uncles, the latter fought among themselves, each striving to enlarge his territory at the expense of the rest of his family. Charles the Bald, after fighting most of his life, survived to become emperor for two years (875–877), but after his death the empire had really ceased to exist. Several shadowy monarchs claimed the title of emperor, and were accorded it by some of their nominal subjects. The Carolingian Empire, which has been called by some the "first Europe," had disappeared; not until Napoleon was so much of Europe to be again under the same crown.

THE BEGINNING OF NATIONAL STATES IN EUROPE

France. Meanwhile "France" and "Germany" had been coming into existence, slowly and painfully. Charles the Fat (884–887), son of Ludwig the German, and great-grandson of Charlemagne, inherited the German monarchy of his father and was also chosen king of the West Franks, thus for a brief moment uniting much of the Carolingian empire. But since he was totally incompetent and unable to defend his realms against the invading Northmen, he was deposed in both territories by his magnates. For most of the rest of the century Carolingians were kings in France, but they exercised almost no authority. In 987 the magnates chose as king Hugh Capet, whose family had distinguished itself in the wars with the Northmen and had exercised much power in the country during the century. His title was acknowledged by the German rulers who had now become once again emperors—though not descended from Charlemagne, ruling only over the territories of Ludwig the German, and intermittently exercising authority in Italy. With the Capets the French monarchy became in fact hereditary, though, like all the German monarchies, it was theoretically elective, a custom that had survived from ancient tribal days.

Germany. In 911 the last Carolingian ruler (Louis the Child) died in Germany, leaving no heirs. The German magnates then chose a duke as their elected king, he in turn choosing a monarch from the house of Saxony (Henry I, the Fowler [919–936]), who was able to consolidate his position and bequeathed the crown to his successors, who ruled for several generations. His son Otto I asserted his authority over his nobles and became by far the strongest lord in his realm. He, like his father, earned much of his prestige by victories over the invading Magyars. In 951 Otto won much of Italy, and took the title of king of Italy. In 961 he was called in by the pope to protect him against his enemies in Rome. In the following year the pope anointed him emperor, thus beginning the empire, later to be called the Holy Roman Empire, which lasted until 1806. The existence of this empire, whose territories were not confined to Germany, had important consequences in the centuries to come, effectively preventing Germany from following the same course as France and becoming a national state.

England. Until the ninth century England was plagued by the weakness of the monarchy. There were several monarchs, each ruling a part of the country. At one time or another one monarch would win power and prestige beyond his small kingdom; but it was not until the Norse invasions in the ninth century that an English monarch ruled the whole country except for that part taken over by the invaders. Alfred the Great (871–899) of Wessex was forced to concede the Danelaw, a large area in the north and east of England, to the Northmen (in England called Danes). But it was reconquered by his son and grandson; and Edgar, the grandson, who ruled from 959 to 975, was recognized as king of all England. In the beginning of the eleventh century, Danes again invaded, and a Danish dynasty ruled England from 1017 to 1042. Then the throne returned to the descendants of Alfred in the person of Edward the Confessor (1042–1066), who was chosen king by the English magnates. It was by this time widely thought in England that the line of Alfred was the only true royal line, and the king already had much more power than did kings on the Continent. This power, of course, was inherited by William the Norman, known as William the Conqueror, who established a strong feudal monarchy in England when he won the throne by force of arms in 1066.

INVASIONS OF NORTHMEN AND MAGYARS

We have already had occasion to allude to the new barbarian invasions of the Northmen and Magyars. Even before the death of Charlemagne, the peoples of Scandinavia had begun to expand southward into Christian Europe. During the ninth century their raids became ever more destructive. At first they did not, like the migrating peoples, expand in search of land and living space. On the contrary, they set forth in boats, with the aim of looting the more advanced and sedentary peoples, especially in those few centers where there was any accumulation of wealth. Armies were unable to deal with these destructive raiders; by the time a feudal army had assembled, the Northmen (Vikings) were already far away. Towns and monasteries close to navigable rivers were especially hard hit, and many did not recover for centuries. In time the defenders learned the tactics necessary to defeat the Vikings, and in due course the latter decided that they wished to settle down. But they had succeeded in putting a virtual end to civilized life in much of Western Europe, and fostered unwittingly the growth of feudalism (which is described in the next chapter). The Northmen were granted their first great domain in France, when their leader Rollo took the name of Robert and became Duke of Normandy, owing a nominal allegiance to the French crown. He and his people accepted Christianity. In England, as we have seen, Northmen sat on the English throne in the early eleventh century and again after 1066. Other Northmen took Sicily from the Muslims and made inroads into the Byzantine Empire, while a group of Swedes led by Rurik founded Kiev in Russia, from which center they raided down to the Black Sea. Many Varangians, as they were called in Constantinople, took service in the Byzantine imperial guard, and were highly esteemed as warriors by the emperor. Everywhere they settled they displayed a remarkable talent for organization; and the Norman states, especially Normandy and Sicily, became among the best-governed of feudal Europe.

At the end of the ninth century the nomad Magyars, from western Asia and southern Russia, began to move westward and penetrated into Moravia, destroying the existing Slavic kingdom in that country in 906. For the next half century they were a constant danger to the Germans, whose rulers were compelled either to fight them or to buy them off. In 933 Henry the Fowler inflicted a severe defeat upon them, a victory repeated in a decisive manner by Otto I (Battle of the Lechfeld, 955). Their last defeat persuaded the Magyars that it was useless to try to expand further, and they began to adopt a settled life, occupying much of the present-day territory of Hungary, in which the Magyars are to this day the leading people. With some difficulty, but aided by missionaries and churchmen from the West, Stephen I (997–1038) converted his country to Catholic Christianity, for which he was rewarded by being given a crown by the pope in 1001. After his death he was canonized as a saint.

EASTERN EUROPE—THE BYZANTINE EMPIRE

During the years following the death of Charlemagne, the Byzantine Empire was little connected with the West, except for Venice and the northeastern Italian territories which were retained by Constantinople from the old exarchate of Ravenna, and southern Italy, which was effectively subjected to Byzantine rule once again by Basil I (876–886). Basil, however, was unable to dislodge the Muslims from Sicily, and they fully subjugated it after his death. During his reign the empire began a period of orderly government and firm rule under the so-called Macedonian dynasty, which occupied the Byzantine throne for more than 150 years, with the succession rarely disputed. The Muslim menace had now receded, and the Asiatic provinces of the empire were kept securely under Byzantine control.

Most of the difficulties experienced by the empire were from the continued invasions of Slavs and Bulgars into its European hinterland, especially the Balkan Peninsula, which the emperors had much difficulty in holding. Already in the eighth century the Bulgars had entered the Balkans, and the Byzantines had conducted several campaigns against them. In 865 the Bulgarian khan, who now called himself a tsar, allowed himself and his people to be converted to Christianity. But he had many difficulties with the patriarch of Constantinople, and for a long time he hesitated between Rome and Constantinople, fearing that religious union with the latter would lead to political subservience. However, when the people insisted upon adopting a Slavonic liturgy, contrary to Roman practices, and when Rome did not fall in with his views on other matters, he turned to the Eastern rite. His son Symeon found coexistence with Constantinople difficult and spent most of his reign fighting against the Byzantines—making, indeed, a serious attempt to win the throne of Constantinople for himself. At one time he even called himself emperor of the Romans, a title which the pope recognized and the emperor in Constantinople was powerless to prevent. After a brief interval, during which the Russians, led by Sviatoslav, attacked Bulgaria and were driven off by the Byzantines, who took the opportunity to destroy the Bulgarian kingdom also, another son, named Samuel, restored the kingdom and established his own patriarchate independent of Constantinople. He extended his empire so that it was hardly smaller than what remained to Constantinople. But the Byzantine emperor, Basil II, an energetic and resolute soldier, accepted the challenge. In a long and terrible war—Basil assumed afterward the title of Bulgaroktonos, "the Bulgar-killer"—he destroyed the Bulgarian empire and annexed the territory in 1018. During the war the Russian prince, Vladimir, accepted Christianity for himself and his people, and thus began the close connection between Russia and Constantinople, a connection whose effects are still with us today. Following the annexation, Bulgaria was entirely incorporated into the Byzantine Empire and lost its identity until the end of the twelfth century, when the decay of the empire under the blows of Seljuk Turks gave the Bulgarians another chance to build an independent state. This state in due course fell to the Ottoman Turks.

In the early eleventh century the Macedonian dynasty fell into the hands of a number of empresses whose husbands ruled through them. The century was one of general decline, with the empire having first to be defended against the Normans from the West and then against the expanding Seljuk Turks, who inflicted a severe defeat on the Byzantines at the Battle of Manzikert in 1071. In 1081 Alexius Comnenus became emperor, founding a dynasty which endured until the Latin conquest of Constantinople in 1204. Alexius was compelled to call in the Crusaders from the West to help him against the Turks, beginning an era of increasing influence of the West in Byzantine affairs. (Discussion of these events will be reserved for the next chapter, when the Crusades will be dealt with as an episode of Western history.)

SUMMARY—"THE DARK AGES"

The centuries covered in this chapter used to be known collectively as the Dark Ages. The term is not inappropriate, even though the epoch was perhaps not quite as dark as used to be thought. Muslim Spain and the Byzantine Empire should, of course, be excluded from the generalization. Both were centers of high culture under rulers who were usually effective; Cordova and Constantinople were graceful cities, centers of learning and enlightenment. But the West was still in the period of gestation. There was little original learning; literacy was almost exclusively confined to the clergy; even in the Church, relatively few men and women could read or write, though the percentage increased after the reforms of Charlemagne. The papacy reached its lowest level of achievement and influence, and the clergy throughout Europe was held fast in the thrall of feudalism, most of the higher clergy not easily to be distinguished from lay nobles, many of them even going to war for their lay rulers. But a reform movement had already begun in the monasteries, especially in France, which was to lead directly to the strong and influential medieval papacy which will be dealt with, for the sake of continuity, in the next chapter.

In the West, therefore, all appeared still "dark," but it was the darkness before the dawn. The historian, with the benefit of hindsight, is able to perceive the stirrings of life in the Western peoples which were to lead eventually to medieval civilization and Western ascendancy. But for the moment there was little above the surface in feudal Europe that would have appeared especially encouraging to contemporary Western man. A Westerner who sought intellectual and cultural refreshment could have turned only to Spain or Constantinople. But his day was coming, and his own civilization beginning. Before the end of the eleventh century he was already strong enough to expand into the East in the episode, typical of Western expansionism, that we call the Crusades.

CHAPTER IX

THE MIDDLE AGES TO THE CLOSE OF THE TWELFTH CENTURY

During the entire period since the death of Louis the Pious in 840 the system called feudalism had been growing, and the monarchs had steadily been losing power. The centrifugal tendencies already visible by the early ninth century continued to operate and became ever stronger, especially under the impact of the renewed barbarian invasions by Northmen and Magyars. Against these raiders it was necessary to band together for local protection, and the defense had to be undertaken by men who had immediate force at their disposal. Lesser lords would often request assistance, and "commend" themselves and their lands to greater lords, receiving back their lands in exchange for their acceptance of certain obligations. The greater magnates, thus fortified, could wage war on others also to increase their holdings. The general condition of Europe may reasonably be described as anarchic, with a certain system in the anarchy that prevented it from disintegrating into complete chaos. Thus, in spite of the fact that monarchs with great theoretical powers continued to exist, Europe became almost fully feudalized by the end of the millennium. The history of the later Middle Ages is the story of how from feudal anarchy arose the national states with strong monarchs which dominated the modern era until the nineteenth century.

THE FEUDAL AND MANORIAL SYSTEMS

The Feudal Heritage from the Roman Empire. It has already been said that because of the collapse of central governments in the period following the death of Charlemagne and the disintegration of his empire, the feudal system was one of semianarchy, under which local magnates exercised the only effective authority. The roots of the system nevertheless lie far back in the past, long before the Carolingians, and indeed, are to be found as early as the last centuries of the Roman Empire, as well as in the peculiar tribal system of the Germanic barbarians. Feudalism was therefore only systematized in the later epoch; its origins must be looked for earlier.

During the barbarian invasions, as we have noted, centralized authority was of necessity replaced by local. The local lords who were strong enough to avoid imperial taxation, or were granted immunity from it, performed the important service of organizing local defense. The smaller lords and tenant farmers looked to the greater lords for this service, and in return were ready to place their lands at their disposal and to provide military assistance. Ownership of the lands, therefore. passed to these magnates, who in return lent them back to their former owners in exchange for certain specified goods and services. Many of the magnates organized very extensive estates called *villas,* to which were attached both free former landowners who provided military services, and *coloni,* or permanent tenants, most of whom lost altogether their free status and became serfs. The villa is the Roman original of the medieval manor, while the network of military and other obligations owed by the free tenants to their protector is the Roman precursor of the feudal system. The magnates themselves owed a nominal loyalty to the emperor, and when the emperors, or the Merovingian kings who succeeded them in one part of their empire, were powerful, they could make them live up to their theoretical obligations; but at other times a great lord could do almost as he wished, usually taking part with his followers in the civil wars constantly being waged by one Merovingian or another to establish his rule.

Thus many lords in the Merovingian period had in actual fact more power than the titular kings and certainly a far greater freedom of action. As a heritage of the Roman Empire, therefore, we find a tendency toward the rise of a class of magnates virtually independent of the central monarchy, accustomed to ruling in their own areas, and paying little attention to royal ordinances unless the monarch, as was the case with the early Merovingians, and above all with the first two Carolingian monarchs, was able to compel them to obey him. On the other hand, most of the magnates were anxious to increase their lands and power, and the king could count on their assistance on occasions when they might hope to win victory, followed by a suitable reward of lands of their defeated rivals. Hence our description of the epoch of growing feudalism as one of semianarchy, marked as it was by constant warfare and the absence of any effective public authority capable of putting an end to it.

The Germanic Contribution. The Germanic contribution to feudalism is to be found in a German institution known as the *comitatus* or companionship-in-arms, and in the historical conditions whereby the tribal leaders of the barbarians came to inherit the Roman Empire. It had been the custom among the Germanic tribes for successful warriors to gather around themselves groups of other warriors who acknowledged their leadership and bound themselves by oaths to support them in combat. Such oaths were considered sacred by the Germans, and to break them was the most heinous of crimes. In swearing them both the leaders and the followers accepted certain obligations, the former to protect and the latter to support. This custom provided what may be called the "institutional" element in feudalism. The system itself grew up to meet the actual needs of the times. But Western feudalism differs from the rule by semi-independent and independent nobles characteristic of many periods and peoples in history, in its network of reciprocal obligations sanctified by oaths. This system culminated in the code of chivalry, which stressed the duties and responsibilities of the "true knight." It was even possible for the Christian Church to find elements in it which were in accord with its own ethics and support them accordingly. The code of chivalry stressed such virtues as keeping one's word and showing courtesy to the unfortunate. The influence of women in the later twelfth and thirteenth centuries likewise served to soften the somewhat barbaric virtues of the military code of arms, while at the same time concealing the actual objectives of feudal warfare in guise of a romantic pursuit of glory in their service.

The Germanic leaders who penetrated into Western Europe and took it over in the fifth century were seldom more than tribal chieftains, equal in status to chieftains from other tribes and groups, and not superior in rank to lesser chieftains from their own tribes. All became nobles in the new barbarian kingdoms, as long as they could command enough military force to take possession of sufficient lands for their own use. Many of them might hope to join the ranks of the very great if they were successful in warfare, like Clovis, founder of the Frankish kingdom, or if they could obtain powerful backing from their superiors. A monarch like Charlemagne was strong enough to impose his will on all his subjects; but Charlemagne's authority was based not on his royal institutions so much as on his own imperious will and personality, and on the military forces which he had at his disposal. By the death of his son, Louis the Pious, the forces that had been in operation under the Merovingians, combined with the renewed dangers from outside the empire, were strong enough to destroy the imperfectly centralized government, and put effective power once more in the hands of the nobles. Having sat out his reign, some of them, indeed, having been granted more power by Charlemagne, they could now return with impunity to their former position of virtual independence from the monarchy.

The Feudal King. In the feudal system which predominated from the ninth century through much of the Middle Ages, the kings, in theory, and in some territories in practice, were elected by their magnates; and they inherited certain rights traditionally attached to the monarchy, which differed in the various countries. Each monarch possessed some territories of his own, often smaller than those held by some of the magnates in his own kingdom. Over these territories he exercised all the rights of a feudal lord. In addition, as king he held the right to appoint the higher clergy, sometimes in the entire kingdom over which he was nominal ruler, sometimes in only a few areas beyond his own feudal domains. He had the right to command the army in a war agreed to by the magnates, and all the lords in the realm were required to contribute to his ransom if he was captured by the enemy. If any lands were left without an heir during their reign they *escheated* (reverted) to the monarch; if they fell to a woman the king had a right to protect her and choose her husband. These were not negligible powers and rights, especially when, as in France, the monarchy continued in the same family for centuries, thus enabling the gains of one king to be bequeathed intact to his successors. But elsewhere they did not prove sufficient to enable the king to build a truly national state with a centralized administration. The king remained "first among equals," and all his equals owed to him a special oath of allegiance. But as long as the feudal system endured the king could not be certain of commanding enough power to put down a concerted effort to dethrone him or take away the succession from his family. Invariably he had to win the support of enough nobles to ensure his position; he could not command them or treat them as subjects, as could the absolute monarchs who followed the age of feudalism.

Rights and Obligations of Feudal Lords. The feudal lords other than the king exercised full authority in their territories, which they maintained by means of feudal courts over which they presided. To these courts were summoned all their vassals, men who owed them fealty, and were obliged to supply them with a stipulated number of armed men. Each vassal was himself a lord in his own domain, but since he held his land by gift from his superior lord in the system, he could not dispose of it. In theory his sons could not inherit the land (called a *fief*); but in practice a fief became hereditary as long as the heir consented to perform the obligations attached to it and took the oath of homage to the lord. The lord in a lord/vassal relationship was obligated to provide protection for his vassal, as the vassal was obligated to aid his lord when called upon. In addition, the vassal had to make certain payments to the lord on special occasions, give hospitality, provide for his ransom, and, especially, to make a payment when he inherited the fief. These *aids* and *reliefs,* as they were called, might amount to a considerable sum during the vassal's lifetime, but did not provide for his lord's subsistence. His primary obligation was to fill his quota of armed men, and it was for the sake of these armed men and the status that his right to call upon them ensured that the lord consented to divide up his land into fiefs. The fiefs, indeed, provided him with far less in actual consumer goods than he would have gained if he had turned the entire land into manors under his direct control. But it was a military society, and the primary need of the lord was for armed men committed to help him in time of war.

The system was greatly complicated by the fact that almost all the major lords both held fiefs and granted them to others. In other words they were vassals to other lords for part of their territories, and yet let out lands by *subinfeudation* to vassals of their own. As can readily be imagined, this gave rise to a conflict of obligations which sometimes led to difficult decisions—as, for example, when one of their own vassals was at war with one of their lords, and they owed obligation to both lord and vassal at the same time.

Decay of the Feudal System. Since small wars were almost always being fought, the military obligations of the system were far from light ones. Only when in the later Middle Ages the kings were able to assert their authority and put an end to them, or when, as in the case of England under the Normans, private wars were forbidden and the king was in a position to prevent them, did the constant warfare diminish. Even then it was likely to break out again as soon as the hand of a strong monarch was removed from the helm. But in the later Middle Ages many lords also preferred in an epoch of rising commerce to make better use of their lands than to give them out in exchange for military services which sometimes they no longer required. Thus the feudal system was destroyed in part by the monarchs, and in part by the fact that it had outlived its usefulness. Most of the later feudal wars were fought by nobles who hoped to control the monarchy rather than for the simple purpose of defending or extending their possessions. The fifteenth-century Wars of the Roses in England had the ostensible object of placing a monarch of one or two families on the throne, but they effectively prepared the way for absolutism, since the noble houses destroyed themselves in the war. The sixteenth-century civil wars in France, though complicated by many factors including the Protestant Reformation, had a basically similar objective, of subjecting the king to control by one of the warring noble families; but in fact they prepared the way for the absolutism of the Bourbons.

The Manorial System. The feudal lords, as we have noted, could not live from the contributions to their upkeep made by their vassals. All lords therefore set aside for their own use a number of manors, or large rural areas, usually including one or more villages which were managed by themselves or their stewards (bailiffs). It was the task of these men to manage their masters' estates and provide them with their means of subsistence. The manor house might be a large mansion or a fortified castle, in which the lord and his family, or, in smaller estates, his bailiff lived. To every manor there were attached a number of serfs, and usually a number of men of free status who were subjected to certain restrictions. The manorial fields were divided into strips reserved for the use of the lord, which had to be worked by the serfs, and strips whose produce was retained by the serfs themselves. In most manors there would also be an obligation for the serfs to work one or more strips set aside for the subsistence of the parish priest, who might originally have been a serf himself. In addition, the serfs had to perform certain specified tasks, such as road building and repairing, and the serfs' wives had to sew and perform domestic service for the lady of the manor. In the village there were more serfs and freemen who worked as blacksmiths and in other occupations deemed necessary by the lord. All the villagers were required to make use of certain facilities provided by the lord, for which they had to pay a fee.

The manor was therefore a more or less self-sufficient economic entity, and, like the feudal system, the manorial system involved a network of mutual obligations decreed by long-standing custom, and not to be changed easily at the whim of the lord. Naturally, oaths of allegiance and homage were not required from serfs, who were the property of the lord and possessed only the customary rights of the manor. But in exchange for their work they had at least the use of the land, and it was to their lord's interest to protect them to the best of his ability.

Decay of the Manorial System. In the later Middle Ages when serfs could escape to the towns and become free without too much difficulty, many took advantage of any such opportunity, while others would join a crusade, often with the permission of their lord, and probably never again return to the manor. But meanwhile the lord was beginning to find the compulsory labor of the serfs less than efficient. It was sometimes more profitable to let out the land on a rental basis and be sure of an income which he could expend on the luxuries that he and his wife had come to desire. Finally with the shortage of labor which resulted from such plagues as the fourteenth-century Black Death, the lord began to consider the possibility of making use of the common land of the manor for more profitable purposes than as pasture for the village animals. Thus began the "enclosure" movement, especially in England, under which the lord turned to wool growing, which needed a minimum of labor and brought in substantial sums of money. Though the peasants objected, they could do little about it. The entire process resulted in the gradual emancipation of the serfs in several countries, especially in France and England, where they were replaced by tenants and small-holding peasants, still owing obligations to their landlord but free to leave if they wished and to make their living in the towns if they preferred. The lords became simple landowners, holding a high social status by reason of their land, often receiving a huge income from rents, and free to increase this income by their efficiency in land use and management. They were no longer a military aristocracy interested primarily in war and only secondarily in the material proceeds of their domains.

THE EMPIRE AND THE PAPACY

The Cluniac Reform and Its Consequences. We have already had occasion to note that in the reign of Charlemagne the higher clergy were appointed by the monarch and used for his own administrative purposes. In the feudal kingdoms that followed the disintegration of his empire the same conditions obtained. The monarchs or greater nobles, indeed, provided the clerics with land, without which it would have been impossible for them to subsist, although they might make a small extra income from donations and fees. But in return for the land the clerics were obliged to perform the same obligations as the lay feudal lords; and neither monarch nor noble could therefore countenance the appointment of men they considered unsuitable to these important positions. Nevertheless the papacy also had an interest in the quality of the appointees, for the men had religious as well as feudal duties to perform; and the system of appointment by laymen could easily be abused. Indeed, when the monarchs and nobles were short of money, they might even sell Church offices to men willing and able to pay for them without regard to any other considerations. This ecclesiastical crime of *simony* the Church was long unable to prevent.

Hitherto we have had no occasion to deal with that characteristic institution of the Christian Church, the monastery; but since it was a monastic reform that laid the foundation for papal supremacy, a few words should be devoted to it here. From early in the Christian era a number of earnest men and women, wishing to devote their lives exclusively to their religion without undertaking all the obligations that accompanied an active pastorship in the Church, had retired from the world, to live either by themselves (the hermits), or with others who held the same ideals as themselves. They devoted themselves to prayer and works of charity for the benefit of mankind, and they themselves as a rule lived from charitable donations and bequests. In due course the Church found it necessary to impose some order and discipline on these groups, and to regulate their behavior. In the West the rule laid down by St. Benedict for his monastery of Monte Cassino in Italy in the early sixth century was widely adopted. This rule received the sanction of Pope Gregory I (590–604), who himself imposed it on other monastic orders—though some orders maintained different rules which had at one time or another been sanctioned by the papacy. The Benedictine rule stressed manual labor as a necessary part of the life of a monk, and it prescribed the form of organization and the type of discipline to which he should be subjected. Many of the men who ultimately rose to high office in the Church were originally trained in monasteries, and at all times the monks (and nuns) played an important part in the various Church reforms, as they did in the Cluniac movement to which we now turn our attention.

In 910 the duke of Aquitaine in France left some lands to the abbot of the monastery of Cluny in southern France, free from any obligations except to say prayers for his soul. The abbey of Cluny was by this act freed from the feudal system and enabled to pursue a policy without fear of dictation from lay lords or kings. The first abbot, a man renowned for his holiness, then insisted that all similar donations should be made with the same freedom from feudal obligations. Since he gathered round him men who were sincerely religious, other men who desired to leave lands to the Church for the benefit of their souls, were inclined to leave them to Cluny, rather than to the unreformed and often secular-minded lay-appointed clergy. The Cluniac movement began to grow, and considerable numbers of daughter abbeys were founded, all owing allegiance to the first abbot of Cluny and his successors. In time monks educated at Cluny began to play an active part in the Church, and were ready to fill the highest positions, even at Rome.

Meanwhile the popes at Rome were chosen only too often by various factions of nobles in the capital, and many incumbents were far from suitable for their high office. When Otto the Great became emperor in 962, he engaged for years in efforts to put candidates who favored his policy on the papal throne, only to find them deposed when he returned over the Alps to Germany. Since the German emperors regarded Rome and all Italy to the north of Rome as a part of their empire, it was wholly natural for them to take a special interest in the person of the ruler of one of their most valuable possessions. At last the emperors established the principle that the pope must be acceptable to them, and for the greater part of a century the emperor virtually held the right of nomination to the Holy See. But several emperors, notably Otto III (983–1002), became seriously interested in the reform movement emanating from Cluny, and secured the appointment of a number of reform popes. These popes recognized that if a reform was to spread fully throughout Europe, the "secular" clergy (that is, the clergy holding ecclesiastical appointments in the state, to be distinguished from the "regular" clergy living according to a *regula,* or rule in the monasteries) must be appointed by themselves. Such a policy was bound sooner or later to come into conflict with that of the emperors, who wished to continue to make use of the clergy in their territories, and even sell their offices when it suited them.

The Quarrel between Henry IV and Gregory VII. The potential conflict became an actual one when Hildebrand, a monk who had long been influential in the forming of papal policy, became pope under the name of Gregory VII in 1075. The groundwork for the freeing of the papacy itself from imperial control had already been laid in 1059 when a papal decree had handed over the election of future popes to a number of Italian cardinals, who, themselves appointees of previous popes, might be expected to work for the interests of the papacy and thereby to maintain a certain continuity of policy at the Holy See. Henry IV, though already emperor, had been only a child under the regency of his mother at the time of the papal decree, and therefore could not object. But when he grew up he was faced by rebellions among his own nobles and needed money to suppress them. He resorted to simony for the purpose. Pope Gregory VII, recognizing that the time was opportune for a showdown, proposed to make an issue of it with the young emperor. In 1076 he issued a statement of practices forbidden by the Church and prohibited the appointment of the higher clergy by anyone but himself. Such an extreme demand he could hardly hope to enforce. But he had various weapons at his disposal which could not be altogether disregarded by lay rulers at a time when the Cluny movement and its offspring had greatly increased religious fervor in Christendom. If he excommunicated a monarch or laid an interdict on his country, those clergymen who obeyed him would refuse to perform any of the Church services, including even the burial of the dead, in his realm. The individual excommunicated, as well as being shunned in his lifetime by his peers, who were forbidden to associate with him, would die unshriven and cut off from salvation. Gregory also claimed the right to depose an excommunicated monarch and to absolve from their oaths all those who had sworn allegiance to him.

When therefore Henry proved recalcitrant and appointed an archbishop of Milan in defiance of Gregory's decree, the pope excommunicated him and absolved his nobles from their allegiance. Since Henry was already at war with many of his own magnates, the latter naturally accepted the papal decree. The German clergy hesitated. If Henry were in fact to lose his throne, it would certainly prove to have been wiser to have made terms with the pope. Most of them, in spite of the fact that they had been largely responsible for Henry's defiance of the pope, now decided therefore either to support Gregory or at least to wait and see. The nobles who had hitherto supported Henry saw the matter in the same light. Henry thus suddenly found himself isolated and unable to prevent his rebellious nobles from taking him prisoner. Rudolf of Suabia, leader of the rebels, thereupon invited Gregory to come to Germany and preside over the election of a new emperor.

Then suddenly, when the pope was on the point of victory, the tables were turned. Henry escaped across the Alps and went to Canossa, where Gregory was staying on the way up to Germany. There he stood in the snow outside the pope's castle and begged for absolution, expressing his repentance. The pope, who was a priest as well as head of the Church, was left with no option but to agree, though he did not promise to restore Henry to his throne. However, the warring German nobles and clergy, believing he was to return to his throne and fearing the consequences, flocked back to his side, and Henry was free to turn on the die-hard rebels whom his forces now outnumbered. Though Gregory soon excommunicated him again, the favorable moment had passed. Rudolf was killed in battle and Henry returned over the Alps to deal with the pope. Gregory summoned the Normans who were vassals of the papacy from Sicily and southern Italy; but they arrived too late to save him. Gregory died in exile in 1085.

The Concordat of Worms. Nevertheless, the struggle had not been altogether wasted. Henry himself was driven later from his throne by further rebellions in Germany, and his successors, unwilling to remain indefinitely at odds with the papacy, tried to make terms. In 1122 a Concordat was signed at Worms under which both emperor and the pope had a veto on appointments of the higher clergy. The emperor invested the appointee with the scepter (symbol of his earthly office), while the pope invested him with the ring and the cross (symbols of his religious functions). Similar agreements were signed about the same period with the kings of England and France. Under the Concordat the king ceased to have the right to choose the bishops, who were elected henceforth by the local clergy, in accordance with canon law. After choice he invested them with the scepter, and the bishops swore an oath of fealty to him; whereupon the archbishop as papal representative, invested him with the ring and the cross.

The papacy had gained much from the struggle, even though it ended with a compromise. Whereas before the lay rulers had enjoyed the sole power to make clerical appointments, and could choose the higher clergy without consultation with the papacy, the latter could now at least prevent the more outrageous royal appointments. Moreover, the monarch knew that if the pope refused to invest his appointees with their spiritual office, he would have to withdraw the appointment or be prepared to defy the pope. During the rest of the twelfth century the papal power in fact continued to grow, culminating in the pontificate of Innocent III, to be dealt with in the next chapter.

THE EMPIRE UNDER THE HOHENSTAUFENS

The Empire itself was soon to fall into the hands of a strong and effective German family, the Hohenstaufens. The second king of this line, and the first to become emperor, Frederick I, Barbarossa, ruled from 1152 to 1190. During this long reign he succeeded in making the empire more nearly what its name implied than any of his predecessors, and far more powerful than any contemporary kingdom. With his desire to make his authority felt in Italy, to which the emperor still held a nominal title, it was inevitable that he should come into conflict with the papacy, whose political aspirations conflicted with his own, and which had no desire to see a strong monarch from beyond the Alps exercising effective authority in Italy. Moreover, in the first half of the twelfth century there had been a great increase of town life in northern Italy, and many of the towns had escaped from the authority of the weak nobility and clergy and had no mind to be deprived of self-government merely because an emperor claimed some rights conceded to him in the far distant past.

So Frederick, though he was able to establish his rule as firmly in Germany for his lifetime as Charlemagne had established his over a wider empire in the eighth and ninth centuries, using means not dissimilar to those of his predecessor, was successful in Italy only as long as his enemies did not unite against him. When the towns refused to allow him his claimed rights, he chastised them severely, destroying Milan and dissolving the *communes* (self-governing townships). But with the emperor beyond the Alps the towns reorganized and formed the powerful Lombard League which won a decisive victory over the emperor at the Battle of Legnano (1176).

Thereafter Frederick changed his policy and made peace with the League, abandoning, in effect, everything but ceremonial rights due to him as emperor. Frederick was also compelled to reconcile himself to Pope Alexander III, whom he had for more than a decade refused to recognize, preferring to work through "antipopes" of his own creation, who retained their authority only when Frederick was in a position to enforce it. But nevertheless, Frederick had the last word. By a piece of shrewd diplomacy he secured for his own son Henry the hand of Constance, the heiress of the Norman kingdom of Sicily and southern Italy (the Two Sicilies), a powerful kingdom that had succeeded to the Byzantine heritage in Italy and captured Sicily from the Saracens. This union meant that when Constance succeeded to her throne and brought it as a dowry to Henry, Italy would be squeezed between the two powers, and it would be difficult indeed for Rome and the Lombard towns to resist.

When Henry inherited the German throne, to which he had already been raised as a coemperor by his father, he set about making certain of the Sicilian crown which had fallen to his wife the previous year. In a series of campaigns, aided by the fortuitous circumstance that he gained possession of the person of the English king Richard I and was able to use him as a hostage to ward off dangerous enemies at home in Germany, Henry safely won the crown of the Two Sicilies. Italy was quiet, expecting the worst, while Henry made preparations to enlarge his possessions in the Mediterranean. Then suddenly, at the height of his power, he died in 1197 at the early age of thirty-two, leaving only an infant son to inherit. The following year Innocent III became pope, and the struggle between empire and papacy entered a new phase which will be dealt with in the next chapter.

THE NORMAN MONARCHY IN ENGLAND

The Reign of William the Conqueror. During the last years of the Saxon monarchy in England the Normans began to look with covetous eyes across the Channel. William (later to be called the Conqueror) became duke in 1035, and consolidated his duchy, making it into a well-developed feudal state firmly under ducal control and virtually independent of the French crown. His cousin, Edward the Confessor, king of England, was without heirs; and William, therefore, early determined to try to win the English throne on Edward's death. Edward himself, though of the lineage of Alfred, was a Norman on his mother's side and had been brought up in the Norman court. He therefore favored the succession of his Norman cousin, and William later claimed that he had bequeathed the English crown to him.

The English, however, had other ideas. The *Witan,* or council of magnates, elected Harold, the leading earl of England, immediately on the death of Edward, and Harold took what steps were available to him to protect his throne. He was, however, threatened by two invasions, one by the king of Norway, who also sought to add the English crown to his own and who was supported by Harold's brother, and the other from Duke William of Normandy. Though Harold defeated and killed the Norwegian king at Stamford Bridge in September, 1066, he was unable to bring effective force to bear upon William, who landed in the south while Harold was away in the north. At the Battle of Hastings, fought in October, 1066, William won a complete victory and Harold was killed. The magnates then accepted William as their king and during the next few years all English resistance was brought to an end.

William was now in a radically different position from that of every other European feudal king. Having conquered England with the aid of Norman warriors who had volunteered for the task, he now became the actual owner of all the English lands by right of conquest. He therefore rewarded his troops with English lands, and the former English lords who accepted his rule and were confirmed in their possessions, had to do homage for them; they were thus in the same position as the Norman barons. William fastened his Norman system securely upon England, though making use of those English institutions that seemed likely to be useful to him, especially the Saxon system of local courts. The Norman administration was to a large degree a Continental structure superimposed on a Saxon base, as is the English language itself, which is a mixture of words of Latin and Germanic origin. It was Norman efficiency that decreed and caused to be compiled the famous *Domesday Book,* which showed the extent, and described the feudal obligations of, every estate in the country—an invaluable source of information for a monarch who wished to be sure that all obligations to him were duly met.

The Reign of Henry I (1100–1135). When William died he still regarded Normandy as his chief possession and bequeathed it to the eldest of his three sons, leaving the crown of England to his second son, William Rufus. When the latter was murdered in 1100, the youngest son of William the Conqueror came to the throne as Henry I and wrested Normandy from his brother, thus uniting the countries again under one ruler. Henry's long reign was noted for the institution of a small council of advisers chosen by the king and responsible to him, to which the monarch committed many of his administrative tasks, thus bypassing the magnates, who were already inclined to be rebellious against the strong royal rule. This council ultimately was transformed into the king's Privy Council, the ancestor of the modern cabinet. Henry also encouraged the use of his royal courts rather than the traditional feudal courts for all lawsuits involving, however remotely, the royal prerogatives. He paid special attention to the royal accounts and established the Exchequer, with its own court, to which were sent all cases involving the royal income. Thus by the end of his reign the king had established the beginnings of a true bureaucracy responsible to him and administering on his behalf many of the most important royal functions. No other contemporary feudal king possessed any comparable instrument for enforcing his will in the country he ruled.

Re-establishment of Royal Control by the Plantagenets. All this "modernization" came to an abrupt halt when Henry died, leaving only a daughter to inherit his crown, at a time when it had not yet been established that a woman could inherit the English throne. The next nineteen years were a period of anarchy, while Stephen, the nearest male heir to the throne, battled with Henry's daughter Matilda, each contender backed by rival groups of nobles. Nobles from both parties began to build castles (forbidden by the first Normans) and to enroll armies (which under Norman legislation was the prerogative of the king alone). The country became not unlike its contemporary Germany before the accession of Frederick Barbarossa. Stephen finally had himself accepted as king, but was compelled to agree to the succession of Matilda's son, Henry Plantagenet, after his death. Since Stephen died soon afterward, Henry came to the throne as Henry II in 1154, perhaps the most able of all the English kings. He needed all his ability and resources if order were to be restored to England.

Henry possessed in his own right several important duchies of France, and acquired more when he married Eleanor of Aquitaine, recently divorced by Louis VII, king of France. Henry indeed was ruler of more territory in France than was the French king himself. He was therefore, with the aid of his French knights, strong enough to compel the English lords to pull down their castles and submit to him. Henry then reorganized the realm, making it as strong as in the time of his grandfather, and his own rule no less secure. His major quarrel was with the Church in the person of his former chancellor Archbishop Thomas Becket, who, with papal support, insisted on all the prerogatives of the Church, including ecclesiastical courts for the trial of all clerics, irrespective of their crime. Since Henry was at the time trying to establish the supremacy of his own royal courts, he fell foul of Becket, and in a moment of anger demanded who would rid him of this "pestilent priest." When some of his followers then murdered Becket in his own cathedral, public execration of Henry was such that he had to do penance for his crime and withdraw his proposed reforms insofar as they applied to the Church. The greatest achievement of Henry was in the field of law, where his reforms virtually made the king's courts and the common law (that is, common to the whole realm) which they enforced the only law remaining in the land. The grand jury dates from his reign, and a number of reforms which ultimately led to the use of the (petit) jury in criminal cases.

In his last years Henry was plagued by dissensions between his sons, and the premature deaths of his preferred heirs brought Richard I, the Lion-Heart, to the throne. Almost his entire reign Richard was out of the country, fighting in the Third Crusade, in prison in Germany, or warring in France with the French king, Philip Augustus, who was trying to take back the English possessions in his country. But the bureaucracy established by his father functioned so effectively that it became visible to all that the king's government could function without the actual presence of the monarch and that a true government no longer depended upon the personality of the ruler. Nevertheless the tremendous ransom for his release which had to be paid to the Holy Roman emperor, Henry VI, bore so hardly upon the nobles and people that Richard's successor John was always in such dire financial straits that he could no longer effectively defend his French possessions. The attempt to extract enough funds from his people to pay for his campaigns drove the nobles to rebel and coerced him into signing Magna Carta. These events will be dealt with in the next chapter.

THE EARLY CAPETIAN MONARCHY IN FRANCE

The early Capetians were, as noted earlier, relatively minor lords in the French realm, ruling virtually little beyond the Île de France around Paris. Nevertheless they held the title of king and possessed ecclesiastical patronage beyond the borders of their feudal domains. Like the English king, but several decades later, they built up a council made up of men, not necessarily noble, who owed their livelihood to the monarch. Many of them were clerics. This council persisted throughout the entire period of the monarchy until the French Revolution. The early Capetians were favored by long reigns and the undisputed succession of their eldest sons. Thus the monarchy began to take on permanence, and the elective principle disappeared.

The monarchs were careful rulers who slowly but surely consolidated their ancestral possessions and made their royal rights accepted. They expanded with caution when opportunity presented itself. Louis VI (1108–1137), the Fat, led a successful defense against German invaders, and won considerable prestige thereby as well as defeating the strong Anglo-Norman state to the north. He therefore came to be regarded as an able protector and increased his possessions to the south of his feudal domains. The new territories which stretched to the Loire became then part of his directly owned feudal possessions. His son, Louis VII (1137–1180), was presented with a wonderful opportunity when the duke of Aquitaine in southern France died without a male heir, leaving Louis free to marry his daughter Eleanor and win all her possessions. But while on the Second Crusade in which he was notably unsuccessful, he also became estranged from Eleanor and divorced her on his return. As we have seen, Eleanor then gave her person and possessions to Henry I of England. Thus the already dangerous Anglo-Norman kingdom became yet more dangerous for the French monarchy, virtually encircling it. It was the lifework of Louis' son, Philip Augustus (1180–1223), to recover and consolidate his realm. Before he died the greater part of present-day France was under his direct control. Since the work of Philip lies mostly in the thirteenth century and heralded the absolute monarchy of later France, it will be reserved for the next chapter.

A few words should be said on the rise of French towns in the early Capetian period. The monarchs were always in need of allies against the feudal nobility and chronically short of funds for their undertakings, which were usually beyond the resources of their small domain. They found the most useful of allies in the bourgeois and therefore gave the towns every assistance and encouragement; they granted charters to many of the towns, permitting them virtual self-government as *communes,* or substantial self-government with some powers reserved to the king. In the thirteenth and fourteenth centuries the monarchs felt less of a need for this bourgeois support, and the towns often stood in the way of their growing absolutism. During this later period, therefore, many of the charters were revoked, but not before royal patronage had helped the towns to free themselves from the feudal domination which continued to inhibit the growth of towns in other countries.

THE IBERIAN PENINSULA—THE RECONQUISTA

During the entire period of the Saracen occupation of Spain the Christians were active in the north, and constantly made efforts to expand into the Muslim domains. When the Ommeyad caliphate of Cordova began to weaken in the late tenth century, the Christian kingdoms of León and Castile were able to take advantage of the weakness. In 1037 León was incorporated into Castile, and in 1085 Toledo was captured by Alfonso VI of Castile, thus bringing almost half of Spain into Christian hands. Although the crusade to the Holy Land called in 1095 by Pope Urban II has always been known as the First Crusade, the principle was nothing new. A series of popes had blessed the arms of the Spanish Christians and of the volunteers, mainly French, who fought in their armies.

The Moors, like the Christians, called in the help of their coreligionists. They were aided by the Berber dynasty of the Almoravids, which succeeded in reconquering most of Moorish Spain by the end of the eleventh century. But Almoravid rule by the middle of the twelfth century had fallen into decay, permitting Alfonso VII to resume the reconquest. Once more the Moors invaded from Africa and took the country in 1172. They held it only until 1212, when they were decisively defeated at the Battle of Las Navas de Tolosa and expelled from Spain. The great Moorish cities of Cordova and Seville were taken by the Christians in the first half of the thirteenth century. Meanwhile, other Muslim groups which had been established in southern Spain for centuries were able to defend themselves against the Christians and remained in Granada until 1492.

The Castilians took the most active part in the *Reconquista,* but all the Iberian rulers played their part. The kingdom of Aragon in the north, a relic of the conquests of Charlemagne, consolidated its power in the early twelfth century and joined with Catalonia to make an impressive state with some possessions on the French side of the Pyrenees, until these were lost in the early thirteenth century. Thereafter the rulers of Aragon expanded along the east coast of Spain and helped to drive out the Muslims, continuing their progress into the Mediterranean area, ultimately winning Sicily at the end of the thirteenth century. Portugal was originally a Spanish country, granted by the Castilian crown to Henry, a Burgundian knight, who had joined as a crusader in the reconquest. His son became king, and he and his successors managed to maintain their independence from Castile in spite of frequent wars. All played an important part in the reconquest. These three major kingdoms of Castile, Aragon, and Portugal therefore emerged from the reconquest as independent states. Aragon and Castile were united in the fifteenth century, and together with still independent Portugal, took the lead in the discovery of the New World.

The *cortes* of the Iberian Peninsula were the oldest parliamentary bodies in Europe, coming into existence at least as early as the twelfth century. In these cortes the burghers of the already flourishing towns of Aragon and Castile were represented. The cortes, however, never became really powerful in Spain except during the periods of royal weakness; and even then they were dominated by the feudal nobility. After the later Spanish monarchs united the country, the cortes were called only at the monarch's wish, and he was quite able to do without them. Thus they never attained even the modest degree of power enjoyed for a period by the French States-General; and the Spanish bourgeois never won the influence enjoyed by their class in England.

One final consequence of the manner in which the Iberian monarchs had won their realms should be noted. The crusade for reconquest was always backed by the Church, which called for a new crusade whenever reverses were suffered at Muslim hands and whenever enthusiasm lagged. Because the enemy belonged to the Muslim religion, the war was never wholly feudal in character, though carried on by feudal lords and divided after the conquest according to the precepts of the feudal system. Religious fervor was never absent, and when the crusaders triumphed, it was Christianity itself that was regarded as the victor. So when the conquest was complete, militant Christianity remained as a legacy to the rulers and peoples. The rulers regarded it as one of their tasks to maintain the religion and, when the appropriate time came, to drive the remnants of Islam from the country. The Catholic Church in Spain has held a position rather different from that in any other country, even to the present time. When the New World was discovered, the crusading spirit provided one motive for the explorations. The Spaniards also regarded it as their first task to convert the Indians, once they had conquered the country, in this respect differing markedly from the English Puritans who settled New England and were far from feeling any such compulsion.

THE CRUSADES—THE FIRST MAJOR EXPANSION OF EUROPE

Background for the First Crusade. In the middle of the eleventh century the Seljuk Turks, a group of Asiatic nomads, began moving westward. In 1055 they captured Bagdad, and thereafter for a considerable time were the real rulers of the old Abbasid empire, though the Abbasid caliph was permitted to continue to exercise his religious functions. The Turks at this time accepted Islam. In 1071 at the Battle of Manzikert they defeated the Byzantines and took control of most of Asia Minor. Various groups of Seljuk Turks then penetrated into the whole Near East, capturing, among other cities, Antioch and Jerusalem, and even took possession of some of the Greek islands. These groups set up separate sultanates, often at war with one another and always rivals; for this reason they rarely were able to unite even against Western attacks on their domains. It was the disunity among the Turks that permitted the Crusaders to capture Jerusalem and divide Syria into fiefs in charge of Western nobles. As soon as the Muslims again united under rulers who were not Seljuk Turks, the crusaders were doomed. This first expansion of Western civilization outside the boundaries of Europe could therefore never have been permanent, as the expatriate nobles were dependent on constant supplies and reinforcements from Europe and greatly outnumbered locally by the Muslims.

After the Battle of Manzikert the Byzantine emperor appealed to the West for aid, but Gregory VII was unable to supply it. When Alexius Comnenus, an able general, became Byzantine emperor in 1081, he could not appeal to the West until after he had repelled a Norman adventurer named Robert Guiscard, who was trying to take the Balkan Peninsula for himself. By 1095 he had secured his

European territories well enough to be able to think of reconquering his lost lands in Asia, now in the hands of the Turks. He therefore sent emissaries to Pope Urban II, to ask him whether it would not be possible to extend the crusading principle, already in operation in the Spanish *reconquista* to the Near East, where the Muslims were at least as dangerous and now controlled the Holy Sepulcher (the tomb of Christ).

The pope was well aware of the situation in the Near East. The Turks were indeed interfering with the pilgrimages to the Holy Sepulcher, which were a feature of the religious life of the West. But their interference had been no worse than that of the earlier Muslims who had held Jerusalem since the time of Mahomet. Though preachers like Peter the Hermit had been badly treated there, there is little likelihood that any pope would have taken official action had not this, as Urban believed, heaven-sent opportunity presented itself to him with the appeal of Alexius. He unquestionably, like all the popes since 1054, still hoped to unite the Eastern and Western Churches which had been finally separated in that year. A crusade was an enterprise that he alone could call and sanctify; it was a wonderful chance to assume the leadership in an all-European undertaking. Feudal wars between European nobles were always horrifying to the popes, but they had been unable to control them, in spite of efforts, like the "Peace of God" and "Truce of God," to confine the fighting to days in the middle of the week. Far better, Urban II would have thought, to have Christians shed the blood of infidels. Lastly, the Church might hope to gain by acting as trustee for the property of nobles who went on the crusade.

The First Crusade. Urban II's speech to the assembled lay and clerical dignitaries at Clermont, in France, was a masterpiece of propaganda, hardly surpassed by any similar appeals in later times. He painted a lurid picture of Muslim atrocities perpetrated upon harmless Christians engaged in their peaceful Christian duties; he played upon the Westerners' pride and sense of mission; and he extolled the (not so unworldly) delights of Jerusalem, the land "flowing with milk and honey"—a land of opportunity compared with their own lands, which were too small for their expanding population. Finally he promised the potential crusaders that they should be freed from any need to perform penances on earth or in purgatory, and that all debts incurred for the crusade should be exempt from interest. The people cried that it was "the will of

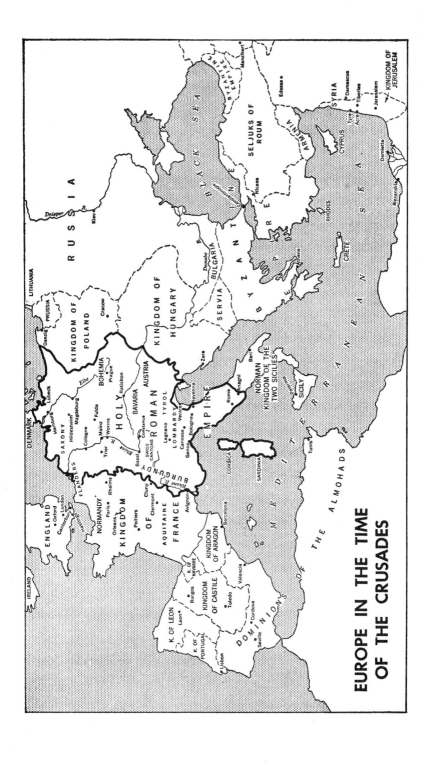

EUROPE IN THE TIME
OF THE CRUSADES

God," and in a great burst of enthusiasm, thousands took the Cross and made ready to go to Jerusalem, of whose very location few had any notion, still less any knowledge of how they were to reach it.

The knights and nobles undoubtedly were delighted at the prospect, as long as they did not have too much to lose at home. The merchants were equally pleased at the thought that there would be a paying cargo of nobles to transport to the East, and prospects of booty to be brought back and distributed within Europe—perhaps even some legitimate trade for the future if the crusaders won new fiefs for themselves in the East. For the serfs a crusade meant a chance for freedom and an escape from the deadly monotony of the manor. Religious enthusiasm undoubtedly played some part in the determination of all classes, but it was probably greatest among the peasantry. What the latter did not yet know was that there was no means of transportation for them save their own feet, which would have to traverse many hostile countries before they reached Constantinople. The peasants were the first to leave on the crusade, led by Peter the Hermit and other preachers. When they reached Constantinople they were already an unruly mob. Alexius, therefore, quickly shipped them across the Bosporus. Once in Asia they were of course massacred by the Turks. Clearly the European population problem of which Pope Urban had spoken was already on the way to solution.

The nobles were more careful with their preparations, and somewhat more acceptable to the emperor when they arrived in Constantinople. Nevertheless their manners were found uncouth by the Greeks, and the emperor was happy to speed them too on their way. Indeed, he had hoped for Western mercenaries who could be paid from his treasury rather than feudal lords bent on extending their possessions, and who would therefore be expected to stay in the country indefinitely. However, because Alexius hoped to recover some of his eastern territories, he made an agreement with the crusaders that all the possessions rightfully Byzantine that they captured should be restored to him. Since Alexius knew more history than the crusaders, including how large the Byzantine Empire had once been, it was unlikely that the latter would keep to their agreement, and he probably did not expect it. But he insisted upon the agreement as long as he dared, and accompanied the crusaders until they showed signs of transferring their military attention to himself. Then he left them on their own.

After considerable hardships and difficulties due to the mountainous terrain and their ignorance of the country, they reached Antioch, the largest and wealthiest city in Syria, and took it with the help of a local traitor. But at once the Turkish governor besieged them in turn, and only with great difficulty did they succeed in extricating themselves. Immediately there was another quarrel with Alexius who claimed the city for himself, whereupon Bohemund, son of that Robert Guiscard who had already tried to win the western part of the empire, returned home and launched another expedition against the emperor. Ultimately Alexius was granted suzerainty over Antioch, but, needless to say, he took no further part in the crusade.

Meanwhile, the Turks themselves had lost Jerusalem to the Fatimid rulers of Egypt who were not Turks but descendants of the Arabs who had taken Egypt soon after Mahomet. So when the crusaders in 1099 fell upon Jerusalem, they had only Egyptians and civilians to contend with, the Turks having withdrawn to a prudent distance. The city itself fell almost without a struggle, but this did not prevent the crusaders from sacking it and butchering the defenseless Egyptians for several days. When the carnage was at last over the Westerners had to decide how to divide their conquests. With considerable acrimony the division was accomplished and arrangements made for the Venetians, Genoese, and Pisan navies to keep them supplied in return for a share of the loot.

The feudal system of the West in its most rigid form was now fastened upon Palestine and Syria—great lords and their vassals, and serfs to work the lands. The system worked very imperfectly, and the crusaders who remained rapidly became orientalized. But reinforcements arrived annually from the West, and a number of crusading orders made up of dedicated knights helped to maintain the conquests. Many of the feudal lords, with the aid of Byzantine engineers, built strong fortresses, from which they were able to protect their own territories, even if they took little part in the defense of the country as a whole. The Turks also expended most of their strength warring unsuccessfully with the Byzantines, who once more made a military and cultural recovery, though Westerners gained in influence in the empire. But the rulers of Mosul, the Muslim successors of the Seljuk Turks, began to make headway from 1144 when they captured one of the Christian fiefs, the County of Edessa. Thereafter they captured Egypt and consolidated their power in the whole area to the east of the Christian fiefs. It was then only a matter of time before they were strong enough to expel the Christians from the country.

Subsequent Crusades. After the fall of Edessa, a Second Crusade was preached, in which the emperor Conrad III and the French king Louis VII took part. It was badly managed and achieved nothing. In 1187 the new ruler of Egypt, a Muslim of Kurdish descent, named Saladin, advancing from the south, captured Jerusalem with little difficulty. He was careful to prohibit any sacking of the city; he permitted all prisoners to ransom themselves; and those poor men who could command no ransom he let go free. But the fall of the Holy Sepulcher shocked all Europe, and the Third Crusade (1189–1192) was proclaimed. It might have been successful if Frederick Barbarossa, who was its first leader, had lived. But he was drowned in a river, and the other two leaders, Philip Augustus of France, and Richard the Lion-Heart of England, were constantly at odds with one another, since Philip was anxious to add Richard's possessions in France to his own kingdom. In the end Philip went home before reaching Jerusalem, leaving Richard to negotiate a truce with Saladin, which permitted Christian access to Jerusalem, though it left the city itself in Muslim hands.

In 1199 Innocent III ascended the papal throne. He was not the man to leave the crusading mission unaccomplished, and he was apparently unable to recognize that Europe had changed and other interests had taken the place of Christian zeal. Kings had always lost by their participation in crusades even if they were fortunate enough to keep their lives. No loot of importance remained in the East, and it was defended by determined and powerful enemies. Men now had to be cajoled and threatened before they agreed to go on a crusade, and only if there were ulterior motives did anyone of importance consent to go. Nevertheless, a group of crusaders heeded the eloquent appeals of Innocent and accepted the offer of Venice to provide transportation on credit for the Fourth Crusade, in exchange for a high percentage of the loot. However, the Venetians, who were busy building a commercial empire in the Adriatic, but enjoyed excellent commercial relations with Egypt and other Muslim countries, had little interest in going in the direction of the objective envisaged by Innocent. What they undoubtedly had in mind from the beginning was Constantinople, now again fallen on evil days and suffering from a disputed succession. When the crusaders, at the behest of the Venetians, captured an Adriatic Christian city named

Zara, formerly a Venetian possession, Innocent excommunicated them en masse, later confining the excommunication to the Ventians. When the refugee emperor of Constantinople urged the crusaders to restore him to his throne in exchange for a considerable sum of money, in spite of some protests from a few, they proceeded to Constantinople and duly carried out their share of the bargain. Almost all of the payment was pocketed by the Venetians.

Constantinople was now wholly in the power of the crusaders. It is doubtful if at this point they could have been persuaded to leave. Jerusalem was far away; they had made little for themselves out of their enterprise, not even their expenses. So when the emperor whom they had just restored was murdered by the Byzantines, their patience was exhausted. They fell upon the defenseless city, the greatest in the Western world, and sacked it thoroughly. Clerics, warriors, and Venetians joined equally in the pillage, all according to the chroniclers "praising God for their great victory." The city itself was divided among the conquerors, Venice taking a portion for herself, together with a considerable part of the Byzantine hinterland in Europe. A Western count became emperor over the remainder, thus establishing the Latin kingdom of Constantinople, which he and his successors ruled, feebly enough, until 1261, when it was recaptured by the Greeks. (After 1204 the Greeks had re-established a kingdom in Asia Minor which they ruled from the city of Nicaea, until they were strong enough to take back their former capital.)

The End of the Crusades. Innocent III was placed in a serious dilemma by the conquest. On the one hand, he could not but disapprove of the deeds of the crusaders in Constantinople—a Christian city—and indeed, did personal penance for them; but at the same time one of his most cherished objectives had been attained, control of the Church of Constantinople, and he could not refuse to accept this most important fruit of the conquest. He therefore did accept it and proceeded to organize the Church to the best of his ability. But there is no reason to suppose that he ever blamed himself for having called the crusade at a time when the crusading spirit had been waning for more than a century and commercial and predatory motives had taken its place.

The crusading spirit, however, was still apparently alive in the very young, who knew nothing of the deeds of their elders. In 1212 bands of children set forth for the Holy Land, believing that the seas would divide for them, as for Moses, and the Holy Sepulcher would be taken without a blow. Some of the participants actually reached the seacoast, where they were sold into slavery. Others, less dramatically, were shipped home.

Innocent, still undaunted, called another crusade in 1215, which failed after an initial success in Egypt. A sixth, led by the emperor Frederick II, who won Jerusalem by diplomacy, will be dealt with in the next chapter. The saintly French king, Louis IX, himself by now an anachronism in his crusading impulses, attempted two crusades which were badly managed and unsuccessful. In 1291 Acre, the last Christian fortress in the Holy Land, fell to the Muslims. Christians won no further toe hold in the Holy Land until 1917.

THE DEVELOPMENT OF TOWNS AND URBAN LIFE

Seaborne Commerce. The crusades greatly encouraged the development of towns in Europe, and especially contributed to the wealth of the great seaports which profited directly by them. These seaports had been the first to recover from the general stagnation of trade and industry in the early Middle Ages. During the Merovingian age there had been few products to export, and international trade decreased to a trickle for this reason rather than, as has sometimes been claimed, because the Saracens took possession of the Mediterranean and were in a position to shut off trade if they wished. In fact the Saracens seldom hampered trade, from which they in fact profited, though Saracen pirates severely damaged Byzantine commerce in some periods. The most important seaport in Europe in the Middle Ages was Venice, founded in the middle of the sixth century. It throve especially on trade with Constantinople, of which for several centuries it had a virtual monopoly in Europe. Venice for a time acknowledged the suzerainty of the Byzantine emperor, but this recognition, which carried few obligations with it, was commercially advantageous to her. Long before she took a leading part in the sack of the Byzantine capital in 1204, she had become an independent state with a hinterland which she colonized; by that time she was the leading distributor of Byzantine and other products which were transported over the Alpine passes into central Europe, as well as by sea. Genoa and Pisa, though smaller than Venice, likewise played an important part in the crusades. They enjoyed the leading share of trade in the Western Mediterranean, clearing the Saracens from the area by the end of the eleventh century. A few years before, the Normans had taken Sicily and founded their kingdom in that island, thus increasing the importance of the Sicilian ports.

A further trading system grew up in eastern Europe as the result of Viking expeditions. Mention has already been made of Kiev in Russia, founded by the Swedes at the end of the ninth century. At the beginning of the tenth century, the Varangians, as the Byzantines called them, were granted trading privileges in Constantinople and thereafter undertook much of the carrying trade for the Byzantines northward up the great Russian rivers, and so into northern Europe, providing Constantinople with northern specialty products in return. But the extension of all this trade depended on the provision of sufficient products from Western Europe to be used in trade, and progress in this direction was slow.

The Inland Cities. In the early Middle Ages there were few inland towns of importance, since the manors were virtually self-sufficient. However, after the Vikings had settled down in their new European homes, town growth was slow but regular. Most of the larger towns had strategic sites such as fords on rivers, or, sometimes, they were founded at important crossroads. Others grew up where there was any possibility for concentration of industry, especially the textile industry. Flanders early became a center of the wool industry, a position it retained through the whole Middle Ages, making use of imports of wool from England as well as local produce. In northern Italy, the center of a fertile agricultural area, where political conditions also favored the growth of free cities, many important towns were flourishing, and, as we have seen, they were able to maintain their independence against even such a powerful overlord as Frederick Barbarossa. Indeed, the growth of towns everywhere in Europe was to a very large degree dependent on political conditions, and the reason for this requires some explanation.

Europe was of course overwhelmingly agricultural, and the manor in most areas was the typical social and economic unit; the political system in operation was feudalism. Thus virtually all villages and towns came under the jurisdiction of some feudal lord, whether it was the feudal king, the bishop or archbishop, or a noble. These men held customary rights over all lands, whether towns were built on them or not. Among these rights was the right to receive the usual feudal aids and reliefs, and military service; and unless the townsmen were nobles or had been granted their freedom by the lords who had the right to bestow it, the great majority of them would be of servile status, which involved many restrictions on their free dom. Such restrictions were intolerable to them if they wished to engage in trade. It therefore became necessary for the leading towns men to negotiate with (or sometimes fight with) their feudal supe riors to win the freedom of their town and its inhabitants. The lords, for their part, were sometimes willing and sometimes extremely reluctant to grant such rights, whatever the townsmen were willing to pay. But in general it may be said that most lords were willing to settle if the price were high enough; relatively few preferred their role of ruler with an uncertain income to that of landlord, with a regular income granted in exchange for the abandonment of their rights as rulers. When an agreement was arrived at, it was embodied in a charter, which permitted a town to incorporate and undertake responsibilities on behalf of all the townsmen, treated as a corporate entity. In most European towns outside Italy the noble or monarch retained in reserve certain rights which he seldom exercised. In Italy the bulk of the towns were in most important respects self-govern ing, and free to adopt even an independent foreign policy. They were, in effect, city-states.

Most towns were ruled by their merchant classes, who united in a merchant guild, with officials elected by the merchants or sometimes by the whole population. The purpose of the merchant guild was to divide up the trade among the members on an equitable basis, enforce merchant law, and lay down and enforce regulations to restrict the entrance of other merchants into their closed system. Craft guilds, which regulated manufactures in a similar manner, were also in operation almost everywhere. The ordinary unit of manufacture was the individual shop, headed by a master. The master trained apprentices, who usually lived with him over the shop. When an apprentice was trained he became a journeyman, who could work for pay until such a time as he became a master himself. To enter into the guild it was customary for him to have to make a "masterpiece" which won the approval of the existing mas ters. Then he might set up shop on his own with the permission of the guild. In later centuries the guild was hesitant to grant the privilege, imposing a restrictive monopoly which the journeyman had to breach by price-cutting or other means, leading to the even tual breakdown of the system. The guild, however, was instrumental in keeping up quality as well as prices; and for a considerable time, while total trade was small and the demand for manufactured goods was necessarily restricted, it fulfilled its function effectively. Surplus agricultural goods from the manor and industrial products from the towns were sold at small local markets and at large international fairs, usually encouraged and policed by leading nobles. The most important of these fairs was at Champagne in France.

By the end of the twelfth century there were several hundred fairly important towns in Europe and they were increasing rapidly, helping by their very presence to break up the feudal system, which in so many respects was incompatible with their growth. Europe was entering the era of a moneyed economy, and lords already needed their military supporters far less than in the past. Feudalism was thus fast becoming an anachronism, its tasks taken over by more modern and forward-looking forms of government and enterprise. We shall follow the process of considering the new forms of government and economy that were to take the place of feudalism and manorialism in the next chapter.

CHAPTER X

THE LAST MEDIEVAL CENTURIES

Throughout most of the twelfth century the power and prestige of the papacy had been growing. With the settlement of the lay investiture problem, the pope had gained a say in the appointment of the higher clergy in Europe; and though secular rulers continued to insist on appointments acceptable to themselves and to make as much use as ever of the higher clergy in their realms, in the various showdowns between secular rulers and the papacy, the latter had usually emerged triumphant. Thomas Becket had been murdered in England, but Henry II had done penance. Frederick Barbarossa had kept Alexander III from exercising his office, but after the emperor's defeat by the Lombard towns, supported by the papacy, he had come to terms with Alexander and recognized him as head of Christendom. Lawsuits in ecclesiastical matters were frequently brought to Rome for final decision. There was now no question at all that the pope was indeed the spiritual and ecclesiastical leader of Europe. No one else could call a crusade; no other Church dignitary, however exalted or however strongly backed by his secular ruler, could expect to be listened to by all Europe. The pope had at his disposal by far the most efficient bureaucracy, and it was he who alone decided on the choice of cardinals, the most sought-after ecclesiastical honor in Christendom. No monarch could compel the pope to choose any of his own subjects as cardinal or papal legate; at most he could request it, but the appointment would have to be negotiated with the pope, and perhaps a price paid. The pope had at his disposal the best corps of ambassadors in the persons of these papal legates; no monarch of his age had such well informed and dutiful servants.

Lastly, the pope was the ruler of much of north-central Italy, and the revenues from these papal states could be used to influence policy in his favor, and at worst, to pay for mercenaries to be put at the service of his foreign policy. He was the feudal suzerain of the Norman kingdom of the Two Sicilies, of the kingdom of Jerusalem, such as it was, and of a few other lesser lands. His temporal power was far from negligible, and few by the end of the twelfth century were inclined to underestimate it. Nevertheless, it was also true that the excessive use of this temporal power might redound to the discredit of his spiritual power. In the thirteenth century this fact was to become abundantly clear; and the decision of Philip IV of France to humiliate Pope Boniface VIII at the opening of the fourteenth century was undoubtedly taken because he and his fellow monarchs had come to regard the pope as a political despot.

THE CHURCH AT THE HEIGHT OF ITS POWER

Innocent III (1198–1216) was the first pope in a position to take advantage of all the powers now inherent in his office. He was fortunate in that there was a quarrel over the succession to the Holy Roman Empire, which gave him a chance to intervene, first on the side of one party and then of the other. As noted in the last chapter, Henry VI had died prematurely. It was Innocent's policy to separate the Empire from the kingdom of Sicily, which had been united in Henry's reign. It was therefore essential to keep the Hohenstaufen heir, Henry's infant son Frederick, from the Empire while looking after the Norman kingdom of Sicily for him. This he was entitled to do as the suzerain for this kingdom. He was successful in this aim until Frederick grew up. But the trouble he had stirred up in the Empire between the two contenders was such that by 1212 he no longer could control it. One candidate, Frederick's uncle, had been murdered, while the other, Otto of Brunswick, whom Innocent had crowned emperor, was pursuing a consistently antipapal policy. The last chance was to build up Frederick as emperor in place of Otto, and try to bind the young man to him with oaths. Though Innocent died before the fruit of his policy became visible, obviously all he had been able to achieve in Germany was civil war and mounting chaos.

Innocent early in his reign disciplined Philip Augustus, king of France, who had renounced his wife. Without bothering to excommunicate the monarch, Innocent laid an interdict upon the country. Philip, knowing that he would soon need papal support for his various enterprises submitted and took back his queen. John, king of England, was both more obstinate and less careful of his own interests. When he refused to accept a papal nominee, Stephen Langton, as Archbishop of Canterbury, Innocent laid an interdict upon

England (1208), excommunicated John (1209), and deposed him (1213). John resisted until he was compelled by widespread opposition to his feeble rule and growing rebellion from his barons, coupled with the danger of invasion from Philip Augustus, to whom Innocent had given his throne, to submit to the pope. He gave England and such of Ireland as he ruled to the papacy as a fief, and Innocent became his feudal overlord. Nevertheless, though thereafter Innocent attempted to protect his new vassal, he could not prevent the barons from forcing John to sign Magna Carta. When John agreed to repudiate the Charter as Innocent demanded, the barons again rose against him, even Langton siding with the barons against the pope. Though Innocent had won an apparent victory, which included a large annual donation from the English crown to the papacy, papal exactions in the following century alienated great numbers of the English, building up a resistance to papal overlordship which ultimately contributed to the English acceptance of Protestantism.

For many years a succession of popes and local clerics had tried to curb an important heresy in southern France, whose leaders had founded what was virtually a church of their own, protected by the French count who was their suzerain. Progress with reconversion was so slow that Innocent in 1208 called a crusade against the heretics. Though the king of France held aloof from the "crusade," many of his barons were not loath to answer the call, in hopes of new fiefs. This so-called Albigensian Crusade was appallingly bloody, since most of the heretics were either unwilling or incapable of resisting. The brilliant Provençal culture of this area in France was destroyed, and the country left in shambles. Raymond of Toulouse, the suzerain of the Albigensians, in 1214, surrendered all his possessions to the pope, who then bestowed them on the leaders of the crusade. In 1226, with the completion of the crusade by the new French monarch, Louis VIII, the territory was incorporated into France. Those Albigensians who had survived were reconverted to Catholic Christianity, especially by the new order of the Dominicans.

Elsewhere Innocent interfered with the same high-handedness, punishing what he considered to be crimes against morality and rewarding his political supporters. The duke of Bohemia was allowed to call himself king, while Castile was laid under an interdict when its ruler put away his wife, as was Norway for the morals of its king. The king of Aragon did homage for his kingdom, as did the king of Bulgaria. In 1215 Innocent, with Europe at his feet, summoned a council at the Lateran which every leading cleric in Europe attended. All monarchs sent their representatives. Innocent dominated the council, which ratified all the acts of his pontificate, political and religious, decreed that the Church everywhere was to be free from lay taxation, proclaimed the dogma of transubstantiation, and prescribed confession at least once a year for every Christian.

This was the highest point of power and authority ever reached by the medieval Church. Innocent claimed the right to dictate to kings and clergy alike, and for the moment he was obeyed. But the demands were so extreme and the area of jurisdiction claimed by the Church was so extensive that it was impossible for any secular state to submit any longer than it was compelled to do so by superior force. Only if the European rulers had truly regarded themselves as responsible in all matters to the pope, and been truly willing to accept theocracy as the proper form of government for all Christendom could such a dream have been realized. But already in the time of Innocent III it was well enough known to many that the pope's power was at least as much political as it was religious. It only required a man who cared not a whit for the pope's religious pretensions to prick the bubble. Though his struggle with the papacy resulted in a draw and though his successors lost their thrones to a temporarily triumphant papacy, Frederick II, the former protégé of Innocent III who became emperor in 1220, was to point the way for all the monarchs in Europe to follow in the succeeding century.

THE FINAL STRUGGLE BETWEEN EMPIRE AND PAPACY

Among the promises Frederick had made as a young man was a promise to lead a new crusade. But it was clear to him upon becoming the ruler of Germany and Sicily that there were many things that needed to be done at home before he could indulge in this luxury. He was half-Norman by birth, and had been brought up in Sicily, where he had imbibed not only the Norman but also the Muslim cultural tradition. Indeed he was an accomplished linguist, a scientist and careful observer of nature, a patron of all kinds of learning, and above all else, a freethinker. Not unnaturally, he was always more interested in his southern than in his German kingdom. For most of his reign he allowed the German nobles and the great German cities to do largely as they wished so long as they continued to acknowledge his authority. As soon as he could he made his own son king in that country. The Sicilian kingdom was organized under the only efficient bureaucracy in Europe outside Rome, and it always provided Frederick with enough money and resources to enable him to carry out a strong imperial policy. He even went so far as to establish in Italy colonies of Muslims pledged to his support, which of course were entirely impervious to any religious sanctions that could be imposed by a pope.

While Pope Honorius III (1216–1227) maintained fairly good relations with Frederick in spite of the latter's first attempts to reduce the Lombard towns to obedience, Pope Gregory IX (1227–1241) was the emperor's inveterate enemy all his reign. Frederick felt himself ready to go on the promised crusade in 1227, having an added incentive in the fact that he had recently married the heiress of the kingdom of Jerusalem and was thus already king of Jerusalem in name. He had only to win Jerusalem in the crusade to become king in fact. Nevertheless, as soon as he started on the crusade, he fell ill and returned. Gregory, who had already threatened him with excommunication if he did not go, chose to regard this disease as a diplomatic one and now excommunicated him in earnest, treating him as a disobedient vassal. Frederick, disregarding the ban, went on his crusade, while Gregory stirred up revolt in his southern domains. Having his own idea of how to win Jerusalem, he brought his plan of negotiating a treaty with the Muslims to a successful conclusion, and Jerusalem once more for a few years was in Christian hands. The Christians in the Holy Land, however, were far from grateful. This was no way to carry on the crusading tradition; and the patriarch of Jerusalem refused to crown Frederick king of Jerusalem since he was still under the ban of excommunication.

It was high time for Frederick to return home, as his kingdom was in turmoil. Without very great difficulty he restored it to obedience, then turned on the Lombard towns in the north. Defeating the revived Lombard League decisively at the Battle of Cortenuova in 1237, he proceeded to organize Italy for the first time as part of a strong kingdom ruled from the south. But the pope was far from finished. At first compelled to make his peace with Frederick, he soon began to stir up war again, using all the financial resources of the papacy to aid the Lombard towns and make trouble in Germany. He feared, and with good reason, Frederick's insistence on incorporating the papal states, and even Rome, into his administration. Though Frederick was at all times willing to acknowledge the papal claim to sovereignty in religious matters, he regarded himself in secular affairs as holding his own sovereignty from God and had no intention of letting any pope behave like Innocent III. Thus Pope Gregory IX, by insisting on his claim to earthly rule, made Frederick into an implacable enemy. He excommunicated Frederick for the second time in 1239.

Both pope and emperor appealed to public opinion and solicited support from the rulers and nobles. Frederick's arguments were well calculated to appeal to the kings. Stressing that their turn would come next if they did not put bounds to papal claims, he no doubt struck an answering chord in royal breasts. Nevertheless they stayed strictly neutral or neutral on the anti-Frederick side, fearing both contestants equally, and perhaps hoping that they would destroy one another. At last in 1241 Gregory decided to summon a council to depose Frederick, who was ready to take his final step of putting an end to the independence of the papal states. But before the council could assemble Gregory died, leaving Frederick in physical control of Italy and quite capable of compelling the election of a man who would be faithful to him and fall in with his policy. He captured the cardinals who were going to Rome for the election and shut them up in a castle until to win their freedom, they chose a friend of his, an experienced jurist who took the title of Innocent IV. But Innocent, once elected, adopted the policy of his predecessors. Being younger and even more energetic than Gregory IX, he contrived to escape to France, whose saintly ruler, Louis IX, was sympathetic to the papacy. There he did indeed depose Frederick and continued to use the power and resources of the papacy to back the Lombard towns in their last-ditch struggle against incorporation into the Norman kingdom. Frederick lost an important battle to the League, and had to continue the struggle. He was still making headway when he died in 1250 and when his son, Conrad IV, died prematurely in 1254, the issue was still undecided.

Manfred, Frederick's illegitimate son, regent of Sicily for his half-brother, could not inherit the Empire. Innocent IV and his immediate successors indeed by their policies created an interregnum which came to an end only in 1273 when the first Hapsburg, a minor princeling who was lord of Austria, was elected to the throne. The papacy now had only Manfred to deal with. Against him, two successive popes, both French, called in Charles of Anjou, brother of the French king, who defeated and killed Manfred in 1266 at the Battle of Benevento. Charles then established an Italian and Sicilian regime at least as oppressive as that of the Hohenstaufens but without its efficiency. Conradino, a youth of fifteen, attempted to establish his family's position in the south, but was captured and beheaded by Charles of Anjou. Ultimately all the French in Sicily were massacred (Sicilian Vespers, 1282), and the throne passed through Constance, the heiress of Sicily, to Peter III of Aragon, her husband. This began the Spanish rule of the Two Sicilies, which lasted with brief intervals until the nineteenth century. Italy itself became divided into separate states, many of which likewise survived until the nineteenth century.

The papacy had triumphed in its struggle with the Empire only to have to submit to French domination, which resulted in the early fourteenth century in the "Babylonian captivity" in Avignon in Southern France. This collapse of papal power in Italy will be discussed later in the chapter as an episode in the rise of the French national state.

ENGLAND—THE BEGINNINGS OF CONSTITUTIONAL MONARCHY

Magna Carta—The First Charter of English (Baronial) Liberties. At the beginning of the thirteenth century John (surnamed Lackland) was on the English throne. Uniformly unsuccessful in everything he undertook, he was no match for the French monarch, Philip Augustus, who as John's feudal suzerain for the English possessions in France, used his rights to the utmost of his abilities. When John married an heiress who had been betrothed to one of his own vassals, the latter appealed to Philip as John's overlord to bring him to justice. Philip, nothing loath, summoned John to his court, and when the English king refused to go, he deprived him of his lands. When John then murdered his own nephew, whose title to the English throne was better than his own, he lost almost all support in France. Under Philip's leadership the French nobility proceeded to execute the decree of the royal court, and John's resources were insufficient to enable him to defend them. Only his possessions in southern France remained to him, since the lords in that part of France disliked Philip's expansionism more than they despised John. John's son Henry III recognized the conquests in northern and central France in exchange for French recognition of his southern domains.

John's ill success in France, and his chronic inability to keep his word, combined with his quarrel with Innocent which ended, as we have seen, in his acceptance of the pope as his overlord, thoroughly antagonized the English nobility, which even intrigued with France to depose him. John had tried to exact so much from his nobles and townsmen to pay for his unsuccessful wars—to say nothing of the ransom that he had had to pay for his brother Richard Lion-Heart—that his more influential subjects determined to compel John to recognize their traditional rights. In 1215 they compelled him to sign Magna Carta, a feudal document which guaranteed the barons, townsmen, and clergy all the rights which they claimed belonged to them from ancient times and incidentally guaranteed all free man a few elementary rights, especially the right to justice in the royal courts. In essence it was a formal promise by the king not to do what he had been doing, and what all English kings had done when they were strong enough. It therefore bound only the particular king who signed the Charter, and later kings were again called upon to renew the undertaking until it finally became accepted as a bill of rights for the whole people and a guarantee that no king would transgress.

The First English Parliaments. Henry III reigned for more than half of the thirteenth century (1216–1272), but for almost all his reign he was unpopular with the nobility. Little more able than his father, he was much more pious, and tried to live up to his agreements with the papacy, which were very costly to the country. He also favored French nobles above the English barons, and kept them as his advisers in preference to Englishmen. Worst of all, from the baronial point of view, Henry, like his father, was tempted to engage in foreign adventures, for example, letting his son be chosen as king of Sicily and his brother compete for the title of emperor—both of which adventures, if carried out, would have embroiled the barons in unprofitable foreign wars and increased the king's demands on them, which they so deeply resented. At last in 1258, the barons decided that the king should be kept under their tutelage and be compelled to observe Magna Carta and maintain their customary privileges, and that royal officials should not be appointed unless they were approved by the great lords. The barons therefore issued the Provisions of Oxford (1258) which in effect gave the barons the right to veto the king's decisions and supervise his appointments, and the king swore to be bound by the provisions.

But the greater barons and the lesser nobles who outnumbered them soon quarreled between themselves. Simon de Montfort, a former French favorite of Henry, took the lead in an armed rebellion against him, backed by most of the leading townsmen and the rural knights and squires. The king was defeated and taken prisoner, whereupon Simon called a parliament, made up not only of nobles but of knights and burgesses, elected as representatives in their local areas. The Parliament came to nothing as Edward, the heir to the throne, who had at first been not unsympathetic to the movement to diminish his father's powers, turned against it. With the help of the greater nobles who were opposed to Simon and his program, Edward defeated and killed Simon in the Battle of Evesham (1265), and shortly afterward Edward became king as Edward I (1272–1307).

Throughout his reign Edward frequently consulted the middle class (townsmen and rural squires) as well as his nobles, and he instituted, often but not always with the consent of the nobility and middle class, a thoroughgoing legal reform. In 1295 he called a Model Parliament, which was to become the example for all later parliaments. It was composed not only of nobles but of knights of the shire and burgesses from many towns, all elected by a severely restricted franchise but for the first time in Western civilization truly regarded as representatives and not as magnates speaking solely for themselves. Though Edward regarded himself as entitled to legislate personally, and did legislate frequently without the consent of Parliament, he often preferred to take advice, while at the same time demonstrating that public opinion was behind him. Eventually Parliament became differentiated into two Houses, the great lords and the higher clergy sitting in the upper house (House of Lords), whereas elected representatives sat in the lower house (House of Commons). As long as the great noble families retained their power, the House of Lords was more influential than the House of Commons. But gradually the House of Commons, as the body which represented the moneyed classes and thus voted funds for the king, overtook the Lords as the more important body in the realm. The right of the Parliament to vote on subsidies to the king was accompanied by the collateral right of Parliament to petition the king for redress of grievances. When the king agreed to the petition, and appended his written signature in the old Norman-French formula "Le roi le veult"—the king wishes it—, Parliament had in effect initiated legislation, and the king's signature meant that it became the law of the land.

Edward I became involved in wars with Wales and Scotland, the former of which had been under full English control, but had relapsed into rebellion in the reign of Henry III. Edward reduced the Welsh chieftains to obedience but as some compensation agreed that the heir apparent to the English throne should in the future be known as the Prince of Wales. Scotland had its own kings, but they had been under the suzerainty of the English kings since the Norman conquest, and Norman lords had gradually come to occupy the leading positions in the country. Edward, as a confirmed centralizer, wished to make the union with Scotland much closer. After backing two separate claimants to the Scottish crown, he defeated the Scots in battle and incorporated the country into England. Under Robert Bruce the Scots rebelled, and in the Battle of Bannockburn (1314) decisively defeated the English under Edward II, thereby in effect establishing Scottish independence. Though the English frequently fought the Scots and at times the king of England was also the king of Scotland, the Stuart dynasty established itself eventually in Scotland, though usually under the control of the Scottish nobility.

The Medieval Constitutional Monarchy. Edward II (1307–1327) was an incompetent king, fond, like his grandfather, of foreign favorites. In the later part of his reign his estranged wife Isabella, a French princess, stirred up a rebellion against him, in which she was supported by a part of the English nobility. Edward II was deposed and imprisoned, and his young son Edward proclaimed king with the title of Edward III (1327–1377). Soon afterward his father was murdered, while Isabella and her paramour ruled the country in the name of Edward III until the latter came of age. From 1337 onward England and France were engaged in the Hundred Years' War, to be dealt with in a later section of this chapter. The needs of the long war played into the hands of Parliament, which had to vote supplies for the monarch. It was regularly called by the monarch during this reign, and the privileges granted to it by the king gradually became to be accepted as its rights.

In his last years Edward lost his grip on the government, and there was much strife between noble factions, usually working through Parliament, which they packed with their supporters. When Edward's son, the "Black Prince," died a year before his father, leaving only an eleven-year-old boy to succeed him as Richard II (1377–1399), the nobles tried to control him too. They were successful in this until Richard asserted himself in the last years of his reign, and with the aid of a private military force established a personal rule by himself, thus setting an example which the Tudor absolutist monarchy of the sixteenth century was to follow. But Richard himself was overthrown by a rebellion, leading to the rule of England by the Lancastrian house in the person of Henry Bolingbroke, who ruled under the title of Henry IV (1399–1413).

Since his hereditary title to the crown was doubtful, Henry may be considered the first king whose only legal title to the throne stemmed from his acceptance by Parliament. His son Henry V (1413–1422) who succeeded him had a slightly better title since his father had been king; but the Yorkist house, which on the basis of strict heredity had the superior title, was only biding its time. Henry V was a successful warrior and won the right to the French throne after his victories over the French monarch (Battle of Agincourt, 1415; Treaty of Troyes, 1420), but his son Henry VI was only an infant when he came to the throne in 1422 and never became an effective ruler. Throughout his life he was intermittently insane.

In 1455 a civil war broke out between the Lancastrians and the Yorkists, known as the War of the Roses, from the red rose, emblem of the House of Lancaster, and the white rose, emblem of the House of York. At first the Yorkists, supported by the most powerful noble of the realm, the Earl of Warwick, known as the "kingmaker," were successful, and Edward IV, head of the House of York, after deposing Henry VI, became king in 1461. A few years later Warwick switched his allegiance and backed the Lancastrian exiles. Edward defeated and killed him at the Battle of Barnet in 1471, and soon afterward decisively defeated the Lancastrian queen at Tewkesbury. Thereafter his throne was secure. Whereas the Lancastrians had worked with Parliament, and Parliament reached the height of its medieval powers during their reigns, Edward consistently bypassed it, using it only when he had need of it (as did the Tudors). Parliament, faced by a strong and ruthless monarch, backed by military force, had no alternative but to acquiese. Whereas

Parliament had initiated legislation, won the power of deciding upon royal expenditures, and impeached and convicted the kings' ministers under the Lancastrians, it now, and in the Tudor period, did what it was instructed to do by the monarch. Henceforward until the seventeenth century Parliament remained as only a potential danger to the monarch, its power of the purse still in its hands ready to be used to discipline the king when the time and the opportunity presented themselves, but content not to make the attempt while England needed and possessed a strong royal government.

When Edward IV died his young son was proclaimed king as Edward V (1483) with Richard, duke of Gloucester, the young king's uncle, as protector and regent. Under the next dynasty of the Tudors Richard was execrated as the murderer of his two nephews, the king and the nearest heir. It has never been proved, however, that he committed the crime, and Henry Tudor never cited it as a reason for his own usurpation of the crown. What Richard did was to produce evidence before Parliament to the effect that Edward IV had a wife living when he married the mother of Edward V, and that the latter and all the other children of Edward by Elizabeth Woodville were illegitimate. Parliament accepted the claim and proclaimed Richard king. Soon afterward Henry Tudor, who had only the barest vestige of a right to the throne, embraced the Lancastrian cause and invaded England with the aid of a French army. He defeated and killed Richard III at the Battle of Bosworth in 1485, and thus won the English throne by right of conquest. Persuading Parliament to declare the children of Edward IV and Elizabeth Woodville again legitimate, he won the support of the Yorkists by marrying Elizabeth, the heiress of the house of York. The Tudor monarchy, thus begun by Henry VII, will be discussed in Chapter XIII.

THE CONSOLIDATION OF THE FRENCH KINGDOM

Improvement of Royal Administration under Louis IX. The French Capetian monarchy in the thirteenth century continued to increase in power. Philip Augustus had won the former English territories from John, and defeated a coalition between John and the Holy Roman emperor, which brought the rich territory of Flanders under French influence (Battle of Bouvines, 1214). Philip's son, Louis VIII (1223–1226) added Provence as a consequence of the Albigensian Crusade. Louis IX (1226–1270) in successful wars with England incorporated Aquitaine and Toulouse, leaving only a few lands to the English monarch of all that had once belonged to his family. The English king renounced all claims to his other possessions.

The centralization of royal power continued throughout the century. Roman law, with its emphasis on royal power, virtually superseded feudal law, but royal justice was generally regarded as superior and Louis IX himself (later canonized as St. Louis) as a fair and impartial judge. As part of his centralizing policy Louis compelled many of the French cities, in spite of their charters, to accept some form of royal control, using the misgovernment of the towns (usually a charge that was true enough) as his excuse. The number of royal officials greatly increased, as did taxes, especially to pay for Louis' two unsuccessful crusades. The French king, however, did not have the right to levy new taxes on his subjects without their consent. What the thirteenth century Capetian kings did was to tighten the administration of their feudal rights; and since the king was the feudal lord of his entire kingdom, he enjoyed a very considerable feudal income.

The Quarrel between Philip IV and the Papacy. When Philip IV (the Fair) came to the throne in 1285 he became involved in a struggle with Edward I of England over the remaining English possessions in southern France. Philip invaded and overran Guienne, and expanded into the rich territory of Flanders to the north. Though the English war ended in 1298 on the basis of the status quo, these enterprises were expensive, and Philip wished to use mercenaries as well as the less reliable feudal nobles. So he was compelled to look around for more sources of income. After he had deprived many of the French cities of their charters and subjected them to his rule and taxation, he turned toward the wealthy Church, which he proposed to tax, contrary to canon law. This involved him in a serious quarrel with Boniface VIII, an able lawyer on the papal throne. The pope issued a famous bull, *Clericis laicos* (1296), forbidding such taxation, to which Philip responded with a most modern measure, one possible only to a monarch who had complete control over his kingdom. He prohibited the export of all money from France to Italy. This brought the pope to terms, and Philip was permitted to continue his exactions.

In 1301 Philip arrested a bishop and proposed to bring him to trial in his own court. Boniface, stung to fury, retaliated with another bull, *Unam sanctam* (1302), in which were asserted the most extreme claims ever made by a pope. Every Christian who hoped for salvation, it declared, must submit himself in everything to the pope. Boniface then prepared to excommunicate Philip. The king took an unprecedented step. He summoned an assembly of the States-General, a group of nobility, clergy, and bourgeoisie, sitting in their separate estates (ranks), and appealed to it for nation-wide support. Then Philip sent his chancellor, Nogaret, to Italy to put pressure on Boniface. With the support of Italian nobles of the Colonna family, rivals of the Gaetani family to which Boniface belonged, Nogaret forced his way into the presence of the aged pope at Anagni, and humiliated him so severely that he died a month later (1303). Though the Italians greatly resented the king's action, they were powerless. Rome was torn by dissension between rival groups of nobles contending for the papal throne, and the city itself was a prey to turbulence and violence. Though one last Italian pope was chosen, he died soon afterwards, possibly of poison, whereupon the cardinal-electors decided that the safest policy was to choose a French cleric as pope. This was Clement V, archbishop of Bordeaux, who never entered Italy, and soon afterward established his headquarters at Avignon, a papal territory within the borders of France. For more than seventy years, a period known as the "Babylonian captivity" of the Church, no pope returned to Rome.

The Hundred Years' War. Philip continued his absolutist way. Though defeated by the Flemish at the Battle of Courtrai in 1302, he did not lose his hold altogether on the rich little country, and the Hundred Years' War broke out later as the result of rivalry between English and French for control of the Flemish wool trade. With papal consent Philip dispossessed the rich order of the Knights Templar, accusing it of numerous crimes. Its chief crime, however, was probably its wealth, which Philip coveted and succeeded in appropriating to himself. In 1328 the direct Capetian line of kings came to an end. The nearest heir was Edward III of England, if inheritance of the crown could pass through a woman. The last Capetian king, Charles IV, who died childless, therefore established with the consent of his magnates the so-called Salic Law, which prevented such inheritance. The throne thereupon passed to the collateral line of Valois in the person of Philip VI (1328–1350).

Edward III paid little attention to his claim until a quarrel broke out with France over Flanders. Philip made war on the county and took it for himself. Edward placed an embargo on the export of wool, on which the Flemish weavers were dependent, which so aroused the Flemish that they rebelled against Philip, calling Edward to their aid. Edward then had himself proclaimed king of France. Thus began the Hundred Years' War, with which the fortunes of the French monarchy were inextricably bound up. It will therefore be treated here as a part of French history. Though the English were of course involved, it was of far less importance for them. The English possessions in France were the private property of the English monarch, and though useful for English trade were not vital to it. The entire war was fought on French soil, and as long as the war went favorably for England, it was popular even with the classes that had to pay for it, since it gave the nobles an opportunity to engage in war, still their favorite pursuit, and the commercial classes the chance to damage French trade to their own profit.

In the early years the war indeed went most favorably for England. The Black Prince, son of Edward III, won undying glory at the battles of Crécy (1346) and Poitiers (1356), when the French armies were hopelessly outclassed by the English who had adopted new methods of warfare, including the use of artillery and the crossbow. The French, on the other hand, continued to rely on their old feudal chivalry, which was outmoded by the fourteenth century. The English victories prior to 1356 had already reduced the French royal government to a shadow of its former self. When John II, king of France, was taken prisoner at the Battle of Poitiers, France fell into virtual anarchy. The States-General was now frequently called but insisted on being granted a share in government in exchange for subsidies to continue the war. It might have succeeded in its aim if a peasant revolt had not broken out which needed the authority of a king to suppress. Charles, the son of the exiled John, took charge of the situation and recovered some of his authority. A few years later a peace of exhaustion was signed by England and France (Peace of Brétigny 1360), under which England won back many of her former possessions in France, which had not been hers since the time of King John.

When Charles the Dauphin inherited the throne in 1364 as Charles V he re-established order in his kingdom and restored much of the old administration, with the aid of new taxes granted him without time limit by the States-General. He then set about the task of having the English expelled. His constable, Bertrand du

Guesclin, adopted new guerrilla tactics which proved efficacious. By 1380 the English were nearly driven out of France. In 1396 a long truce was concluded with England. But the new king, Charles VI, who had inherited the throne in 1380 was intermittently insane, giving an opportunity for the most powerful noble in France, the duke of Burgundy, to engage in wars and intrigue which threatened the monarchy. Two factions sprang up in the country, one (the Armagnacs) supporting the dauphin, Charles, and the other (the Burgundians), who were strong in the north and were willing to ally themselves for their own purposes with England. Thus when Henry V of England invaded France once again in 1415, he was supported by the Burgundian faction, which was willing to control the monarchy. After winning the Battle of Agincourt in 1415 and subsequently winning the whole of France as far as the Loire, the French king agreed to a treaty (Treaty of Troyes, 1420) under which Henry was to marry Catharine, daughter of Charles VI, and their son, if any, should inherit the throne of France. But Henry V died in the same year as the now quite mad French monarch, and his son by Catharine was only a few months old.

Thus began the last stage of the Hundred Years' War. The English regents for the infant king fought hard for his rights. With Burgundian support they had him crowned king of France in Paris. Only a few lands south of the Loire remained to the Armagnacs, led by the dauphin, who was known contemptuously as "king of Bourges" (the largest city which he retained under his control). The English were attacking everywhere, and it seemed impossible that the Armagnacs could long survive. It was at this moment that Joan of Arc, a young country girl, presented herself at the court of the dauphin and offered her services, claiming that she had been instructed in visions to save the legitimate king and have him crowned as king of France. Since nothing better offered, the dauphin permitted her to join his troops, whereupon she breathed such new spirit into them that they raised the siege of Orléans. Joan was able to have the dauphin crowned as Charles VII in the cathedral of Reims (the traditional place for the coronation of French kings) by one of the few loyal churchmen who remained to him. Joan did not believe her mission was over, and she insisted on continuing the fight against the English until she was captured. The English, anxious to discredit her and thus destroy her influence, handed her over to a vindictive bishop who had collaborated with them and was willing to preside over an irregularly constituted Inquisitorial trial. Although she defended herself ably, the result was a foregone conclusion, and she was burned as a relapsed heretic in 1431. Charles and his advisers were more interested in detaching the Burgundians from the English alliance than in winning the war through small and costly victories. When they were successful in this aim, the English were doomed. With the aid of extensive army reforms and new taxation, Charles, before his death, was able to drive the English not only from northern France, but from the whole of the country except the seaport of Calais, leaving a newly united realm to his son, Louis XI (1461–1483). This king, by dint of shrewd diplomacy and occasional campaigns, unified his kingdom, and re-established royal absolutism. His greatest enemy was the duke of Burgundy, who had added greatly to his possessions in the northeast, most of which were outside the jurisdiction of the king of France. But by buying off the English king, Edward IV, and devoting himself to organizing opposition to the duke, Louis finally triumphed when the last duke was killed in battle by the Swiss. He then incorporated as many of the Burgundian territories as he could into France. He lost Flanders, however, which went with the duke of Burgundy's daughter to her husband, the Hapsburg Maximilian. When the latter became emperor, Flanders passed into the Holy Roman Empire.

At his death in 1483 Louis bequeathed to his successor a united kingdom, well organized and efficient, with almost all power concentrated in royal hands, and with enough taxing authority to provide for the needs of his country. France was by this time by far the leading country in Europe, and already a true nation. For a period she lost this dominance, first to the great ramshackle Hapsburg Empire of Charles V, and then disputed leadership with Charles's successors in Spain, enriched as they were by the Spanish conquests in the New World. It was not until the advent of the Bourbon monarchy in 1589 that she recovered her dominance which she retained till the nineteenth century.

THE IBERIAN PENINSULA

The Union of Castile and Aragon. Until the fifteenth century the monarchies of Castile and Aragon were separate. Castilian leadership in the *Reconquista* had given much power to the military aristocracy, and few of the kings were able to rule really effectively.

Successful military leadership did not give them the kind of pre-eminence won by the kings of France. The Castilian towns were strong and usually allied with the monarchy in the early medieval centuries; their growth had been encouraged in particular by the constant war with the Muslims which had devastated so much of the countryside, whereas the towns were able to defend themselves and stave off the Muslim attacks. In the later Middle Ages the towns lost some of their importance, but the power of the aristocracy constantly grew. Most of the nobles were entirely free from taxation, as was the Church. The towns therefore became the major source of income for the monarchs; but they were not strong enough to be of any great value to the king in his struggle with the aristocracy.

The kings of Aragon, on the other hand, after winning the Sicilian kingdom at the end of the thirteenth century, gained some much-needed strength; but even so, the nobles for a considerable time continued to dominate the monarchy, objecting, indeed, strenuously to the Mediterranean interests of their kings. Alfonso V (1416–1458) was much more interested in his crown of Naples than in Spain, which was ruled by his brother John as regent. All this, however, was to change, when the two states of Castile and Aragon were united under Ferdinand and Isabella and each monarch could rely on help from his other realm. Henry IV (1454–1474) of Castile was an almost powerless monarch; and John II (1458–1479) of Aragon was occupied almost all his regency and reign with rebellions, and with intrigues on the part of Louis XI of France, who aimed to add Catalonia to the French domain. But John proved able to defend his possessions and handed them over intact to his son Ferdinand, later to be known as Ferdinand the Catholic. Henry of Castile was kept uninformed of the intention of his strong-minded half-sister, Isabella, to marry the heir of Aragon. But he had little choice afterwards but to recognize her as his heir to the Castilian throne, since his own daughter was clearly illegitimate. Thus on his death in 1474 Isabella succeeded to the throne of Castile, while Ferdinand succeeded to his own throne of Aragon in 1479.

Throughout their joint rule over Aragon and Castile each monarch governed his own kingdom, but policies were concerted jointly; and the Castilian aristocracy, in particular, was to a large degree tamed. Granada, the last stronghold of the Muslims in the south, which had given little trouble as the vassal of the Castilian rulers, was captured in a joint enterprise in 1492. In the same year the monarchs also expelled some 200,000 Jews from their domain following with the expulsion of the Castilian Moors a few years later.

These expulsions were carried out under the aegis of the Spanish Inquisition, set up with the permission of the papacy in 1478, but always in Spain under royal control and used as the instrument for the furthering of royal power. This Inquisition was much more severe than was the relatively mild papal Inquisition, founded as early as the thirteenth century by Pope Gregory IX for the purpose of ferreting out heretics and compelling them to recant on pain of death by burning. Since the Inquisition could not execute capital sentences itself, it always had to have the support of secular rulers if it were to function effectively. In the rest of Europe this support was not always forthcoming, whereas in Spain it was not only forthcoming but the Inquisition was the actual instrument of the rulers. The expulsion of so many useful citizens who controlled much of Spanish trade and industry was a severe blow to Spanish prosperity and it may be argued that Spain never recovered from the loss. But in 1492 Christopher Columbus, a Genoese sailor in Spanish employ, discovered America, thus paving the way for the great Spanish colonial empire, to some degree making unnecessary, in the short run, any expansion of home industry, and concealing the grievous economic damage done by the expulsions.

In 1504 Isabella died leaving a daughter Joanna to inherit her throne. Since she was already married to Philip, the Hapsburg archduke of Austria, some friction arose between Ferdinand and the Hapsburgs which was settled by allowing Philip to administer Castile as regent. But since Philip died almost at once afterward and Joanna became insane, Ferdinand was able to restore Castile to his full control. When Ferdinand died in 1516, both his kingdoms passed to Charles, son of Joanna and Philip, who was the legitimate heir to both Castile and Aragon. Since Charles later inherited the Hapsburg dominions and was chosen Holy Roman Emperor as Charles V, he became incomparably the most powerful monarch of Europe; his subsequent career will be discussed in Chapter XIII.

Portugal—Prelude to the Discoveries. Portugal was far more fortunate than Spain in its rulers in the later Middle Ages. Although there were several dynastic disputes, on the whole the rulers controlled the small country firmly and were helpful in increasing the commercial prosperity of their subjects, especially through the fostering of overseas trade. The final battle with Castile which firmly established Portuguese independence was fought in 1385 under the leadership of John I, an illegitimate son of a former ruler who founded the new Avis dynasty, under which Portugal reached the greatest heights of her influence and prosperity. One of John's sons, Henry the Navigator (1394–1460), established a school for navigators in Sagrès near Lisbon, which trained all the early Portuguese discoverers. Portugal was still greatly interested in crusading against the Moors. Much effort was expended in attempting to obtain an African bridgehead at Ceuta, which attempt eventually failed. Henry himself belonged to an important crusading order, and his primary object was to drive the Moors from Africa. But in fact his efforts resulted in the great Portuguese discoveries in Africa, and it was the Muslims to the east of the African continent that were to be driven from their strongholds by the Portuguese in the succeeding century.

John II (1481–1495) was the greatest supporter of Portuguese voyages of discovery and backed several important expeditions. In his reign Bartholemeo Diaz rounded the Cape of Good Hope, but John did not live to see the immensely successful voyage of Vasco da Gama to India. It was the work of Portuguese navigators after Henry, and the strong support given by the Portuguese crown to the acquisition of such bases as Madeira, Cape Verde Islands, and the Azores, that laid the groundwork for the Portuguese monopoly of the new sea route to India that will be discussed in the next chapter.

EASTERN EUROPE

Conquest of Constantinople by the Turks. The Latin kingdom of Constantinople was destroyed in 1261 when the Byzantine emperor of Nicaea, Michael VIII, returned across the Bosporus and re-established Greek rule in Constantinople. But the restored empire was never more than a feeble echo of its former self. Independent rulers were in possession of much of Michael's European hinterland, while another Greek monarch held the eastern part of Anatolia. Moreover the emperor had to contend with European adventurers who sought to win more territories for themselves, especially Charles of Anjou who, it will be remembered, had been called in by the pope to destroy the remnants of the Hohenstaufen rule in Italy. Indeed, at one time the danger from Charles was so great that Michael agreed over the protests of his clergy to unite with the

Western Church, and thus win the support of the papacy. But this arrangement lasted for a mere eight years, as Michael's successor at once restored the Orthodox Church. A second Bulgarian empire had flourished during the period of the Latin kingdom of Constantinople but fallen into decay before the Byzantine restoration; therefore the new empire did not have to deal with the Bulgarians. But the Serbs, a Slavic people in the Balkan Peninsula, rose to power in the fourteenth century, threatening Constantinople itself. Stephen Dushan (1331–1355) built a considerable Serbian empire and openly proclaimed himself emperor of the Serbs, Greeks, Bulgars, and Albanians. It is possible that his still undefeated arms would have taken the capital even though the Byzantine emperor called to his aid the Ottoman Turks, who proved to be a far more dangerous and permanent enemy than the Serbs. Though the Turks inflicted a defeat on the Serbs, Stephen did not halt his expedition, which had been in the making for many years. He had already captured Adrianople, and nothing of importance stood between him and Constantinople when he suddenly died. His empire, held together only by his ability and personality, fell apart and was never a major threat again.

Meanwhile the Ottoman Turks, supposedly united as a people by Osman I (1290–1326), who gave his name to this branch of the Turkish people, had been encroaching on the Byzantine possessions in Asia Minor. Originally, according to tradition, employed in earlier periods as Byzantine mercenaries and long settled in Asia Minor, the Ottoman Turks moved slowly against their Greek mentors and former employers, and their invasions were sporadic, dependent, no doubt, on Byzantine strength at the time. In 1331 they took Nicaea, which had been the capital of the Greek empire during the period of the Latin period of Constantinople. Their first moves into Europe (1345 and 1349) were made at Byzantine request as we have seen. In 1354, again with Byzantine permission, they settled in Europe. As soon as Stephen Dushan's threat to Constantinople was over, the Turks under Murad I (1359–1389) themselves took the offensive. The papacy called several crusades against these Muslim intruders into Christendom, but nothing substantial was achieved. In 1389 (Battle of Kossovo) Murad won a decisive victory over the Serbs, Bulgars, and others, which put an end to their ambitions, and secured for the Turks a permanent domain in Europe, from which they were not to be ousted until the nineteenth century.

The Byzantines, however, were to be permitted a further lease of life. The Turkish sultan, Bayazid I (1389–1402), besieged Constantinople for seven years but was unable to take it, though he extracted a tribute from the emperors. Then suddenly an Oriental conqueror, one of the greatest in world history, emerged from the steppes and invaded the Asiatic Turkish provinces. This astonishing man, Timur Lenk (Tamerlane) decisively defeated Bayazid and captured him, humiliating him by carrying him along with him in an iron cage. If he had wished, Timur could have destroyed the Ottoman Empire for good. But he was more interested in conquering China and left Western Asia for his expedition to that country, on which he died. Though Timur's descendants became the Great Moguls of India, he had no further influence in the West, and the Ottomans recovered their power. Murad II (1421–1451) again besieged Constantinople, but had to abandon the siege to meet crusaders from the West, who appeared in greater force than hitherto and were successful in freeing part of the Balkans for a time from Turkish rule. But Murad ultimately recovered and defeated the crusaders. His son Mohammed II, left free to deal with Constantinople, besieged it once more, and in an epic three-month struggle finally took it by storm. It then became the Ottoman capital, which it remained until after the First World War, when it was replaced by the Anatolian city of Ankara. For the rest of Mohammed's reign the Turks occupied themselves in consolidating all the former Byzantine possessions which they could acquire. After a successful war with Venice they made the Balkan Peninsula fully Turkish, which it remained until the nineteenth century.

The Grand Duchy of Moscow and the Mongolian Occupation. As we have noted in Chapter VIII the early Russian state was centered on Kiev, which had been founded by the Swedes in the ninth century. Until the twelfth century Kiev continued to be the leading Russian city, although it was sometimes dominated by local tribes from the steppes. In the thirteenth century southern Russia fell under the domination of the Mongols from central Asia, who under Jenghiz Khan (1206–1227), subdued almost all central Asia, stopping short at China in the east and Iran in the west. When Jenghiz died the Mongol armies returned to the central Asian capital of Karakorum for the choice of a new ruler. This custom which was observed when each Great Khan died, was to prove more than once the salvation of Europe. As soon as a new leader had been chosen the conquests were resumed, but the defenders had had a chance to prepare themselves. In 1237 the westward march was resumed under Batu Khan, and southern and central Russia were conquered. Poland and Hungary were invaded. In 1241 the Poles and Germans were defeated by one Mongol army, the Hungarians by another. Once more the Europeans were saved by the death of a Great Khan, and the Mongols never again penetrated so far to the west. But they did subjugate much of Russia and established a state with a capital at Sarai on the Volga. Moscow was a vassal state of the Mongols in Russia who were collectively known as the Golden Horde.

Meanwhile in the north the great trading city of Novgorod was never subjected to the Mongols; but its rulers had to defend themselves against German knights and Swedes who were advancing from the west. Alexander Nevski, prince of Novgorod, defeated the Swedes in 1240 and the Teutonic Knights at the battle of Lake Peipus in 1242, thus putting a stop to German and Scandinavian expansion into Russia. Alexander himself made terms with the Golden Horde, acknowledging Mongol suzerainty over the land that he possessed south of Novgorod. The city, however, soon came under German commercial influence and for a time was an important Hanseatic center.

The grand duchy of Moscow acquired importance during the second century of Mongol rule. Ivan I (1325–1341), grand duke of Moscow, was entrusted by his overlords with the task of collecting the tribute due from their various Russian vassals, and he used it to further the fortunes of his house. In the later part of the fourteenth and the fifteenth centuries the Mongols were gradually expelled, and the grand duke of Moscow fell heir to their dominions. Under Ivan III, the Great (1462–1505), the Mongols were finally expelled from central Russia, and the German merchants were expelled from the northern territories of Novgorod, which Ivan added to his duchy. Thus when Ivan married the daughter of the last emperor of Constantinople after that city had fallen to the Turks, the grand duchy of Moscow was by far the greatest power in Russia, and the country had some right to be considered, as its ruler proclaimed it, the Christian heir of Constantinople. It was left to another strong ruler, Ivan IV, the Terrible (1533–1584), the first Russian ruler to call himself tsar of all the Russias, to take the remnants of the Russian territories from the Mongols and bring the boundaries of his domain close to those of modern European Russia.

The Expansion of the Teutonic Knights. The kingdom of Poland had first been converted to Christianity in 966, but through the eleventh century there were several returns to paganism, in part because of the unpopularity of the Christian clergy. Ultimately Christianity became firmly established, but the Polish kings were always in danger from their own nobles as well as from the Germans to the west. In the early thirteenth century the Teutonic Knights, an order of military crusaders, left the Holy Land after it had fallen to the Saracens and took up the task of Christianizing the still pagan peoples to the east of the Empire. They were given their new tasks by Emperor Frederick II in 1226, and thereafter began their notable career of expansion. All the lands that they conquered and converted belonged to them, although they acknowledged the nominal suzerainty of the papacy. Prussia was soon won by the Knights who were joined by the Livonian Brothers of the Sword, another crusading order. In spite of revolts in Prussia, which the Christian Poles helped the Knights to suppress, it became a permanent German possession. In the fourteenth century the Knights began to attempt the conversion of the great territory of Lithuania, at that time the last remaining pagan stronghold of importance in Europe. But here they met with determined opposition from the Poles, who resented the German advance, even though it was under the aegis of Christianity. In 1386 the Poles achieved a master stroke. The elected queen of Poland—Poland was always an elective monarchy—married the grand duke of Lithuania, who agreed to become a Christian. This created a personal union of the two countries which became for a period a vast empire stretching from the Baltic to the Black Sea to the west of Russia and included the Russian capital of Kiev. The union marked the beginning of the end for the Teutonic Knights who could advance no further to the east. In due course the Baltic countries settled down under secularized German nobles, who remained the dominant upper class in these regions (Prussia, Estonia, Latvia) until the end of the First World War.

PROGRESS OF THE TOWNS IN THE LATER MIDDLE AGES

The Hanseatic League. The internal structure of the medieval towns and the organization of commerce and industry were touched upon in the last chapter. It only remains to be noted here that the great cities of northern Europe in the late Middle Ages began to win for themselves much more than a merely nominal sovereignty and a limited internal self-government. Whereas the towns in England and France were always at the mercy of the royal governments, the German cities had no similar territorial rulers to dominate them. The cities in the Holy Roman Empire might in name be imperial cities, and the emperor had some rights in them that might be honored. But the cities were usually quite strong enough to resist him if he had attempted to interfere with them. On the other hand, the absence of any strong protector, needed by the towns to ensure their trading rights abroad, tempted them to ally themselves with one another for mutual protection, even though their territories were not contiguous. The North German city of Lübeck took the lead in this movement for closer co-operation in the thirteenth century, by entering into agreements with some of her neighbors. By the end of the thirteenth century German traders had established their own *hansas* (or associations) in foreign cities, often protected by the local ruler who was only too glad to trade with them. In the fourteenth century a wider league of Hansa towns was formed, including Lübeck, which was for a period a powerful organization, capable of making war with the aid of mercenaries for the purpose of obtaining new trade concessions and maintaining its existing monopolies. In 1370 at the Peace of Stralsund the Hanseatic League compelled the Danish king to grant it a monopoly of trade in his domains, and even the right to depose any Danish king who dared to abrogate the monopoly. Several monarchs, especially the king of England, were strong supporters of the Hansa privileges, since the merchants contributed substantially to their revenues without exacting anything in return save the monopoly of trade in certain cities, a monopoly for which they were willing to pay a good price. Not until local merchants were able to match the price and put pressure on him, did the English king decide to abrogate the Hansa privileges. As late as 1474 Edward IV of England gave the Hansas a monopoly of the London steelyard. But it was in the fifteenth century that the League as such began to break up, since the interests of its member cities became increasingly divergent, and there were many internal struggles between the different classes in most of the cities. The last meeting of the League was held in 1669, but by this time there were only six members and all power had been lost.

The Flemish Towns. The towns of Flanders have already been mentioned as being in some measure responsible for the Hundred Years' War. In the later Middle Ages some of the most prosperous cities of Europe were to be found in the small county of Flanders, the center of the northern European wool trade. Most of the wool was imported from England; much of it from Cistercian monasteries which owned huge sheep runs. The English kings thoroughly approved of this trade, even though little wool was made into cloth in their country. What the kings needed was money, and this was provided for them by export taxes on wool and import duties on the finished cloth. It was perhaps only a matter of time before the English decided to manufacture the wool for themselves, and keep the extra manufacturing profit. This was accomplished during the Tudor period, and thereafter Flanders ceased to be of such importance in the wool trade. But while it lasted, and while the Flemish sent their woolen products all over Europe, receiving luxuries in return from Italy and elsewhere for distribution in Europe, the great Flemish medieval towns were built and flourished. Most of them were self-governing and owed little to their feudal overlords. Even while the wool trade was in decline the great city of Antwerp was to know a further period of great prosperity as the leading seaport and financial center of the sixteenth century.

The Italian Towns and the Renaissance. It was in the later medieval centuries that the Italian cities reached their maximum period of growth and prosperity, even though their political development was very different from the cities to the north. The so-called Italian Renaissance, to be discussed in the next chapter, came into being at a period when the rest of Europe must be considered as having not yet emerged from the Middle Ages. Nevertheless, the Renaissance, though an urban phenomenon was not accompanied by a growth in the self-government of the Italian cities. On the contrary, the self-government of the cities which had been a feature of the earlier period gave way during the Renaissance to rule by individual despots, some merely soldier-adventurers (*condottieri*), others scions of prosperous merchant families. These men took over the rule of their cities and ruled with the support of and in the interest of their class. The Italian cities in the medieval period invented almost all of those commercial devices which have fostered the growth of trade in the centuries since: the bill of exchange, the draft, the discounting of bills, and even double-entry bookkeeping. These advances were gradually taken over by other countries.

Venice for a long time had a near monopoly of trade with the East, and under a merchant oligarchy she built an empire. Genoa, Pisa, Amalfi, and other ports all at one time or another fought for their share. Florence was the greatest inland commercial city, as for a long time it was the center of Italian Renaissance art. The cities quarreled among themselves, and within each town there were at all times factions fighting for power. But the quarrels seldom damaged their commercial prosperity. What did slowly ruin the Italian cities was the transfer of the Oriental trade to the Atlantic seaboard following the discovery of the New World. Even so, the accumulated capital of such cities as Venice enabled Italy to continue to finance much of European trade for a long time after the fifteenth century, and her cultural inventiveness endured for several centuries. But it remains true that the heyday of Italian greatness was in the last medieval centuries and during the Renaissance; and this greatness was solidly based on the power and prosperity of the Italian cities, and upon their urban civilization which was of an altogether different quality from anything to be found elsewhere in Europe at that epoch.

DECLINE OF MEDIEVAL CIVILIZATION IN THE FOURTEENTH AND FIFTEENTH CENTURIES

It should not be thought from the above account that the towns were engaged in constant expansion of trade in the last medieval centuries. The great period of expansion occurred earlier, and in most areas there was some contraction in the fourteenth and fifteenth centuries. In industry the guild system had already degenerated into closed commercial monopolies against which newcomers strove largely in vain. There were not enough precious metals in circulation in the West to finance expansion of production and consumption on an extensive scale, and the commercial associations such as the Hanseatic League were more interested in maintaining the monopoly of what trade there was than in creating new business enterprises and introducing more and different products to the market. The

Western world was surely ready for the shot in the arm represented by the discoveries at the end of the fifteenth century and during the sixteenth; they came none too soon if Europe were to continue the development so auspiciously begun in the twelfth and thirteenth centuries.

But, far more important than the slowdown of production in the towns, was the depression in rural areas due to the failure of social and political institutions to adapt themselves to the changes that were taking place. The Black Death (bubonic plague), which ravaged most of Europe in the years 1347–1350 and raged intermittently during the later Middle Ages and even afterward, reduced the population of Europe to an extent which cannot be accurately estimated, but may have been as high as fifty per cent. We know of quite large towns which were almost completely wiped out, small businesses in certain areas reduced in number by ninety per cent, and whole countrysides depopulated. Though Europe was overpopulated before in relation to its productive capacity, it now became seriously underpopulated. No one had any idea how to deal with the plague. Some of the religious orders suffered tremendous casualties, especially the Franciscans who devoted themselves, among other tasks, to healing, but did not have the skill to save either the patients or themselves. The plague was widely regarded as the judgment of God for the wickedness of the people; bands of flagellants wandered through Europe, inflicting suffering on themselves as a means of appeasing divine or demonic powers who had sent it. Other thousands left their stricken homelands and were lost forever to the manors.

This was the period described in the last chapter when the manorial serfs were recovering their freedom. But freedom was granted because the lords found the system no longer profitable and preferred to rent their private lands and enclose the commons. The gesture for a long time made the conditions of the poor landless worker worse, not better, than before. The lords merely ceased to accept the responsibilities that the manorial society had expected them to undertake, and absolved themselves of any interest in the welfare of the sharecroppers and tenants on their estates. Yet they continued to demand that the peasants provide them with some services in addition to renting their land in exchange for often exorbitant payments, that they continue to pay for the use of their facilities—they still forbade them to create their own. If they wished to turn their estates into sheep runs, expelling the former tenants, there was nothing to prevent them. Since the landowners everywhere either controlled or had a strong influence on the government, the peasant was left without redress. All he could do was rebel, with the virtual certainty that the rebellion would be bloodily suppressed, and he would gain nothing. Not even a king could help the peasants against the entrenched opposition of the nobility, as young Richard II of England found in 1381 when he quelled a revolt by making promises of reform and then discovered he could not implement them. Peasant revolts were endemic for centuries in Europe, but none knew any lasting success.

The local lords and merchants who administered justice in rural and urban areas had no intention of raising wages, in spite of the shortage of labor occasioned by the Black Death. Laws were constantly passed to discipline the workers and compel them to accept the same wages as before the plague, in spite of the very considerable increase in prices. Rather than submit, many men took to highway robbery as a career, or became what the English law called "sturdy beggars." Such occupations were savagely punished with the result that has always attended such methods; nothing of permanence was achieved, and there was no visible diminution in the number of beggars or highwaymen.

The Middle Ages thus ended in an ever more virulent social struggle to the detriment of rural and urban production; with a Great Schism in the Church, which saw two and eventually three popes competing for the leadership in Christendom; with lords talking of chivalry and crusades but actually engaging in ruthless exploitation of their peasantry; with industrial associations in the cities striving to keep to an outmoded system of production and jealously guarding their dwindling monopolies; and with kings everywhere trying to establish their positions against competing nobles, and usually failing. Yet it was the kings who triumphed in the next period of history, and it was largely they who gave their peoples the strong government that they required. Where the kings established law and order, the unruly competing classes could be made to accept some modicum of that responsibility which they had accepted as a matter of course in an earlier age—an age when clergy were still respected, and nobles and knights had not yet learned the delights of personal luxury combined with irresponsibility.

CULTURAL ACCOMPLISHMENTS OF THE MIDDLE AGES

Science and Philosophy. The Middle Ages was not a period of great intellectual achievement. Scholastic philosophy, though it showed great clarity of thought, lacked originality and was too dependent on the great authorities of the past, Plato, Aristotle, the Bible, or the Fathers of the Church. Almost all philosophy was concerned with religion and attempted either to interpret truths believed to have been revealed or to discover such truths by the process of thinking. Medieval thinking was essentially deductive, drawing out the logical consequences from premises accepted as self-evident or revealed. It thus could add little that was new; and relatively few thinkers were at any time interested in the world phenomena to be observed around them, still less in using the data of observation to confirm their hypotheses or to submit generally accepted beliefs to verification.

It was therefore not a great age of science. There were many good observers of nature who compiled their observations into great compendia of facts—as there were also similar compilers who collected false information without ever troubling to verify their "facts." There was an important school of scientists in England founded by Robert Grosseteste, bishop of Lincoln, who did some original and interesting work in optics and certain branches of physics, in part relying upon the prior work of the Muslims in this field. Some Englishmen, such as Roger Bacon, and his French friend Peter de Maricourt, were interested enough in scientific method to recognize the necessity for verifying generally accepted tales. Peter wrote a useful treatise on the magnet, a phenomenon that interested him, and tried to explain magnetism. Bacon wrote a famous treatise for the pope in which he drew attention to the great work of the Muslims, which in his view was insufficiently known in Europe, and suggested that with proper moral and financial backing, a true body of scientific knowledge could be built up based on what he called "the science of experience." In Germany Albertus Magnus studied minerology, botany, and alchemy, and made valuable contributions to these sciences on the basis of his observations, though his ability to theorize was not the equal of Bacon's. In the later Middle Ages much progress was made in the effort to improve upon Aristotle's theory of motion, which was seen not to conform to the observed facts. This work was carried on at the universities of Paris and Padua. The later achievements of Galileo could not have been made without the solid work of his predecessors at the University of Padua.

But on the whole Aristotle was regarded in the Middle Ages as the "master of those who know," and it took a courageous man to question his findings. Most scientific teaching consisted in expounding on Aristotle rather than striking out on a new path. The Hellenistic astronomer and scientific writer, Claudius Ptolemy, who wrote the fullest exposition of the geocentric theory of ancient times, was regarded as the ultimate authority in astronomy. As long as his theories worked in practice, no one thought it worth while to raise the questions later asked by Copernicus, except the churchman Nicolas of Cusa (1401?–1464), who died a few years before Copernicus' birth. In medicine the Hellenistic scientist Galen provided the modicum of medical theory for medieval doctors, most of whom in fact used a horrifying mixture of superstition, magical practices, and primitive surgery on their patients, without reference to much theory at all.

Medieval philosophy had one outstanding virtue: it taught men to reason. During the Middle Ages the work of the religious philosophers, especially Thomas Aquinas, succeeded in persuading theologians that their teachings must not be in contradiction to what the reason dictated as clearly true. Thomas, through impeccable logic, showed on the basis of premises that he regarded as self-evident that there must be a God, that God was necessarily good, that He possessed a will, that He cared for the world and mankind, and that the soul was immortal. These truths, in his opinion, can be discovered by the unaided mind. Other truths, however, are above reason, and God had chosen to impart these to man by revelation; they must be accepted on the basis of faith. Thus Thomas and those thinkers who followed him, regarded theology as in part a "science," that is, to be discovered by man's own mind and known as true. The rest of theology lies in the domain of faith, and all the philosopher can do is show that it is not contrary to reason. He can demonstrate that the revelations hang together, he can expound them, but he cannot discover them. Catholic philosophy, ever since the time of Thomas, has borne the impress he laid upon it. In the late nineteenth century, the great Pope Leo XIII proclaimed Thomism as the official philosophy of the Catholic Church and commanded that it be studied by all Catholic candidates for the priesthood.

Art. The greatest achievements of the Middle Ages lie elsewhere than in the domain of the intellect. Most moderns would agree that its church architecture is unique in the Western world, an achievement different in kind from Greek and Roman architecture, which was revived in the Italian Renaissance, and intermittently ever since. The Romanesque with its round arches, heavy and substantial pillars, and mysterious gloom, owes much to classical antiquity, though it was greatly developed in the early medieval centuries. Not so the Gothic, with its pointed arches, flying buttresses, and insubstantial interior framework, which suggest the aspiration toward heaven. The Gothic building is filled with light, entering from the numerous windows made possible by the skeletal structure of the building. In the greater cathedrals there are rose windows through which the sun shines, filling the building with colored light. The other windows were almost always made of stained glass, showing scenes from Scripture or even from everyday life. The quality of this stained glass has never been equaled, and we are not entirely certain, even today, just how it was made. Most of the cathedrals were constructed by co-operative enterprise led by the bishop. All the inhabitants of the city took part in the work, and the finished result is the greatest monument to what has been called, if somewhat hyperbolically, the Age of Faith.

Medieval painting and sculpture were religious in inspiration, and it is in the great cathedrals that we find most of the examples that have survived. Sculptured saints and the Virgin are to be seen in both the interior of the cathedral and often above the doorway, most of them realistic enough since the medievals knew no technique but realism, save in the representation of imaginary figures like the Virgin and the Child. In such sculptures the artist was free to imagine for himself the symbol of the divine Mother and of her Son who sacrificed himself to save mankind.

Literature. Most earlier medieval literature was written in the Latin language. But in the later centuries, though Latin was still in use among educated classes and was the language for almost all works of religion and learning, the great vernacular tongues were also coming into wider use. The songs and poems of the troubadours were written in the vernacular, especially old French and German. There was a great body of literature concerned with deeds of chivalry, romanticized out of all recognition from the original historical events. Such a work is the famous poem *Chanson de Roland,* which purports to tell of the heroic defense of Roncesvalles pass against the advancing Saracens by the rear guard of Charlemagne's army. The German minnesingers sang of chivalrous love, as did the troubadours, when they were not extolling knightly deeds. There is an entire cycle of poems concerned with the search for the Holy Grail (the cup in which the blood of Christ was held after the crucifixion), which was said to have been taken by Joseph of Aramathaea and secreted in some hidden castle in Europe. The greatest poems in this cycle are by Chrétien de Troyes and Wolfram von Eschenbach. The Grail becomes a great ideal sought by the Christian knight, who can attain it, as did Parzival, after learning wisdom through numerous trials and much affliction, with his one potent weapon, his simplicity and purity of heart.

More clearly religious is the tremendous poem of Dante called the *Divine Comedy,* in which the poet is led in a vision through hell and purgatory until at last he attains paradise, where his ideal lady, Beatrice, comes to lead him onward to the momentary vision of God. The poem is suffused with the religious teaching of Thomas Aquinas, which though never obtrusive gives form and substance to the vision of man's destiny in the spiritual worlds. Underlying this teaching can be observed the firm structure of Aristotelian philosophy.

But while religion and chivalry were giving birth to their own literature, other interests were paramount in the towns. The townsmen enjoyed earthy stories, and fables which extolled the sharpness of the urban mind and its ability to take care of itself in a world where each man had to get the best of his fellow men to survive. The great strength of many of these *fabliaux* is in their drawing of character and their understanding of human nature. The fourteenth-century masterpiece of the English Geoffrey Chaucer, the *Canterbury Tales,* is unequalled for its delineation of the many characters of the medieval world. Chaucer chose the occasion of a pilgrimage to Canterbury by a group of persons from assorted occupations, on which each member of the party tells stories to while away the time.

The Universities. Lastly, mention should be made of the great institutional achievement of the Middle Ages, the founding of a hundred or so universities throughout Europe, most of which have survived to the present. The earliest university in Europe was that at Salerno in southern Italy (founded in the ninth century), which was largely a medical school and much influenced by Muslim medical science. The great Italian university of Bologna was founded for the study of Roman law, especially the newly rediscovered *corpus juris civilis* of Justinian. Since Roman law was the basis for the canon law of the Church, obviously it was of interest to clerics who hoped to rise high in the Church hierarchy. It was, however, also interesting to monarchs engaged in trying to establish their own authority as against the feudal law in operation in their countries. The Roman law in the Middle Ages was therefore often superimposed upon existing Germanic codes and emphasized above all by the kings, whose power and authority it tended to enhance, since all Roman law emanated from the emperor. Kings therefore often sent their ministers to the University of Bologna, and men who wanted to advance in the royal service would go there to prepare themselves for their later duties. The University of Paris was the major school of theology in Europe. Founded as a university by Philip Augustus in 1200 but based on the existing cathedral school which was much older, it also offered degrees in Arts, based on the standard medieval curriculum. The English universities of Oxford and Cambridge probably grew to some degree by fission from the University of Paris. When the latter was closed down for a time in the thirteenth century by the pope because of disorders and a curriculum of teaching which the papacy considered dangerous, Oxford and Cambridge grew mightily. But Paris soon regained its supremacy, which it held throughout the Middle Ages, constantly enlarging its curriculum, but finally becoming a stronghold of conservatism at a time when other universities, notably the Italian university of Padua, greatly surpassed it in its encouragement of modern learning, especially science.

Summary—the Medieval Achievement. The Middle Ages therefore saw the founding of much that has survived into modern times, and in many respects prepared the way for future advances. But its tendency to look back to classical antiquity for inspiration and to accept too much knowledge on the basis of authority rather than original investigation, had to be overcome before Western man could step forward boldly toward the future. This was not achieved at once since it needed a fundamental change of outlook, and motives far different from those that animated most medieval men. But the achievement of the greatest medieval thinkers in granting primacy to the reasoning faculty in an age which, like almost all other ages, was predominantly anti-intellectual, should not be underestimated; nor should we treat too lightly the efforts made by the medievals to break from the bonds imposed by authority, nor the fact that they gave us many of the tools used for our later advances. Though the Middle Ages in many respects marks the end of an epoch which began with classical antiquity, it also looks forward to the future; and in this aspect it may not unworthily be called, as Oswald Spengler described it, "the springtime" of Western civilization.

CHAPTER XI

THE AGE OF THE RENAISSANCE AND THE DISCOVERIES

It is apparent to the historian, even if it would not perhaps have been equally apparent to a contemporary, looking at only a few manifestations of the process, that toward the end of the Middle Ages the interest of Western man was turning away from those matters that had hitherto engaged his attention. He was beginning to emancipate himself, though slowly and with many glances backward, from his traditional ideas and preoccupations. While it may be an exaggeration to think of the Middle Ages as an age of faith, there can be no doubt that the medieval centuries saw relatively little social change. The general picture of man presented by medieval Christianity and sanctified by long-established authority was that he was born to a certain status in society from which he was not expected to rise; that as a result of Adam's sin he was himself a sinful being deserving of damnation but redeemable not through any merit of his own but by the sacrifice of Christ and through the ministrations of the Christian Church. He could not and should not expect to be relieved of suffering on earth, which was a vale of tears. But when he had been redeemed by God's mercy he might look forward to a blessed hereafter, in which all his earthly sufferings would be forgotten.

Clearly such beliefs were not conducive to go-getting. Ambition, pride, competitiveness, public display, the pursuit of earthly wealth —were all characterized as more or less deadly sins, likely to lead man to everlasting punishment in hell rather than to everlasting bliss in heaven. It is a curious paradox that such "sins" have become the staple stock in trade of Western man and his civilization, and all are to a greater or lesser degree overtly or covertly approved in modern Western civilization, in spite of the fact that Christianity has remained the major religion of the West—from which it would appear that the drive and energy of Western civilization have proved too strong for its framework of religious ideas.

In the last medieval centuries and the beginning of modern times the typical qualities of Western civilization were already becoming apparent. We have noted the expansionism of the Crusades and how by the time of the Fourth Crusade (to Constantinople) naked aggression and the desire for booty had completely ousted the initial (at least partly) religious impulse. We have noted the growing authoritarianism of the Church and its willingness to use its political power for other than religious ends. We have noted how the feudal lord was ready to abandon his ancient responsibilities toward his serfs in the pursuit of profit and personal luxury; how in the later Middle Ages the worldly cities grew to form the nucleus of a society which was in the fullness of time to supplant the static feudal order.

In this chapter, the first devoted to what may be thought of as modern history, we shall consider the further development of these tendencies toward the secularization of life and the decline of religion; and in the next chapter we shall give our attention to various aspects of the Protestant and Catholic Reformations which, after they had run their course, finally succeeded in relegating religion to the role it has since occupied in the Western civilization—a series of personal religious commitments chosen by the individual, institutionalized in the various churches, but no longer the warp and woof of civilization itself.

DECLINE OF THE MEDIEVAL CHURCH

The Papacy at Avignon. The high point of the medieval Church, as we have already noted, was reached in the pontificate of Innocent III at the turn of the thirteenth century. By the early fourteenth century a French pope had left Rome and taken up his residence at the papal city of Avignon. Its presence within the territorial boundaries of France constituted a great offense to many of the rulers and people of Europe, who regarded Rome as the city of St. Peter, chosen as the headquarters of the Universal Church by the apostle to whom Christ himself had entrusted the task of founding his Church. Other rulers, rivals of France, felt that French influence, already high enough, could not but be predominant in the counsels of the Avignon papacy.

In fact, the papacy for the period of its exile in Avignon did not abate its universalist claims and was not especially pro-French; it stood up indeed fairly effectively to the efforts of the French crown to use it for its own purposes. Although always looking for a possible return to Italy when political conditions had improved there, a number of able popes, especially John XXII (1316–1334) felt themselves freed from the exigencies of local Roman politics and devoted themselves to the reform of the Church as an institution. Unfortunately, this reform did not extend itself to the other pressing needs of the Church. Finances were greatly improved, and the collection of church taxes systematized. The procedure for appeals to the papal curia was clearly laid down, and the judicial methods prescribed. For the first time virtually all appointments to the higher clergy were made by the pope, and the leading dignitaries of the Church were definitely subordinate to the papacy, and expected to carry out papal policy. The papacy required the regular payment to the papal treasury of *annates,* the first year's income from all higher ecclesiastical offices, though arrangements were made with local rulers by which they received their share, thus in effect cutting these rulers in on church revenues to the disadvantage of the local clergy. The papacy also prescribed numerous fees to be collected for all kinds of services performed by the Church, and sent out papal tax collectors to ensure that no money due was left uncollected. However, the tax collectors themselves were often notoriously corrupt, gambling sometimes with the money they had collected and making various profits from its use before handing over the residue to their superiors.

The Avignon papacy thus achieved a remarkable degree of centralization and efficiency as an organization. But in the process it alienated many of the local clergy who now had to submit to the appointment of foreigners to high positions in the Church; and rulers, even while they pocketed church revenues, could not fail to regard the papacy as a rival power bent on its own interests, to be tolerated when it was useful or opposed when it stood in the way. The luxury and pomp of the Avignon popes and the cardinals did nothing to endear them to the peoples of Christendom in an age when the Black Death stalked through Europe. When at last Pope Gregory XI decided to return to Rome in 1377, he died before he had been long in the city, thus throwing open the election to the College of Cardinals, meeting for the first time in many years in the Holy City. In such circumstances, under the threat of violence, the cardinals chose an Italian who took the name of Urban VI. When he threatened to pack the Sacred College so that the papacy would never again fall into the hands of the French, a number of cardinals seceded and chose their own pope (Clement VII), who returned at once to Avignon.

The Great Schism. Since neither pope would give way to the other, there was nothing for the various rulers of Europe to do but to make a choice between them. This meant, in fact, that they decided their allegiance on the basis of their own national and dynastic interests. Because France backed Clement, England, the enemy of France, preferred to back Urban. Scotland, enemy of England, chose the Avignon pontiff. The emperor accepted Urban, but many of the German princes in the Empire preferred Clement. This Great Schism, as it was called, created the most appalling scandal in the entire history of the Church, and almost everyone of importance in Europe, both rulers and clerics, realized that it must be brought to an end as soon as possible. In particular the University of Paris took the lead in demanding a Church council to restore the unity of the Church, a demand supported by most of the secular rulers, and even by the rival cardinals. This Conciliar Movement lasted for almost half a century, and came to an inglorious end long after the popes had returned to Rome. At issue was the basic question of whether the popes, once they had been elected, were indeed the absolute rulers of the Church or whether their decisions could be overruled and they themselves subjected to discipline by the higher clergy and even secular rulers. No pope ever accepted the right of any Council, however exalted its membership, to dictate to him; and in the end the absolutist principle triumphed, largely because of the disunity and lack of endurance on the part of those who would reform the Church from outside the clergy.

The Council of Pisa (1409) deposed both popes and chose a thoroughly unsuitable candidate. Since neither pope accepted this third choice (John XXIII—no longer regarded by the Church as a canonically elected pope, hence the title of the twentieth-century pope), there were now three popes, and the scandal was even worse than before. In 1414 another Council met at the summons of Emperor Sigismund and deposed John XXIII. The Roman pope resigned, but the Avignon pope refused to do so. But this time the new choice, an Italian who took the name of Martin V, was accepted by Christendom, and the schism was over. Martin and his successors stalled off reforms urged by a new Council which met intermittently at Basel from 1431 to 1449. By this time the great issues no longer seemed so important to rulers and the clergy, not even to the Parisian professors. The pope was back at Rome and in full control of the Church and the papal lands. From the pontificate of Nicholas V until the Protestant revolt, papal interests became largely those of any other Renaissance prince with estates to administer and money to spend on the commissioning of artistic masterpieces for his city. We shall therefore now deal with the Italian Renaissance as a whole and return to its effect on the Church later on in the chapter.

THE RENAISSANCE IN ITALY

The Humanists. The Renaissance is seldom regarded by modern historians as in any sense a "rebirth," as its name would imply. The literary humanists who were intellectual leaders were few in number and rather self-consciously aware of what they were trying to do. For them the Renaissance was primarily a revival of classical antiquity as a reaction to everything they considered barbaric about the Middle Ages from which they were just emerging—"Gothic" art and architecture for which they coined the name, the Goths being prototypes of all barbarians; medieval Latin, a barbarous debasement of the pure Latin idiom of Cicero; the "otherworldliness" of Christianity as distinct from the supposed Greco-Roman enjoyment of earthly life. The prestige of the humanists was such among the molders of opinion that they succeeded in killing interest in Gothic, at least in Italy, until the romantic revival of the early nineteenth century. They were instrumental in restoring the perfection of the Latin tongue at its classical best, but at the cost of making Latin a learned language and a dead one—whereas it might have become the universal language of the educated in Europe, living because it constantly changed, as it had changed during the Middle Ages. The humanist insistence on the enjoyment to be gained from earthly life reflected the new interest of the richer bourgeois in the Italian cities; but it was propounded with so much enthusiasm and verve that it convinced men and women in Western Europe that a new day had dawned. The ideal of the many-sided man who expressed all the potentialities of human nature was one that was fulfilled in many artists and men of action of the age, not excluding the despots who won control of most Italian cities in the fifteenth century. The thirst for fame and repute tempted not only kings and merchants, who patronized Renaissance art and left statues and paintings of themselves for the admiration of posterity, but soldiers of fortune, and even popes, to say nothing of the artists themselves, who now proudly signed their names to their masterpieces.

All this had little enough to do with the actual deeds of Greeks and Romans; but the Italians regarded at least the latter as their own ancestors and wished their own age to surpass that of their Augustan forebears. But one important result was the recovery, often from old monasteries, of many classical masterpieces, seldom if ever read in the medieval world. With the spread of the late medieval invention of printing from movable metal type, these masterpieces were reproduced and sold, especially by the Venetian presses. Thus they became once more the treasured possessions of Western civilization.

The Despots. The Italian Renaissance was less literary than the same Renaissance when it spread north of the Alps. In Italy it was the artist and man of action who gave the tone to the Renaissance, the two often combined in the same person. In Florence the banking family of the Medici supplied their city with a long line of wealthy princes who established their supremacy and ruled as despots, supported more by the lower classes than by their fellow nobles or the rich bourgeois. Cosimo de Medici, a man of faultless artistic taste and strong will and personality, experienced difficulty with the aristocracy that held his city, and on one occasion he was expelled. But he returned and established himself securely in control of the government run by his nominees. Lorenzo the Magnificent, his grandson, was the greatest Renaissance prince of his day, a man of supreme versatility, a poet in his own right, an effective ruler of his city-state. The family branched out later far beyond Florence. The pope in Luther's day was a Medici, while the ruler of France for much of the sixteenth century was Catharine de Médicis, as regent for her royal sons, who succeeded in turn to the throne.

Other Renaissance princes were simply soldier-adventurers who hired mercenary armies and won their cities by force, maintaining their positions by the same means. Most of these men were nobles whose families had held at least one title in a single city; during the fourteenth and fifteenth centuries they attemptd to add others to their domains. Such a family was that of the Visconti in Milan. When the Visconti family finally fell from power, Francesco Sforza, a true *condottiere,* won the dukedom for himself after putting an end to a short-lived republic. Cesare Borgia was the greatest *condottiere* of them all. The son of a cardinal who later became pope as

Alexander VI, he used his father's power to the full. Able but unscrupulous, he was rapidly building up a position of supremacy by warfare and frequent assassination of his rivals, which might have resulted in the unification of Italy. But his father died suddenly, and without the support of the papacy, Cesare was unable to make much further headway. The administration of many of these Renaissance princes was efficient if despotic. Almost all were patrons of the arts, and some, such as Francesco Gonzaga, duke of Mantua, were educational reformers and experimentalists. The wars of the despots, though constant, did not greatly affect their subjects, since they were fought almost entirely by mercenaries and there was little looting of the civilian population. Only when France at the end of the fifteenth century began to interfere seriously in Italy was there much disruption of civil life. Thereafter the Italian cities fell upon evil times, often ruled by foreign princes, some of whom governed well enough, but seldom in the interests of their inhabitants; and this rule persisted, except for the interlude of Napoleon, until well on into the nineteenth century, in part accounting for some of the difficulties experienced by Italy as a nation in more recent times.

The Artists. The greatest of Italian Renaissance art was far from secular and worldly, either in its subject matter or in its aspirations. Nevertheless, the great paintings were much more naturalistic than in the medieval period, and one may recognize the portraits of Italian beauties even in the pictures of the Virgin. During the course of the Renaissance new techniques in painting were developed, especially the effective use of perspective. The great names in this period of abundant creativity are too many to be recorded here. From Giotto whose work came at the beginning of the fourteenth century down to the Venetian Titian, who died, still turning out masterpieces, late in the sixteenth century, there is always a religious undercurrent, not to be accounted for solely by the influence of the Church as one of the largest patrons of art. Though Leonardo da Vinci painted a Mona Lisa, he is also known for his great *Pièta* and for several superb Madonnas; Raphael Santi was the religious painter par excellence, his Madonnas unequalled for their inspiration and beauty. Michelangelo's *Last Judgment* with its wealth of figures, any single one of which may be taken from its surroundings and still rank as an individual masterpiece, is suffused with its creator's feeling for mankind in its final hour before the throne of

God. Both Michelangelo and Leonardo were men of the utmost versatility in the best tradition of the Renaissance—Leonardo winning fame in his lifetime as inventor and engineer, and posthumously as scientist, while Michelangelo was the supreme sculptor, but painter, poet, and thinker as well.

The Papacy. The popes ever since the Donation of Pepin had of course been Italian princes as well as leaders of Christendom. During the age of the Renaissance they took their role as princes very seriously indeed, intervening constantly in Italian politics and trying to extract as much revenue as they could for their enormous building program, which altered the face of much of Rome almost beyond recognition. From being the poverty-stricken provincial city that it had been when the papacy was at Avignon, it became once more one of the greatest cities in Christendom, and a repository of the best art of the Renaissance, including St. Peter's Church, the rebuilding of which was now taken in hand. The early humanist popes, Nicholas V and Pius II, were great collectors of manuscripts, and patrons of the new learning and the classical revival. Sixtus IV, Alexander VI, and Julius II were typical Italian despots, builders, patrons of the arts, and above all diplomats and administrators, not hesitating to play the game of Italian city-state politics. All interfered constantly in the secular affairs of the peninsula for the benefit of their families, if not always of the Church. But none of these popes attempted the by now long overdue moral reform of the Church. All needed money for their manuscripts or for their building programs, and for the upkeep of the curia; they did not hesitate to utilize their religious position to obtain ever increasing sums of money, whether due to them from the local churches and clergy or from voluntary donations by believers. This was the heyday of the *indulgence,* a payment sanctioned by the Church, made as a part of penance, and believed by the purchaser to relieve the pain of the departed in purgatory. It was the widespread abuse of the indulgence which provided the occasion for the revolt of Martin Luther that resulted in the Protestant Reformation. The general laxity of the Renaissance papacy in religious matters led in turn to an ever more serious demand for reform voiced by earnest Christians within the Italian Church, and by others outside Italy who proved themselves willing even to leave the Church if it were not reformed. Ultimately the reformers within the Church hierarchy itself regained control of the papacy and brought about the Catholic Counter Reformation. But by that time it was too late to restore the unity of the Church and the Protestants had left, never to return.

THE RENAISSANCE BEYOND THE ALPS

The Humanists. It was not until almost the end of the fifteenth century that the Italian Renaissance began to spread in earnest beyond the Alps. The influence intensified especially after the invasion of Italy by the French king, Charles VIII, who achieved few of the political aims of his invasion, but was greatly impressed by the Italian cultural achievements. He then and there determined to have them imitated in his own country. The Renaissance took various forms in different countries. The literary Renaissance was taken much more seriously in almost all other countries than in Italy. Whereas for the Italians it had been a somewhat dilettante movement confined to a small group, few of whom acquired any profound knowledge of Greek, in Germany, France, and England, the revival of classical learning had more substance, and resulted in the permanent improvement of the educational curriculum and a growing influence of the Greek and Latin classics on new literary work in these countries. Moreover, the increased knowledge of the classical languages led to a serious study of the Bible.

The German Reuchlin, a scholar of Hebrew as well as of Greek, drew attention to the many discrepancies in the existing Latin texts of the Bible, and was drawn into a controversy with the Church which led to the banning of his works. The Frenchman Lefèbre d'Etaples, likewise an earnest student of the scriptures, suffered a similar fate. Desiderius Erasmus, the European humanist par excellence, spent much of his life and energy in producing a new Latin testament and in translating many of the Greek classics. He became the model of the enlightened man, detesting violence and extremism of all kinds, opposed to the Catholic Church because of its appeal to ignorance and superstition and to Luther as an authoritarian, no more enlightened and no less dogmatic than the Church he was engaged in overthrowing. Aided by the extensive correspondence of Erasmus, humanists everywhere in Europe kept in touch with one another, and monarchs engaged in improving education in their countries constantly called upon them for help.

Among other humanists may be mentioned Michel de Montaigne, a French aristocrat who in his *Essays* chose to pillory gently the ignorance he saw around him. He strove to live his life as a free man, self-conscious and aware, but free from prejudice, looking at life and society with eyes unblinkered by the conventions and superstitions of others. With Montaigne we have one of the first true individualists, pursuing an ideal implicit in the Italian Renaissance but more strongly expressed elsewhere in Europe. Another Frenchman, François Rabelais, in his life and writings came more close to the Italian ideal, espousing the right of all men to follow their impulses without imposing upon themselves the artificial restraints of the medieval world, enjoying the good things of life provided so abundantly by nature. Rabelais reserved his choicest satire for the self-imposed discipline of monks who were seldom able to live up to their protestations and yet could not enjoy themselves like men who had been emancipated from the repressions demanded of them by the Church. The Spaniard Cervantes, in his masterpiece *Don Quixote,* poked fun at the long outmoded chivalrous ideas which had persisted in life and literature in his native Spain far beyond the life of the society that had given birth to them. The Englishman Sir Thomas More wrote of a *Utopia* where men could live lives worthy of free human beings; he himself refused to bow to the will of his Renaissance monarch Henry VIII, who commanded him to take an oath acknowledging him as head of the English Reformed Church, and he ended his life on the scaffold. The English poet and dramatist, William Shakespeare, perceiving his characters in their many-dimensional reality as none before him and few, if any, since, studied and described humanity—in this fulfilling another Renaissance ideal brought to fruition beyond the Alps.

The Despots. There were few Renaissance despots beyond the Alps, for political conditions did not favor them. No *condottiere* won a throne by his intrigues and valor, but several monarchs patronized art, architecture, and learning, most notably Francis I of France (1515–1547). Henry VIII of England (1509–1547) was in some respects a despot of the Italian type, especially in his personal tastes. But his penchant for theology was un-Italian, and English conditions and institutions prevented Henry from enjoying the full freedom of action assumed by the despots in the smaller states of the Italian peninsula.

The Artists. Renaissance art beyond the Alps was seldom quite free from Italian influence, and Italians continued to be in much demand as artistic advisers and innovators. Francis I of France persuaded Leonardo da Vinci to spend his last years in his country and brought in many Italian craftsmen to aid him with his building program. Gothic was still in vogue in all the northern countries, and Renaissance buildings of the Italian type had to wait until the neoclassical revival in the eighteenth century. The great French châteaux of the Renaissance period owed much to the Italians in detail, but the general conception remained native French. In the sixteenth century, French architects gave serious attention to how they could make use of Italian innovations while retaining what was best in the French traditional style. In painting the greatest German Renaissance artist was Albrecht Dürer, who had studied for a long time in Italy. The portrait painters of the Low Countries gradually moved away from their predominantly religious interests, especially in the work of such men as Frans Hals. But it was not until the Italians had moved forward into the Baroque, which developed out of the Renaissance impulse, that they had their fullest artistic influence in Europe. Indeed, Baroque, with its sense of tension and its vital and unclassical exuberance, which was more congenial to the northern temperament, had a success beyond Italy greater than in its homeland, in spite of the predominantly Baroque architecture of St. Peter's in Rome; and the greatest Baroque painter of them all was the Dutchman Rembrandt van Rijn, whose masterpieces of human insight on canvas have rarely if even been equalled.

THE AGE OF DISCOVERY AND THE "COMMERCIAL REVOLUTION"

Urban Trade. It has already been suggested that it was the growth of the towns in the later Middle Ages that ushered in the modern age, and that the Italian Renaissance was an urban phenomenon, unthinkable without the cities which provided the wealth and the artists and craftsmen who created the artistic masterpieces of the period. The efforts of the cities to increase their wealth through trade led directly to the other great achievement of the age of the Renaissance—the discovery and colonization of the Americas and the opening of direct seaborne trade with the East.

Portuguese Expansion to the East. We have already noted in the last chapter how the work of Henry the Navigator led to an increased interest in exploration, and the acquirement of the geographical information without which no such exploration could have been undertaken. The Portuguese during the fifteenth century also developed a greatly improved sailing ship, the *caravel,* capable of long voyages through the open sea, a vessel which was imitated in due course by most of the maritime powers. The crucial Portuguese voyage was that of Vasco da Gama to India (1497–1498), accomplished during the reign of Manoel I, which demonstrated clearly that in spite of the dangers and expense, such voyages could bring immense profits to the bold men who undertook them and the kings and merchants who financed them. The voyage was followed by many others, which involved the Portuguese with extensive fighting with the Muslims, in which their superior armaments and tactics were enough to yield them the victory. The Portuguese acquired a number of colonies in Africa, together with enclaves in India, some of which they have retained to the present day. These territories were needed originally as ports of call under metropolitan control, and later as entrepôts for the slave trade. Since the Spaniards had already discovered America before the voyage of Vasco da Gama, but at a time when it was clear that it was only a matter of time before such a voyage was made, both the Spaniards and Portuguese appealed to Pope Alexander VI to arbitrate the boundaries of their intended empires. The pope handed down his decision, later embodied with changes in the Treaty of Tordesillas (1494), under which all territories to the west of a certain line, not held by a Christian prince, should belong to Spain, and all to the east of the line to Portugal. By this treaty Portugal was able to acquire Brazil, which fell to the east of the Line of Demarcation, although it was not officially "discovered" by the Portuguese until 1500 (voyage of Cabral), who was ostensibly occupied in voyaging to India.

For almost a century the Portuguese maintained their monopoly of the sea route to the East. But when in 1580 the crown of Portugal was inherited by Philip II of Spain, and he was able to make good his claim, the Portuguese colonies were neglected. Spanish governors and officials often replaced the Portuguese. They had little interest in the Portuguese possessions and did not seriously attempt to defend the Portuguese monopoly against the Dutch, whose navy and merchant marine were at the time greatly superior to anything likely to be brought against them. By this time it was in any case clear that the Portuguese could not hope to maintain their monopoly much longer. With a small population and few resources they could not afford the losses in manpower resulting from the expeditions and the performance of their military obligations in the East. Already they had been compelled to concede to other nations, especially the Dutch, the right to transport Oriental merchandise from

Lisbon and distribute it throughout Europe. When Philip II, at war with the Dutch, inherited Portugal and forbade them the facilities of the port of Lisbon, he thereby doomed the Portuguese monopoly —since the Dutch were quite strong enough to protect their own merchant marine and take the Oriental goods to their own ports in the north without touching Lisbon. So Lisbon, for nearly a century the great entrepôt for the Eastern trade, lost its importance—as did Portugal herself, who was never again to know the power and prosperity she enjoyed in the sixteenth century.

Spanish Expansion to the West. In 1492 Christopher Columbus, a Genoese, at last persuaded Ferdinand and Isabella of Spain to patronize and finance his proposed voyage westward. In October of that year, a little more than two months after leaving Spain, he sighted land in the Bahamas, continuing on to Cuba and Santo Domingo. This great discovery ushered in an era of exploration and conquest which need not be recounted in detail here. John Cabot, an Italian in English service, discovered Cape Breton Island in North America in 1497. In later voyages he discovered Nova Scotia and explored part of the New England coast. Amerigo Vespucci, another Italian in Spanish service, discovered the mouth of the Amazon in 1499, but it was the Portuguese Cabral who took official possession of Brazil in 1500. Perhaps the greatest achievement of all was the circumnavigation of the world begun by Ferdinand Magellan, a Portuguese in Spanish service, but completed by only one of his ships (1519–1522), the explorer himself having been killed in the Philippine Islands. But the islands themselves became a Spanish possession, and so remained until 1898.

The Spanish, firmly ensconced in what were called the West Indies (from Columbus' belief that he had reached a western route to Asia), proceeded during the sixteenth century to conquer Mexico and part of what is now the United States, and a little later took possession of Peru and in due course almost the whole of South America. In both cases the small but militarily expert Spanish armies destroyed indigenous cultures (the Aztecs of Mexico and the Incas of Peru) which were socially highly developed but in technical respects backward, and in any case no match for Spanish arms. South America was thus subjected to the Spanish crown, which drew great riches from the mines of the continent for well over a century. Since the Spanish monarch was entitled to one fifth of all treasure extracted by his subjects, Spain, whose armies were paid for by this treasure, was able to exercise an influence in Europe out of all proportion to the economic strength of the homeland.

England, France, and the Low Countries were later on the scene than Spain and Portugal, though none were idle, the English in particular seeking a northwest passage to the East, and the French gradually penetrating into Canada, following the voyages of Jacques Cartier from 1534 to 1541. But the exploration and settlements of these late-comers demonstrated their importance after the sixteenth century and will be dealt with in their place in subsequent chapters.

The "Commercial Revolution." The most important result of the sixteenth century explorations was the increase in gold and silver which poured into Europe from the Americas. The new colonies were exploited, often mercilessly, for the benefit of their European conquerors. Christianity was brought to the Spanish territories, and both the monarchy and the Church tried, though seldom very effectively, to dissuade their colonists from the extremes of exploitation. However, on the whole it was the latter who profited, transferring their social system, which was one of the most backward in Europe, to the Americas. But the insistence by the Spanish monarchy on the annual tribute of bullion from their possessions must bear a share of the blame. As an ironical paradox this bullion which found its way into Spain and Portugal damaged their economies and aided the countries that used the bullion more productively.

Naturally every country in Europe suffered from a rise in the price level and the accompanying inflation, but Spain suffered most severely. Spanish industry was neglected, the nobles preferring to pay out their gold and silver for luxuries manufactured elsewhere. Other industrial countries competed among themselves for their share of the Spanish market and improved their efficiency accordingly. The Spanish monarchy preferred to engage in dynastic wars and wars of aggrandizement in Europe. Not only did this policy result in huge unproductive expenditures, but it also tended to lower the royal income, since enemy navies preyed upon Spanish shipping and attempted to break the monopoly of trade with the Spanish colonies. Thus in the seventeenth century when the treasure ships ceased to sail from America to Spain, Spain had little to show for all her efforts. She retained the colonies till the early nineteenth century, but her industry was backward and her agricultural system still unreformed. From being a first-rank power she sank precipitately to the third rank, far surpassed by England, France, Holland, and the other late-comers who entered into much of her inheritance.

The rise of maritime trade and the importation of new products from the Americas, together with the increase of the supply of money in Europe, provided an impetus to commerce which has sometimes, with some exaggeration, been called a "commercial revolution." What actually occurred was a great improvement in the mechanism of the exchange of goods, ranging from the founding of the first stock exchange (in 1531 at Antwerp, the greatest center for the distribution of ocean-borne goods) to the provision of credit institutions, commercial banks, and almost every other instrument known to modern capitalism. But there was no corresponding increase in the production of saleable goods. Such an increase had to wait until a truer revolution known as the Industrial Revolution, to which Chapter XVI is devoted. Although throughout the sixteenth and seventeenth centuries there was some improvement in industrial production it was very slow, since Europe had not yet adjusted its political and social systems to take care of any really significant expansion. Indeed, it was widely thought by economic theorists of the period that total international trade was limited, since the classes able to consume the products of industry were still small and not likely to increase with any rapidity.

The Mercantile System. This perception, which was not altogether untrue of the period, led to the efforts by commercially-minded monarchs who profited by the trade of their nationals, to increase their own trade at the expense of foreigners. Various methods were available to them to achieve their ends, which are collectively known as the "mercantile system." Governments could subsidize home industry, protect it by tariffs, pass navigation laws to aid their own shipping, and even engage in trade wars for the purpose of damaging foreign shipping and forcing trade concessions from a defeated enemy. All monarchs in that age were convinced that that country was richest which possessed the greatest supply of bullion. If a monarch controlled no gold or silver mines of his own, and if piracy on the high seas to steal the products of the mines of foreigners proved insufficient to allay his thirst for the precious metals, he had only one alternative—to win "a favorable balance of trade." This meant that his subjects had to export more than they imported and receive the balance in bullion.

Though it was difficult for all to achieve this desirable goal, all tried. Fortunately the Spanish market was available for a time, and Spain manifestly could not win a favorable balance of trade, however hard she tried. Thereafter trade wars became ever more numerous. During most of the seventeenth century the Dutch were the leading commercial power, in spite of the relative shortage of home industry. They built economical ships for themselves, and even for other European powers, and for a time their navy was the strongest in Europe. But it was certain that in due course the Dutch would be outclassed by their more populous neighbors, the French and the English. They never fully recovered from the destructive wars fought with Louis XIV of France in the late seventeenth century and gradually left the field to the English and French, who competed severely among themselves both in European markets and in the scramble for colonial territories overseas.

By the late seventeenth century the colonies themselves were be-coming important markets and sources of supply, as, with the partial exception of the Spanish, they were not in the sixteenth. This competition, however, will be reserved for a fuller discussion at the end of Chapter XIV.

CHAPTER XII

THE PROTESTANT REFORMATION AND ITS CONSEQUENCES

Enough has been said in earlier chapters to indicate the manner in which the Church in many important respects had become secularized. In the feudal era the Church had become enmeshed in the feudal system. It had played a crucial part in the destruction of that system, but in the process it had become a political power in its own right, using the political instruments of secular rulers to achieve its ends. Its clergy had become worldly; by the beginning of the sixteenth century there was too often little to distinguish a prince of the Church from any lay royal prince save for the claim he still put forward of being able to aid the faithful toward their salvation through the Church he represented. Even during the Avignon period its religious claims were in no way abated; but increasingly, especially during the Great Schism, many earnest Christians ceased to concede them. They were beginning to ask themselves whether a Church which was so worldly and wealthy, as well as politically powerful, could possibly be the heir of those unassuming early Christian communities which had lived in poverty, despised by and despising the world, and of its Founder who had lived and died a poor man and refused to use his power even to save his life.

BACKGROUND OF THE REFORMATION

Religious Dissent. When opposition to the Church had arisen in the twelfth and thirteenth centuries, two reforming religious orders, the Dominicans and the Franciscans, had established themselves and been accorded recognition by the Church. The Dominicans had devoted themselves primarily to preaching and to the instruction of the faithful in the truths of their religion. The Franciscans, inspired by their founder, St. Francis of Assisi, who gave away all his possessions to devote himself to aiding the poor and himself set a positive example of Christian humility, had at first eschewed all learning and contented themselves with simple preaching and healing. But

by the opening of the sixteenth century, both these orders had trav-
eled far from the paths blazed by their founders. The Dominicans
largely staffed the Inquisition and were noted for their learning,
while the leadership of the Franciscan order had also become learned
and took little care of the needs of the poor. Both orders had become
wealthy, and their members performed many of the financial tasks
imposed upon them by the papacy, including the selling of indulgences. This path had led the Franciscan order to split as early as
the fourteenth century, the "Spirituals" wishing to live in poverty
and continuing the ideal of St. Francis. A later offshoot, known as
the Fraticelli, or "little brothers," was still active, but now banned
by the Church and able to do its work only when protected by lay
rulers, who made use of its services when they themselves were quarreling with the Church.

A reforming Dominican, a fiery preacher named Girolamo Savonarola, had caused a short-lived revolution in the city of Florence
at the end of the fifteenth century. The townsmen drove out their
nobles and for a period purified the city. But they soon tired of
Savonarola's puritanical rule, and turned against him when he was
excommunicated by the pope. In 1494 he was put to death with papal
approval. An English theologian and reformer named John Wyclif
had declared as early as the last quarter of the fourteenth century
that the Church should not possess property and held that the sacraments of the Church were of less importance than personal faith.
In his later life he even went so far as to deny the doctrine of
transubstantiation. The Church was unable to touch Wyclif, since
he continued to enjoy the support of the English king; but his
teachings gave rise to a movement known as *Lollardy,* under which
"poor preachers" went through the land calling for reform, and
denying many of the most fundamental teachings of the Church.
The heretical movement spread from England to the Continent
where it had some influence on John Hus in Bohemia. Everywhere
the rulers tried to suppress it with the support of the nobility, and
in England for the first time heresy was made punishable by burning (1401).

John Hus, a Bohemian professor, who taught many of Wyclif's
doctrines at the University of Prague, attacked the Church for its
worldliness, denied the supremacy of the pope, and claimed, as
Martin Luther was to do later, that the sole religious authority for
Christians was the Bible. He also insisted that sinful churchmen

were unfitted to exercise their priestly functions. His teachings fell on such fertile soil in Bohemia that when the Council of Constance convened in 1410 for the purpose of settling the Great Schism, Hus hoped to make his voice heard at the assembly, although he had been excommunicated by the pope as a heretic. The emperor Sigismund who was responsible for calling the Council granted Hus a safe conduct, and he was allowed to address the assembly. When the emperor abrogated his safe conduct and permitted Hus to be burned as a heretic—on the pretext that promises made to heretics were not valid—the Bohemians were outraged. A few years later when their own king Wenceslas IV died, and Sigismund was himself elected, large numbers of reformers refused to recognize him and took to arms. Though "crusades" were proclaimed against them, the emperor found it impossible to subdue them, and the Hussites invaded Germany. But when the Council of Basel offered to come to terms, the more moderate of the Hussites split off from their extremist wing, not being willing to live solely from voluntary donations and far from ready to accept a definitive break with Rome. Ultimately the extremists (called the Taborites) were defeated and forced to go underground. The movement, and the puritanical sect of the Bohemian or Moravian Brethren was never entirely suppressed, continuing its existence until the Reformation. The Moravian Brethren indeed remain as a separate Protestant sect to this day.

The Issue of Indulgences. The Church had therefore briefly triumphed in the fifteenth century, but it was not to survive unscathed the assaults of the German, Martin Luther, in the early sixteenth. By this time political conditions had changed. Whereas in the fifteenth century Bohemian (Czech) nationalism had been too weak to resist the power of the emperor, in the sixteenth century several German princes united against him in the name of religion, and they could not be so easily subdued. The princes were individually weak, and could separately resist neither the domination of the emperor nor the demands of the papacy—unlike the monarchs who could treat with the papacy as equals or superiors and could impose economic sanctions on the pope, as Philip the Fair had done at the beginning of the fourteenth century. Insatiable in their need for money for their building program, the popes imposed ever more severe demands upon the local churches, and this money went by a one way route to Rome, none of it ever returning to Germany. The higher clergy in Germany, appointed by the pope, only too frequently bought their offices, hoping to extract enough from their dioceses both to pay the promised sum and make enough profit for themselves. The only way for them to do this was to obtain voluntary donations from the people over and above their dues. The most lucrative method proved to be the indulgence, or what the common people called "pardons," which could be purchased from itinerant sellers, authorized by the Church. It was widely believed that these "pardons" actually won salvation for the sinners who were already dead but had not yet been received into heaven, and there was a very great demand for them. Even though the Church did not claim that the indulgence saved sinners who were damned, but only relieved from the pains of purgatory those sinners who would in due course be saved after they had been purged, it was obvious to many earnest Christians that the indulgence was taking advantage of the simple faith and ignorant superstition of the purchasers. The indulgence, a part of the sacrament of penance, was supposedly a free gift in partial atonement for sins that has to be accompanied by contrition. But none of this was emphasized by the "pardoner," whose major interest was the collection of money.

MARTIN LUTHER AND THE BEGINNINGS OF THE REFORMATION

Some thinkers were beginning to doubt indeed whether there was a purgatory at all, others whether the Church was needed as an intermediary between men and God, especially such a Church as that of the early sixteenth century; and, as we have seen, for a long time it was held by many that the pope could be overridden by a Council. Martin Luther in the course of his career gradually came to deny all the claims of the Catholic Church, so that it became possible for him and his followers to set up a separate Church of their own, free from all those elements in the Catholic Church of which they disapproved, and which did not have unmistakable scriptural authority. They endeavored to return to the Bible as the sole authority in matters of religion, and the Church that they founded was, in their view, no less efficacious for salvation than the Catholic Church.

The occasion for the break with the Church was provided by the arrival of a new seller of indulgences in Germany. When Luther saw faithful Christians flocking to him, all his personal feelings that he had long harbored against the practice coalesced in his mind, and he nailed up a list of ninety-five theses on the door of the church in Wittenberg. They were addressed to his own archbishop, who had in fact paid 30,000 ducats for his office, most of which he had borrowed. In his theses Luther emphasized, as he put it, that "indulgences confer absolutely no good on souls as regards salvation or holiness, but take away only the outward penalty which used to be canonically imposed." This was a matter of the most absolute conviction to Luther, since in earlier years he had been convinced of his own utter unworthiness and had undergone an inner experience as the result of which he knew that he had been saved by the mercy of God. This was a personal matter between him and God, and no intervention by priest or pope had been necessary, nor had it been the result of his partaking of the sacraments. This personal relationship became the core of all later Lutheran doctrine—Luther coined the remarkable slogan "every man his own priest"—and made it possible for the Lutheran churches to leave the Catholic fold. "Justification," or, in effect salvation, according to Lutheran teachings, comes by faith alone. Because he had believed, God had intervened to save him; and thus it was to be for all men.

The Ninety-five Theses created a sensation, and Luther was called to account by his ecclesiastical superiors, and ultimately by the emperor, Charles V. In the course of disputations with Catholic theologians, he was led ever further into criticism of the Church and almost all its doctrines. In different political circumstances he could not have hoped to escape punishment for heresy; but in the early sixteenth century his words fell upon receptive ears. From the beginning he was protected by his prince, the elector Frederick the Wise of Saxony, who could not be coerced by the emperor unless the latter had been willing to go to war with him. Charles was very far from being an absolute ruler in Germany and constantly needed the support of the German independent princes, especially the four powerful electors who with three church dignitaries decided on the succession to the Empire. So when Luther was summoned by Charles to appear before an imperial diet, Frederick the Wise granted him a safe conduct, which he and the emperor honored, unlike the similar pledge given by the Emperor Sigismund to John Hus a century before.

By this time many of the other German princes had begun to think that there was much merit in Luther's position—not necessarily because it was theologically sound, which few of them would have been qualified to judge—but because separation from Rome would transfer to them the rights held by the pope over the German clergy. A prince who appointed his own bishops and could keep for himself all the revenues that had formerly accrued to the papacy, would have at his disposal a valuable instrument that could be used for securing his political supremacy in his state. Only religious scruples stood in the way of accepting the gift offered by Luther— and the temptation was so great that it is not surprising that so many of them fell into it.

Luther himself gave what support he could to the princes who set up their own churches. An authoritarian himself, he had the greatest respect for secular rulers, and as a German patriot he regarded the papacy as a foreign institution that had no place in his native land. He was in no sense a revolutionary or democrat; and when the peasants used his doctrines as an excuse for overthrowing lay as well as religious authority, he urged the princes and nobles to suppress them. He was as convinced as any pope that his own theological insights were revealed truth. He quarreled violently with Ulrich Zwingli, a Swiss reformer, who began the Reformation in Zurich only a year after the posting of the Ninety-five Theses, and with Erasmus, who in the popular view had "laid the egg that Luther hatched." Both were more liberal in their theological teachings and more flexible in their dogma than Luther. Erasmus preferred to stay in the Catholic Church, in spite of its abuses, than to join Luther, whose extremist views on the powerlessness of the human will were repugnant to him; while Zwingli organized a Reformed Church in a number of Swiss cantons, which retained his theological views even after the reformer himself had been killed in battle. Zwinglianism represented a mean between Lutheran and Calvinistic teachings on the question of transubstantiation and the meaning of the Eucharist. If Luther had accepted Zwingli's *via media,* it is possible that there would have been no need for Calvinism, and the constant fission within Protestantism might have been averted.

THE RELIGIOUS PEACE OF AUGSBURG

The considerations which applied to the small German princedoms did not apply in the same degree to the more powerful monarchies. All the kings were strong enough to obtain certain rights over the Catholic Church in their territories, including some of its revenues. This was especially true of the French (Gallican) Church, which was almost a national church, Francis I having signed a concordat with the papacy in 1516 (Concordat of Bologna), one year before the

Ninety-five Theses. Francis therefore supported Catholicism strongly against the Lutheran reformers. The Spanish monarchy had the Inquisition at its disposal and no wish to abandon the source of power this represented. It also was able to obtain the terms it desired from the papacy. The English king quarreled with the Church as we shall see, because the pope, under pressure from the emperor Charles V, would not grant him a dissolution of his marriage with Charles's aunt, Catherine of Aragon—not because he could not come to terms with the papacy on other matters. Charles V as king of Spain, as well as Holy Roman emperor, was often in a position to control the papacy, and had no desire to abandon his Catholicism; nor was his political position such that he could have headed a German national Church if one had been established. But the German princes could use their national churches to increase their independence, which was always threatened by a powerful emperor as well as by a foreign papacy.

Charles early recognized the danger to his own position presented by Lutheranism. But for a long time he was not free to take much effective action against it. The imperial ban on Luther himself was ineffective as long as he enjoyed princely protection, and Charles was too busy in wars with France, and with the Turks who menaced his dominions in the East to think of forcing the princes to abandon the Reformation. Most of the princes who had accepted Lutheranism (Evangelicanism) joined together in 1531 in a league known as the Schmalkaldic League, to defend their new churches and their right to have them. War erupted in 1546 when Charles was at last free to take decided action, both to destroy the Lutheran Church and to reduce the independence of the German princes. Though he won some victories, the war soon began to spread, involving France on issues that had nothing to do with religion. Charles ultimately agreed in 1555 to the Religious Peace of Augsburg. This peace permitted the evangelical princes and the free German cities that had accepted Protestantism to retain their religion. The name of Protestantism had been widely adopted following a formal protest made by the Lutheran princes at an imperial diet called at Speyer in 1529 against the decrees of Charles opposing the reformed religion.

Under the terms of the peace all Church properties confiscated before 1552 were permitted to be retained; but no concessions were made to Calvinism, which was growing in importance but had not yet captured many of the princes. At the Peace of Westphalia in

1648 the same privilege was extended to Calvinist princes. It may be noted that it was the prince who chose the religion for his people and established it as the official religion of his state; his subjects were not consulted. The only concession permitted to the latter was that if they wished to emigrate to another state where they could be with their coreligionists they were, at least in theory, free to do so. It cannot therefore be seriously contended that the Peace of Augsburg contributed much to religious toleration. It was a victory for the princes, one of many that the German nobles had over the centuries won against monarchs who had tried to unify their country and decrease the endemic tendency toward ever increasing political fission. Wars fought on the pretext of religion were to continue for more than a century, but in all, the religious were inextricably entangled with political issues. This condition is somewhat less true of Calvinism, the other major branch of Protestantism to which we shall turn our attention shortly.

It remains only to be said here that Lutheranism spread during the sixteenth century to the small Scandinavian kingdoms, whose monarchs were influenced by motives similar to those of the German princes. In Sweden, which had been under Danish rule for two centuries, Gustavus Vasa, the Swedish leader of the independence movement, was able to defeat the Danish king, in part because he had adopted the reformed religion, while the Danish monarchy resisted the movement. Later Denmark too turned Protestant, taking Norway with her, as the Swedes took Finland, which was at that time a Swedish province. Lutheranism also made headway among the nobility and middle classes in Poland, and both Lutherans and Calvinists made many converts in Bohemia. Both these countries were forced back into Catholicism by the Counter Reformation, the latter as the result of the Thirty Years' War, to be described in the next chapter.

THE GROWTH OF CALVINISM

The Teachings of John Calvin. John Calvin, a French theologian and lawyer whose *Institutes of the Christian Religion* was the fundamental work on the doctrine that bears his name, was a much more rigorous thinker than Luther, and his religious teachings have always had a profound influence on those branches of Protestantism that stem from him. The basic tenet of Calvinism is the notion of predestination, that each man has been predestined from birth to salvation or damnation and that the human will is powerless to change this destiny. This teaching has always been difficult to refute, since if omniscience and omnipotence are to be ascribed to God, then He must know in advance who is to be saved, and it must be God's power that saves, unless man can be presumed to have a determining influence on God. The problem, in particular, had troubled the fourth-century Catholic bishop and theologian, St. Augustine, bishop of Hippo. St. Thomas Aquinas had been able to reconcile human free will with God's divine knowledge only by making an important distinction between detailed foreknowledge and "knowledge of vision." Luther also had recognized the powerlessness of the human will, but Calvin stressed it as his fundamental tenet. Yet, paradoxically, this did not make for passivity or fatalism; on the contrary, a man's knowledge that he himself was one of the elect company of the saved lent him strength and fortitude to stand up to ungodly oppressors. Moreover the godly behavior of a man on earth demonstrated to all that he was indeed one of the elect—and by the same token the ungodly behavior of a sinner demonstrated that he had not been predestined by God for salvation. Human beings, therefore, on earth as in heaven, were divided as between the godly and the ungodly—and the latter in a Calvinist state had no right to offend the former by their ungodly ways.

Thus Calvinism was authoritarian like Lutheranism. But within Calvinism authority stemmed not from the social or political position a man had inherited. It came from the good works that he did on earth. The leaders of a Calvinist church were the godly, organized as a group of elders, authorized by their position to supervise the morals of the community. When Calvin was called to Geneva to lead the Church in that republican city, he was at first opposed by a rival group and expelled when it came to power. But when wrangling again ensued he was invited back and thereafter controlled the city to his death. Geneva became the headquarters of the entire Calvinist movement, and men and women exiled from other countries for their Calvinist views were welcomed and educated there. Thus for a time there was a real center of the new religion in which missionaries and leaders could be trained, thereafter returning to their native countries after actual experience of the functioning of what was close to a theocracy.

The Spread of Calvinism in Europe. Though converts in Lutheran countries soon were led to accept the reformed religion after it had been imposed upon them by their rulers, it is probably true that far more people were converted to Calvinism as individuals than converted freely to Lutheranism. It is also true that many adopted Calvinism when they were engaged in a struggle against their legal rulers—even though Calvin himself was not an advocate of rebellion. It is clear that if a state should be ruled only by the godly, there is an implication that the true Calvinist should resist an ungodly tyrant—and it is certain that the Calvinists in the Netherlands in revolt against their ruler, Philip II of Spain, regarded themselves as engaged in just such a struggle. William of Orange, the Dutch leader in the rebellion, long remained a Catholic from conviction; but when in due course he converted to Calvinism, already the religion of most of his followers, his position was greatly strengthened and the rebellion took on something of the aspect of a religious war.

In France the Calvinists, known as Huguenots, made many converts among the nobility and the bourgeois, but very few among the peasants. The French so-called wars of religion in the sixteenth century were largely class struggles. At one time probably the majority of the nobles were Protestant, including Henry of Bourbon, the next heir to the throne if the Valois line, as seemed probable, were to die out. The last Valois monarchs were Catholic, but several were at best lukewarm. They were, however, supported by a number of strongly Catholic families, especially the great house of Guise. The opponents of the Guises often adopted the Protestant religion for the very reason that the Guises opposed them. Henry himself, when he became king in 1589, found that his Catholic opposition was so strong, especially in Paris, that he could not hope to keep his crown as a Protestant. He therefore allowed himself to be reconverted to Catholicism ("Paris is worth a mass," he is reputed to have said), but granted a limited toleration to the Protestants, by which the still undefeated Protestants were allowed to keep their strongholds but were forbidden to extend them (Edict of Nantes, 1598). When Louis XIV in 1685 revoked the Edict of Nantes, many of the Huguenots had already been converted. The rest were driven into exile, especially to countries like Holland and Prussia whose rulers were Calvinists.

In Scotland the Calvinist preacher and church organizer, John Knox, won the support of a powerful group of the Lowland nobility in the late sixteenth century, but was not initially strong enough to make his country a fully Calvinist state, with a Calvinist monarch. However, when the Catholic Mary, Queen of Scots, disgraced herself by eloping with the murderer of her former husband, Knox was able to take full advantage of the situation. Mary fled to England, and the council of regency for her infant son James, made Presbyterianism, the Scottish form of Calvinism, the official religion of the country, and the Presbyterian Church the established Church of Scotland, as it remains to this day. Calvinist doctrine was also influential in England, as will be seen, though relatively few among the group of reformers collectively known in England as the Puritans favored the establishment of a church organized along the lines favored by John Calvin. Though the Presbyterians in England and members of more radical religious groups played a part in the dethronement and execution of Charles I, it later became clear that they were in a minority in the country, and the established religion was restored.

Thus the Calvinists at the end of the sixteenth century were in power in the Netherlands, in several of the German states, including Prussia, and in Scotland. They were a strong minority in England and France, and in parts of Hungary. Though the latter was soon reconverted by the combined efforts of the Hapsburg monarchy and the Jesuits, in the other countries Calvinism remained strong afterward, and was soon to enjoy new triumphs when the Pilgrim Fathers took their religion across the Atlantic to North America.

ANGLICANISM

The English Reformation took a peculiar course of its own, relatively little influenced by events on the Continent. Henry VIII in the early sixteenth century took the trouble to issue a rebuttal to the doctrines of Luther, for which he won the title from the pope of Defender of the Faith, a title still curiously retained by the English crown. But when the pope refused to annul his marriage to Catherine of Aragon, Henry appointed as archbishop of Canterbury a married Protestant priest who was willing to pronounce the marriage void and celebrate a new marriage for him with Anne Boleyn, a lady in waiting of the recent queen. Henry then proceeded to dissolve the monasteries and sequestrate their wealth. Although he continued to regard himself as a Catholic to his death, he had repudiated papal leadership of the Church in England and assumed its leadership himself. When he died he saw to it that his young son by his third wife was surrounded by a regency council made up of Protestants. In the short reign of this son (Edward VI, 1547–1553) Protestantism made much headway, and the first Book of Common Prayer was adopted for use in the English Church.

The next ruler, Mary (1553–1558), daughter of Catherine of Aragon, was an ardent Catholic and restored England to the old religion, in the process putting to death several hundred Protestants who were willing to die for the reformed religion. Married to the equally fervent Catholic, Philip II of Spain, she espoused a pro-Spanish policy, strongly resented by all classes in her country, and Catholicism became equated with this policy. After a short reign she was succeeded by the lukewarm Protestant Elizabeth, second daughter of Henry VIII, who recognized that if she were to be acceptable as queen she must renounce both the religion and the policy of her half-sister. Her ministers therefore prepared a religious compromise which granted toleration to Catholics and Calvinists as long as they were not treasonable but made the Reformed Church of England into the established Church of the country with herself as "Supreme Governor." This establishment endured in spite of the efforts of the papacy and the Jesuits to dethrone Elizabeth. After surviving the Puritan interlude in the middle of the seventeenth century, it took on new strength, and it has remained the established religion of England to this day— in theology and ritual the nearest of the Protestant religions to Catholicism, but entirely separated from the Roman Church and acknowledging no authority beyond the limited and constitutional rights granted to the monarch and its own religious dignitaries. Nevertheless, the bishops and archbishops are appointed by the monarch—though now not on his own initiative, but on the advice of the prime minister and his government.

THE CATHOLIC OR COUNTER REFORMATION

The Council of Trent. The Catholic Church was slow in taking active measures to counteract the growth of Protestantism. Leo X, a Medici, who was on the papal throne at the time of the Ninety-five Theses, was a typically Renaissance pope, a patron of art but no reformer. He appears to have had no idea of the depth of the anti-papal feeling in Germany, and supposed that the customary banning of Luther's works and his excommunication would suffice, as such penalties had in the past. Least of all did he recognize that the Church itself was in serious need of reform. His immediate successors attempted a modicum of reform, but their half-hearted measures aroused opposition from within the Church.

Emperor Charles V, however, was very seriously concerned, in view of his political position. He put pressure on the papacy to call a Council to see if any measure of compromise was possible with the Protestants, by which they could be induced to return to the Church. But the popes, remembering the danger such Councils had presented to them in the past, were understandably reluctant to call one, unless it was quite certain that it would be at all times under its own control. At last Pope Paul III agreed to call a Council which was held at Trent, with interruptions, from 1545 to 1563. The Council finally achieved its aim, since during its life the reformers within the Church were ultimately able to oust the Renaissance papacy and make their views prevail. It was found impossible to come to terms with the Protestants, who themselves were invited to the Council but were so obviously outnumbered and impotent and their views so totally unacceptable to the papacy that they quickly abandoned any effort to co-operate.

The reformed papacy took the position that all the theological doctrines which the Church had espoused during the centuries had been inspired by the Holy Spirit and that therefore there could be no change in these. Compromise with the Protestant views on such matters as justification by faith was unthinkable. But it agreed that these doctrines could and should be stated more clearly and made known to all Catholics through the priesthood. It also accepted the need for moral reform within the Church. The Council therefore gave its sanction to a catechism in which all Catholics should be instructed; to an Index of Forbidden Books which might disturb their faith; and to the strengthening of the Inquisition or Holy Office. By the time the reformers had finished their work the Church had become in essentials what it has since remained, an authoritarian religious organization with the pope at its head, the repository of a body of dogma to be accepted by all the faithful, attempting to set an example of morality to Christendom. Priests since the Council of Trent have been appointed by the religious authorities only and instructed in all the basic tenets of their religion. Though the Church did not lose all its political power, it recognized that it could no longer exercise it in the direct manner of the medieval papacy, and, save in the papal states that remained under its control until the nineteenth century, it ceased to act as a secular power. There can be no doubt that the reform greatly strengthened the Church as a religious organization with claims upon the obedience of the faithful, and from the moment the reform was completed Protestantism ceased to grow in Europe.

The Society of Jesus and the Counter Reformation. There remained the question of how to restore the countries that had been lost to the Church. It is this aspect of the work of the Catholic Reformation that gave it the name in the Protestant countries of the Counter Reformation. Here the Church was greatly aided by the foundation of a new order, the Society of Jesus, organized on quasi-military lines by St. Ignatius of Loyola, a former Spanish soldier. The Jesuits, as they were called, took a vow of absolute obedience to their General, and the latter on behalf of the order took a similar vow to the papacy. The Jesuits were highly trained, and went through a period of severe discipline before they were admitted to the order. Many of them learned, and wholly dedicated to their work, they quickly founded schools which for a long time were the best in Europe, and undertook missionary work not only among the Protestants but in pagan lands throughout the world. Their technique was to go above all to the influential in each country and if possible to achieve an ascendancy over the consciences of rulers and thus inspire them to reconvert their countries to Catholicism. Though Jesuits soon became unpopular even in Catholic lands, since they were greatly favored by the papacy and constituted its militant arm, participating in the internal affairs of the Christian nations, sometimes against local rulers and clergy, the movement was on the whole immensely successful; and all the countries whose rulers did not protect the Protestants were returned to the Catholic fold. Poland and Hungary, many parts of south Germany, the southern section of the Low Countries and other scattered Protestant areas throughout Europe became fully Catholic once more, most of them strongly influenced by the Jesuits. The movement totally failed in England, where the Jesuits were regarded as treasonable, and the last Catholic monarch (James II) was finally deposed by the people in 1689. Most of the north German states were also impervious to Jesuit blandishments, as was Scandinavia. But if the majority of the inhabitants of Europe outside Russia remain Catholic today, it is largely the result of the work of the reformed papacy and the Jesuits in the sixteenth and seventeenth centuries.

The restoration of Catholicism, however, was by no means achieved without bloodshed, and there were prolonged wars in various parts of Europe. But since these wars were waged at all times at least as much for political as for religious ends, they will be dealt with in the next chapter as part of the process of the consolidation of national states.

CHAPTER XIII

THE EUROPEAN STATE SYSTEM TO THE BEGINNING OF THE EIGHTEENTH CENTURY

In the centuries which comprise the early modern age the major topic for consideration is the development of the state system and the governmental structures under which the modern European states attained their nationhood. In Germany and Italy national states were not brought into being until the nineteenth century, and even then only at the cost of several wars. But France, England, Spain, and European Russia were already national states by the early part of the eighteenth century, with substantially their present boundaries—and Prussia, which was to swallow up the rest of Germany in the nineteenth century, was already a strong state and had just become a kingdom. The greatest obstacle to German unity was the existence of the Holy Roman Empire under the Hapsburg family, a collateral branch of which ruled Spain for the whole of the period under discussion. This empire was not destroyed until 1806. But it became clear during the period that it would never again be permitted by the other European powers to rule as much of Europe as it did under Charles V. Although it enjoyed periods of successful expansion and for brief periods ruled some of the other German states, the trend throughout these centuries was toward contraction. The Peace of Westphalia in 1648 and the Peace of Utrecht in 1713 both marked important stages in this process. When the wars of Napoleon dealt the Empire its knock-out blow all that remained to the emperor, who still kept his imperial title, was Hungary and a number of Slavic territories in addition to his homeland of Austria. All the rest of German-speaking Europe had been lost to him.

We shall in this chapter, therefore, first consider the Holy Roman Empire and continue with a discussion of the other empires: the dominions of the Spanish Hapsburg monarchs, and the Ottoman Empire, which was still expanding into Europe during the early sixteenth century, but thereafter suffered a slow decline, culminating in the nineteenth century, at the end of which all that remained to it in Europe was a small hinterland around the capital city of Constantinople.

THE HOLY ROMAN EMPIRE OF THE HAPSBURGS

The Era of Charles V. The emperor Charles V, as has been already noted, inherited not only the Hapsburg dominions in Central and Eastern Europe but also the various kingdoms of the Iberian Peninsula with the exception of Portugal, and the commercially important Low Countries, including both the Belgium and Holland of today. It was too much for one monarch to rule effectively, and Charles grew immensely weary of the task of trying to maintain his rule. Ultimately, in 1556, he abdicated, having already invested his brother Ferdinand with the rule of his eastern possessions and his son Philip with his western possessions, including the Spanish overseas colonies and the Low Countries. He died a few years later, worn out and broken by a lifetime of almost constant warfare.

The western territories of the Empire gave Charles relatively little trouble. He experienced his greatest griefs in the territories where foreign powers, especially France, disputed his rulership, and in his own German lands whose princes desired the Empire to be simply a nominal one, while they enjoyed actual independence. Francis I (1515–1547) fought Charles for much of his reign over disputed possessions in Italy; and though France had the worst of most of the warfare, the French king even being taken prisoner at one time by his enemy (Battle of Pavia, 1525) and forced to sign a humiliating peace before he was permitted to return to his country, she continued to support every effort made by any other groups to reduce the imperial power. She even joined the Lutherans of the Schmalkaldic League, though the French monarchy was as Catholic as Charles himself. This policy of diminishing the Hapsburg power was a constant in French policy for the whole of the period considered in this chapter and was entirely unaffected by religious considerations. The French were even allied with the Muslim Turks for much of the period. What was at issue was the so-called "balance of power," a concept that was just beginning to receive definition in Europe.

When Charles died and his dominions were divided, the rest

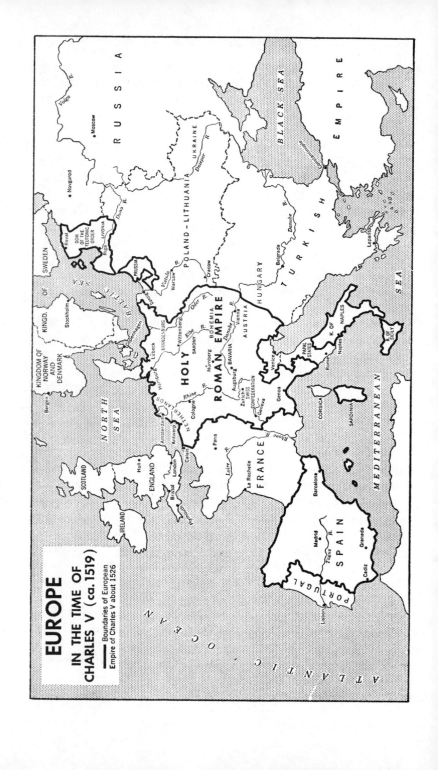

EUROPE
IN THE TIME OF
CHARLES V (ca. 1519)

Boundaries of European
Empire of Charles V about 1526

of Europe breathed more easily, even though both the territories of Ferdinand and those of Philip II of Spain were more extensive than those of any other European country. Ferdinand I, who succeeded his brother as emperor, had his hands full for much of his reign with the Turks. Elected king of Hungary, he inherited the war with the Turks being waged by the Hungarians, but was compelled to leave most of the country in Turkish hands in spite of numerous campaigns. The reigns of the other emperors during the century were undistinguished and Emperor Mathias (1612-1619), who was childless, was unable to secure the imperial throne for his nominee without a dispute. By this time the Counter Reformation was in full swing, and the Protestant German princes, and the Protestant nobles and people of Bohemia were of no mind to allow Mathias' choice, his cousin Ferdinand of Styria, to take the throne. Ferdinand was a determined Catholic, educated by the Jesuits; and it was understood that he would undertake the task of using all the powers of the Empire to force a return to Catholicism. Indeed in 1618, even before the death of Mathias, Ferdinand made himself so unpopular in the country that the Bohemians undertook direct action against his commissioners, thereby initiating the Thirty Years' War.

The Thirty Years' War. It has already been noted that the emperor was elected to his position by an electorate of seven, three Catholic archbishops and four laymen. In 1619 three of the laymen were Protestants (two Calvinists, namely the count palatine of the Rhine and the margrave of Brandenburg, and the duke of Saxony, who was a Lutheran). The seventh elector was the king of Bohemia, who was an elected monarch, chosen by the Bohemian estates. Emperor Mathias had been king of Bohemia himself but his successor would have to be chosen as usual by the estates; and the latter, being largely composed of Protestants, did not wish to sign their death warrants by choosing Ferdinand of Styria. The situation was further complicated in that the electors were no longer the most powerful princes of Germany—the duke of Bavaria, a strong Catholic, for example, having a far more secure position and a better army than the count palatine.

The Bohemians in this crisis looked around for someone else to make king who would vote with the Protestant electors. But they knew that Ferdinand would attempt to crush any alternative candidate and that he would probably succeed in doing so, as he had the power of his ancestral Hapsburg lands behind him. The Protestants in Germany could not decide to unite against the Hapsburg and his probable Bavarian ally, most of them not believing that Ferdinand as emperor would present any special danger to themselves. The Bohemians were left therefore with no recourse but to choose Ferdinand as their king. Once they had done so, Ferdinand began to interfere in Bohemia and attempted to abrogate the long-cherished political and religious liberties of the Bohemians. Before Ferdinand had yet added his vote to those of the Catholic archbishop electors to make himself emperor, the Bohemians took action and deposed him, offering the crown to Frederick, the count palatine (a Calvinist married to the daughter of the king of England), the only German prince of substance who could be induced to accept it. Ferdinand naturally refused to allow himself to be deposed and cast his vote as Bohemian king in the imperial election, thus becoming emperor in the eyes of all Catholics, if not of the Protestant electors and the Bohemians.

Thus fortified, Ferdinand II turned on the Bohemians and Frederick, and with the aid of the duke of Bavaria defeated them decisively in the Battle of the White Mountain (1620). Bohemia was incorporated into the Hapsburg dominions, and the two allies then fought Frederick in his own territories and expelled him. The duke of Bavaria was rewarded with Frederick's electoral vote. The English sent a small expeditionary force which met with little success; other German states, at last aroused to the danger that Ferdinand would next turn his attention to them and recover their states for Catholicism, decided to fight, with the aid of whatever forces they could muster.

Thus began the destructive Thirty Years' War that raged through Germany until it was concluded at the Peace of Westphalia in 1648. Various Protestant princes intervened, first Christian IV of Denmark, who was defeated by Count Wallenstein, an inspired leader of mercenaries in the employ of Ferdinand. Then the great Swedish king, Gustavus Adolphus, known as the Lion of the North, invaded Germany and won battle after battle until he was killed while his soldiers were winning one of his greatest victories.

Meanwhile the Spanish Hapsburgs had come to the aid of their family in Austria, bringing the French into the war, since they could not tolerate the disturbance of the balance of power involved in a union between the Hapsburgs. Cardinal Richelieu, the architect of French foreign policy, had no religious objections to aiding the Protestant cause in the interests of France. First he subsidized the Swedes and other allies, and finally brought France into the war. Though the French generals lacked military experience and lost several battles, in the end their intervention and their continued support of the Swedes decided the issue. The Hapsburg emperor was defeated and had to submit to the loss of all imperial authority in Germany. Eleven years later, in 1659, the war between the French and the Spaniards was brought to an end by the Treaty of the Pyrenees.

The loser in the Thirty Years' War was not only the emperor but the entire German nation. For thirty years German territory had been fought over by ruthless mercenaries under generals who, even on the rare occasions when they wished to do so, could not prevent the pillage of prosperous cities and the devastation of the countryside. Few areas of Germany had escaped the armies, and the last phase of the war especially had been appallingly destructive. Even Brandenburg-Prussia, which had been neutral through most of the war, had had its territories fought over by the mercenary armies, which it was unable to expel. The Prussian elector, however, was shrewd enough to enter the Thirty Years' War at a time when French intervention was on the point of bringing it to an end. Since he chose the victorious side, he made some gains at the Peace of Westphalia.

France, however, was the chief beneficiary of the war, no significant part of which had been fought on French soil. She gained territory and prestige at a relatively low human cost, and she humbled both her Hapsburg enemies. She built up a strong army with experienced generals. Her efforts made possible the long ascendancy of the French during the seventeenth and eighteenth centuries, and laid the groundwork for the unique position of Louis XIV in the second half of the seventeenth century, when he was incomparably the most powerful single ruler of Europe.

The Decline of the Empire in the Late Seventeenth Century. The only major achievement of the Empire during the rest of the period covered by this chapter was the recovery of that part of Hungary that had been under Turkish control. Although at one period (1683) the Turks once more laid siege to Vienna, the Ottoman Empire was unable to press the assault successfully, and the city was relieved by an army of Germans and Poles under the

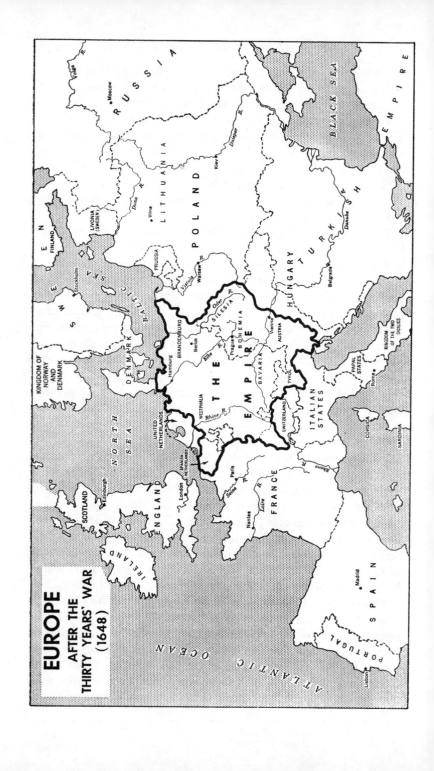

EUROPE
AFTER THE
THIRTY YEARS' WAR
(1648)

native Polish king, John Sobieski. The Austrians then invaded Turkey and compelled the Turks to relinquish Hungary by the Treaty of Karlowitz in 1699. Thereafter the throne of Hungary became hereditary within the Hapsburg family, and the countries were not divided again until the First World War.

THE SPANISH HAPSBURG MONARCHY

The Revolt of the Netherlands. When Charles handed over his western possessions to his son who became Philip II of Spain, it was a rich heritage indeed, composing not only the homeland of Spain itself but the Spanish colonies in the New World and the Low Countries, which had been inherited by Charles V from his grandmother, who had been the daughter of the last duke of Burgundy and thus brought the Burgundian territories to her husband, the emperor Maximilian. Philip also inherited certain lands in Italy that belonged to the Aragonese crown.

With the aid of troops paid for by American treasure Philip played an important part in European affairs, intervening everywhere to assist the Counter Reformation and the fortunes of his Hapsburg family, two causes not always easily to be distinguished from one another. His policies led to the revolt of the Netherlands, which were, however, not strong enough to achieve complete independence during Philip's reign, and to a serious naval defeat at the hands of the English. Nevertheless, Spain was still rich and powerful at the death of Philip II, who had in the meantime inherited the crown of Portugal, and it was not until the seventeenth century that she entered into her long political decline, a decline that was tempered by magnificent cultural achievements, in quality and quantity almost the equal of any in Europe during that century.

The revolt of the Netherlands was the direct result of Philip's religious policies. Even though the people were severely taxed to pay for Philip's wars that were little of their concern and usually contrary to their interests, it is doubtful if there would have been a revolt if Philip had not undertaken to suppress Protestantism, which had taken a strong hold in the northern Netherlands—first Lutheranism and then, much more thoroughly, the newer doctrines of Calvin. In particular, there was a constant fear in the country that Philip would introduce his dread Spanish Inquisition, which was claiming its thousands of martyrs in Spain itself. The Netherlanders also provoked Philip directly by destroying the images in many Catholic churches, a practice which their own leaders tried with indifferent success to prevent.

In 1567 Philip decided to take strong measures, and he sent his most famous soldier, the duke of Alva, to restore the province to order. Alva executed some of the more illustrious leaders of the country who fell into his hands, forcing the rest into exile; whereupon Alva confiscated their lands. This had the effect of driving them to a revolt which they had in fact not originated, and brought about a death struggle with Spain, requiring ever more and more repressive measures. When the unpaid Spanish soldiery sacked the major towns of the country, including Antwerp and other cities in the Catholic south (1576), the entire Spanish Netherlands agreed to join the revolt. The Netherlanders could win few victories by land against the Spanish troops, but they caused great damage to the Spanish naval forces and even captured some treasure ships. Not until 1578 did Philip recognize that more than repression was necessary and that a measure of statesmanship was required. A new governor, Alexander Farnese, duke of Parma, arrived in the country in 1578 and by a mixture of diplomacy and force detached the southern Catholic provinces from the by now solidly Calvinist north. The northern provinces proclaimed their independence in 1581 under the hereditary rule of William of Orange, as stadtholder.

Thereafter, though William was murdered in 1584, the Spaniards were unable to make much headway in what became the Republic of the United Provinces. The southern areas, however, were restored to their obedience and remained in Spanish hands until they passed to the Austrian Hapsburgs in 1713 at the Peace of Utrecht. The United Provinces went on to become for a period the greatest maritime nation in Europe, as has already been noted in Chapter XI; and their independence was recognized in 1648 at the Peace of Westphalia.

The Spanish Armada. During much of the war with the Netherlands, the English gave assistance to the Dutch, since they were themselves embroiled with Philip, in part because of his determination to do all he could to dethrone Queen Elizabeth and impose the Counter Reformation on England and in part because of trade rivalry. The English constantly tried to break the Spanish monopoly of Latin-American trade, and English "gentlemen-adventurers" patriotically and profitably preyed on Spanish shipping in the Indies.

Sir Francis Drake even went so far as to raid Cadiz, the greatest Spanish port and destroyed much of the Spanish fleet at anchor there (1587). Philip therefore decided to teach the English a lesson. He outfitted the famous Spanish Armada and devised a plan for conquering England with the aid of the duke of Parma who was to assist with the invasion from the Netherlands. But the plans miscarried, in large part owing to Philip's insistence in appointing an unwilling commander to take charge of the expedition, and in part owing to his refusal to permit this commander any measure of flexibility in his tactics. When a storm arose in the English Channel and the lighter but smaller English fleet began to harass the great Spanish galleys, the Armada was scattered, and none of the plans could be carried out as arranged in advance. The majority of the ships were lost in further storms off the coast of Scotland. Philip, of course, was not overwhelmed by such a defeat, nor did he lack resources to protect his treasure ships in spite of it. But it was a severe blow to his prestige, and he attempted nothing on such a scale again. The Spanish defeat was of more consequence to the victorious English than to the Spaniards, as it confirmed to them that their future lay on the seas, and it encouraged them to build their maritime supremacy, which was to stand them in such good stead in later centuries.

Seventeenth-Century Decline. After the death of Philip II in 1598, Spain entered a long era of decline. Though the Spanish soldiery still won great victories in Europe during the Thirty Years' War, the homeland sank into economic stagnation. The last of the Moorish descendants, the Moriscos, were expelled in 1609, damaging the economy in which they had played such a large part. Spain lost too many people by emigration to the colonies, as well as by war. She became a country of large estates, living by wool growing, the estates worked by poverty-stricken peasants held fast in the thrall of the Church and the nobility. The Treaty of the Pyrenees (1659), which put an end to Spanish participation in the Thirty Years' War, marked the end of major Spanish military adventures on the Continent, though she played an undistinguished part in the wars of Louis XIV. Toward the end of the seventeenth century, when it was clear that the last Hapsburg monarch, Charles II, would have no heir, the other European powers quarreled among themselves as to who should succeed to the Spanish inheritance, which included the still valuable colonial possessions. The succession of a Bourbon chosen by Charles precipitated the great War of the Spanish Succession, in which all the European powers played their part. Since this war was largely an outcome of the policy of Louis XIV, it will be dealt with in more detail under France.

THE OTTOMAN EMPIRE

Relations with Venice. A few words are necessary to describe the role of the Ottoman Empire in European affairs during the period. This empire, inheriting many of the Byzantine interests, found itself in almost constant conflict with Venice, which by this time had been hard hit by the development of the new Atlantic trade. Though Venice tried to come to terms with the Turks, she was by this time so much less powerful in the eastern Mediterranean that any agreements were usually made in favor of the Turks. In 1570 the Turks captured the most important of the Venetian possessions in this area, the island of Cyprus; and the ancient republic decided to make a great effort. Allied with the Spaniards, the Venetians won the battle of Lepanto (1571) in which a large Turkish fleet was routed by Don John of Austria, natural son of Philip II. But even this great victory was useless. The Venetians and Spaniards quarreled, and only two years later the former were compelled to give up Cyprus. The Turks had built a new fleet which the Venetians, for all their still considerable wealth, were unable to match. In the middle of the seventeenth century the Venetians were driven out of Crete; but when the Turks extended themselves in the late seventeenth century siege of Vienna, the Venetians joined the Austrians and their allies and attacked Turkey through Greece, even taking Athens. It was during the Venetian occupation that the Parthenon was irretrievably damaged through the explosion of ammunition stored in the ancient temple. Though the Turks conceded the Peloponnesus (Morea) to Venice for a period, they recovered it twenty years later.

Influence on Europe. We have already noted the two Turkish sieges of Vienna and the long occupation of most of Hungary. Nothing more therefore need be said here of these. The Ottoman Empire, however, was still a factor to be considered in European affairs, as it was to prove again in the nineteenth century when the various Balkan states either recovered their independence or fell to the Austrian Empire. In the sixteenth and seventeenth centuries the Turks were regarded as an ever present infidel menace. It was never known when they might start to expand into Europe. All wars against them were regarded by the papacy as crusades, and many calls to arms were summoned against the Turks and officially proclaimed as crusades. But few took part in them because they were crusades. Turkey was a factor that could not be dismissed in all considerations of the European balance of power—and Christian monarchs, especially the French, did not hesitate to ally themselves with the Turks to redress the balance in their favor. The concept of a unified Christendom had finally given place to a concept of national and dynastic interests—and not all the clarion calls of the heirs of the medieval papacy could change the reality.

THE ASCENDANCY OF FRANCE

Richelieu and Mazarin. When Henry IV, the first Bourbon monarch, came to the French throne in 1589, he began the rule of a dynasty which was to make France into the greatest single power in Europe. Faced with the heritage of the long civil wars, he and his finance minister, the duke of Sully, set to work at once to try to restore the prosperity of their country. Sully's careful policy quickly began to show results; and when Henry was murdered by a Catholic fanatic who resented his toleration of the French Huguenots, France had already largely recovered from the wars. Nevertheless the nobles were not finished, even though the bourgeois Huguenots accepted the Bourbon regime with relief. Louis XIII was a minor when he came to the throne in 1610, and the nobles and the regent, the queen mother Marie de Médicis, struggled for control of the monarch. In four years the financial surplus left in the treasury by the frugal Sully had been dissipated, and Marie and her foreign favorites were compelled to call the States-General, for the last time, as it happened, until the eve of the French Revolution. No funds were voted, however, and the monarchy struggled on for a few more years, hardly any more powerful or competent than in the sixteenth century. But this time a leader emerged who was able to exclude both Queen Marie and the nobility from power, and for the rest of the reign of Louis XIII was the virtual ruler of France. This was Cardinal Armand de Richelieu.

The source of Richelieu's power was the monarchy, which in competent hands possessed enough financial resources and military might—a legacy of the work of Charles VII and Louis XI in the later Middle Ages—to enforce its will. Louis gave his full backing to his minister for the whole of his reign and thus laid the foundation for the virtual absolutism of Louis XIV. We have already noted the successful intervention of Richelieu in the Thirty Years' War, which brought France new gains in prestige and territory. Richelieu also fought a few brief campaigns with the Huguenots to wrest from them the fortresses and private arms allowed them by the Edict of Nantes, though he permitted them the exercise of their religion. He had a more difficult task to quell the nobles, who made frequent efforts to upset his regime. But here too he was successful, compelling the recalcitrant to pull down their castles, refrain from enrolling private armies, and submit to the monarchy. Lastly, Richelieu, in the interests of the royal revenues, restored a system already begun by Henry IV under which a number of royal offices, called *intendants,* were delegated authority to supervise all the affairs of the provinces, including the collection of direct taxes. This system was greatly resented by the local nobility and local magistrates, who had been accustomed to do virtually as they wished in their areas. But it persisted throughout the remainder of the *ancien régime,* and was the most important means used by the king to enforce his authority in the provinces.

When Louis XIII and Richelieu died within a few months of each other, once more leaving a minor to inherit the throne, the nobles made yet two more attempts to restrain the absolutism of the monarch. Richelieu's hand-picked successor, an Italian cardinal named Mazarin, ruled the young Louis XIV, again through the queen mother and regent, Anne of Austria. Hardly less able than Richelieu himself, and just as successful in his direction of the last phase of the Thirty Years' War, Mazarin was more vulnerable to opposition, since he was both a foreigner and a nepotist, filling high French offices with his relatives and amassing (unlike Richelieu) a vast personal fortune. The opposition to Mazarin was twofold. On the one hand the nobles sought, as usual, their personal and family advantage, and on principle objected to a strong monarchy. On the other hand, the *parlements,* legal bodies made up of the "nobility of the robe," men who purchased or inherited their offices and regarded themselves as the protectors of the traditional rights of French citizens, objected to the growth of royal absolutism and wished to have the rights of their class and the general citizenry respected. The Parlement of Paris, the chief of these courts, which had the traditional task of registering royal decrees was particularly disgruntled by the actions of the new monarchy. The "nobility of the sword" and the "nobility of the robe" were thus fortuitously in agreement with one another during the rule of Mazarin. But their objectives were entirely different. Moreover the parlements had no real power at their disposal and knew it. They could refuse to register the king's decrees, but the king was in a position to compel them to do so if he summoned them to a special session for the purpose. They could encourage and propagandize, but they were dependent in the last resort on the swords of the feudal lords. Moreover, the last thing that they desired was the restoration of feudal anarchy.

Nevertheless, during the regime of Mazarin outbreaks occurred supported at one time by the feudal nobility and at another time by the parlements. But the efforts were unco-ordinated. Though Mazarin with the young king was driven from Paris, both were soon able to return when the veteran general Turenne decided to support the monarchy rather than the nobles, whose leader was openly in treasonable alliance with Spain. Thus the rebellions, known as the *Frondes,* collapsed with little bloodshed; and Louis XIV was given a salutary lesson on the real impotence of his potential opposition, from which lesson he evidently drew considerable profit.

The Absolutism of Louis XIV. When Mazarin died in 1661 Louis XIV declared himself ready to rule; and for the next forty-four years he did in fact rule as an absolute monarch, without any opposition of substance. He even went so far as to announce that he himself *was* the state, and he always acted as if there was no need to consult anyone not of his own choosing. In fact he maintained the traditional privileges of his subjects as long as they did not conflict with his autocratic practices, and in no sense was his rule a tyranny. He was a legitimate monarch, endowed with his powers by the divine right of inheritance. In the elaborate ceremonial observed in his new Baroque palace of Versailles, Louis took care to emphasize the extraordinarily exalted position of the king, far above all his subjects. This was the great Classical Age of France, marked especially by the growth of drama (Corneille, Racine, Molière), literary criticism (Boileau), polite letters (Mme. de Sévigné), and other literary modes, and by a disciplined Baroque art (Poussin, Gellée). The monarch subsidized most of the artists and encouraged them to come to his court at Versailles, which was the model for all Europe. All these demonstrations of royal power and munificence were paid for by the unremitting labors of Louis' finance minister, Jean-Baptiste

Colbert, as were the numerous wars of aggrandizement fought by the man whom it was natural for all Europe to call "le grand monarque."

The Wars of Louis XIV. The wars themselves were fought mainly in the dynastic interests of the Bourbon house, although in the process France was able to extend her boundaries significantly, especially at the expense of the Holy Roman Empire, which still at the beginning of Louis' reign possessed several important eastern sectors of the country, part of the former duchy of Burgundy. Alsace was added to France during the reign, though Lorraine remained in imperial hands until 1766. The boundary with the Spanish Netherlands to the north was also ill-defined and many important cities now in France were part of the Netherlands at the beginning of the reign of Louis. Each time that Louis fought, a coalition was raised against him; even when his enemies were not directly threatened, they felt it necessary in the interests of the balance of power to prevent France from becoming too strong. By far the most persistent enemy of Louis was the Dutch leader, William of Orange, who later became king of England. The Dutch were always threatened by Louis and his wars; being so much weaker than the French, they had to find allies wherever they could, and poured out their riches for the purpose. They succeeded in maintaining their independence throughout the reign, but in the course of the period they lost ground to England, which inherited the Dutch maritime supremacy in the eighteenth century.

When William of Orange became king of England and Louis extended his protection to the Stuart family, England entered the coalition against Louis until the powers enjoyed a short breathing space in 1697. But the greatest of all the wars in that epoch, the almost Europe-wide War of the Spanish Succession, was still to come. Charles II of Spain, as noted earlier, was hard put to it to decide on who should inherit his crown and possessions. It was uncertain which of three princes was entitled to the throne by strict heredity. One was an Austrian Hapsburg, one a French Bourbon, and one a German princeling. Before Charles had actually given up the ghost, the European powers decided on a partition of the Spanish domains, to which Charles himself was not a party. When he heard of it he decided to leave everything to the least dangerous candidate, the German prince, who was only seven years old. Even so, the latter died the next year; whereupon the powers again decided upon a partition, to which Charles riposted by choosing the French candidate, the grandson of Louis XIV, in the hope of maintaining the Spanish empire intact. A few months later he finally died.

England and Holland were unalterably opposed to the French succession, as was naturally the emperor, who had hoped his own younger son would succeed. A Grand Alliance was organized against the aging Louis, who himself had no allies except the new

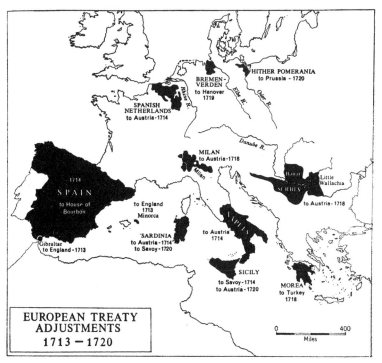

EUROPEAN TREATY
ADJUSTMENTS
1713 — 1720

Map by Vincent Kotschar. From Stewart C. Easton, *The Heritage of the Past; From the Earliest Times to 1715* (New York: Holt, Rinehart & Winston, 1957). By permission of the publisher.

king of Spain, who was unable to lend him much aid, and a few German and Italian princes. Nevertheless the war was not one-sided, though the greatest victories fell to the English duke of Marlborough and Prince Eugene of Savoy, the imperial general. France's resources were so severely strained that Louis had to make a personal appeal for funds and recruits in the sacred name of patriotism. But in the end the political tide turned. The Austrian candidate for the Spanish throne suddenly fell heir to the imperial possessions also—which would have altered the balance of power in Austrian favor if he had also won the Spanish throne. Thereafter a compromise was quickly reached. Philip of Bourbon was confirmed as king of Spain provided he renounced all claims to the French throne; the emperor was granted the former Spanish Netherlands. The Peace of Utrecht which closed the war in 1713 and a treaty between France and the emperor the following year, dotted the *i*'s and crossed the *t*'s of this arrangement, giving incidental recognition to the right of the elector of Prussia to be called king, and to the Protestant succession in England, by which France accepted the Hanoverian dynasty and ceased to put forward the claims of the Stuart pretenders.

By the end of the reign of Louis XIV, France's European position had been little impaired, though the revocation of the Edict of Nantes in 1685 which forced the remaining Huguenots into exile, severely damaged her economy. It was not until late in the eighteenth century that the *ancien régime* of France became clearly an anachronism, and no longer able to meet the problems the country had to face. But a discussion of this phase of French history will be left to the next chapter.

ENGLAND—THE TUDOR MONARCHY AND THE PURITAN REVOLUTION

Tudor "Absolutism." When Henry VII ascended the throne of England in 1485, his position was not unlike that of the first French Bourbon a century later. His country had just emerged from a long civil war over the succession, fortunately as yet uncomplicated by religious issues. But there was one outstanding difference between England and France. England possessed in Parliament an institution through which grievances against the monarchy could be expressed; and both nobles and middle classes could be heard and make their influence felt. Parliament could be mobilized by an intelligent monarch to support royal policy and thus share in the responsibility for it; or it could organize opposition to a king who disregarded it or offended it. The essential difference between the Tudor and the Stuart monarchies lies in their respective methods in handling Parliament. The Tudor monarchs were in effect absolute, since they handled Parliament in such a manner as to keep it reasonably content, whereas the early Stuarts clashed head on with it to their undoing. When Charles I was beheaded by the authority of a purged and extremist Parliament, there followed a period of minority rule bolstered by the army. Charles II, restored to the throne in 1660, trod warily with Parliament and survived; his successor James II was compelled to abdicate. Thereafter the English monarchy gradually gave way to constitutional government in which the king became a revered figurehead, thus pointing the way for all monarchs in Europe who hoped to retain their positions in an increasingly democratic age. England thus blazed the path quite unwittingly toward modern Western democracy; and the process by which this was achieved therefore deserves somewhat more than cursory attention.

Henry VII (1485–1509) proved to be a shrewd monarch, careful in his financial expenditure and willing to take effective action without hesitation against any efforts to revive the feudal wars. As soon as rebellion showed its head, he quickly suppressed it with the aid of loyal troops, executed its leaders, and confiscated their property. Lesser rebels were heavily fined, incidentally improving the royal finances. Private armies were forbidden by act of Parliament. Parliamentary sanction was also requested and granted for the setting up of a new royal court, empowered to try certain kinds of offenses. This court, later to become the notorious Star Chamber and an instrument of royal tyranny, was composed of royal nominees. It used the Continental procedures inherited from Roman law, and, like the Inquisition, it used torture to compel a witness to testify against himself. The court, however, in the sixteenth century filled a need in English law, since it was becoming impossible to obtain convictions in local courts against influential persons who would either bribe or intimidate local juries.

Henry VIII (1509–1547) was a typical Renaissance monarch, often capricious and tyrannical but with a shrewd sense of the limits of his power and of the use that could be made of his inherited institutions. We have already noted in the last chapter how he nationalized the English Church. He was careful throughout the whole process to utilize his Parliament, sending it instructions through his chancellor as to what laws to pass, always with the implicit threat of unpleasant sanctions which the king was both powerful and ruthless enough to impose. Parliament established an Anglican Church with Henry as head, it dutifully dissolved the monasteries at Henry's behest, and it gave him whatever subsidies he requested for his royal purposes.

But in spite of his six marriages Henry had only three children, one by each of his first three wives. The youngest, because he was the only boy, succeeded to the throne as Edward VI without difficulty and without rebellion, since he was clearly legitimate in view of the previous deaths of Henry's first two wives. During his short reign the members of his regency council quarreled constantly among themselves, the senior, Lord Protector Somerset, the king's uncle, being sent to the scaffold by his colleagues when his policies ceased to be acceptable to them. Edward himself never succeeded in asserting himself and shortly before he died he even agreed to bequeath his throne to Lady Jane Grey, a learned young lady who had only the remotest of hereditary right to it. But she was married to the son of the leader of the king's council, the duke of Northumberland. Northumberland's attempted coup collapsed at once after Edward's death, and Mary Tudor, the eldest daughter of Henry VIII was able to secure her position without great difficulty.

The problem of the succession was, indeed, at this time a serious one. The Catholics recognized Mary Tudor as the legitimate heir, while Protestants recognized Elizabeth, the daughter of Henry's second wife. Elizabeth, therefore, was in a dangerous position during the whole of Mary's reign, but in fact the queen took no action against her. Mary's marriage with Philip of Spain was unpopular, but she was able to ride out the storm, especially when it became clear that she would not provide him with an heir. When she died early in 1558 Elizabeth, brought up as a Protestant, secured the throne, in spite of the proclamation of Mary of Scotland, the nearest heir if Elizabeth was illegitimate, as queen of both England and Scotland. Elizabeth was to experience constant trouble during her reign from Catholic-inspired plots in favor of Mary. At last in 1587 Elizabeth, who had given asylum to her cousin when she was driven out of Scotland in 1568, had her executed.

Elizabeth I (1558–1603) was one of the most effective of English rulers, using every weapon at her disposal, including her own nubile status, to advance the interests of her country. Naturally her hand was sought by all the European rulers who were either themselves marriageable or had marriageable relatives. But Elizabeth refused to the end to enter into alliance with any foreign potentate, nor would she elevate the rank of any of her subjects by a marriage union. However, she never made clear her fixed intention, and was able to hold out and discourage hope as her diplomacy demanded. She was parsimonious and preferred to avoid the expense of war, especially since she would be compelled to call Parliament for war subsidies and had no desire to give it the opportunity either to refuse or to impose conditions. She would not permit Parliament to discuss the Church settlement concluded at the beginning of her reign, fearful of the growing influence of the Calvinists in the country who were opposed to the still largely Catholic ritual of the Anglican Church. When Parliament, in spite of her skillful management of that body, showed itself determined to influence her financial policy, which it felt to be damaging to the commercial interests of the country, she gracefully withdrew her opposition and took the lead in enacting the laws Parliament demanded. Elizabeth was able to win as much as she did from her subjects largely because of the prestige won by the defeat of the Spanish Armada and the successes of the English navy. This was also the first great age of English literature and drama (Spenser, Marlowe, Johnson, Shakespeare, and many others), and for the first time England felt unified as a nation, secure in her island fortress, able to turn back the greatest of the military powers of the Continent, at last of real importance and influence in the world, in spite of her still very small population. Shakespeare and Spenser, each in his different way, gave utterance to this new sense of pride and patriotism, and each gave honor to the great queen under whom it was achieved.

The Beginning of the Constitutional Struggle. James I (1603–1625) was the son of Mary, Queen of Scots, by her murdered husband and cousin, Lord Darnley. He was thus on both sides the nearest heir to the English throne, and there was only one minor attempt to unseat him. Nevertheless, he was regarded in England as a Scot and a foreigner and was never able to win any popularity. He regarded himself as an experienced and successful king and had indeed shown some shrewdness in playing one party against another in his native land. But he was personally unattractive, extravagant and fond of display, inordinately addicted to favorites, and worst of all he believed so thoroughly in the divine rights of kings that he was unwilling to concede that his subjects and Parliament had any vested rights that did not emanate from the crown. He therefore came into conflict with Parliament, which claimed the right to legislate on its own initiative subject only to the royal veto, and to a share in the shaping of policy through its power to withhold subsidies from the crown. James also experienced much trouble with his judges. These men were accustomed to regard themselves as independent servants of the law rather than of the king. James was totally unwilling to admit the right of Parliament to bring the king's ministers to trial for alleged malfeasance in office, although it had frequently exercised this right in medieval times. The king himself might be above the law, but his ministers, in the opinion of Parliament, were not.

Although James was himself a pacifist, and had no interest in going to war, he was constantly short of money. A king in England was expected to "live of his own," but in recent centuries prices had risen far more quickly than the royal income, which was mostly derived from the crown lands, many of which had been alienated by his predecessors. The Tudor monarchs had resorted to numerous expedients to ensure themselves a sufficient private income without having to call on Parliament. They had sold monopolies to merchants and titles to the socially ambitious; they had on occasion debased the currency; they had cut themselves in on the profits of sea voyages, including the activities of gentlemen-adventurers, privateers, and plain pirates. They had called upon their subjects for "benevolences," loans which the latter knew would never be repaid but thought politic to offer. Henry VIII had had at his disposal a windfall from the sale of monasteries. But these were dwindling, or once and for all, assets. Monopolies offended the merchants who did not enjoy them and were clearly a hindrance to increased trade. Once peace was declared with Spain there was no more income from privateering. Titles became cheaper and less desirable the more they were sold. The reformed Church could not call upon the faithful for the kind of money payments that had been a matter of course in the Catholic Church, since the Church was no longer a mediator between man and God and laid claim to no such efficacy in aiding the faithful to salvation. Besides, the Anglican Church was no longer wealthy and needed most of its revenues to sustain itself. Parliaments in the past had granted the king at his accession the right to tonnage and poundage (broadly, the equivalent of customs and excise), a welcome addition to the royal exchequer, but the rates of these taxes it claimed to be able to determine itself, and the total depended greatly upon the prosperity of the country.

When James came to the throne there was already in existence an undercurrent of opposition to royal absolutism, which had been held in check by the prestige and tactfulness of Queen Elizabeth. In particular the growing number of Calvinists (Puritans) objected to the ritual in the Anglican Church inherited from Catholicism, and to the system of bishops who were authorized by the crown to enforce religious conformity and who had been granted a special court by Elizabeth (Court of High Commission) to impose penalties for nonobservance. It is possible that if James had not alienated the Puritans so early in his reign all the other difficulties he experienced with his subjects, especially with Parliament, in which there were now many Puritans, might have never been brought to an issue.

The English people were in no way ill-disposed to the monarchy, and all, including members of Parliament, were fully prepared to accord to James "the reverence which was his due" and refrain from interfering with what had traditionally been the royal prerogatives. Even his tactlessness could have been endured. But James fancied himself as a theologian and was prepared to argue with the Puritans; and he did not argue well. He usually lost his temper and threatened his opponents with the direst penalties. He was never able at any time in his life to understand that he was offending their deepest susceptibilities. It was for this reason that a number of Puritans decided that rather than submit to James's autocratic interference in their religion they would leave for America, where they founded their own Puritan community in New England. When Parliament attempted to criticize James's religious and other policies, he either dissolved it—which was his right and privilege as long as he was prepared to do without the money he expected it to provide—or tried to intimidate it. He dismissed judges who did not give decisions that pleased him, including Chief Justice Coke, who became the implacable opponent of royal absolutism and, after being elected to Parliament, led the Parliamentary opposition to it.

Nevertheless when James died in 1625 he had not greatly impaired the royal position, nor had kings' prerogatives significantly diminished. But what he had achieved was the creation of a determination in the ranks of many members of Parliament that they would not tolerate from the son what they had been willing to take from the father; and this boded ill for Charles I, who was at least as autocratic as his father but lacked his father's experience, and had been endowed with even less ability and wisdom, in addition to more than his fair share of duplicity.

The Attempted Absolutism of Charles I. When Charles I came to the throne in 1625, Parliament at once showed its feelings toward him by refusing to grant tonnage and poundage for more than a year. This did not prevent Charles from collecting the money, but laid the basis for later Parliamentary attacks upon him for his supposedly illegal actions. Charles was also unfortunate enough to be engaged in a war which his father had entered in the last years of his reign. The enemy was the always unpopular Spain, but since Charles proposed to entrust the command to a dissipated nobleman of no apparent military talent, it was vastly uninterested in paying out good money for a proposition that was likely to be unprofitable. When Charles borrowed the money and met the expected disaster, Parliament had little sympathy for him, nor did it vote him any substantial funds.

Charles did not at first fully realize what was happening, nor did he recognize the only way in which he could manage to exist without Parliament, namely, by living within his means until such time as he could get the country under his full control and establish alternative methods of collecting money without using the machinery established in past centuries by Parliament. As soon as he called a Parliament, it insisted on making him listen to his petitions, and it tried to impeach his ministers. Charles was compelled to sign the Petition of Right in 1628, under which he undertook, no doubt with mental reservations, not to do what he had been doing—in this respect following the precedent of King John in the thirteenth century. But by the following year he realized that he could never come to terms with Parliament save by abandoning most of his royal prerogatives and becoming a constitutional monarch. He therefore dissolved Parliament, as he hoped forever, and decided to use the full resources of the monarchy to establish his undisputed rule. In this he was ably abetted by Thomas Wentworth, earl of Strafford, commander of the royal troops who had just returned from a successful if ruthless campaign in Ireland.

For the next eleven years Charles tried to rule absolutely. He exploited to the full all his ancient feudal rights; he collected tonnage and poundage, levied benevolences, dispensed monopolies. He also pared his expenses to the bone. There can be no doubt that his government was far more efficient than the rather loose administration of the past; and it is quite possible that the majority of his people approved of it. He was doing no more than Richelieu on the Continent, and other absolute rulers of his day. When he levied an ancient tax called ship money, supposedly to pay for the English navy, he received no protests from the maritime towns, which customarily had paid the tax. Only when he extended this tax to the inland towns did he meet with opposition. Even so the opposition was not very effective since the royal courts duly convicted the recalcitrants. Parliament was effectively silenced because it was not summoned. Perhaps in time, if the king could have held out, it would have fallen into desuetude. But Charles could not refrain from interfering with religion. Himself a High Anglican, he gave support to the efforts of his archbishop of Canterbury, who was busily engaged in compelling even Puritans to worship according to the Anglican rite, using the authority of the Court of High Commission to discipline those who refused. But when Archbishop Laud, satisfied with his work in England, turned to Scotland and attempted to enforce the use of the Anglican Book of Common Prayer on the Scots, he met with armed resistance. The Scottish leaders formed a Solemn League and Covenant, swearing that they would defend their Presbyterian Church to the last. The Covenanters quickly organized an army and invaded England. Charles was thus compelled to call a Parliament (the Short Parliament) in 1640, but it refused Charles any money until he had promised to redress its grievances. As before, Charles raised an army on credit, but it was overwhelmed by the Scots.

His position was now hopeless. He was compelled to call a new Parliament (the Long Parliament), which dismantled the entire apparatus of absolutism so carefully built up by the English monarchy over generations. It also impeached Strafford. Failing to obtain a conviction in the House of Lords, it then passed a bill of attainder and Charles was forced to sacrifice his minister. Nevertheless, Parliament still refused to give Charles enough money for his purposes, and the Scottish army remained entrenched in the north of England.

The Civil War. At this point the coalition of different groups in Parliament which had been held together for the purpose of setting bounds to the power of the king, began to break up. There were Anglicans who desired a constitutional government of king and Parliament and Presbyterians who wanted to establish a Presbyterian Church of England like the Church of Scotland. There were Independents belonging to various Protestant sects, many of whom even desired a republic without a king. When the last two groups by a few votes forced a bill through Parliament which took away virtually all the royal power that remained, Charles decided he had had enough. He attempted to arrest the Parliamentary leaders, but they escaped to the city of London, which refused to open its gates to the king. This was rebellion, and Charles escaped to the north where he rallied his loyal followers to his standard.

During the war the Parliamentary side found its greatest champion in Oliver Cromwell, who was an Independent and had no intention of allowing a Presbyterian Church to be established in England, as the Scots and the English Presbyterians wished. The civil war therefore took on the aspect of a war not only between Parliament and the king, but between Cromwell and his army and the Presbyterians. Charles attempted to play one party off against the other for several years, but at last the discipline of Cromwell's army won the day. The Scots were defeated and had to give up their hopes of establishing a Presbyterian Church in England, while Cromwell proceeded to purge the English Parliament of its Presbyterians and with the small number of Independents who remained, he brought the king to trial and had him executed.

The Commonwealth and Protectorate (1649–1660). But as Cromwell soon found, nothing had been settled. Within his own army itself there were numerous dissident groups, including even the first organized English communists. They were willing to allow Cromwell to head a republican government (first called the Commonwealth, later the Protectorate), but Cromwell himself wished to base his government on at least some Parliamentary institutions. Despite several attempts, successively using the old Rump Parliament, nominating a Parliament of "godly men," and restricting the franchise to men of considerable property, he was never able to find a body with which he could work. All Parliaments wished him to disband his army, but this he dared not do. There were rebellions to put down in Scotland and Ireland in favor of Charles Stuart, son of Charles I, and Cromwell knew that his own position depended on the army. He was also aware that his regime was thoroughly unpopular at home, in spite of his brilliant foreign policy, and the prestige which he enjoyed on the Continent after successful wars with the Dutch and Spaniards, and in spite of the aid he consistently conferred on commerce and industry. England, so recently "merrie" was unwilling to become a nation of Bible-reading and psalm-singing Puritans, and was beginning to look longingly toward the royal exile on the Continent, who had perhaps learned his lesson. Ultimately Cromwell was forced to rely upon a military government and administration run by major generals, competent and efficient, and now able through improved administration to collect any taxes that might be refused by Parliament. Cromwell died in 1658 after having made his position of protector hereditary. But the country was still unreconciled to his rule, though the security of his power had been in no way impaired during his reign.

Cromwell's son Richard was unwilling to assume the kind of burden that had fallen to his father. He quickly resigned his position of protector, and for more than a year the various generals of Cromwell jockeyed for position. But in the end General Monck, the leader of the army in Scotland, invited Charles Stuart to return. Charles issued a declaration granting a virtually universal amnesty and accepting the constitutional limitations imposed by the Long Parliament on the monarchy, and then proceeded to enter London in triumph in 1660.

The Era of the Restoration. The Restoration ushered in a new phase of the century-long revolution. Neither of the sons of Charles I who reigned in succession accepted the new limitations on the monarchy and the increased power of Parliament; but Charles II was a consummately adroit, if entirely unscrupulous, politician, and he knew when he came to the throne, as his father never learned during his lifetime, that Parliament's power was real. If a monarch were to be absolute in England, as his brother monarchs were on the Continent, Parliament would have to be circumvented, not defied; an English king retained very substantial powers which he must learn how to use. So Charles ruled for twenty-five years and his position was stronger at the end of his reign. His brother James had his father's inflexibility and lacked his brother's subtlety. He ruled for a bare four years; by defying the wishes of Parliament and people he forfeited his throne, and in due course the constitutional monarchy was fully established and accepted by both monarch and people.

The details of Charles' maneuvers and the intricacies of English politics during his reign lie outside the scope of this book. The first royalist Parliament, known as the Cavalier Parliament, at once began to show itself more royalist than the king, and enacted severe laws against dissenters. Charles did not prevent these, even if he personally was not in sympathy with them. Married to a Portuguese Catholic wife, and himself the son of a Catholic mother, he had little more use for Anglicanism than for Puritanism, and he came to an agreement with Louis XIV that when the right time came he would declare himself a Catholic. Meanwhile he would do the best he could for them. But when he went so far as to issue a declaration of indulgence, Parliament replied with a Test Act, which Charles, short of money at the time, was compelled to sign. Under this act neither Catholic nor dissenter (Puritan) could hold office under the crown or in the universities. Charles never tried such a tactic again. His wars were fought for peculiar ends. What he really desired was to be subsidized by Louis XIV, so that he need not call Parliament. But Louis did not wish to pay his price unless his own position compelled it. Charles therefore went to war on the other side until Louis was prepared to meet his price. Under the secret Treaty of Dover with Louis XIV, he promised to do his best to convert his people to Catholicism, for which purpose Louis would lend him some troops if necessary. Under the public Treaty of Dover, Charles only promised to go to war with the Dutch. But Parliament so distrusted the French alliance that the war was immensely unpopular and Charles had to withdraw. Fortunately for him Louis was also willing to pay the subsidy for Charles' neutrality, so he did not suffer greatly.

The real issue that filled the last years of Charles's reign was the succession. James, the king's brother and heir, since Charles himself had no legitimate children, was a devout Catholic who had resigned as lord admiral after the Test Act. The dominant party in Parliament in these years, which now began to be called the Whig party, though it was not a cohesive party in the modern sense, continually introduced an Exclusion Bill to prevent James from inheriting the throne, which it was a permanent feature of Charles's policy never to allow to be passed. Whenever there was a danger that it would be forced upon him, he dissolved Parliament and hoped for a break in his favor before the next one. In 1679 a man named Titus Oates, once an Anglican and later converted to Catholicism and trained by the Jesuits, suddenly turned informer against the Jesuits and proclaimed that there had been a "Popish Plot" to murder the king and put his brother on the throne. The Whigs listened eagerly, and the people, distrusting deeply the many convolutions of Charles's policy, believed the story. Convictions and executions followed, all based on the sole word of the informer. Charles, instead of intervening, let the mania run its course until the people were surfeited, then suddenly arrested Oates and compelled him to admit that the plot had been a fabrication, thus throwing the Whigs into confusion. Their leaders took refuge abroad. Soon another "plot" was unearthed by royal efforts, this time, of course, engineered by the Whigs. In the confusion Charles dismissed the last Parliament and with the support of the Tories, the opponents of the Whigs, he instituted a colossal gerrymander, as a result of which it would be virtually impossible for there ever again to be a Whig majority in Parliament. Meanwhile the Tories, owing everything to the king, would be triumphantly harnessed to his chariot wheels. Then, having made the country safe for his successor, Charles died, and his Catholic brother James took the throne. The Exclusion Bill had never become law, and James held Parliament in the palm of his hand.

The Glorious Revolution. But Charles's efforts were dissipated in a brief three years. At first James's position was even strengthened by two short-lived rebellions, to suppress which Parliament voted him funds. The rebellions over, and the participators punished with the utmost severity, James made no move to disband his new army but ominously brought over Catholics from Ireland to prepare it for its role in the re-establishment of the old religion. James issued a new declaration of Indulgence and began to fill high offices in state and Church with Catholics, deliberately contravening the Test Act. Still the people did not stir. The Tory Parliament, though staunchly Anglican, was not prepared to forfeit its ascendancy, as long as there was any chance that the successor to James would be one of his Protestant daughters by a first marriage, the elder of whom was married to William of Orange, ruler of Holland. James, however, had recently married a Catholic, and she was expecting a child. If it proved to be a boy he would succeed before his half-sisters. When in fact it was a boy, a Jesuit plot was at once suspected by all. It was widely believed that the Jesuits had smuggled the child into the royal bedchamber.

At all events, the birth finally persuaded both Tory and Whig leaders that it was time to act. Having already been sounding out William of Orange for years, they now made him a definite offer of the crown, which he accepted, anxious above all to add the English to the Dutch resources in his wars against Louis XIV. When William landed in the southwest of England, James's hired army melted away. Finding himself deserted, he had no option but to flee to Ireland, where he might find Catholic supporters. Though captured he was allowed to escape again, thus giving Parliament the chance to declare that he had abdicated. Parliament then drew up under Whig influence a list of the king's misdemeanors, which included unconstitutional actions such as claiming the right to "dispense with the laws" duly passed by Parliament and signed by the king. Though most of the Tories did not agree with this interpretation, and still hoped for the restoration of the Stuart dynasty in the person of some monarch who would declare himself an Anglican, they had to accept William as king. When the latter signed a Bill of Rights prepared by Parliament, which confirmed the rights of the people won during the last century—as, for example, that the monarch could not suspend the operation of the laws, could not tax without the consent of Parliament, and that members could not be penalized by the king for speaking freely in Parliament—William in effect became a constitutional monarch.

William was in fact, if not wholly in theory, king by will of Parliament; and though his powers were not at first substantially less than those of Charles II, the revolution was really over. Monarchs were to exercise their remaining powers throughout the eighteenth century and were far from figureheads, as will be seen in the next chapter. But the way was now clear for the cabinet and parliamentary government, which was fully established by the end of the eighteenth century. When Parliament in 1701 passed the Act of Settlement which decreed that no Catholic monarch could ever inherit the throne of England and passed over the legitimate heirs of James II to grant the crown to the German heirs of that Elizabeth, daughter of James I who had married Frederick the Winter king of Bohemia and count palatine of the Rhine (Hanoverian dynasty), the last act in the revolution which was thereafter known as the Glorious Revolution was played. The remainder was natural evolution and development; there have been no revolutions in England since that day.

BRANDENBURG—PRUSSIA

In the period covered by this chapter the state which was to become the kingdom of Prussia began its meteoric rise. The electors —margraves—of Brandenburg were poor and possessed little power until after the Thirty Years' War. Their territories were largely undeveloped and scattered across northeastern Europe. Only the western areas formed part of the Holy Roman Empire.

The elector, John Sigismund of Hohenzollern, turned Calvinist at the beginning of the sixteenth century, but hesitated to give even such support as he had available to the Protestant cause during the Thirty Years' War. Although the margravate was neutral for much of the war, this did not save it from being fought over by the mercenary armies; both the great power of Sweden and the second-rank power of Poland had constantly to be reckoned with. The Swedes were busily engaged in building a Baltic empire for themselves that prevented the margravate from having access to the sea in the areas which would have been most useful to it. The Great Elector, Frederick William of Hohenzollern, who ruled from 1640 to 1688, was able by dint of careful alliances, and a little fighting, to improve his situation in a marked manner. At home he reorganized the administration of his weak and scattered territories and built himself an army, officered by landowners (the Junkers), whose principal occupation was making ready for war, and improved the commerce of the country. But abroad the elector for a long time was little respected. Though he won some concessions from Poland, he could for a long time make little impression on Sweden. At times he entered alliances organized by Louis XIV and at times alliances organized against him, but his rewards from both were meager. However, by his death there was no doubt that Prussia (by this time the name of Brandenburg had fallen into disuse) was a state that would have to be taken seriously.

The Great Elector's successor, determined to win a royal title, allied himself with the emperor in hopes of receiving recognition for his claim. He was rewarded in 1701 when he was allowed to become king *in* Prussia, a distinction which was made necessary by the claims of Poland to superior sovereignty in this part of the margrave's dominions. The distinction, however, soon disappeared. The second king of Prussia, Frederick William I, soon made his title into a reality in the eighteenth century. Prussia under Frederick the Great, the third king of the line, became the most formidable military power in Europe, challenging even France and Russia on fairly even terms, as will be discussed in the next chapter.

EASTERN EUROPE

Russia to the Reign of Peter the Great. We have already noted in Chapter X the manner in which the grand duchy of Moscow freed itself from the Mongols and how its rulers expanded until they were able with some truth to style themselves the tsars of all the Russias. Yet the rulers did not achieve this position without encountering opposition from the independent and semi-independent nobles. The means they used may be described in general terms as the fostering of a new class, usually called the gentry, who were ennobled by the monarch and could be used to lessen the power of the boyars, or hereditary nobility. Out of the gentry Ivan IV (1533–1584) fashioned a corps of picked fighters by means of which he broke the boyars. The establishment of a strong monarchy, however, did not improve the lot of the peasants in either the short or the long run, as it did in the West. The tsar relied upon the gentry and submissive boyars to recruit troops from among the peasants and therefore encouraged them to take steps to see that their peasants stayed on the land where they had been born. So the Russian peasants, who had been personally free and possessed even some rights against their lords in the Middle Ages, were reduced to serfdom, from which they were not emancipated till 1861. Much the same process took place in Poland, where serfdom was not an ancient condition from which the peasants had to free themselves in modern times but a status newly imposed on them from the sixteenth century onward by the triumphant nobility. After the death of Ivan IV there ensued a period of weak central rule when various nobles strove for power, and the country was constantly subjected to Polish intrigues and invasions. Ultimately in 1613 all the influential classes chose a tsar from a new family, most of them hoping that he would be an improvement over Ivan and would be too weak to re-establish the latter's despotic rule, while at the same time freeing the country from foreign interference. Michael Romanoff was only sixteen years when he became tsar but he learned quickly and restored much of the system of Ivan IV. He continued to use the gentry to the exclusion of the boyars, who lost almost all their power and influence during the century; and though the wars were seldom very successful they aided Michael and his son and successor, Alexis (1645–1676), to strengthen the position of the monarch in relation to his subjects. The Russian military establishment was too technically backward to be able to cope with the Swedes or even with the Poles; and Alexis, at least, knew it. He therefore encouraged foreigners to come to Russia to settle there, both as merchants and military instructors. Though their presence was resented by the native Russians, they succeeded in preparing the ground for Peter the Great, who shared the first years of his rule with an ineffective brother until he took over the entire responsibility of government in 1689.

It was Peter's policy to make use for his own purposes of everything that had been developed in the West in recent centuries during which Russia had been stagnating. He and his country could then stand up to their former teachers and no longer be subjected to humiliating defeats at the hands of powers inferior in population and resources to their own. To build an army capable of this, Peter reorganized his administration in such a manner as to make it wholly obedient to his will. The last vestiges of the old medieval free institutions disappeared, and the Orthodox Church was subjected to royal control. From this time onward the Russian tsar was the most absolute of all European rulers, and thus entered fully into his Byzantine heritage. To symbolize and strengthen his program of modernization Peter built a new city (St. Petersburg) on the Baltic and degraded Moscow, the center and symbol of Russian backwardness, to the status of a provincial city.

The power that stood in Peter's way in the north was Sweden, a country with a proud military tradition but small in population, which had overextended itself in the Baltic. The Danes, Poles, and Russians were all agreed that Sweden should be cut down to size, each having otherwise different objectives in the war that began in 1699 with the three powers in alliance (Great Northern War). But they had to contend with a young king, Charles XII of Sweden, who was a great if over-reckless military leader, and all suffered severe reverses at his hands. The Russians were utterly outclassed at the Battle of Narva in 1700 by a small Swedish army led by the king, but were saved from further loss by the necessity for Charles to deal first with the Poles to the west. Thus Peter was granted a six-years' breathing space to equip and improve his army, which he used to such good effect that he was able to sustain the invasion of Charles when it came in 1707. The Swedish monarch hoped for allies among the Cossacks of the Ukraine who resented Peter's autocratic rule, and he therefore marched into the Ukraine rather than making directly for Moscow. The Russians destroyed the Swedish army piecemeal and ultimately overwhelmed Charles at the Battle of Poltava in 1709. Charles escaped to Turkey, where he became a valuable hostage in Turkish hands. By the time he was allowed to return to his country and resume his campaigns, Russia was safe, and had no further serious trouble with him. After Charles's death the Swedes agreed to the Treaty of Nystadt (1721), by which Russia acquired Livonia, Estonia, and some useful Baltic islands and other territories from Sweden, which thereupon ceased to be a great power. Russia herself inherited much of the Swedish territory in the Baltic, and by virtue of her vast hinterland was forever afterward a power to be taken seriously in European affairs.

Poland. After the union of Poland and Lithuania at the end of the fourteenth century, little success was achieved by the monarchy in its efforts to control the dissident nobility. Though, as in Russia, the monarchs supported a gentry class, the latter soon could only with difficulty be distinguished from the older hereditary nobility, and they never became an effective instrument of royal policy except for a very brief period. It was the nobility that was successful in reducing the peasants to serfdom in the early sixteenth century. The king merely acquiesced in the process.

The great kingdom of Poland-Lithuania remained virtually intact for most of the rule of the Jagiellon dynasty, and even managed to acquire an outlet to the Baltic. Then gradually it began to be whittled away, most of its losses being to Russia until the mid-sixteenth century, when the Swedes and Danes began to take their share. When the last Jagiellon monarch was already advanced in years and had no male heir, he consummated the Union of Lublin under which Poland and Lithuania were to be amalgamated into one kingdom (1569). When he died three years later, the nobles insisted on returning to the elective monarchy, which in theory had always been operative in Poland; thereafter, with rare exceptions, no native Pole sat on the throne.

The position of Polish king was one that was coveted by all the princelings of Europe in spite of the difficulties of the position, for there were still relatively few royal crowns available. But the kings were seldom much interested in the domestic affairs of their adopted country. They fought in the interests of themselves and their families in other areas of Europe, or for their religion—as did the Swedish Catholic Sigismund III (1587–1632), who aided the Jesuits and the Counter Reformation in their successful efforts to force the Polish people back into the Catholic fold. They were on the whole notably unsuccessful in spite of the occasional resounding victories; and the country gradually lost its Baltic provinces to Sweden (1660), some of its eastern provinces in the Ukraine to Russia (1667), and others for a period to Turkey (1672–1699). In the Great Northern War the elector of Saxony occupied the Polish throne, but was no match for Charles XII of Sweden, who took the great cities of Warsaw and Cracow (1702), whereupon the Polish nobles compelled him to abdicate for a few years. With the defeat of Sweden by

Russia, the latter began to exercise increasing influence in Poland, eventually leading to the successive partitions of what remained of the ancient kingdom in the last decades of the eighteenth century.

The Polish system of rule by nobles over the backward serfs, with a king who lacked power to reduce his country to order, was made possible by the impotence of the national diet, the one institution empowered to pass laws and resolutions for the whole country. Each single representative in the diet was possessed of a veto. If any objection was raised by a single member to any resolution the diet was thereupon dissolved. It may be imagined how rarely any action could be taken binding upon the whole country. If the country had been ruled by a tight, well-knit oligarchy it might have held together. But the system was closer to anarchy than to oligarchy, since the nobles from different sectors of the country consulted only their own interests and not even those of their fellow nobles elsewhere. In spite of efforts at reform in the eighteenth century, it was not until after the country had been partitioned that the reform movement acquired any momentum. By that time it was too late, as will be discussed in the next chapter.

THE SMALLER COUNTRIES OF EUROPE

Sweden. Reference has already been made throughout this chapter to events in the smaller countries in Europe, and it only remains here to deal briefly with these countries in themselves. Sweden escaped from the domination of Denmark only at the beginning of the sixteenth century, but subsequently under the Vasa family she had a meteoric rise. Taking Finland with her after the break with Denmark, she later expanded into the Baltic and for a period ruled much of what is today northern Germany, as well as several provinces of Denmark. Under the rule of the Vasa dynasty the country became an effectively organized national unit, with a strong military machine. The monarchs during the period of expansion experienced little trouble from the feudal nobility, and by the time of the Treaty of Oliva in 1660 they were rulers of an extensive northern empire. Most of this empire, however, was quickly lost during the reign of Charles XII, as we have seen, though Western Pomerania and Finland were retained during the eighteenth century and lost only during the Napoleonic wars. Sweden was compensated at the Congress of Vienna by receiving Norway, which she kept until the early twentieth century (1905).

Denmark–Norway. Denmark after separation from Sweden retained Norway but was unable to do much to defend herself from the expansionism of Sweden, who sheared off several of her provinces during the numerous wars between the two nations. Christian IV, who intervened, as we have seen, in the Thirty Years' War, returned home to spend the rest of his long reign (1588–1648) in consolidating and improving the administration of his remaining possessions. His successors at last succeeded in quelling the unruly Danish nobility, but the country played little part in European affairs. As a punishment for aid given to Napoleon, Denmark lost Norway to Sweden at the Congress of Vienna.

The Swiss Confederation. Another small country is worthy of attention here, since its political development was so different from that of any other European nation. The first confederation in Switzerland was composed of three forest cantons (small self-governing states), which banded together in 1291 for mutual defense with some common institutions. They were all within the Holy Roman Empire; but the most dangerous enemy to their independence was the Hapsburg duke of Austria, who was usually also the Holy Roman Emperor. While the Confederation did not object to the nominal rule of the emperor, whoever he might be, it did not relish the efforts of the emperor in his position as Hapsburg duke to enforce his rights in Switzerland. Faced with frequent wars to maintain their independence, the original cantons soon permitted others to enter the Confederation and all won much military experience, and were far more often victorious than defeated. The Swiss soldiers had an almost legendary reputation in Europe by the end of the Middle Ages, and for centuries more they were in demand as mercenaries. Controlling as they did the most important Alpine passes into Italy, they had a position of strategic importance out of proportion to the size of the country.

When the Protestant Reformation came to Switzerland it accentuated the intercantonal quarreling which had always been a feature of Swiss life. The Catholic and Protestant cantons now warred openly with one another, though the Confederation with its supercantonal institutions continued to function, and did not officially take sides in the struggle. In the Thirty Years' War both Catholic and Protestant cantons fought for the control of the important passes into Italy, which were essential to the Spanish Hapsburgs if they were to give effective aid through Italy to their fellow Hapsburgs in Austria. Though the Spaniards ultimately won the right to use the crucial Valtelline Pass, the Peace of Westphalia recognized the independence of Switzerland as a whole. The Confederation remained, however, to a large degree paralyzed by religious strife for the rest of the century, and co-operation between the two groups of cantons was minimal. The separate cantons, no longer compelled to band together to resist foreign invaders, administered their own cantons and made little effort to convert their Confederation into either a unitary state or a true federation. For a full century (1663–1776) the federal diet never met. But in the seventeenth and eighteenth century wars there was a tendency for Catholic Swiss mercenaries to fight on one side and Protestant on the other, thus exacerbating the friction between the cantonal religious groupings. In the early eighteenth century the Protestants, led by the Bernese, defeated the smaller and less populous Catholic cantons and thereafter for the rest of the century established their ascendancy. But the ancient Confederation was not dissolved, and even survived the many changes brought by the French Revolution and the rule of Napoleon.

EXPANSION BEYOND THE EUROPEAN CONTINENT

Dutch Expansion. Although it was not until the eighteenth century that the rivalries between the various European powers over their colonial possessions outside Europe became acute, brief mention should be made in this chapter of a few phases of the expansion, which was constant from the Age of Discovery onward. When the Portuguese possessions were taken over by the Spanish crown in 1580 the growing maritime power of the Dutch found fields for its enterprise in the eastern Spanish possessions. Since they were at war with Spain, they had no reason to withhold their attacks on the Portuguese, and during the seventeenth century they built up a huge and commercially profitable empire in the Far East, based on the island of Java. Batavia, the capital of the Netherlands East Indies until after the Second World War, was built in 1619, and became the headquarters of the huge Dutch East India Company, a semi-governmental concern, entrusted with the task of administering the new colonies. The Dutch were able to destroy with ease the small English settlements in that area, and left almost nothing to the Portuguese. Although the English continued to found settlements in lands claimed by the Dutch, and even controlled Java during part of the Napoleonic period, the peace settlement after the wars restored the whole area to the Dutch in exchange for concessions elsewhere.

The French in the New World. Major French expansion in the seventeenth century was into North America, under the leadership of such men as Samuel Champlain, who founded Quebec in 1608; Maisonneuve, who founded Montreal in 1642; and LaSalle, who explored the Mississippi valley. At the end of the century the French colony of Louisiana was founded, and the great cities of Mobile and New Orleans. Detroit was founded in 1701 by Cadillac. In the Mississippi valley the French came into frequent conflict with the Spaniards who had expanded to the north from Mexico; in the north there was occasional conflict with the English in the first half of the seventeenth century, but this conflict became serious only with the wars of Louis XIV, and especially the War of the Spanish Succession—known in the Americas as Queen Anne's War (1702–1713). After this war several French territories, including Nova Scotia (formerly Acadia), were permanently ceded by the French. In every war thereafter between the British and French, or the British and Spanish, colonial territories were involved, some of which will be discussed in the next chapter. By the end of the seventeenth century, however, the French had colonized much of what is today Canada. Aside from the few important cities, the settlements were purely agricultural. Peasants, especially from Normandy, had been encouraged to settle by the home government, and their descendants remain in Canada today, the typical Canadian *habitant* with his rural and Catholic culture, so distinct from that of the British newcomers who began to arrive in force only at the end of the eighteenth century.

Competition in the West Indies. Britain, France, Spain, and Holland all contended for the various West Indian islands, most of which were ideally suited for the growing of sugar, a commodity in increasing demand in Europe. The French governments, indeed, were far more interested in profitable islands than in their wild and sparsely populated mainland; to some degree this was also true of England in the seventeenth century. A great deal of capital was invested in the islands, including their labor supply of Negro slaves. The islands changed hands many times throughout the centuries, the most valuable ultimately falling to the British, but still leaving to this day two of the largest under French rule, and a few of little importance are still in the hands of the Dutch.

The English in North America. The English did not win a sure foothold in North America until the early part of the seventeenth century. Most of the few settlements were made by trading companies chartered by the crown, under whose auspices even the religious dissenters sailed, although in some cases they were able to establish themselves at once as semi-independent self-governing units. Jamestown in Virginia, for example, was founded in 1607 by the London Company under the leadership of John Smith. Plymouth Colony, the first settlement in New England, founded by the Puritan Pilgrims who sailed on the *Mayflower* in 1620, was in fact an independent venture, though the Pilgrims had first obtained from the London Company the right to make their settlement. In other areas the crown granted various territories to noble proprietors who purchased their lands from the crown or were rewarded with them in exchange for services rendered to it. In due course the crown resumed responsibility for all the settlements and sent out governors to administer them. But some of the rights to which the colonies had become accustomed, for example, the right to hold representative assemblies, were confirmed by the crown. There was little conflict between England and the other European powers in the colonizing of North America south of the French settlements and north of the Spanish territories; and though for more than two centuries the Europeans had to engage in constant hostilities with the "Indians," the original inhabitants of the country, the issue was never in doubt. The colonists through their superior armament and organization could always win the victory whenever they brought sufficient force to bear. There were, however, a few scattered Dutch territories, including Manhattan Island, which was owned by the Dutch from 1626 to 1664. It fell in the latter year to the English, and was in part responsible for the first war between Charles II and the Dutch.

Colonies of Settlement and Colonies of Exploitation. It should be noted that the settlements on the American mainland were all made by European emigrants who planned to make their permanent homes there. The climate was temperate, and the agricultural resources of the country were unlimited. In the West Indies the European planters often lived their whole lives in the new country, but they rarely regarded it as their home. It was their task to organize production by the African slaves, and from their work they hoped to become rich and probably retire to England to spend their wealth in a civilized community. In the East the colonies were merely coastal settlements as entrepôts for the up-country trade, which was of course in the hands of the natives. The Europeans were there to make their fortunes, protected by the military strength of their home country; and they had no intention of living permanently in the countries they ruled. This distinction will become important when we come to consider the War of American Independence in the next chapter when the colonies separated from the mother country and set up their own government; and in later chapters when we shall give some attention to the organization of the older British dominions, peopled by immigrants of British extraction, but with separate governments of their own. The Spanish colonies, like the North American ones, were colonies of settlement and achieved independence under their own Spanish-American governments. But there was no permanence for the other type of colony in which a European power merely ruled over native peoples. It is colonies of this type that are now achieving their independence in the second half of the twentieth century.

CHAPTER XIV

THE EIGHTEENTH CENTURY— THE AGE OF ENLIGHTENMENT

The eighteenth century was an exceptional period in European history, and is thus separated in this narrative from the other early modern centuries. A great intellectual revolution had been taking place in the seventeenth century whose full fruits were experienced only in the eighteenth. This revolution was the result of a radically new way of thinking about the world which is best described as scientific, although in its early appearance it had little of the intellectual rigor we associate with modern science. Men of science took a new look at the world, and though basing themselves to some degree upon the opinions of their predecessors, ceased to regard the latter as in any way authoritative. They concluded that the ancients simply did not have any superior source of knowledge at their disposal. Aristotle was an early Greek scientist whose findings might be accepted if they were found to conform with their own discoveries, but in many respects he had been seriously mistaken. Ptolemy's views of the universe were far from being the best explanation for the visible phenomena and should be replaced by a different series of hypotheses. Galen was badly mistaken about the functioning of the human organism. Let us try to be "objective," see what already is present in the world, these men said, and then try to provide an explanation which will stand up to criticism and is capable of verification. In the seventeenth century the Ptolemaic system was superseded by the new astronomy developed by Copernicus, Kepler, Galileo, and Newton, with its more rigorously applied mathematics; Harvey's observations and experiments on the circulation of the blood replaced the older theories of Galen; Descartes invented analytical geometry and tried to explain the whole universe in terms of matter and motion; while Francis Bacon tirelessly insisted on experimentation and verification, discovering nothing himself, but urging his system as the only one which could lead to "useful" and not "contentious" knowledge, capable of being placed at the service of man.

IMPACT OF THE SCIENTIFIC REVOLUTION

Religious and Social Thought. The result of this new mode of thinking and of the enthronement of the intellect as the supreme tool for the understanding of the universe was initially of more importance than any material benefits it incidentally conferred on the men of the eighteenth century. In the field of religion it led to the criticism of the Christian revelation as being irrational and unscientific, an accumulation of myths and beliefs which had no grounding in reality. Some thinkers even went so far with their criticism that they became true atheists, with Baron d'Holbach, regarding "nature" as the only true god, while others stopped short at that extreme only out of deference to the opposition it aroused and from their own personal unwillingness to disbelieve all that they had been taught. The cult of reason in religion excited also its counterpart, especially in the work of John and Charles Wesley, whose Methodism was a return to the religion of pure feeling, calling for a conversion or inner transformation of man and making little appeal to his reason.

In the fields of social and political thought, the new scientific ideas, and especially the precision of the new mathematics, directed man's attention to theoretical considerations as to how society should be organized and how governments ought to be run—disregarding in the process the slow organic development of existing societies. Some thinkers, such as Thomas Hobbes, regarded human beings as machines, moving in a determined manner according to the impact of the elementary particles of which they were composed, and absorbing the "stuff" of knowledge and sensation as if it too were made up of similar material substances. Economists, calling themselves Physiocrats, attempted to create what they called a "social physics" and to discover laws on which all economic transactions were based. In all realms there were efforts to discover fundamental laws, analogous to the "laws" of nature, and from them to deduce important consequences for man's social and political life. These supposed laws were arrived at largely by the processes of reason rather than observation, still less experimentation, and it was thought that when reason had given its assent to them they could be regarded as self-evident, like certain "self-evident truths" in the American Declaration of Independence, as unequivocally true for all time.

Enlightened Despotism. One of the most noteworthy results of the prevalent thought of the eighteenth century was the widespread belief among rulers that their rule should be enlightened, and for the benefit of their subjects. To be sure, each ruler interpreted enlightenment in his own manner, and he ceased to be enlightened as soon as his own authority was threatened. But the "enlightened despots" of the eighteenth century sincerely thought that absolutism was the only rational form of government, and that they alone could hope to know what was for the benefit of their subjects—and in this belief they were backed by the vast majority of the political thinkers of the time. Even Napoleon, who overthrew so many of the despots, was in the same tradition and regarded himself as the most enlightened despot of them all. We, who have been brought up to regard democracy as the highest form of government among men may think that the people through their representatives should make the decisions that affect our lives and not leave them to men who rule only through the accident of heredity and might in truth be no more enlightened than the next man. But in the eighteenth century this notion was not even accepted in the country that had given birth to the institutions which were to develop into democracy; and it was a considerable advance over the past that hereditary rulers should recognize their obligations to their subjects and not regard themselves as free to consult the interests only of themselves and their families. The notion that government should be enlightened was itself carried over into the democratic era; no one today would question the concept, even though many might disagree as to the interpretation different governments have placed upon it.

THE ENLIGHTENED DESPOTS

Enlightened despotism had its fling in almost all the European countries, though not all can be dealt with here. In the Hapsburg realms the most extreme of the despots, Joseph II (1780–1790), attempted in his reign of ten years to make over his country by reforms decreed from above. Impatient with the slow progress made by his mother, Maria Theresa, in her long reign (1740–1780), he vastly accelerated all the reforms that had been tentatively set in motion by her. In Prussia, Frederick the Great (1740–1786), after concluding a series of wars which greatly added to his territories, spent the rest of his life in reducing them to order and integrating them into his realm, by means of usually intelligent plans thought out by himself and to a large degree adapted to the social conditions of each part of his country. Catherine II, the Great, of Russia (1762–

1796), found herself unable to achieve much improvement at home and, in fact, fastened the despotic rule of the tsars even more firmly on the peasants. She was, however, very hospitable to the propagandists of the Enlightenment (known as *philosophes*), and publicized her efforts at reform while concealing the reality of her failure. Duke Leopold of Tuscany (1745–1790) gave his small Italian duchy the best administration it had ever known, successfully abolishing serfdom and aiding its commercial development. The Bourbon monarchy in Spain, especially in the reign of Charles III (1759–1788), did its best to modernize the administration at home. Charles was notably forward-looking in his work in the Spanish colonies, to which he introduced the intendant system of Bourbon France. In Portugal, in the reign of Joseph I (1750–1777) the marquis of Pombal became one of the most remarkable of all the enlightened despots, greatly reducing the power of the nobility and the Church, improving the finances, instituting a reformed program of education, and encouraging and aiding industry and agriculture. In Denmark King Christian VII (1766–1808) attempted a similar reform under his prime minister John Frederick Struensee, but was not powerful enough to push through the reforms. After hardly more than a year in office Struensee fell from power and was executed as a result of the opposition of the nobility. Later in Christian's reign some of the reforms, including the abolition of serfdom, were carried out under a new minister, Count Andreas Bernstorff (1784–1788). Lastly Louis XV, the Bourbon king in France (1715–1774), though himself not to be classed as an enlightened despot, attempted a considerable number of reforms, some of which were still in operation by the end of his reign, though quickly reversed by his successor. These will be dealt with in a separate section.

The heart of the movement toward enlightened despotism was the effort by the monarchs to work through bodies of trained bureaucrats who held their position by virtue of the authority delegated to them by the monarchs. What had to be destroyed was the system of privilege that had persisted from the Middle Ages, and had even been accentuated in some countries where monarchy throughout the early modern period had been weak. In most European countries there were still serfs attached to their estates and unable to dispose freely of their own persons and services. Even where, as in France, serfdom as an actual institution had disappeared, the free peasants were oppressed by numerous regulations and duties still owed to their lords. The lords were grossly undertaxed and were able to pass on to their serfs such taxes as they had to pay; they were highly resistant to all royal attempts to take this privilege away from them, and especially to change the status of their serfs. The monarchs knew that they could not modernize their states and rule in the interests of all their people without coming into conflict with their nobles; to win such a conflict they had to appoint public servants and invest them with great power, and then back them to the limits of their own authority. Few monarchs of the eighteenth century could command the services of sufficient numbers of these men, and where their own power was inadequate for the purposes, they failed, as in Denmark. But the work done in the eighteenth century by the despots was nevertheless of crucial importance for the future. In all countries where the nobles possessed vested rights, their powers were significantly reduced. By means of the French Revolution and the regime of Napoleon, the monarchs themselves were to be caught up into the same process and lose their power, as the nobles had lost theirs through royal initiative in the eighteenth century. Thus the way was opened for the growing democracy of the last two centuries.

EIGHTEENTH-CENTURY FRANCE

France was the center of the political thought of the eighteenth century, as she remained the cultural leader of Europe. The French philosophes were well aware that their monarchy was in most respects unenlightened and most of them backed the efforts at reform initiated by Louis XV and his ministers. What the king had to fight was the entrenched system of privilege, under which the feudal nobles were virtually exempt from taxation and the parlements gave their full legal support to every privilege extracted by the nobles and bourgeois from the monarchy in previous centuries. Louis was in constant need of money for his wars and his dissipations, and he found it impossible to extract it from his subjects. His only recourses were borrowing at high rates of interest and obtaining advance payments from the tax farmers, who handled the collection of indirect taxes, as under the Roman Republic. Thus he would sometimes have spent in advance several years' income; and in spite of the prosperity of the country, very little of this prosperity was reflected in the state of royal finances.

Louis therefore attempted to institute various forms of income tax and other kinds of taxation, designed to hit the upper classes and exempt the peasants and wage earners, who were heavily enough taxed already. All the affected classes resisted, claiming that the taxes were contrary to the established laws and customs of France. In the earlier years of his reign, Louis, who disliked being unpopular and was personally indolent, withdrew his reforms under protest and conditions became worse. At last he decided to abolish the privileges of the parlements and set up his own parlements staffed by competent bureaucrats and lawyers. This too met with the expected resistance, and the privileged oligarchy began to talk of rebellion in the name of the rights of the people. Louis XV, however, persisted until his death; and his new parlements, known as *Maupéou parlements,* after the name of his chancellor, survived his reign. But Louis XVI lacked enough fortitude to continue the program of his grandfather and restored the old parlements. Though for a time he appointed re-forming ministers who hoped to alter the system by less radical methods than those of Maupéou, he was unable to support them ade-quately without the necessary institutional reforms, and time after time he bowed to the opposition and dismissed his ministers. Since the financial condition of the government became steadily worse, it was only a matter of time before the government itself became bankrupt; and this bankruptcy led directly to the Revolution, which will be discussed in the next chapter.

Meanwhile France became the undisputed cultural leader of Eu-rope, and Paris its unquestioned cultural and intellectual capital. The greatest intellectual achievement was the production of the multi-volumed *Encyclopédie,* an epitome of all the scientific knowledge and pseudo knowledge of the century, strongly anticlerical and thus usually banned by the European governments, but sold without dif-ficulty through subterranean channels. This enormous twenty-eight volume work, with seven additional supplemental volumes, edited by the French philosophe Denis Diderot, was primarily designed to put forward the point of view of the philosophical movement. It was therefore sceptical, scientifically deterministic, anticlerical, and, above all, rational, the product of minds which had seriously at-tempted to emancipate themselves from all the traditional thinking of the past and especially of what the writers thought of as medieval obscurantism. It was the principal medium for the spread of the notions of the Enlightenment, and it enjoyed a huge success. Few if any other works in history have so well summed up the climate of thought of an epoch. The thought was suffused, it is true, with the prejudices of an economically privileged intellectual elite; but at that period these were the makers of European opinion, and in the *Encyclopédie* they had an unequalled means for its diffusion.

THE ADVANCE OF CONSTITUTIONAL GOVERNMENT IN ENGLAND

The Beginning of the Cabinet System. Meanwhile in England the institutional means were being devised by which Western civilization was to move into the democratic era of modern times. Little affected by what was happening on the Continent, England nevertheless supplied continental thinkers, especially Montesquieu and Voltaire, with a wealth of experience, from which they could draw lessons for their own countries. Some of these ideas, indeed, were filtered through French minds to become the general principles used by the Fathers of the American Constitution when they came to devise a government for their newly independent country. What was achieved during the eighteenth century in England was a workable system of cabinet government, which was continually developed in subsequent centuries and became a model for all constitutional monarchies and most of the parliamentary democracies.

The last two Stuarts, William III and Anne, knew when they began to reign that they could not achieve their ends in opposition to Parliament, by this time a settled institution of the realm which had to be summoned by the king at regular intervals. Parliaments under the new constitutional arrangements were summoned every three years, and could remain in office for that time as long as they held the monarch's confidence. He could dissolve Parliament and call for a new election as frequently as he wished. But what the monarchs now found was that they had to work with a group in Parliament capable of delivering to them the supplies and of enacting the legislation which they needed. It was thus useless to dissolve a Parliament if a party hostile to the king's program were to be elected after the dissolution. The king could appoint such ministers as he wished, and he had full control of the executive; unless his ministers were impeached by Parliament and convicted, they could run the day-to-day business of the country as they had always done. But they could do little if they were not supported by Parliament. Hence as a matter of practical experience the king came to recognize that it would be best if he appointed ministers who had the support of the majority group in Parliament, who sat in that body, and could take the lead in enacting the king's program. Thus, insensibly, the leader of the majority group took over the king's executive power and the power of initiating legislation. Impeachment fell into disuse, as did the royal veto, since ministers could be overthrown as soon as Parliament ceased to give them its support, and it was useless for a king to interpose his veto unless he could be sure of obtaining a majority for his viewpoint after a new election. Dissolution of Parliament therefore took the place of the veto. The last royal veto was, in fact, cast by Queen Anne.

The tasks of the king's council in due course were taken over by the Parliamentary ministers, and the Privy Council of the king, though it continued to exist, was reduced to a more or less honorary position.

It was, however, a long time before king and Parliament recognized what was happening. George I, the first Hanoverian monarch, was more interested in his German electorate of Hanover than in England. His reign coincided with the rise to power of Robert Walpole, who was in fact the first English prime minister, without the title. Walpole held office for twenty-one years, the longest continual period of office of any prime minister to this day. Parliament was still elected under a restricted franchise, barely changed from the Middle Ages. The constituencies which elected members had been redistricted many times throughout the centuries, and were by the eighteenth century outrageously unfair and unsuited to the existing distribution of population. These facts permitted a shrewd and well-informed politician like the duke of Newcastle to organize the vote in such a manner as actually to control the election of the party and government he favored. The result was what has been termed the Whig Oligarchy, although in fact Tories from certain areas were well represented in it, and party distinctions were always blurred. When Walpole's pacific policies ceased to be popular and began to damage Britain's growing trade interests in the world, Walpole lost the support of the duke who had loyally provided him with majorities for eighteen years. Newcastle, indeed, was persuaded to throw his crucial influence to the war party. King George II greatly disliked William Pitt the Elder (later Earl of Chatham) in spite of his obvious talents, but he was left with little option but to put him in power, even though he balked at making him the titular head of the government.

The Government of the "King's Friends." When George III came to the throne in 1760, the first Hanoverian to be born in England and regard himself as an Englishman, he set himself to undermine the influence of Pitt, even though the latter was conducting the Seven Years' War with considerable success. George was of the opinion that what Newcastle could do for his nominees, he himself could do also, especially since he had control of a very extensive royal patronage. Rather than oppose Parliament directly, he proposed to pack it with his "friends" and chose his ministers from among those who supported him personally. Though at first unsuccessful and thwarted by Parliament, when the war was over he was able to create a fairly stable government, which in 1770 was taken over by Lord North. It was this government which handled the grievances of the American colonists so ineptly that the latter resorted to rebellion. The war itself was no better managed, but the king was still able by the lavish use of patronage and bribes to keep his friends in power until 1782. But the failure in the war so damaged his reputation and the reputation of his government that when a moderate young Tory leader, William Pitt the Younger, son of the Earl of Chatham, showed himself able to manage Parliament, George bowed to the inevitable and appointed him prime minister. Shortly afterward George became intermittently insane, and Pitt and his Parliament ran the country. Parliamentary government was never seriously disturbed by any monarch thereafter; and though the king retained some minor powers and prerogatives and all government was carried on in his name, it was nothing but the constitutional truth when Edward VII in the early twentieth century told a man who asked his personal opinion of an international crisis that an English king held no opinion other than those of his ministers.

INTERNATIONAL RELATIONS

Concept of Balance of Power. In the eighteenth century, as befitted an age of Enlightenment, international relations were guided far more consciously by the concept of the balance of power than hitherto, and, on the whole, national interests began to take precedence over dynastic or family interests in the wars waged by the various sovereigns. No nation had as yet resorted to conscription, and the wars continued to be fought with mercenary armies, led with some exceptions by professional officers of the same nationality as their employers. The soldiers of fortune who hired out to whatever rulers were willing to pay for their services were now almost a thing of the past. Though the wars were still ostensibly fought for the succession to a particular throne, every combatant had certain definite ends which were far more material and substantial than simply seeing that a member of one's family sat on a particular foreign throne. There were certain constants in the foreign policy of all the rulers, and these constants were well understood by the diplomats who handled the negotiations for their royal masters.

The English were unwilling to see the power of France extended through the Low Countries and were prepared to fight to see that this did not happen. They were therefore almost always on the opposite side of a war from France and this constant could be relied upon by any would-be combatant. France was almost certain to be on the opposite side of a war from the Hapsburgs, as long as the Hapsburgs were the dominant power in Central Europe, especially now that the Hapsburgs controlled the former Spanish Netherlands. Though Spain could now be regarded only as a possibly useful auxiliary and was no longer a power to be reckoned with, two other important powers had now entered European affairs. One was post-Petrine Russia which was usually engaged in lopping pieces from the Ottoman Empire, and thus could not spend too much energy and resources on the less important West; the other was Hohenzollern Prussia, now far more consequential than any other German territories outside Austria. The other German territories were fairly equally divided between Catholic and Protestant; the Catholic duchies could usually be relied upon to support the Hapsburgs, while the Protestants might be expected to support Prussia.

Throughout the eighteenth century far more attention was given to the organizing of diplomatic alliances than hitherto. Some theorists even went so far as to suggest that wars would become outmoded, to be replaced by the moves and countermoves of diplomacy, not unlike the game of chess, which is ended by the capitulation of the enemy when faced by overwhelming force. Civilian populations would scarcely be involved, it was thought. After a brief encounter between national forces, one side would be seen to have the advantage, and would sign a treaty, winning some concessions from the enemy—which would change the rulership of a province or two but do no lasting damage to any. Some but not all of the eighteenth century wars followed this pattern. Louis XV on one occasion had already won most of today's Belgium; he probably could have overwhelmed Holland. But in so doing he would have made an implacable enemy of England who would not have tolerated the conquest, thus involving him in a long war which he could not hope to win. So he preferred to withdraw his troops and make peace in exchange for colonial concessions which had not been won by his arms.

The Silesian Wars and the Partitions of Poland. But the great reality in the eighteenth, and in the later part of the nineteenth century, was the emergence of Prussia as a great power under the rulership of Frederick II, the Great (1740–1786). He coveted Silesia, a rich territory more commercially valuable than the entire kingdom of Prussia, and he knew he was strong enough to take it from the Hapsburgs, now under the rule of Maria Theresa, who could not succeed as a woman to the Empire. But whether he would be permitted to keep it was a serious question. All the other powers would necessarily be concerned at the strengthening of his realm and the consequent weakening of Austria. Even Russia might become involved if only for the purpose of winning Austrian support in her other designs. Frederick in fact took Silesia, and Maria Theresa, deeply involved elsewhere, allowed him to keep it after the first war. When she was ready to take on Frederick with somewhat better allies, she fought again, and again lost, confirming the conquest the second time. But by the third war, Austrian diplomacy had organized a grand alliance against Prussia, including both France and Russia, now under the empress Elizabeth. The only aid that Frederick could count on in this war, known as the Seven Years' War (1756–1763), was England, and England was so heavily engaged in fighting France in the New World that she could spare few troops and relatively little money. This time Frederick had to fight for his life and his own homeland of Prussia as well as newly won Silesia. His remarkable military prowess enabled him to compensate to some degree for his lack of men and resources. But even so he was gradually being worn down and would without any doubt have been defeated, had not Empress Elizabeth providentially died. Her nephew and heir, Peter III, was an inordinate admirer of Frederick and had been brought up in Germany. Rather than fight against him he withdrew the Russian troops. Without them the alliance collapsed, and this time Frederick kept Silesia for good, while the British won almost all of French North America.

Catherine the Great, wife of Peter III, who connived with the guards officers to have her estranged husband deposed and then murdered, took over the reins of the Russian government. She preferred not to fight Frederick but to obtain his consent, for a price, to her designs on Poland. The Poles were almost helpless against constant Russian infiltration and intimidation. But Catherine did not feel herself strong enough to take the country and defy the other European powers. The result was the First Partition of Poland (1772) between Frederick, Maria Theresa of Austria (who would have preferred to have had no hand in the matter but had no wish to see her rivals strengthened), and Catherine, the lion's share going to the last. The Poles, finally thoroughly alarmed and determined to keep the rest of their country intact, put through a new constitution, abolishing the "free veto," and establishing a hereditary monarchy. This however did not meet Catherine's plans, since Russian influence in Poland would have been reduced to a minimum. She therefore planned another partition, to which Frederick III of Prussia agreed. This time (1793) Austria did not join. The Poles were still not finished. A national uprising led by Thaddeus Kosciuszko was a forlorn hope but the people went down fighting. The third and final partition took place in 1795, in which Austria took her share. The partitions had aided Prussia to round out her territories, and had added all of ancient Lithuania and much of the Ukraine to Russia. Austria's share, though second only to Russia's in population, was of little use to her, and much of it was lost to Russia after the Napoleonic wars.

THE EXPANSION OF EUROPE IN THE EIGHTEENTH CENTURY

French and British Rivalry. During the eighteenth century the struggles between Britain and France for colonial possessions reached its height. Every European war in which the two sides were involved brought changes in the colonies, but in general it was the war in Europe that determined changes in the ensuing treaties rather than the fighting in the colonies. Thus in the so-called War of the Austrian Succession (1743–1748), known as King George's War in America, the British had won the great French fortress of Louisburg on Cape Breton Island but restored it to the French by the Treaty of Aix-la-Chappelle. But in the Seven Years' War (1756–1763, known as the French and Indian War in America) when Britain's European ally, Frederick the Great, had with British assistance beaten France and Austria, France was forced to cede all her mainland possessions conquered by Britain during the war, retaining only the French sugar islands of the West Indies, which were in fact more profitable to the French than the mainland.

Needless to say, both the English and French colonists resented the manner in which their respective mother countries disposed of them without much regard for their interests; but the French Canadians were less able to make their influence felt than the British Americans. When the Seven Years' War was over, the British government felt that the colonists who had benefited so greatly from British participation in the war, should pay some of its costs. The Americans did not see the matter in at all the same light, resenting all the taxes laid upon them by the British, as long as they were unrepresented in the British Parliament by delegates of their own choice—few realizing that the British people themselves were equally unrepresented in the unreformed Parliament of the eighteenth century. The grievances of the colonists, which were many, and included the subordination of American trade interests to those of the mother country, finally came to a head when the British decided to teach them a lesson and take serious punitive action against those who engaged in minor rebellious acts, especially refusal to pay the indirect taxes. In 1776 the colonists declared their independence in a famous document drawn up by Thomas Jefferson, in which a number of "unalienable" rights to which all men were entitled were said to have been infringed by George III, thereby giving the colonists a "natural" right to rebel for the purpose of winning them back.

The British, believing the colonists incapable of offering serious resistance, took the early part of the war too lightly, and General Burgoyne was compelled to surrender at Saratoga. This first great victory brought the French into the war on the side of the colonists, hoping to undo the settlement of 1763. French aid, especially by sea, was enough to turn the tide for the colonists, who ultimately were able to build an army capable of meeting the British on equal terms. The North Government fell in 1782, and peace was agreed to at Versailles in 1783, which recognized the independence of the new United States of America. The Americans then wrote themselves a federal constitution in 1787, which with comparatively few amendments is still in operation today. George Washington, the commander in chief of the American forces in the war, became the first president of the United States.

The French gained little from their participation, since their navy was seriously defeated by the British in 1782. Canada remained under British control, and was strengthened by the addition of American colonists who wished to remain under British rule. By the Quebec Act of 1784 the British guaranteed the French the right to continue to use their language, and religion, and the settlement was accepted as final. Thereafter the *habitants* used the share in the Canadian government granted them by the British to advance their interests without reference to France; and when the French Revolution destroyed the *ancien régime* forever, most of them lost sympathy with their mother country and settled down as Canadians.

In India the French and British again struggled for trade and influence when the old Mogul empire, founded by a descendant of Timur Lenk, began to collapse after the long reign of the intolerant Muslim Aurangzeb (1659–1707), leaving the way open for the Europeans to play off one Indian group against the other, thus preparing for the conquest of the whole country. The British, however, had one great advantage over the French. Though the latter were often represented by fine soldiers and administrators such as Dupleix, they failed to give them adequate support from home. Too few Frenchmen were interested in the Indian trade, whereas the British East India Company, a semigovernmental institution like the Dutch East India Company, which had the monopoly of the Indian trade, enjoyed powerful support in the British Parliament; and there was no likelihood that its interests would be neglected from lack of a hearing. Louis XV himself had to be approached in France, and the support of his reigning mistress would have to be enlisted before any action was taken; whereas in Britain the trading classes knew very well the value of the Indian trade and were strong enough to persuade Parliament to grant the necessary military aid to the Company. Thus, though Dupleix at one time was within measuring distance of obtaining control of all India, Robert Clive, the British commander on behalf of the Company, was given greater support. Dupleix was recalled, leaving the field open to Clive who overwhelmed the French at the Battle of Plassey in 1757 and virtually drove them from India, leaving only a few settlements in French hands at the Treaty of Paris in 1763. In 1774 the British assumed full responsibility for the government of India, although it remained the financial responsibility of the Company; a succession of governors-general gradually took over the whole subcontinent during the course of the following century. The island of Ceylon was added to the growing British Empire in 1798.

Russian Expansion in Asia. A few words should also be devoted to Russian expansion to the East. In 1581 a band of seminomad Cossacks under their leader Yermak, began to penetrate beyond the Urals into Central Asia. The territory was very sparsely populated, and the Cossacks had very little difficulty in subjugating the people with whom they came in contact. They founded a number of important settlements, which they usually fortified, and reached the Pacific as early as 1540. Yermak himself offered his first conquests to Tsar Ivan IV in exchange for support, and all the territories later acquired were officially under the suzerainty of the tsars. The tsars, however, did almost nothing with the territories, using them mostly as penal colonies, and in the later nineteenth century as areas of settlement for emancipated serfs. Not until the Soviet regime in recent years has the whole territory been gradually developed, now contributing, indeed, a great deal to the power and wealth of the country.

Summary—European Possessions at the End of the Century. Thus by the end of the eighteenth century, the British were securely ensconced in India and North America, with a few scattered colonies elsewhere, while the French had lost almost all they had at one time ruled. Their most important remaining possessions were the sugar islands of the West Indies and the Île de France (Mauritius) in the Indian Ocean. Spain still was master in most of Latin America, but her hold was gradually slipping, Portugal had Brazil and a number of coastal settlements in Africa, used mainly for the export of slaves. The Dutch still possessed the East Indies, which was a profitable commercial empire. In the nineteenth century the Latin American countries achieved their independence (as did Canada), but their culture and language remained Spanish, Portuguese, and Anglo-French. None of the other European possessions was to be lost until the twentieth century, and there was a new outbreak of colonial expansion in the nineteenth. Discussion of this phase of European expansion will be reserved for Chapter XIX, devoted exclusively to this subject.

CHAPTER XV

THE FRENCH REVOLUTION AND THE ERA OF NAPOLEON

The demarcation line between the early modern and the modern world has traditionally been considered to be the French Revolution, and there is much to recommend such a division. Though the Revolution occurred in France, it rapidly affected the rest of Europe; and all monarchs recognized at once that their own positions were threatened, as they had not been by the English Revolution of the seventeenth century, which likewise involved the beheading of a king by his subjects. There had been such an outpouring of political thought in the eighteenth century and such serious consideration of the foundations of society that monarchs could no longer believe that their persons and regimes were sacrosanct, merely because they were hallowed by time and tradition. Indeed, as we have seen in the last chapter, European rulers themselves were inclined to feel that their regimes should justify themselves by being beneficial to their subjects. It was inevitable that these subjects, if they lived under an unenlightened rule, might reach the conclusion that the monarchy was not justifying itself in practice and might reasonably be replaced by an alternative. So, once the Revolution occurred in one country it was natural that intellectuals elsewhere should take a long hard look at their own regimes and possible that they might conclude that these regimes had outlived their usefulness—and that they themselves, as had happened in America, might hope to set up a new and functioning republican government which would give them far greater prestige and influence.

It was, however, a long step from criticizing one's own regime to plotting to overthrow it; and it is doubtful if there would have been many revolutions outside France if the French themselves had not decided that their own was available for export and backed their decision by force of arms. The rulers who took the initiative to try to overthrow by arms the revolutionary regime in France, opened the door to reprisals, which were duly visited upon them by the conscript French revolutionary armies, even before Napoleon put his military talent at their disposal. Thus when the Napoleonic tide had receded nothing in Europe could ever be the same again; and though the Congress of Vienna tried, with some success, to control the revolutionary flood for a further half century, the era had in fact opened in which kings had the choice either of keeping their thrones and subjecting themselves to constitutional limitations or being replaced by republican regimes. This is the modern world which we know— and if despots have occasionally ruled in the last century, few of them have been kings, and none have ruled simply by the divine right of heredity.

THE FRENCH REVOLUTION

Causes of the Revolution. We have already considered the failure of the French monarchy to put through its programs of reforms in the eighteenth century, and the continued refusal of the privileged classes to give up their immunity from direct taxation. This resulted in the swift decline of the government into bankruptcy, accelerated by the huge costs of French participation in the War of American Independence, for which no financial compensation had been received. Some of the nobles and virtually the whole middle class honestly believed that when the king proposed to tax them, he should at the same time concede them some share in the government, a share enjoyed by their counterparts in England for centuries. All they could do now was to stand firm on what they considered their traditional rights and to turn a deaf ear to the king's requests. No other outlet for their grievances was permitted them, especially since the heavy hand of the censor fell upon their publications. The majority of the nobles and the higher clergy, whose Church was immune from taxation but offered a voluntary though inadequate contribution to royal expenses, were the beneficiaries of the present system. They felt that any change, especially one that gave substantial power to the bourgeois, would be likely to be for the worse. The lower clergy, to the contrary, were usually more closely identified with the interests of the peasants to whom they ministered; and they appreciated the grievances which the peasants had against the relics of the feudal and manorial systems in the form of forced labor, fees paid to their lords, and land taxes extorted from them to compensate for their masters' immunity. Neither the peasants nor the lower clergy had, as a rule, anything against the king, and the Church played as important a part in their lives as ever. Lastly, the urban masses suffered from an inchoate general grievance against all the privileged classes, but the indirect taxes and high prices consequent upon the financial instability of the government weighed upon them most heavily. A number of bad harvests in the 1780's had raised the price of bread even higher than usual, so that there was actual want in the big urban centers.

Though the accumulation of these grievances added up to a considerable dissatisfaction with the government, which was of course blamed for them all, only the middle class knew what it wanted, and it was this class which determined that the financial embarrassment of the government on this occasion must be exploited to give it a share in the government. It was an opportunity that might not recur, and the bourgeois had no intention of helping to relieve the situation without winning substantial reforms from the government. But they were not agreed among themselves as to just what they did want, and various pressure groups were formed as the Revolution progressed, each with a different and very flexible set of demands. On the left wing were the Girondins, who wanted a constitutional monarchy or a moderate republican regime and the Jacobins, who wanted a republic under their own control and had no use whatever for a king.

The Calling of the States-General. From the time he inherited the throne Louis XVI tried to appease the reformers and save the solvency of his government. But the American War plunged him further toward the abyss, and he could not persuade the privileged classes to accept any reforms that would involve their taxation. As the 1780's wore on, and one minister after another was compelled to acknowledge the failure of his efforts, the demand grew for the summoning of the ancient States-General, which had not met since 1614, but which had been the traditional institution from which the king had to request financial subsidies. Louis at last bowed to the demand and the States-General met, after all classes in the country had submitted lists of grievances which they wished to be considered, and if possible redressed. Louis at first held the notion that he could play the two more conservative "estates," the clergy and the nobility, against the third estate, the middle class, which had the most representatives (600) and could outvote either of the other two estates if each representative had a vote. But Louis thought the estates should vote as groups, and that the two senior estates should therefore be able to outvote the third estate by two to one. The third estate had no intention of permitting itself to be outmanoeuvred by such a transparent device, and refused to deliberate until Louis permitted voting by delegates. It was finally allowed to have its way, but not until Louis had lost face by first making a show of resolution and then backing down. Meanwhile the Parisian mob, thinking that the king was deliberately trying to stall until his foreign troops could disperse the States-General, marched on the ancient royal prison of the Bastille and captured it (July 14, 1789), massacring the royal defenders.

The third estate was soon able to obtain a majority through the defection to its side of a number of the lower clergy, and the States-General was converted into a constituent (National) Assembly, with the task of writing a constitution. In one of its early meetings a few nobles, perceiving that the time had come to make some concessions, especially since the peasants were beginning to take matters into their own hands in the countryside, announced to the Assembly that they were giving up all their remaining feudal and manorial rights. Their announcement proved contagious, and in one night feudalism was virtually abolished. Most of the peasants were now satisfied. What disturbed them, and the king, was the evident intention of the Assembly to disestablish the Catholic Church, an intention finally translated in 1790 into the Civil Constitution of the Clergy, under which the monasteries were to be dissolved, Church lands sequestrated, and all the clergy, high and low, were to be converted into servants of the state, with salaries paid by it. A number of clergymen appealed to the pope, who, after much hesitation, finally came out against the Constitution.

This interjection of a religious issue into the Constitution had the effect of dividing clergy and people on religious grounds. The state insisted that all bishops and lower clergy should take an oath to support the Constitution on pain of being dispossessed of their livings. For much of the rest of the Revolution, an active counterrevolutionary movement called the Vendée, often led by nonjuring or refractory priests was in operation in the countryside. Even more serious was Louis' belief that his soul would be endangered if he supported the Constitution; thereafter he too must be regarded as having been a counterrevolutionary, determined to do nothing that would serve to put him in the position of supporting the Revolution.

The Legislative Assembly. Meanwhile, in due course the Assembly produced a resounding resolution known as the Declaration of the Rights of Man, largely based upon the principles of Jean-Jacques Rousseau, assuring to all men their natural rights as citizens, and, in 1791, a constitution. This first of the revolutionary constitutions was a very moderate document. It established a constitutional monarchy and left the king substantial powers, including a suspensory veto on legislation. It did not satisfy the king, though he accepted it, since the pope had not yet pronounced upon the Civil Constitution of the Clergy. Many of the nobles preferred to emigrate rather than to submit to it, intending to arouse monarchical opinion abroad and perhaps win foreign intervention against the revolutionaries.

Louis knew he was in some danger, for it was clear that the Parisian mob which had already taken the Bastille, was not prepared to be cheated of its hoped-for gains, and was far less moderate than the bourgeois-controlled Assembly. Moreover, some of the extremist clubs were willing to accept its support. The mob had already marched before the end of 1789 on the palace of Versailles and compelled the king and the Assembly to meet thereafter in Paris. Thus Louis was a virtual prisoner, and if his full power together with the established religion were to be restored, it was clear to him that he must escape abroad. He made the attempt in June, 1791, and was recaptured. His position was now one of extreme danger, since he had given public notice that his acceptance of the Constitution had been made only under duress, and he did not believe himself bound by its provisions.

Nevertheless, he was not as yet deposed, and the constitution to which he had finally consented came into effect. A new Legislative Assembly came into being (October, 1791) and began its work. Meanwhile the rulers of Prussia and Austria, urged on by French emigrés and by the French queen, Marie Antoinette, daughter of the Austrian empress, Maria Theresa, had taken official notice of the recapture of the king, and threatened intervention in certain well defined circumstances (Declaration of Pillnitz, August, 1791). The Girondins who were in control of the Assembly chose to regard this still decently veiled threat as a cause for war, and declared war against Austria. But the country was hopelessly unprepared for war; and though it put several armies in the field, they were badly disciplined, uncertain of their aims, and were uniformly unsuccessful. The Prussian commander, the duke of Brunswick, in July issued a threatening ultimatum which greatly excited the Assembly and the mob. The latter stormed the king's palace and killed his Swiss guards. The Assembly thereupon decided to call a National Convention, elected under universal manhood suffrage, to write a republican constitution. Many prisoners were massacred by the mob. In September the Prussians were defeated in the battle of Valmy, and the next stage of the Revolution began.

The Reign of Terror. In the National Convention the extremist groups were in control from the first. The monarchy was abolished, and by a majority of one vote it was decided to put the king to death. The Revolutionary government proclaimed that it would give help to all who wished to change their governments, and the war for a time was successful. But the Jacobins were determined to win full power for themselves and their program, and they did not wish even the measure of bourgeois control favored by their opponents. The defeat and defection of the leading Girondin general provided the Jacobins with their opportunity. They denounced the Girondins in the Convention and guillotined their leaders. Those who escaped fled to the provinces, where they stirred up opposition to the Jacobins. The latter, now in full control of the Convention, set up an emergency government, known as the Committee of Public Safety, and revolutionary tribunals to punish dissenters.

There ensued what was to become known as the Reign of Terror, directed by the two Jacobin leaders, Danton and Robespierre. This was the most bloody period of the Revolution (1793–1794); but the *levée-en-masse* (universal conscription) ensured the provision of enough troops for the army, which was organized by Lazare Carnot into an effective military instrument, able to win victories against the disunited and often dispirited forces that were thrown against them. Meanwhile the National Convention passed over eleven thousand laws, changing the entire administrative system of France. The worship of God was abolished and that of Supreme Reason put in its place; the months were renamed and Sunday replaced by a secular holiday every ten days. Men addressed one another by the simple title of "citizen," all aristocratic titles being abolished. The Committee of Public Safety and the Convention assisted their lower-class supporters by attempting to fix prices on many articles of consumption, and succeeded to some degree in arresting temporarily the collapse of the currency.

In April, 1794, Robespierre made himself supreme by sending his leading opponents, including Danton, to the guillotine. In July Robespierre himself met the same fate at the hands of opponents who were afraid that it might be their turn next, so quickly was the Revolution devouring its children. The Convention, hitherto cowed, then asserted itself, and moderate leadership, fortified by the return of the Girondin exiles, replaced the Jacobin ascendancy (Thermidorean Reaction). The army continued to win victories, and Flanders was overrun. Prussia withdrew from the war in March 1795. The first of the Revolutionary republics was founded in the Low Countries under French domination, to be known as the Batavian Republic.

The Directory and the Rise of Napoleon. The Convention decided that the domestic gains of the Revolution ought to be consolidated, but that the war should continue until French war aims had been achieved. A more moderate constitution was agreed upon with a Directorate of Five and a two-chambered legislature. But in order to ensure their continuation in office the legislators of the Convention decided that two thirds of their number should belong to one or other of the new chambers. This provision excited much opposition in Paris, and a rising had to be suppressed by the Directors, who called upon an artillery officer named Napoleon Bonaparte who had distinguished himself in the wars, to disperse it. This he did with what he called a "whiff of grapeshot" and was rewarded with a command against the Austrians in northern Italy.

Napoleon carried out a brilliant campaign in Italy, setting up the Cisalpine Republic of northern Italy and the Ligurnian Republic in the area around Genoa. In the Treaty of Campo Formio in 1797 he compelled the Austrians to recognize the Cisalpine Republic and to concede the former Austrian Netherlands, now part of the Batavian Republic to France. In the following two years other French armies set up a Republic of Rome, a Helvetic Republic in Switzerland, and the Parthenopean Republic in Naples. Napoleon himself after his Italian victories went to Boulogne just across the Channel from England and made somewhat ostentatious preparations to invade the country which had been one of his most persistent opponents, subsidizing all the enemies of France with money, but taking little part in the military action. Apparently deciding that he was not strong enough for the purpose, he decided to attack her indirectly by threatening her Indian empire. For this purpose he set out for Egypt, where he won some easy victories against the Egyptians, but was defeated in a naval action at Aboukir by the English fleet under Admiral Horatio Nelson and was thus cut off from France. It was during this expedition which, like those of Alexander the Great, was accompanied by scientists, that the Rosetta Stone was discovered by one of Napoleon's officers, a find which was eventually to provide the key for the understanding of the ancient Egyptian language. In 1799 Napoleon himself left for France. His troops were undefeated by land, but he had involved France in an unnecessary war with the Turks, and their position became increasingly insecure until they were repatriated under an agreement with the Turks in 1803.

Meanwhile the Directory, in spite of its early foreign successes, had become increasingly unpopular at home. It had initiated the restoration of a sound currency, issuing a new money based on the security of confiscated lands. When this money, like its predecessors, fell catastrophically the Directory then repudiated two thirds of the national debt, laying the groundwork for the later Napoleonic successful reform of the currency. This move, like most of the other successful experiments of the Directory, was never credited to the Directors by Napoleon, since Napoleon invariably took credit for anything constructive done under his regime. In 1797 a new election was held for the legislature, resulting, in large part due to the participation of great numbers of antirevolutionary peasants, in a royalist majority. This could not be countenanced by the Directors. They split among themselves, but the majority of three received the military backing of Napoleon and nullified the election.

In 1799 when a new Anglo-Austro-Russian alliance was forged by England, who remained its chief paymaster, the French suffered a number of serious defeats at Austro-Russian hands in Italy, making it imperative for the Directory to obtain the assistance of the one general, who, it was still widely believed, was an invincible hero. Napoleon, who had returned to Paris but was without a command, conspired with one of the Directors to overthrow the government. This was accomplished, incidentally without much help from Napoleon, who fainted at the critical moment, and a new regime was installed with Napoleon as First Consul of three. He soon sidetracked his colleagues and became sole Consul. From that eminence it was not difficult to promote himself to the exalted position of emperor of the French, which he achieved in 1804. But it is properly from 1799 that his absolute rule should be dated, since there was from then onward no power in the state that could stand against his will. Each change in his title was ratified by a plebiscite, in which Napoleon received immense majorities.

THE ERA OF NAPOLEON

Domestic Achievements. The constitution approved by Napoleon was designed to place all the effective force of the government in the emperor's hands. The bodies with which he worked were either nominated or approved by him and had only consultative functions. Universal manhood suffrage was retained, but the vote was not meaningful, in view of the fact that the men elected had no power and very little authority. The adminstrative reforms of the Revolution were maintained; there was trial by jury; neither judges nor anyone else could buy their offices or inherit them; and the tax system, though still marked by anomalies, was no longer one that gave special privileges and immunities to a particular class. The educational system was strengthened by new schools under state control. Napoleon was interested in having enough men available to staff his civil service and army, and equality of opportunity was provided in both to the able. Napoleon insisted also in having all the local laws of the various parts of the country consolidated in a new code based on Roman principles, known as the *Code Napoléon,* which the exiled emperor in later years was to proclaim as his greatest achievement. Perhaps even more important in his time, however, was the peace he signed with the papacy in 1801, defining the rights to which the Church was entitled in France. The Church lands sequestrated in 1790 remained in the hands of their purchasers, but the papacy was given control of the appointment of bishops, a right it had not possessed since the sixteenth century—though their salaries continued to be paid by the state. The Church was not re-established, and religious toleration was continued, even the salaries of Protestant ministers being paid by the state. After the signing of the Concordat of 1801, the refractory clergy accepted the Revolution, and the pope himself crowned Napoleon emperor.

Revolutionary Influence in Europe. Abroad the Napoleonic reforms proved even more revolutionary than they were at home. France was incomparably the greatest military power in Europe. Only Britain could be considered to be immune to French innovations, since she had already developed, if sedately, along her own lines, making a new revolution unnecessary and unlikely, especially since she ultimately emerged the victor in the war with France. Wherever the French armies conquered, the old order was seriously shaken by reforms instituted by Napoleon. Invariably, in spite of the fact that he was a foreign invader, there were some people who sympathized with his aims with regard to their own country. If only for the purpose of defeating France, it was necessary for some reforms to be put into operation. This was especially true of Prussia, to a lesser degree of Austria. In the short-lived republics established under the Directory, the peoples gained their first democratic experience—and even when they were directly subjugated by the French and ruled by Napoleon or his relatives, the experience was not lost. It can therefore be easily understood why Napoleon was so detested by the monarchs who could have tolerated a mere change of dynasty in France as long as they retained their own thrones. But they regarded Napoleon as the heir of the Jacobins, and indeed often referred to him contemptuously as "that Jacobin"—even though at home in France he was almost as much an "enlightened" heir of Louis XIV as he was of the Revolution.

The Napoleonic Wars. Napoleon's first task was, of course, to put an end to the wars that had been raging since 1791, to give him a chance to consolidate his own regime and the French gains in the warfare. After renewing the war with Austria and defeating her again he concluded a peace, following it up with treaties with all the other enemy countries in Europe, including England. Since Napoleon's star was in the ascendant at that moment, all the treaties were very favorable to France. The new republics were recognized, Spain ceded Louisiana in America, which was soon after sold to the United States, the Holy Roman Empire conceded the Rhine boundary and Belgium to France, and Britain restored the West Indian islands which, as usual, she had captured during the war. From 1803 to 1813 Napoleon never found all the European powers united against him again. Each believed that it could fish in the troubled waters, and gain some of its own ends by allying itself with him, or at least preserving neutrality with him. The old order was disintegrating, the Empire was obviously on the point of dissolution, and some rulers, especially the German princes who had been promised compensation for the loss of their principalities taken over by France in recent years, were far more anxious to win these territories, even at the expense of other Germans, than to defeat Napoleon. Only Britain was determined to right the balance of power that had now turned so decisively in favor of her greatest Continental rival; to her the Treaty of Amiens signed between her and Napoleon in 1802 could be nothing but a breathing space, as it was also to Napoleon, whose ambitions were as yet far from sated, as long as he had surplus power that could be used and the European state structure remained in a condition of flux.

The British were the first to renew the war, claiming that Napoleon had not carried out the terms of the Treaty of Amiens. Thereafter they tried to organize one coalition after another with whatever allies they could find, and sought out the soft spots in the defenses of Napoleonic Europe. At first Napoleon again prepared for an invasion of England; but when the latter succeeded in organizing a great coalition of herself, Austria, Russia, and Sweden, he gave up the notion of a direct invasion. He sold Louisiana to the United States, recognizing that the effort to restore any part of French rule on the American mainland would involve him with the United States, and would dangerously weaken the forces at his disposal. Though he lost the naval Battle of Trafalgar to the British in 1805, he utterly defeated the Austrians and Russians at the Battle of Austerlitz a few weeks afterward. He bought off the Prussians, who had been about to join the coalition, by conceding to them the English electorate of Hanover. Austria was then forced to conclude a humiliating peace. A few months later the Holy Roman Empire was declared abolished by the Hapsburg emperor, who became thereafter simply the emperor of Austria. Meanwhile the Bourbon king of Naples was dethroned, and Joseph

Bonaparte, elder brother of Napoleon was proclaimed king. Louis Napoleon, another brother, was made king of Holland, the Batavian Republic being extinguished.

In 1806 Napoleon organized the various West German princedoms into a Confederation of the Rhine under his protection. This brought Prussia into the war without Austria, who was licking her wounds and kept the recent peace; but Prussia enjoyed such aid as the Russians could give, which at the moment was not much. In a brilliant campaign Napoleon virtually knocked Prussia out of the war and occupied Berlin, then turned on the Russians and defeated them in the Battle of Friedland (1807). He then signed a very favorable peace treaty at Tilsit with both Russia and Prussia. A new kingdom was created for another of Napoleon's brothers, Jerome, which was known as the Kingdom of Westphalia, carved out of the domains of Prussia and minor German states.

Meanwhile, Napoleon was doing his best to subdue his most stubborn enemy, Great Britain. In 1806 he inaugurated the Continental System, which was supposed to cut off the entire continent of Europe from British trade; to which Britain retorted with Orders-in-Council cutting off all trade with Europe, including that carried in neutral vessels from Asia and America. Napoleon insisted that all the European countries observe his decrees, and the continental powers for a time even declared war on Britain. Denmark and the Iberian Peninsula were the only areas of importance that had usable ports for the English trade. Britain struck first at Denmark and captured the small Danish fleet. But the country then voluntarily allied itself with France, closing the trade outlet of Copenhagen to the British. Spain and Portugal Napoleon dealt with directly. Portugal, refusing to abrogate her long-standing alliance with Britain, was occupied by French troops, the Spanish Bourbon king was compelled to abdicate, his position being taken by Joseph Bonaparte, hitherto the king of Naples. Since Napoleon had now run out of brothers, one of his generals, Murat, was made king of Naples.

British sea power, however, caused Napoleon much trouble in the Iberian Peninsula. Though often defeated, the British nevertheless secured a toe hold in Portugal and ultimately were able to push on into Spain, where the new monarchy was unpopular and constantly had to call upon French troops for aid. Even Napoleon himself had to invade on one occasion to secure the position of his brother. In 1809 Austria attempted to throw off the Napoleonic yoke, but after winning some victories, lost the Battle of Wagram to Napoleon, and was shorn of some of her territories in the peace that followed. The Austrian emperor allowed his daughter to marry Napoleon, who had by now divorced his first wife, Josephine, and hoped for an heir from the bluest blood in Europe. For a few years Europe was relatively quiet, but Tsar Alexander I of Russia was restive. He objected to Napoleon's policy in Poland and to the Continental System. When he began to try to organize an alliance against the French, Napoleon made preparations for an attack which would, if successful, have completed the subjugation of all Europe.

In 1812, aided by contingents from his temporarily submissive allies, Austria and Prussia, Napoleon invaded Russia. Though he took Moscow, he found the city deserted. Soon afterward the Russians burned it and Napoleon was forced to begin a retreat which soon became a disaster, the Russians harassing the French and refusing any major battle before the retreat had become a rout. Though Napoleon himself made his escape and rallied enough of his armies from the rest of Europe to make a fight of it, Austria and Prussia deserted him, as was to be expected, and a new alliance was formed, this time with all the major powers in Europe arrayed against him. In 1813 at the Battle of Leipzig (Battle of the Nations) Napoleon was decisively defeated. Since French troops had had to be recalled from Spain, the British began to advance in that country. Napoleon still had many opportunities to sign a favorable peace in the next months, as he continued to win some useful victories which gave him leverage in negotiations. But in the end France was successfully invaded and Paris taken on March 31, 1814. Napoleon abdicated and was granted the island of Elba as his personal principality, while the victorious allies retired to Vienna to decide how the Napoleonic empire was to be liquidated.

The first decision, incorporated in the Treaty of Paris in 1814, was to restore the nearest Bourbon heir to the French throne under the title of Louis XVIII; to make his position tenable only mild peace terms were imposed upon France, by which she retained the gains of the first revolutionary years. While Congress was still discussing the permanent peace terms, to be discussed in Chapter XVII, Napoleon escaped from Elba and succeeded in rallying France once more to his standard. Louis XVIII fled and Napoleon entered Paris. But the anti-French coalition was quickly re-formed, and the combination again proved too great for the emperor. At the Battle of Waterloo (June 21, 1815) he was defeated by the British under Wellington and by the Prussians under Blücher. After his surrender he was condemned to permanent exile in the South Atlantic in the British island of St. Helena, where he died in 1821.

CHAPTER XVI

THE AGRICULTURAL AND INDUSTRIAL REVOLUTIONS

This chapter will be devoted to the economic background of Western advancement, the conditions which made possible all the political and social changes that characterize modern civilization. If today only a little more than ten per cent of the population of the United States live on farms, whereas two centuries ago the proportion was almost reversed, this has been due to two concurrent revolutions, the Agricultural and the Industrial Revolutions. Both are still in progress today; but in spite of their persistence it is fair enough to call them revolutions since their effect was to overturn the whole foundations of Western society—even though they were not events that took place, like the French Revolution, once and for all and were then finished. It is these revolutions that distinguish Western civilization from all civilizations that preceded it; and in the long run they are far more effective agents of Western expansionism than all the crusaders, explorers, imperialists, and colonialists sent out by the West from the Middle Ages to the present. Every country in the world has been affected by them, and every government today has to formulate a policy on how to deal with them. No country wishes to fall behind and keep its people from enjoying the material benefits they bring; none can be indifferent to their effects. All they can hope to do is to turn them into such channels that they will not utterly destroy the fabric of their present social structure and to try to transform their present society in such a manner that they too can have the same revolutions with the minimum of dislocation.

THE AGRICULTURAL REVOLUTION

The medieval manor was a virtually self-sufficient entity, consuming the vast bulk of its production on the manor itself. Its agricultural methods, by modern standards, were hopelessly inefficient, and the crop yield was low. There was, at least until the Black Death, a surplus of labor; the application of more labor to the land could not result in higher production as long as the actual methods were so inefficient. We have already noted the changes in land tenure that took place in Western Europe, the gradual emancipation of the serfs and their conversion into small holders; whereas in Eastern Europe there was a tendency for serfdom to increase, a result of the ever growing power of the nobles. Eastern Europe therefore lagged behind the West in agricultural methods, as it still does. Only in countries like the Soviet Union where there has been an agricultural revolution in recent decades has the gap between East and West begun to be closed—though it is too early as yet to say whether the collective and state farm system of the Communist countries will prove itself as efficient as private land tenure and capitalistic incentives.

The Agricultural Revolution has consisted of an advance on many fronts. The first, and probably the most important, was the division of the land into more manageable economic units than the large manor. The late medieval sheep growers led the way by using a part of all of their lands for one crop, wool, which was most in demand in their day. For the purpose of specialization they "enclosed" the common land and marginal land formerly used for food crops, and there they pastured their sheep. Dispossessed rural workers either went to the towns, thus contributing to the growth of urban manufacturing, or had to make their living on the land that remained. This required more intensive cultivation of what they had left and provided an incentive for technical agricultural improvements.

As population grew, more food was of course needed. From the seventeenth century onward, improvements were made in many directions. The innovations came from Holland, France, and, above all, eighteenth-century England, where the great pioneer was Viscount (Turnip) Townshend, who publicized his system widely. The system involved the scientific rotation of crops to make use of the humus in the soil and the available supply of organic manure to the best advantage. At about the same time the horse-drawn hoe and seed drill were invented, which were both labor-saving devices and at the same time made more effective use of the seed. A working farmer named Bakewell also began to experiment with the different strains of animals, thus beginning the specialization of farm animals for the purposes for which they were required. The next stage was the discovery about 1840 by Justus von Liebig of the chemical components of plants, which he found by analysis of their ash. This of course was the fundamental discovery behind the immense fertilizer industry.

The other great development was the use of machinery to save the often extremely arduous hand labor of earlier times. The cotton gin, invented by the American Eli Whitney revolutionized cotton production just at the time when a cheap and durable material was coming to be required for the increasing population. In time almost all agricultural operations began to be performed by machines, at first using the labor of horses and oxen, and then of tractors. The increasing amounts of capital needed by a working farmer if he were to produce his crops at a competitive price involved ever increasing specialization and larger acreages, since machines could not be used profitably if they were to be used only a day or two during the whole year.

All these inventions and improvements were cumulative; but all involved the employment of ever fewer workers on the land in Western countries, in spite of the greater increase of the production of the crops. One purebred Holstein cow bred for her milk-yield could give more milk in a year than half a dozen less specialized cows living on a rough pasture; one White Leghorn chicken might give over three hundred eggs a year in comparison with perhaps forty if she had lived in a state of nature. One tractor driven by two or three men could work twenty-four hours a day during the season, and plow over a thousand acres in a growing season, and chemical fertilizer could take the place of the earlier summer fallow which left one third of the fields idle every year. But the displacement of labor meant that there would be widespread suffering and social dislocation if there were no alternative employment available for the displaced. Thus a concurrent Industrial Revolution has historically been necessary whenever an Agricultural Revolution has been successful, whereas in countries where there is an overabundance of labor but as yet only an embryonic industrial revolution, the agricultural methods developed in the West cannot be used immediately without damaging the fabric of local society. Hence the insistence of all the new nations on developing industry, for which again they have to look to the West for their examples.

THE INDUSTRIAL REVOLUTION

The Progress of Invention. The Industrial Revolution, like the Agricultural Revolution, is a continuing process. Before there could be any great increase in industrial production there had to be a market available, a sufficient accumulation of capital to build and distribute the machines, a large enough pool of scientific and technical knowledge for the inventors to draw upon, and an organization of industry capable of being expanded as the market for the finished products grew. These conditions were fulfilled in the seventeenth and subsequent centuries, and as the Industrial Revolution progressed, so did the momentum of social change, even though it never kept pace with the advancement of engineering and science. It would be tedious to recount all the inventions that have marked this period, and most of them are familiar to every reader. The crucial early invention was the steam engine, which utilized the energy of coal and water to create power. At the beginning of the eighteenth century the English mineowners were using an inefficient steam engine invented by Thomas Newcomen to pump water from their coal mines. As coal was available in unlimited quantities, the inefficient use of the fuel was not a great drawback to the use of this machine. James Watt in 1765 redesigned this steam engine so that it used less coal, enabling it to be employed in other places than in the immediate vicinity of the coal. The steam engine by the early decades of the nineteenth century was being used to propel steam locomotives by land, and Robert Fulton in 1807 first used a steam engine to propel a river boat in the Hudson.

The leading world industry in the early modern period was textiles, and the method used for production was what is known as the domestic system. "Putters-out," as the English called them (jobbers), would distribute the raw material to be finished among numerous farm homes and collect them when they were completed, giving the workers a contract rate of pay for their work. But the farmers and the cottagers could make use of only the most primitive machinery; everything else was beyond their means. When machinery began to be invented to improve textile production, beginning with the flying shuttle (John Kay) in 1733 and culminating in the power loom of Edmund Cartwright in 1784, it was clear that the domestic system was doomed, since no small producer could afford such an innovation. The progress to the factory system, under which the machinery was owned by a capitalist who hired specialized workers to tend the machines, was rapid, and little was left of the domestic system by the mid-nineteenth century.

The development of the key raw materials used in industry was at first slow, since much scientific knowledge had to be accumulated; and inventions could not be made on the job, as so many were in the case of the machines. Iron had of course been known for more than two thousand years, but only wrought or beaten iron could be made by earlier technical processes, the individual blacksmith with his anvil and bellows being the typical productive unit. It was necessary to develop methods to obtain far greater temperatures than was possible with bellows; and this was done by using coke instead of coal and making the coke by burning off the gas in a high chimney. Even so, it was more than a century before steelmaking became economical, when processes for smelting out the impurities in the iron ore were invented (Bessemer in 1856, Siemens-Martin, 1866). Today the methods have been refined out of all recognition, and the exact quantities of all ingredients for making different kinds of steel are known, and the knowledge utilized for manufacturing exactly the steel needed for the different industrial processes. In recent years other materials have begun to be used instead of steel for many purposes—notably aluminum, derived mostly from bauxite, and an impressive array of materials never found in nature, invented by the chemist in his laboratory, and using all the known raw materials. Celluloid was the first of these materials, which have now become known under the general term of "plastics."

Meanwhile, the need grew for increased transportation, especially in England, the leading industrial country in the nineteenth century. Canals were developed, along which heavy goods could be transported at a minimal cost, new methods of constructing and surfacing roads, and, of course, steam railroads. With the development of the internal combustion engine late in the nineteenth century, a new era opened, to which again scientific research greatly contributed, especially in the improvement of fuels. Today coal is used ever less frequently as a fuel in the more industrialized countries, especially the United States, and very rarely indeed directly. Gasoline and diesel fuel are used for transportation by road, railroad, and in the air, while electricity and gas, the former produced by water power or from steam plants fueled by coal, and the latter either piped in its natural state or derived from coal, are the preferred sources for heating and power. In the last decades the atom has been harnessed to man's use by the process of nuclear fission, but the process is yet too costly to be used save for special purposes such as underwater propulsion.

The proliferation of new inventions and new materials made necessary new techniques for industrial production. Whereas in the early decades of the Industrial Revolution the entrepreneur could build himself a factory by accumulating his own capital or borrowing from a few sleeping or active partners, the ever increasing need for reducing the unit cost of industrial products to meet competition made it necessary for him to have access to more capital than he could expect to find among his friends and potential partners. So the public joint-stock company, which had been known for several centuries but had never been the preferred method of business organization, now became the most easily available source for the required finance. In this type of company the risks were shared by thousands of small investors who played no part in day-to-day management, but who received profits from the business in proportion to the amount of money they had invested. Banks and trustees who have money to invest on behalf of depositors may also finance the more solid of these companies. But with the possibility of having really large business enterprises, it became essential to find the means of organizing them in such a way as to make the most efficient use of labor and machinery. The pioneer in these efficiency studies was the American Frederick Taylor, and all enterprises in subsequent times have depended in some degree on the work done by him.

The Technique of Mass Production. Nevertheless, even the most efficient production is useless without equivalent consumption. The great bottleneck in consumption during the nineteenth century was the inability to tap mass markets because of the poverty of the worker. Industrial goods could be sold only to the relatively wealthy middle and upper classes, who formed only a small minority even in the industrialized nations. The answer to this problem was found by many industrialists, but the most spectacular demonstration of its effectiveness was made by Henry Ford, who, contrary of the advice of all his fellow manufacturers who thought him mad, decided to raise the salaries of his workers in the hopes that they too might be able to buy a Ford if the cost were sufficiently reduced. But it seemed in the last degree unlikely that costs could be reduced by raising the cost of labor. The answer to this was standardization and specialization, or what has come to be known as mass production. This technique involves the manufacture of interchangeable parts, each made by specialized machines. These parts are then brought together in an assembly line, where the complete article is assembled by workers specialized in that task. Each worker performs probably only one operation, and he spends the whole of his working day on it. He is aided throughout by a machine designed for the single purpose intended for that particular part.

Production of the item therefore increases enormously, but the unit cost goes down. If the product is not sold the manufacturer of course goes bankrupt; it is up to him to see that the product is not left unsold in his warehouses. The mass market is therefore artificially created by advertising; but even so the product cannot be sold unless there are enough persons with the money available to buy it. Ford's raising of the salaries of the workers was a step in this direction, and in the industrial countries of Western civilization the process of increasing the money available for purchase of durables has been continuous since his day—in spite of occasional periods, such as the Great Depression of the 1930's, when consumption and the distribution of income were unable to keep pace with production. In the last decades numerous devices for enabling the customer to spend his income in advance during the presumed life of the product have helped to keep industry humming. In the most recent times the ingeniousness of inventors and engineers has again, however, tended to defeat its own objective. Under the system that is now called "automation" ever more ingenious machines have been invented to do the work of men. Thus fewer workers are needed, and fewer workers receive wages to enable them to buy the ever increasing supply of goods produced by the machines. This, indeed, will be the crucial problem of the next decades and may require more fundamental changes in Western societies than have yet been envisaged by industry and government. Hitherto it has been thought that industrial unemployment will be compensated for by increase of employment in the "service industries." It remains to be seen whether this in practice will be found sufficient or whether more may not have to be done in the direction of lessening the hours of work—or even the most radical suggestion of all, divorcing income from labor, so that a man will be paid not by his work but according to what his society can afford from its total income.

Social Thought of the Industrial Age. This last suggestion was already put forward in the nineteenth century by thinkers who prematurely concluded that the problem of production was solved, and that what remained was the changing of the social order in such a manner that the goods produced by the Industrial Revolution should be as equitably distributed as possible. Different forms of socialism were widely discussed and political parties calling themselves socialist were formed to put their principles into effect. It was also widely believed that nationalism would be replaced by internationalism. Following the teachings of Karl Marx, whose so-called "scientific socialism" gained most supporters, since it involved revolutionary plans to overthrow existing societies, it was thought that classes would take the place of nations. Above all, the productive working class in one country would unite itself with its opposite numbers in other countries and overthrow the bourgeoisie, which had performed a useful function in destroying the feudal system but was now itself outmoded, digging its own grave. The bourgeoisie now controlled the means of production which it used exclusively for its own benefit. But, according to Marxian thought, it had raised up against itself the more powerful and numerous working class which would in due course put an end to its supremacy. All history, it was said, was the history of class struggles; but the final struggle was now approaching when the working class would put an end to its oppressors, and the era of the "dictatorship of the proletariat" would be ushered in. In due time the state itself was expected to "wither away."

To give force to these predictions, international meetings with delegates from all socialist parties were called, and an embryonic international organization was formed. But there was so much jockeying for power and so much difference of opinion regarding immediate and long-term aims, as well as between the proponents of different socialist theories, that these successive "Internationals" were never very effective, even though their very existence struck terror into the more conservative upholders of the status quo in the European countries.

The Rise of Big Government. The slow social revolution that took place within the Western nations as a result of the advances in industry was less spectacular than the socialist thinkers predicted, but was none the less real. In the early nineteenth century the first results of the factory system in the social conditions of England of the period were such as to shock the conscience of the people, including members of Parliament. Workers flocked from the countryside to the new factory towns, where the companies provided, at most, minimal housing. The influx of would-be workers was such that economic theorists, such as David Ricardo, pointed out that there would always be too many workers chasing too few jobs, and thus wages would tend to be driven down. This so-called Iron Law of Wages indeed fitted nineteenth century England, though time was to show that the capitalistic system was capable of making many adjustments, so that none of the nineteenth-century theorists, not even Karl Marx, could be thought to have arrived at a formulation of economic laws valid for all time. Conditions in the mines were especially disgraceful, but in textile factories they were not much better. If every member of a family worked long hours the wages earned were just sufficient to enable the family to make ends meet. In such circumstances it meant little short of starvation if any member of the family were dismissed. This was the heyday of the individual capitalist, who enjoyed the full backing of his government, which believed in a policy of strict laissez faire, or "hands off business."

But in time labor unions, which for decades were prohibited as "conspiracies in restraint of trade" were legalized, thus making strikes and other forms of direct action feasible, while the parliamentary legislators, often led by the landed aristocracy, which was quite willing to chasten the upstart industrialists, passed laws regulating hours and conditions of labor. In due course the working classes themselves won the vote and thereafter were able to influence legislation in their favor. The very threat of such action by the working classes, indeed, was able to win for the workers in Germany the very first social security legislation, which was put through by Bismarck as early as 1883. In the twentieth century labor unions have become rich and powerful, and governments, as a rule, ever more responsive to pressure from the organized working classes. But at the same time business itself ceased to be interested in laissez faire and desired different forms of protection from the government, whether in the form of tariffs to protect their home market from competition by foreigners, subsidies to meet foreign competition or to keep them working with at least a skeletal organization so as to be ready to expand in case of war, or price supports to save them from excessively dangerous and unprofitable competition from their peers. Thus in modern times we find three great powers in the industrial countries, labor, capital, and government, with the latter often vainly but sometimes effectively endeavoring to protect the interests of the whole people in their capacity as consumers. The Industrial Revolution has therefore tended to increase the power of governments and the area in which they are expected to intervene. In the Soviet Union the immediate aim of the Bolshevik Revolution of 1917 was to dispossess the bourgeoisie and to place all means of production in the hands of the community as represented by the state. Thus from the beginning there was no private enterprise, and labor unions have never had any independent power, being reduced largely to the status of cheerleaders and generators of social pressure at the behest and under the control of the government of the state.

Social Consequences of the Industrial Revolution. Lastly a few words should be said on the general social and political consequences of the Industrial Revolution. A phenomenon common to all the Western nations is the so-called "emergence of the masses," a marked change from earlier centuries, when men of rank or wealth were responsible for the creation of all culture, handled all governmental administration, and were alone able to enjoy an education. The Industrial Revolution, as we have seen, had need of the masses as consumers, and could not long withhold other rights from them. It became possible for individual men from the working classes to gain fortunes in industry and move out of the class into which they had been born. Democratic forms in government enabled them to rise to leading positions in the state. But social mobility has always been the exception rather than the rule, and it has varied from country to country in accordance with the stability of the social structure. Most members of the working classes remain within their class, which being the most numerous has tended to set even the cultural standards of the whole population. The standardization of the products of consumption has tended toward a certain standardization of the individual citizen. He wears the same clothes, eats the same food, enjoys the same entertainment provided by industries, geared to supply as standardized products as those of mass-production manufacturing industry. Thus the standard of living has tended to equalize itself. This applies as fully in countries like the United States, where little governmental effort has been expended in trying to achieve this result, as it does in Britain, New Zealand, or Scandinavia, where government has tried to aid this equalization by the use of its powers of taxation.

This chapter has necessarily taken us forward a long way in time, even to the social and economic problems that are afflicting us in the second half of the twentieth century, but it was thought best to cover them in one general discussion rather than constantly referring to them in each chapter. The reader should therefore take them for granted in the chapters which follow, as we proceed now to the history of the nineteenth and twentieth centuries which will occupy the remainder of the book.

CHAPTER XVII

NINETEENTH-CENTURY EUROPE TO 1871—
THE GROWTH OF NATIONALISM
AND LIBERALISM

The nineteenth century was marked by two movements of the utmost importance, both arising from the French Revolution and the Napoleonic Wars—nationalism and liberalism. Although the unification and consolidation of national states had been in process for several centuries, the personal identification of the individual with his nation was a comparatively new phenomenon. This sense of nationality had already been visible in Elizabethan England and frequently found expression in Shakespeare; it could be observed in seventeenth-century France, but in less noticeable form. The cultural ascendancy of France throughout Europe in the seventeenth and eighteenth centuries had served to obscure the fact that other nascent national cultures were being subordinated to the all-pervading French influence. Frederick the Great preferred to speak and write French, regarding German as a barbaric language; the Dutch used French as the language of the court and diplomacy, the Russian intelligentsia had much the same attitude toward Russian language and achievements as Frederick the Great had toward the German. They too spoke French and did not hesitate to recognize the superiority of the rest of Europe in all the arts and techniques of civilization.

But when in the era of Napoleon French cultural ascendancy, which had been accepted as a fact of life even when it was not actively welcomed, was translated into French political domination, the leaders in other countries were made forcibly aware of their inferiority and resented it. They began to take their own cultures seriously, and all found virtues in them which had hitherto been obscured. They looked at their own national resources and discovered that they were not necessarily inferior to those of the French; they were merely undeveloped, and this could be changed. France had had the great advantage of being unified as a nation, whereas the Germans and Italians by the accident of history had been doomed to either internal squabbles or domination by foreigners; but there was nothing inherently inferior about a German or an Italian. The Russians had suffered from a Mongol occupation that had retarded their political development; it was now up to them to catch up with the rest of Europe. The Poles had been afflicted with an impossible form of government, but Copernicus had been a Pole. Hungary had been dominated by the Turks and Austrians, and the Balkan states had been incorporated against their will into the Ottoman Empire. The first essential for each country was therefore to build a national state as the prerequisite for the national self-expression and recognition by the rest of Europe as an equal.

This nationalism became and has ever since remained as a dominant factor in the life of modern man, spreading from Europe and the rest of the world as its leading export in the realm of ideas. Those peoples who do not enjoy the luxury of nationhood regard it as the one aim worth working toward, to be subordinated to all other ambitions. It is not too much to look upon nationalism as little short of a substitute religion, taking for many the place of that Christianity under the sign of which Western civilization was formed. Thus the medieval ideal of Christendom with a universal Church and a universal Empire disappeared into the new ideal of the modern world of national self-determination. The end of the process is still not in sight. Even the modern secular ideal of Marxism, which looked toward world revolution and world communism, was revised by Stalin, in recognition of world realities in his day, to an aspiration toward "socialism in one country," with the world revolution to be postponed to more propitious times.

Liberalism, the second movement that arose from the French Revolution, is not to be sharply distinguished from nationalism, which it often accompanied, being included in programs of nationalist regeneration. Liberalism was a more modern version of eighteenth-century enlightenment, but it stressed the "free" aspect that forms part of its name (Latin, *liber* = free). Liberalism believed that the human being should be freed from the bonds artificially imposed upon him either by government or any other agency. It was an essential part of its credo that men should be permitted to govern themselves, and not subjected to the tyranny of any autocratic ruler, however enlightened. But since most nineteenth-century liberals belonged to the middle class, they were not especially inter-

ested in permitting the lower classes to have their share in government. Many of them indeed believed that this would only fasten
upon themselves the tyranny of an ignorant majority, which might
be even worse than that of a royal autocrat. In economics the liberals believed that government should not interfere with business,
not even by the imposition of protective tariffs. Enterprise should
be as "free" as possible. But the liberal also believed that unenlightened laws and customs should be swept away. He did not think,
with the conservative, that the old order should be preserved simply
because there was virtue in "conserving" what had been hallowed by
tradition. He was, as a rule, determinedly and actively antitradi-
tional, and therefore often anticlerical. He preferred secular to religious education because the former was likely to be more in keeping
with the changing times. The liberal, clearly, was the heir of the
more constructive aspect of the French Revolution; but he had little
use for Napoleon except insofar as he had been secular-minded and
had supported the modernizing reforms of the Revolution, nor
could he condone the Reign of Terror which fastened a tyranny of
the Left on the French people in the name of reform and progress.

THE METTERNICH SYSTEM AND ITS FAILURE

The Congress of Vienna. The members of the Congress of
Vienna, which assembled in 1814 after the defeat of Napoleon for
the purpose of liquidating the Napoleonic empire grievously underestimated the forces of nationalism and liberalism. They were eighteenth-century men, and few had any appreciation of the meaning
of the French Revolution. On the whole they were inclined to regard
it as a temporary aberration and to believe that the *status quo ante,*
the enlightened despotism of the eighteenth century, could be restored—that an eighteenth-century peace settlement could be imposed on Europe and would be found acceptable by the European
peoples, who would swiftly return to their old ways. The map of
Europe would of course have to be redrawn as it had been after
other long wars. Territories would be exchanged, one power would
be compensated for its losses in one part of Europe or its colonies
by territories in another part, with the victors as usual making most
of the gains. The French representative, Talleyrand, put forward a
suggestion of more general application. It was his view that if the
principle were accepted that all rulers who were legitimate (that is,
who were entitled to rule by hereditary right) were restored to their

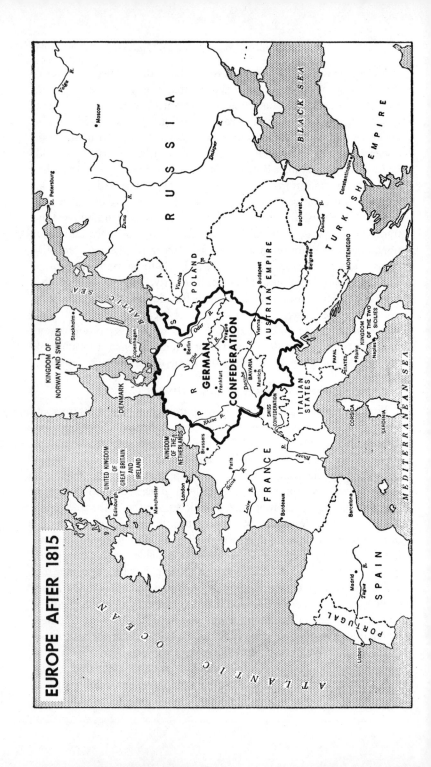

EUROPE AFTER 1815

thrones, there could then be no doubt as to who should occupy these thrones. The diplomats would not then be compelled to make invidious distinctions on the basis of such judgments as competence, contribution to the general war effort, or similar criteria.

The dominant figure at the Congress was Count Metternich, the foreign minister of Austria, although the Russian tsar, Alexander I, held the highest rank and had probably contributed most to the defeat of Napoleon. Alexander was vaguely affected by liberal ideas, and had little notion of just what he desired to emerge from the deliberations. Metternich, on the contrary, knew just what he wanted, and the ideas of Talleyrand on the principle of legitimacy made considerable appeal to him. Under this principle the Spanish and Neopolitan Bourbon monarchs would return to their thrones, replacing the Napoleonic siblings who had preceded them. Louis XVIII of France would keep his throne which he had occupied insecurely since 1814. The Dutch stadtholder of the House of Orange could become king of Holland, with the former Austrian Netherlands (which had not been worth much to Austria in the century during which she had held them) falling to his rule in exchange for concessions elsewhere.

Thus it was decided; and it was conveniently overlooked that neither the Spanish nor Neopolitan Bourbons had any reputation for enlightenment, nor was much attention given to the fact that perhaps the Spaniards and the southern Italians might not care to receive their monarchs back after a couple of decades of more efficient, and even more liberal, rule. If they did not like the settlement then they could be compelled to accept it by the arms of the victorious powers, which would, according to Metternich's plans, be placed at the disposal of the restored monarchies. Indeed, it was the great achievement of the Congress of Vienna that it recognized the obligation of the victorious powers to police the settlement they imposed. Though England demurred at the thought that she should put her troops at the disposal of a settlement whose inequity was apparent to many leading English thinkers, Austria, Russia, and Prussia undertook to take the necessary steps, and each offered 60,000 troops for the purpose. Even France, after a period of probation during which she paid her indemnity and it was seen that she was a reputable and reliable member of the new Concert of Europe, was allowed to take the place to which she was entitled by virtue of her military position in Europe.

The Revolutions of 1830. The Congress system worked fairly well until 1830, when the French seriously upset it by staging a new revolution. Before that time the British had withdrawn their approval of the system and retreated into an isolation from Europe which was customary for them unless their interests were directly involved. An uprising in Naples had been suppressed by the Austrian army, which came to be derisively called the "fire brigade of Europe"; another in Spain was put down mainly by the French, whose first major assignment it was. But the second Bourbon monarch of post-Napoleonic France, Charles X (1824–1830), proved himself too reactionary for any but the most conservative of Frenchmen. Although Louis XVIII had granted a constitution and a Parliament, Charles believed that it was his task as a divine-right monarch to put back the clock to before the Revolution, extending his program even to the restoration of lands sequestrated from nobles and Church. He had no interest in governing with the aid of Parliament, which he regarded as an undesirable achievement of the Revolution. The French therefore in 1830 took matters into their own hands, compelled Charles to abdicate his throne and flee to England, and set Louis Philippe, a more liberal member of a collateral branch (Orleanist) of the royal Bourbon family on the throne.

This so-called "July Revolution" triggered a number of other revolutions in Europe. The Catholic Belgians had been objecting for fifteen years to rule by the largely Protestant Dutch; and their trade interests, in their view, were being systematically ignored by the autocratic William I of Holland. They therefore staged a revolution, out of which emerged the new kingdom of Belgium, ruled by a royal German prince—but obviously not the legitimate monarch of the country unless the revolution itself were recognized as a legitimate fulfillment of Belgian aspirations. The inhabitants of several German states rose against their rulers, making intervention by Prussia difficult if not impossible, while the Austrians were plagued by troubles in their Italian territories which required all their available energies. Only Tsar Nicholas I of Russia was willing to intervene in Belgium, but he was compelled by an insurrection in Poland to forego his intentions. Therefore, nothing effective was done to prevent the revolutions in Holland and France. No new republics had been created, and Europe settled down again to a further period of a monarchy which in several countries had now by royal will become constitutional and a little more limited than before. Meanwhile the Greeks, supported by the British and many volunteers from all over Europe, had also overthrown the rule of a legitimate monarch, the sultan of Turkey. Though the peace had been broken, it was in an out-of-the-way part of Europe, and the European powers did not feel that their system was seriously endangered by this resort to arms, in spite of the liberal ideas that accompanied it.

The Revolutions of 1848. In 1848 it was the French who again set foot on the path that was to lead to the total destruction of the Metternich security system. Louis Philippe had not lived up to his early promise, and his governments were dominated by the more conservative elements of the bourgeoisie. Radical, including socialist, ideas had been gaining ground among the masses, in part as a result of a severe depression and unemployment. Liberal leaders were disgusted with the general corruption of the parliamentary government and were prepared to countenance the experiment of another republic, the first since the Revolution. Louis Blanc, the socialist leader, was demanding radical reforms to provide work for the masses. In February, 1848, the workers put on a demonstration, and Louis Philippe, to avoid bloodshed, abdicated. There followed a confused period during which the poet Alphonse de Lamartine became head of a provisional government and national workshops were established to provide jobs for the unemployed. But the middle classes were not yet prepared to abdicate their positions of power, and the Parisian workers, facing the loss of their national workshops and the taking over of the new republic by right-wing elements, rose once more in an insurrection which was bloodily suppressed by General Cavaignac, acting as the agent of the National Assembly elected under the old restricted franchise of the monarchical period. The Assembly then wrote a new republican constitution which included universal manhood suffrage and called for a presidential system. A man who was little known, but possessed a potent name, the nephew of Napoleon Bonaparte himself, won the first election for president. In due course Louis Napoleon by a coup d'état made himself emperor, thus beginning the Second French Empire (1852–1870). The coup d'état was confirmed by plebiscite in the best manner of Napoleon I.

The new French revolution was followed by revolutions and attempted revolutions in almost every country in Europe. Numerous uprisings took place in the German states, many of whose rulers granted a measure of constitutional reform. The Prussian king, Frederick William IV, was taken unawares, and rather than suppress the demonstrators by force agreed to a constitution. A number of liberals and other intellectuals met together in Frankfort to draw up a constitution for a united Germany which they hoped to bring into being (to be discussed later in this chapter). In the Hapsburg Empire the Hungarians, under the leadership of Louis Kossuth and Francis Deak, had long been demanding autonomy or independence. When news of the February Revolution in Paris reached Austria, Kossuth put forward his demands with more urgency, and there were clashes between troops and demonstrators in Vienna. Metternich, who had been in power ever since 1815, saw the writing on the wall and left the country. Though the emperor granted a constitution, almost all the subject peoples of the empire demanded autonomy for themselves, and engaged in varying degrees of violence, while the Italians under Austrian rule began a full-scale rebellion in northern Italy. Meanwhile, the Hungarians invaded Austria and threatened Vienna.

These events were too much for Emperor Ferdinand, who abdicated in December 1848, to be succeeded by Francis Joseph I, who reigned throughout the rest of the century. In June 1849, faced by the impossibility of suppressing all the insurrectional movements and holding the empire together, the emperor accepted the willingly proferred help of Tsar Nicholas of Russia. This intervention turned the tide; all the revolts were suppressed; and even the king of Prussia felt safe enough to withdraw his offer of a constitution and dispersed the Frankfort Assembly after refusing the crown of a united Germany. Only Charles Albert, king of Piedmont and Sardinia, felt himself bound by his promises, and despite Austrian victories in Italy which forced his abdication, the Italian constitution granted in the excitement of the 1848 revolutions was preserved. It was this willingness to abide by his promises when he was no longer compelled to do so that eventually ensured the acceptance of a constitutional monarchy rather than a republic in a unified Italy, with a descendant of Charles Albert as king.

The End of the Metternich System. By 1849 the last victories had been won by the legitimate monarchs of the Metternich settlement of 1815. All the kings who retained their thrones thereafter had to submit to some kind of a constitution, though the process was delayed in Russia until 1905. The security system of Vienna had not worked beyond 1830 and was now in ruins. Germany (without Austria) and Italy were soon to become unified as national states (as will be discussed later in this chapter). France was ruled by an emperor who was compelled, by events as well as by his subjects, to modify his absolutism and become almost a constitutional ruler before his regime was overthrown by a war with Prussia. Only the English had pursued the even tenor of their ways, developing their constitutional monarchy further and moving toward the era of democratic Parliamentary rule, through reforming the franchise and equalizing the electoral districts. We shall now turn our attention to an account of these events in Britain and follow this with a discussion of the last bulwark of autocracy in Europe, tsarist Russia, returning thereafter to the unification movements in Germany and Italy. This will take us to the year 1871, leaving for Chapter XX the events of the last quarter of the century and the early years of the twentieth century which culminated in the First World War.

GREAT BRITAIN IN THE NINETEENTH CENTURY

Parliamentary and Electoral Reform. Britain as she emerged from the Napoleonic wars appeared to be strong and secure. Her institutions had proved themselves, and her leaders were well satisfied with the way in which they had responded to the challenges of the war. What few of them recognized was that the Industrial Revolution was beginning to create changes in the social structure that would sooner or later be certain to demand political expression. The Tories who were in power were already being challenged not only by the Whigs, soon to call themselves Liberals, but by a group of earnest reformers who called themselves Radicals, relatively few in number but with access to publicity and able to make their views heard in Parliament. Many of the Radicals followed the lead of a social reformer and political scientist named Jeremy Bentham, who had given much thought to social problems and propounded the view (known as Utilitarianism) that all legislation should be for the "greatest good of the greatest number" of people, as determined by a "calculus of pleasure and pain." Bentham encouraged his followers to apply this yardstick to all the existing laws and customs of England: to accept nothing as sacrosanct merely because it was old, but rather to see how such laws and customs worked in practice. If they added to the sum of human misery and were not counterbalanced by corresponding benefits, then they should be altered. The Radicals, therefore, did not attach themselves to any particular Parliamentary party; they were willing to support either Tory or Whig according to the particular legislation it produced. In this way they won an influence out of all proportion to their numerical strength and were behind all the progressive legislation in the first half of the century.

The most important reform that was obviously overdue was to make Parliament more representative of the people. This meant the abandonment of the medieval franchise requirements and a thorough revision of the existing parliamentary constituencies. Most of the members sat for districts that were very lightly populated, some of them with no bona fide voters at all in the early nineteenth century, though they might have been centers of some importance a few centuries before. On the other hand, the new industrial centers that had sprung up in the nineteenth century might have no members to represent them at all. The Tories opposed any reform of Parliament but had no objection to improving social conditions by legislation when it appeared necessary. The first reforms of the social order were therefore passed by the Tory governments, which, fortified by the accession of a number of liberal-minded men, remained in office until 1830. A beginning was made with the reform of the hopelessly antiquated criminal law. There was also some dismantling of the mercantile system, which too often protected inefficient and outmoded industries at the expense of new and expansive businesses, anxious to take advantage of British leadership in the Industrial Revolution. Religious equality was at last conceded by the repeal of the seventeenth-century Test Act and the removal of the political disabilities of Catholics dating from that period. When the Tories went out of office and were replaced by the Whigs, who represented the substantial middle class, the Radicals teamed up with the latter to win Parliamentary reform. Though the Tories fought to the last, initially in the House of Commons and then in the last stronghold of Toryism, the House of Lords, ultimately the First Reform Bill was passed, the Whig prime minister having threatened to swamp the House of Lords with new Whig peers and gained the consent of the king to this step.

The Reform Act of 1832 carried out a full redistricting but did not greatly extend the franchise. As a result the upper middle classes, the men of property who were strongly represented in the Whig party, were reasonably well satisfied and desired no more electoral reforms. But the Tories were not so sure that all was well. Neither of the major parties desired to extend the vote to the working class, but the Tories needed to have some program likely to appeal to the electors; and since their party was mostly composed of the landed gentry, they cordially disliked the business interests. The Tories and the Radicals now worked together to obtain some valuable factory legislation, which was naturally opposed by most of the business interests but was felt by its proponents to be a move that might head off the growing demands of the workers for a share in the government. From 1839 on, large numbers of workers, often led by Radicals, joined the Chartist movement, presenting petitions to Parliament asking for redress of grievances and electoral reform (universal manhood suffrage). The Chartists were very successful in arousing lower-class opinion but had little success with Parliament, which time after time refused to heed their petitions. The movement finally died in 1848, and many of the former Chartists emigrated to the British colonies in the Antipodes, where they were often able to lead the movement for reform in their new homes.

Meanwhile, in the face of widespread famines in the 1840's and the determined demand of the Anti-Corn Law League, which had been agitating for the reform for many years, the protective duties on grain were removed. By this act Britain became, as she has ever since remained, a grain-importing country with a visible adverse balance of trade, unable to feed herself from her own resources, but making up for the difference by supplying services and capital to every country in the world, as well as by exporting industrial goods.

By the 1860's it was clear to both Liberals and Conservatives that a new measure of electoral reform must be granted. New leaders had arisen in these parties who were both in their own way reformers. Gladstone and Disraeli were venturesome politicians, willing to undertake the task of reform of all kinds and not greatly inhibited by ancient tradition. Disraeli took the lead in proposing a Reform Bill which would extend the franchise to the more prosperous workers, hoping to gain political capital thereby. He miscalculated, since the newly enfranchised workers voted solidly for his opponent, but the Act was now on the statute book, and Gladstone went ahead with his own domestic reforms. In 1870 an education bill was passed setting up local state schools where Church schools were not available. This was followed by the founding of a true civil service, based on merit as determined by examinations. The Disraeli government which followed continued the Tory/Conservative tradition of legislating for the benefit of those who were the victims of the industrial system, but gradually it began to occupy its attention, primarily and then almost exclusively, with foreign affairs and the new imperialism. Gladstone in 1884 secured the passage of the Third Reform Bill, which granted the franchise to virtually all men except the poorest of agricultural laborers; but otherwise the pace of reform slowed down in the last years of the century, leaving a tremendous backlog for the Liberal government which at last came to power in 1906 (and will be briefly touched upon in Chapter XXII).

The Irish Question. The last quarter of the century was dominated not only by imperialism but by the so-called Irish Question, which prevented Gladstone from carrying out much of his domestic program, since many of his governments fell on the question of Irish Home Rule. Ireland had been united with Great Britain in 1800 after several centuries of British rule, almost always unenlightened. Ireland was treated as a colony for the benefit of British landowners and capitalists; though the population of most of the country was Catholic, they had to submit to an established Anglican Church with their own religion barely tolerated. Irishmen sat in the British Parliament but had little influence there until the end of the nineteenth century when they gained a balance of power, their votes being necessary to both parties in view of the small majority at the disposal of successive governments. Gladstone came to the conclusion early in his career as prime minister that the Irish must be given Home Rule, as it was called, or a self-governing status under the British crown. This caused dismay among the six northern counties (Ulster) which were mainly Protestant and did not wish to submit to Catholic rule by the southerners. They were backed by the Conservatives in both the House of Commons and the House of Lords, who resisted fiercely every effort at reform, and especially the Home Rule Bill continually introduced by Gladstone. Moreover, England herself was divided seriously on the question, while the southern Irish did not improve their position in English public opinion by engaging in terrorism, replied to in kind by the Ulstermen.* Though Gladstone in his first administration was able to have the Anglican Church in Ireland disestablished, and made many land reforms, these

---

* The twentieth-century French position in Algeria was an almost exact parallel, and for those familiar with the bitter French-Algerian struggle of the last decade which divided French opinion both in Algeria and in France, the parallel offers many instructive lessons.

proved to be far from sufficient for the Irish, who won their demands only after the First World War, and then after a long civil war and at the cost of partition of their country.

RUSSIA, BULWARK OF AUTOCRACY

During the nineteenth century Russia continued to be the last stronghold of absolutism. Though some of the tsars were seriously interested in reforming the administration and catching up with the West in technical matters, none was willing to grant anything resembling a constitution that allowed a modicum of power to other elements in the state. Nothing like a constitutional monarchy was granted until 1905, and even then Tsar Nicholas II acted under duress and modified his constitution as soon as the immediate crisis (to be dealt with in Chapter XXII) was over and he found he could not control the parliament (Duma) he had created.

As early as 1825, when there was doubt over which of his brothers should succeed Tsar Alexander I, there was a minor uprising by reformers (Decembrists) who wished to force the establishment of constitutional government. It was suppressed by Tsar Nicholas I (1825–1855) without difficulty. Poland also staged an uprising in 1830. The Congress of Vienna had granted Poland to Tsar Alexander I as a personal possession ruled by him as its king, but not incorporated into Russia. Alexander had proclaimed a constitution and agreed to uphold Polish traditional rights. But he had never fully put it into effect, nor did he pay much attention to Polish rights. Nicholas suppressed the 1830 uprising with severity, and thereafter there was no pretense that Poland was a constitutional monarchy. In 1848, as we have seen, Nicholas helped Austria to suppress her minorities. Only when Alexander II came to the throne in 1855 was there any further effort to change the system from within, though Russian and Polish revolutionaries constantly agitated abroad.

Alexander II (1855–1881) was seriously interested in internal Russian reform. He emancipated the serfs in 1861 under a formula which permitted the Russian village community (*mir*) to purchase land from its former owners. He also aided local self-government. But the Poles, thinking they had a liberal tsar to deal with, from whom they could extract concessions, initiated another rebellion, which was suppressed no less severely than in 1830. Before Alexander was assassinated by terrorists, he had already come to doubt the efficacy of his reform programs; and since he was not prepared to concede a constitution, the revolutionaries abroad had likewise despaired of obtaining anything from the tsars save by force. Alexander III (1881–1894) encouraged the industrialization of his country and was willing to contract foreign loans, especially with France, for the purpose. But neither he nor Nicholas II, who succeeded him, was willing to reduce his own power, and the autocracy continued into the twentieth century. Russia was by this time a great power, capable of waging war effectively. In the so-called Crimean War (1854–1856), when her opponent Turkey was able to win a limited support from several European powers, she had to acknowledge defeat. In 1877–1878 she won another war with Turkey, but was compelled by the European powers to relinquish most of the fruits of her victory. Nevertheless, in spite of her military prowess she remained far behind the rest of Europe in political development. Though she had a fairly efficient army and bureaucracy, many of the most active members of her intelligentsia were either abroad fomenting revolution and organizing terrorism as the only effective method of combating the tsarist regime or in prison camps in Siberia, where they had been sent by the secret police. It was of course in these years that the revolution was prepared that was to erupt in 1917; and the violence of that revolution and the swift failure of moderate constitutional government were in large measure due to the long period of repression that preceded them.

THE FOUNDATION OF THE GERMAN EMPIRE

The Vienna Settlement and the Zollverein. After the Congress of Vienna had done its work Prussia was the largest German state, possessing territories in both eastern and western Germany. These territories, however, were not connected with one another. The small German states and Austria surrounded the Prussian territories which were organized into a confederation with each state retaining its full sovereignty in all important matters. Few of the rulers had granted constitutions to their peoples, and most of them had been little changed by the Napoleonic wars. All that Napoleon had achieved was the reduction of the number of the states to thirty-eight.

The diet of the Confederation was dominated by the Hapsburg Empire of Austria, which could usually rely upon the aid, in particular, of the south German Catholic states; but Austria, in addition to being a German power, possessed also Slavic and Magyar territories, not represented in the diet. Nevertheless, the small German states could not ignore the power and prestige of the largest member of the diet, even though in the diet she spoke officially only with the voice of her German population. The situation was naturally uncomfortable for Prussia, the obvious leader of Germany if Austria were excluded; but right up to the 1860's Austria had the upper hand in the diet and could humiliate and thwart Prussia as she wished.

Prussia's first great achievement was the formation of a *Zollverein* or customs union between the various north German states—from which she was able to exclude Austria on the ground that Austria was an empire, and the Austrian minorities, not being German, could not join in a German union. This contention was quite acceptable to the German states which, for economic reasons, did not wish to include the Slavic and Magyar territories in their customs union. The south German states also kept out of the Prussian-dominated Zollverein as long as they could, feeling their interests were bound up with those of Austria. But as an economic venture the Zollverein was immensely successful, and the minor German princes who sometimes reluctantly agreed to enter it all found out that their revenues were increased and they had no grounds for complaint.

The Frankfort Assembly. The Zollverein was already a functioning organization to which most of the states now belonged by the time of the Frankfort Assembly of 1848, already mentioned. This Assembly throughout its deliberations and even after it had formed itself into an all-German Parliament, was concerned with bringing a united Germany into existence. But the delegates split on the question of whether Austria should be a member, and if so whether the Hapsburg emperor should be its ruler, in which case the new entity would no longer be all-German—an idea distressing to the nationalists in the Assembly. Austria herself, as it happened, ruled herself out, since she was not prepared to enter without her minorities, whereupon the Assembly turned to Frederick William IV of Prussia. But he, as a Hohenzollern, could not accept even the crown of a united Germany from an elected Assembly, or, as he delicately phrased it, "pick up a crown from the gutter." When he had made his refusal known, the Assembly began to dissolve, and its rump was dispersed by Prussian troops. Thus ended the effort to unite Germany by peaceful means. Thereafter Otto von Bismarck with his wholly different ideas took the leadership in the movement, and succeeded in 1871 in uniting Germany by "blood and iron."

War with Austria. The revolution of 1848–1849 left Prussia with a constitution promulgated by Frederick William IV. The king retained ultimate power and authority, which he exercised through a chancellor appointed by and responsible to himself. The *Landtag,* or Parliament, was a conservative body elected under a system of votes weighted in favor of property-holders; but at least it had the theoretical right to discuss the budget and withhold funds—though, as Bismarck was to demonstrate, the king and chancellor could continue to collect them, even when the Landtag refused authorization. The Landtag also had a proportion of vocal liberals in its composition, since liberals were far from propertyless. Although Austria continued to dominate the German diet on most matters, she was still excluded from the Zollverein, in spite of her efforts after 1849 to join it. Prussia was able to control tariff policies even though she lacked the votes in the diet to set the direction for the policies of the German states as a whole.

When Bismarck became chancellor in 1862 he recognized that Austria was the great enemy of German unity and that it might well require force to expel her from German affairs. He, therefore, over the opposition of the Landtag, enlarged and improved the Prussian army, while trying to create an incident which would lead the German princes to support him and not Austria over some crucial issue. His opportunity arose when two largely German duchies, Schleswig and Holstein, ruled as personal possessions by the Danish king, were incorporated into that country by their ruler. Austria and Prussia together, with the authorization of the German diet, invaded Denmark and forced the concession of the duchies to both Austria and Prussia. Bismarck blandly suggested a division of the spoils, Holstein going to Austria; the Austrians fell head first into the trap. They now possessed a duchy entirely surrounded by Prussian lands, and it was not long before the two countries were embroiled with one another. Until the last moment Austria suffered from no doubts regarding her victory in an eventual war, and both she and Prussia entered into vague agreements with the French emperor, Napoleon III, by which the French would preserve neutrality. But Bismarck had entered into an agreement with the Italians, who were engaged in their own unification and wanted nothing better than an excuse to drive Austria out of Italy with the aid of a powerful ally to the north. So well had Bismarck laid his plans that Austria used her majority in the German diet to condemn Prussian actions in Holstein, and Prussia thus became the aggrieved party, and on the whole had the moral support of most of Europe.

The German military machine, fully prepared, invaded Austria and utterly defeated her in the Seven Weeks' War (1866), then turned on those German states which had sided with Austria and defeated them too. Both Austria and the south German states were granted reasonable terms, since Bismarck was not anxious to remain at enmity with them. A new North German Confederation, including Hanover, now definitively annexed by Prussia, was formed, naturally dominated by Prussia, while the southern states were made to join the Zollverein. Austria, excluded from Germany, entered into agreements with her leading minority, the Magyars, who were granted control over the Slavic population in the eastern part of the Hapsburg possessions. The Empire thereafter became Austro-Hungarian and was known as the Dual Monarchy, the emperor becoming king of Hungary while he retained his title of emperor in relation to his other possessions. Soon afterward constitutions were granted in both Austria and Hungary.

Franco-Prussian War. Prussia was now overwhelmingly strong in Germany, but the south German states retained their independence, and it was Bismarck's aim to have them join voluntarily. To achieve this he had the idea that they might fight on Prussia's side against a foreign enemy, and this enemy was close at hand in the person of Napoleon III of France. This matter was handled by a combination of finesse and ruthlessness characteristic of the "Iron Chancellor." First he influenced British opinion against Napoleon by publishing the latter's demands for concessions at German expense as a reward for his neutrality in the recent war. Then he maneuvered French public opinion against Prussia in the hopes of inciting an attack by France. Meanwhile he made his army ready with a completed plan for a quick knockout blow of the French army, followed by an attack on Paris. His Landtag was now much more favorable to him than before. It had legalized his previously unauthorized taxation and now gave him new funds without demur. The main difficulty was his own king, William I, who feared a war with France which he was doubtful whether his smaller army could defeat. Hence Bismarck's care to see that Napoleon attacked, not he.

All his objectives were attained when a vacancy occurred on the throne of Spain, and a Hohenzollern prince was invited to assume it. Napoleon and the French Chamber objected strongly, and Bismarck was able to make it appear—by the doctoring of a telegram (the Ems Despatch)—that King William had been insulted, while the French thought that they had been insulted too—and that in any case it was time for Prussia to be cut down to size. Napoleon duly declared war, and after a few minor encounters the Prussian army, aided, as hoped, by the south German states, smashed into France, took Napoleon himself prisoner and laid siege to Paris. The king of Bavaria, at the suggestion of Bismarck, invited William to become German emperor; on January 18, 1871, ten days before the capitulation of Paris, German unification was completed. For good measure the French provinces of Alsace and Lorraine were taken from France and included in the new empire, now incomparably the greatest power on the European continent—as the world was to discover forty-three years later. France herself soon proclaimed her Third Republic, which was to last until 1940, the longest lived of her post-Revolutionary regimes.

THE UNIFICATION OF ITALY

Italy after the Congress of Vienna was still hopelessly disunited, and north of Rome was effectively dominated by Austria, which had annexed Lombardy and Venetia outright. There were two kingdoms, Sardinia (the Mediterranean island plus the rich mainland northern Italian territory of Piedmont) and Naples, which included southern Italy and the island of Sicily, now ruled by a newly restored Bourbon. The remainder was divided among the papal states and several small independent duchies.

A momentarily successful revolt in Naples in 1820 was quickly suppressed by Austrian arms. This was followed by others in some of the duchies, likewise suppressed by the Congress powers, soon to include France. The revolts were mostly the work of secret societies, especially the Carbonari, who lost ground after their ineffectiveness had been so signally demonstrated. Giuseppe Mazzini, in 1831, formed yet another society, revolutionary but not secret, known as Young Italy and pledged to work for an eventual Republic of Italy. Mazzini soon went into exile, first in France and then in England, where he propagandized tirelessly. But all the uprisings sponsored by Young Italy were suppressed with monotonous regularity.

It was not until the revolutions of 1848 that the independence movement had its first successes. Constitutions were extracted from the two kings, from the pope, and from several dukes: and Charles

Albert, king of Sardinia, finally agreed to support Milanese and Venetian rebellions against the Austrians and declared war on Austria. A short-lived republic was also set up in Rome. But in the following year the Austrians decisively defeated the Piedmontese. President Louis Napoleon of France sent troops to Rome to put an end to the republic. The French troops remained in Rome until 1870, protecting the position of the pope and effectively preventing the papal states from taking any significant part in the unification movement. Though Charles Albert abdicated in favor of his son, Victor Emmanuel II, as already mentioned, the constitution granted in 1848 was not abrogated. Thereafter the kingdom of Sardinia took the leading part in the independence movement.

In 1852, Count Camillo di Cavour, a highly skilled and experienced liberal diplomat, became prime minister of the Sardinian kingdom, and thereafter worked tirelessly for the independence of all Italy under his royal master. He had little use for the republican ideas of Mazzini, nor did he trust the filibustering independent military adventures of Giuseppe Garibaldi, even though he was prepared to make use of them when conditions required it. His plan was to win European allies among the great powers, and use them to throw off the yoke of Austria, employing military forces of his small state where they would do the most good. His first success was with Napoleon III, who agreed to help expel Austria from Italy in return for Nice and Savoy and for a political settlement far short of unification. The latter promise, of course, was not in the power of Cavour to fulfill, nor presumably did it have any meaning for him. The French duly entered a war provoked by the Italians (1859), and Napoleon's troops were sufficiently successful to compel the cession of Lombardy but not Venetia. Much to the chagrin of the Italians, France withdrew from the war before the Austrians had been driven out of Italy. Meanwhile a number of central Italian duchies overthrew their rulers and petitioned for annexation by Piedmont, while Garibaldi with his thousand Red Shirts invaded Sicily. The expedition turned into a triumphal procession which overthrew the Kingdom of Naples. Naples and Sicily thereupon requested annexation by Piedmont. The papal states not under the protection of Napoleon were defeated by the Piedmontese and the kingdom of Italy was proclaimed (March, 1861).

Italy was still not united. Venetia remained in Austrian hands, and the pope still ruled some of his states. Moreover it had only been after considerable hesitation that Garibaldi had yielded to the demands of Cavour to place his territories under the king, since he himself preferred a republic. In June, 1861, Cavour died, and his successors were even more fearful of involving the still only partly united kingdom of Italy in a war with Austria and France at the same time.

As it happened, events played into Italian hands. Prussia, expecting war with Austria, was glad to have an Italian ally to the south. Though the Italians themselves were defeated in their sector of the war, Austria was compelled to cede Venetia in 1866. Garibaldi took matters into his own hands and defied his own Italian government, engaging in war with the papal troops and their French auxiliaries on his own account; but he was taken prisoner by them in 1867. However, when France became involved in war with Prussia in 1870, at last the French troops had to be withdrawn. At once the Italians entered Rome; the city by a plebiscite agreed to be annexed to the kingdom of Italy; and the unification was complete. Pope Pius IX retired to the Vatican, where he proclaimed himself a prisoner. His successors did not finally accept their new status as rulers only of the Vatican until a concordat was signed between Mussolini and Pope Pius XI in 1929.

CHAPTER XVIII

THE AMERICAS IN THE NINETEENTH CENTURY

The American continent in the fifteenth century had been sparsely inhabited by "Indians" of numerous tribes, well adapted to their environment. Only two major groups had a strong political organization. These were the Aztecs of Mexico and the Incas of Peru, both of whom had established extensive empires. By Western standards, however, both Aztecs and Incas were technologically backward, although in intellectual and cultural attainments they had much to their credit.

The European peoples who conquered these Indians in the sixteenth and succeeding centuries were thus able to establish their rule without great difficulty; and though at first of course outnumbered by natives, in the sparsely populated lands of the temperate North America, they soon came to outnumber the Indians. But in Central and South America, except in the extreme south, the Indians have continued to outnumber those of European descent to this day. Even in these areas, however, there was considerable intermingling of the peoples, thus producing in effect new peoples of mixed blood, in addition to the pure Indians and the pure Europeans. In North America, on the other hand, where there was little intermingling, the Europeans took over the whole country for themselves, penning the Indians into relatively small "reservations," and creating in effect an overseas European civilization.

Each of the European peoples who took over the Americas laid the impress of their own culture upon the land they acquired. British North America, prior to the secession of the United States, was with a few exceptions thoroughly British in its political institutions as well as its language. Socially, however, it was far more egalitarian than the mother country, though class distinctions were for a long time of great importance and reflected in some measure those in Britain. The pioneering life imposed by the new environment rewarded different virtues from those most valued in Britain.

Above all, there was far greater freedom of opportunity, especially in the nineteenth century, when the Americans were colonizing their vast country and unimagined fortune might await the enterprising. Nevertheless, the British political heritage, with its parliamentary institutions and its general freedom of discussion, made the new United States of America entirely different in all essential respects from America south of the Rio Grande, colonized by the Spaniards and Portuguese.

Canada, separated from the United States in 1783, was a country that had only recently been won by the British from the French and for several decades was not at all certain that it would not be swallowed up by its greater neighbor to the south. The French Canadians, who were still a majority in 1783, were totally unaccustomed to English institutions and for a long time paid no attention to the rights granted them by their British conquerors. These institutions were used exclusively by the British element in the population for several decades—the French being satisfied that their Church and language had been guaranteed to them and wishing only to be left in peace to cultivate their lands. They remained a stubbornly individualistic and unassimilated block in the country, until they found that their interests were being disregarded by the Anglo-Canadian immigrants who poured into the country every year. Not until they were in fact outnumbered by the new Canadians did their leaders bestir themselves and make use of the rights they had been granted. Even so, they have remained largely in the areas (especially the provinces of Quebec and New Brunswick) which they had made their own by the end of the eighteenth century and have shown little sign of wishing to extend into the other areas of the country, soon to be dominated by the Anglo-Canadians. Thus outside the areas of French-Canadian settlement the country is almost as much an offshoot of British civilization as is the United States—though its longer period under British rule and its continued close association with the British through the Commonwealth, have kept it more British in orientation.

Latin America was for centuries dominated by the typical Spanish social and political structure. Here great estates, ruled by the American equivalent of Spanish grandees, were the custom, the Catholic Church was the all-pervading cultural institution, there was no tradition of self-government, freedom of speech or worship, no incipient democracy. Even after the achievement of independence from

Spain there was little sign of any major internal change. The ruling class persisted, though Spaniards of European descent and permanent residents of the Americas (Creoles) largely replaced Spaniards from Spain. The typical form of government was the president supported by the army, and such presidents in the nineteenth century usually ruled, often very insecurely, by force alone—the peon fatalistically accepting each change of ruler without protest unless he was impressed into the army of one or other of the competing war lords. Though most of the countries had some kind of parliamentary institutions, they never enjoyed any substantial power; at the most they were bodies of advisers to their presidents, usually nominated by him, sometimes, in more recent times, after the pretense of an election. Only in the twentieth century have some attempts been made to redistribute the land among those who work it and to alter the rigid class structure inherited from the Spaniards. Even so, most of the numerous revolutions in Latin America have been merely attempts by those not in power to take it by force. This process merely changes the personnel at the head of the government. The major revolutions of most countries are still in the future; and none, with the partial exception of Mexico, can as yet be considered to have done more than make a dent in a long-established social structure which is a direct descendant of royal and Catholic Spain.

THE UNITED STATES

The Constitution. The young United States, just separated from Britain, first had to write itself a constitution. In view of the historic differences between the thirteen colonies it was at once decided that the constitution should be federal. A confederation having proved unsatisfactory in the few years during which it was in operation, a fully federal constitution was agreed upon in 1787. Each of the colonies, now become states, ratified it, thereby giving up some of their sovereign powers to the federal government. In the Constitutional Convention itself, there was considerable difference of opinion between the nationalists (Federalists) led by James Madison, Alexander Hamilton, Gouverneur Morris, and others, and the proponents of virtually unimpaired state sovereignty. Eventually a compromise was hammered out under which only certain specified powers were granted to the federal government, while in other respects the states remained sovereign. After the Constitution was adopted, the Federalists continued to put their views strongly before the country, both to win ratification and afterward. Under George Washington, the first president, and his successor John Adams, the Federalists, now organized into a party, largely dominated the government. The federal Supreme Court was, however, early permitted the right to interpret the Constitution, and some of its interpretations have granted more to the federal government than was probably envisaged in 1787. Only with the ratification of the Fourteenth Amendment after the Civil War were the federal courts permitted to enforce a certain number of fundamental rights when these were held to have been infringed by the states. The Court itself, however, for many years after the Fourteenth Amendment took a very narrow view of the powers permitted to it. Only in the twentieth century has the Court construed it to protect individual rights against infringement by the states. When a "constitutional" question, usually under this amendment, is not involved, the Supreme Court of each state is the highest court of appeal.

Conflicts of Sovereignty between States and Federal Government. It may be said that a very great part of the history of the United States in the nineteenth century (and indeed this is not entirely untrue of the twentieth) is concerned in the widest sense with the conflict of sovereignty between the federal and state governments, a conflict of course altogether absent in a unitary state like Britain. The economic interests of the generally agricultural south and the industrial north constantly clashed. The North desired a protective tariff, the South in the nineteenth century wished to be able to import cheap goods from abroad, especially from Britain. When the Midwest and the West were opened up, their interests again were divergent from those of the industrial northeast. This economic conflict was naturally reflected in the political life of the new nation, since the powerful Senate (the upper house) was made up of two members from each state, irrespective of the size and population of the state.

The result was that the more heavily populated Northern states were not easily able to make their views prevail over the South, and compromises had constantly to be devised which satisfied none but kept the country together for more than half a century. This situation spurred the development of regional parties, but they soon came to realize that they could achieve nothing unless they joined one or other of the major parties capable of winning national elections. Hence politics in the United States has always been extremely active, and political parties have continually fluctuated, entering into flexible combinations, and, on the national level, little subject to party discipline. Though universal white manhood suffrage became the rule in most states before 1830, the peculiarities of the Constitution and the technical procedures adopted in Congress which put a premium on experience and professional expertise, have prevented the popular will from expressing itself at once in congressional legislation, save in exceptional circumstances. This remains hardly less true today than in the early nineteenth century.

The conflict between states and federal government led directly to the greatest crisis in United States history, the Civil War, or War between the States, fought from 1861 to 1865. The issues were complex and manifold, but the major one was that of Negro slavery. At the time of the War of Independence most enlightened men, Northern and Southern, were in general agreement that slavery was on the way out, and that before long it would disappear. But the invention of the cotton gin by Eli Whitney in 1793 suddenly made American short staple cotton a commodity with an enormous economic future. In a few decades the economy of the South became overwhelmingly dependent on cotton, which was grown under the plantation system, using Negro slave labor. What amounted to a new American subculture grew up, which became dear to its beneficiaries and known as the "Southern way of life"—the aristocratic and benevolent slaveowner paternally ruling his submissive and rightless slave. In the North there was constant agitation against slaveholding, on moral and economic grounds; and though for a long time the antislavery interests were willing to condone the possession of slaves in the states where slavery already existed, the problem of what to do about new states that petitioned to enter the Union could not be forever avoided. A related question was whether a runaway slave who escaped to free soil would be returned to his home slave state. In the Dred Scott Decision (1857) by the Supreme Court, it was ruled that he must be returned on the ground that slaves were not citizens but property. The antislavery groups at once recognized that by this decision their hopes for a gradual disappearance of slavery were probably doomed to disappointment. Moreover, the slave states were aggressively demanding that, at the least, new states should be free to choose whether or not they would permit slavery.

The slavery issue split the dominant Democratic party in two in the 1860 presidential election, thus permitting the election of Abraham Lincoln, who belonged to the relatively new Republican party, from which he was the first president. He had won no Southern electoral votes at all. Although Lincoln had not expressed himself clearly on the slavery issue, his party had made it clear that it would never permit slavery to be extended to the various territories of the United States which would in due course become states. Thus the slave states would in time be certain to be outvoted. The Southern states therefore believed that the time had come for a showdown. Several of them seceded from the Union even before the inauguration of Lincoln, and set up a Confederacy of their own.

Civil War. This step immediately put the issue on a different basis. From being a question of slavery, it became the question of the right of a minority of states to secede from the Union and resume the sovereignty they had agreed to abridge when they ratified the federal Constitution. The war pitted the people of the far more populous industrial North and the lightly populated West and Midwest against the South, which lacked resources and manpower. If the war were not ended by compromises short of victory, there could be no doubt as to who would ultimately win. In spite of heroic efforts by the Confederacy, the federal forces eventually compelled a surrender. Lincoln was assassinated shortly afterward, soon after his inauguration for a second term.

During the war, and in part as a war measure, all slaves in the Confederate states (except in areas occupied by the Union army) were freed by presidential proclamation, and slavery was prohibited in the entire country by constitutional amendment after the war (1865). But the question of what to do about the Southerners and how to integrate their former slaves into American life was far from clear. Congress, meeting without the Southerners who were assumed to have lost their civic rights through the rebellion, had little sympathy to spare on the former slaveowners. In spite of efforts by President Andrew Johnson, himself a Southerner from the "border" state of Tennessee, who was impeached for his efforts and only escaped conviction by a single vote, the Southerners for a time were treated almost like a conquered people, largely as the result of the work of the radical Republican Congress, which wished to "punish" the South for its secession. In the view of Congress the South could be treated as a defeated enemy—an opinion of doubtful legal validity, for the Supreme Court eventually ruled in 1869 that there had been no legal secession at all since the Constitution was, in law, indissoluble. By this time, however, "Reconstruction" had been largely completed. Under the policy of Congress illiterate freedman were given the vote, and in some states where the whites were unable to exercise their franchise, even took over the government. Northerners on the make combined with "renegade" Southerners to exploit the prostrate Southern states, while military government protected them. Eventually the Southerners were integrated once more into the Union and their rights were restored. But the era of "Reconstruction," following on the bitterness of civil war itself, prevented a permanent healing of the rift. Negroes were once more suppressed by economic and political means, though now theoretically free and entitled to vote. Segregation laws were passed and enforced. For several generations the Southerners refused to give a majority to any party calling itself Republican, and this remains true of state elections to this day.

The Mainland Expansion of the United States. The United States was for the entire nineteenth century by far the greatest power on the American continent, though she did not become a major world power until the First World War. She used this power to extend her territories in all directions until she achieved her present boundaries. In 1812 she entered, ostensibly on the question of freedom of the seas, another war with Britain, which neither power really desired. Numbers of Americans, especially the frontiersmen, however, thought that the time had come to annex Canada. In this enterprise they failed since the war effort was badly mismanaged. Peace was eventually proclaimed in 1814 with no change in boundaries. The French mainland possessions (known as Louisiana), as already noted, were purchased from Napoleon in 1803; and Florida was ceded by Spain in 1819, since Spain was so fully engaged in trying to protect her possessions in Central and South America that she could not withstand an ultimatum from the United States.

Texas, a part of Spanish America, was colonized with the permission of the newly independent Mexican government from 1821 onward. Soon the Americans outnumbered the Mexicans and established an independent republic (1836), in due course petitioning to be annexed by the United States. This was done by congressional resolution in 1845. The high-handed action brought on a war with Mexico in 1846, but the Mexicans were no match for the armies of the United States, which marched into the country until they captured Mexico City. New Mexico and California were ceded by the Mexicans in exchange for the sum of $15,000,000 and the writing off of all American claims on Mexico. The annexation of Texas was recognized.

Meanwhile in 1818 Britain and the United States agreed on the forty-ninth parallel as the boundary between the United States and Canada as far as the Rocky Mountains; in 1846 the Oregon Treaty between the two powers regulated the boundary to the Pacific coast. The latter was concluded only after many claims and counterclaims by both parties and occasional minor hostilities. Thus by 1848 the United States had obtained her living space. The rest of the century was occupied in bringing this huge territory under full control and establishing communications. This heroic task lies outside the scope of this book. It need only be said that its success was due to the pioneer settlers, ranchers, and homesteaders, who braved the numerous dangers (especially from the Indians, constantly driven from their hunting grounds by the white men's inexorable westward march) and to the great railroad builders who opened up the country for their successors. The last mainland territory to become a state was Arizona in 1912. At the end of the century, the United States began overseas expansion, to be discussed briefly in the next chapter.

CANADA

Canada before the early part of the nineteenth century was afflicted by political difficulties arising out of the British failure to understand the full extent of the grievances of the American colonists, which included the continued domination of local legislatures by appointed British governors. The situation was made worse by the fact that the country was divided into two provinces, Upper and Lower Canada, the latter predominantly French. The French naturally resented even more than the English their domination by British governors and their councils.

The system, nevertheless, was maintained in Canada until the 1830's, when the conflict between royal governors and their appointed councils on the one side, and the elected assemblies on the other erupted in a brief rebellion. Though this was easily suppressed, the British sent out a Radical peer, Lord Durham, to look into the situation and make proposals. The result, the Durham Report of

1839, marked an epoch in Anglo-Canadian relations, though not all the proposals were accepted. Upper and Lower Canada were united; but the councils and assemblies were maintained as before. Shortly afterward the governors, in obedience to British instructions, gradually ceased to exercise their power of veto, and the assemblies took over the major work of government. From this it was a brief step to the granting of truly responsible government under the British North America Act of 1867. Canadians wrote their own federal constitution, which differed from that of the United States in that all the powers not specifically granted to the provinces were vested in the federal government. The right to their own language and religion conceded to the French settlers in 1774 became "entrenched" clauses in the constitution. Canada remained in the British Empire and juridically under the crown, but for all essential purposes she was an independent country. The few anomalies in her relationship with Britain were settled under the Stature of Westminster in 1931.

LATIN AMERICA

The French Revolution at first created little stir in Latin America. For many years local Spaniards and Creoles had talked of possible independence from the not very enlightened and strongly autocratic Spanish monarchy which ruled its colonies through viceroys and appointed councils. Francisco de Miranda, a Venezuelan of Basque ancestry, thoroughly at home in European courts, had tried throughout the period of the Revolution and the first years of Napoleon to gain European support for his plan to liberate the Spanish colonies. But he had achieved little, his one early attempt at an uprising ending in abject failure.

The great opportunity seemed to present itself in 1808 when the Spanish monarchy was overthrown by Napoleon. But a new attempt by Miranda failed after a brief period of success, and Miranda himself died in a Spanish prison. One of his aids, Simon Bolívar, however, escaped the disaster and returned a few years later. Though he gained a good deal of local support, his movement was suppressed as the Bourbon monarchy in Spain was restored, and Bolívar again went into exile. The restored monarchy, however, caused much antagonism by its repressive methods, especially in Venezuela; when Bolívar returned three years later he therefore found far greater local support. This time he was able to build an effective army and defeat the Spaniards. Having been chosen president of Greater Colombia (Colombia and present-day Venezuela), he then marched westward to give aid in the liberation of Peru.

Meanwhile José de San Martín, a native Argentinian, had been placed in 1814 at the head of an Argentine junta. From the Argentine he aided Bernardo O'Higgins in the liberation of Chile and marched up the west coast to Lima. Here he encountered Bolívar, who had just crossed the Andes and taken the Spaniards in the rear. By agreement San Martín returned southward, leaving Bolívar and his most loyal aid, Antonio Sucre, to organize the western territories. The Spaniards were decisively defeated at Ayacucho, Peru, in 1824 and thereafter gave up the struggle in the west. Bolívar returned to Venezuela, where he re-established his personal position, which had been rapidly disintegrating during his absence. Even so, when he relinquished the presidency in 1830 Venezuela was on the point of separating from Colombia. When he died a few months later, all his ambitions for a large successor state to Spain were in ruins. For most of the succeeding century all the Latin American states were torn by dissension and ruled by one military dictator after another. Only a few could establish their rule securely enough to do much for their countries.

Brazil followed a rather different path from the rest of Latin America The Portuguese royal family took refuge in Brazil after being expelled from Portugal by Napoleon, and Brazilians regarded their huge country as the center of the Portuguese empire. Though the king himself returned to Portugal in 1821, his son Pedro was left as regent and Brazil was officially proclaimed an independent empire in 1825, with Pedro as emperor. It remained an empire until 1889, when Pedro II was pensioned off and the state became a republic under a president. As a consequence of this peculiar course of events, Brazil never had to fight for independence from Portugal. For a time she attempted to add Uruguay and Paraguay to her empire but both eventually succeeded in attaining their independence, though Paraguay engaged in a ruinous war later in the century (1865–1870) with Brazil, Argentina, and Uruguay at the same time. Almost her entire male population was destroyed in the war, and over half her women died. Paraguay has never recovered from this war.

The Mexican territories experienced greater difficulties in escaping from Spanish control than did any other countries in Latin

America; and, as we have seen, Mexico was also compelled to relinquish her northern lands to the United States. The revolution was first proclaimed by two priests in 1810, but the Spanish had no difficulty in suppressing it. Little was accomplished until 1821 when Augustin de Iturbide, the Spanish general in charge of operations, decided to join the rebels. He himself was shortly afterward proclaimed emperor of Mexico, but he quickly lost his support among the Mexicans, leaving the Spaniards the opportunity to intervene again. But the invasion was unsuccessful, and in 1829 Spain recognized the independence of the Mexican Republic.

For a short time during the reign of Napoleon III Mexico was again subjected to European rule, this time in the person of a Hapsburg archduke, Maximilian, kept in his position by French soldiers. The United States, at the time deeply involved in her own Civil War, could not intervene—even though the French intervention was a clear breach of a doctrine proclaimed by President Monroe in 1822, according to which European intervention in the Americas would be regarded as an unfriendly act. But once the Civil War was over, the United States advised Napoleon to take note of the doctrine. Weary of his unpopular war against the Mexican people, he abandoned his puppet emperor. The Mexicans at once restored their republic and executed Maximilian.

Thus by 1830 all America was free of Spanish rule. But the small successor states were unstable, and the continent as a whole was unable to play a part in the world commensurate with its size and resources. Its social and political problems were unsolved and it was chronically in need of outside capital, which the United States and all the industrial countries of Europe were willing to supply in their own interests and for the benefit of their own nationals. Though there has been somewhat greater stability in most states during the twentieth century, on the whole, this pattern remains substantially unchanged, and Latin America has still to find her true place in the modern world.

CHAPTER XIX

THE EXPANSION OF EUROPE

We have already noted in earlier chapters the tendency on the part of Western civilization to expand into areas of the world beyond Europe and to take possession of these for its own use. By the early nineteenth century the boundaries of the major European nations, which had been in a state of flux for several centuries, had been settled, and great changes were no longer to be expected. A kind of uneasy international concord had been reached, based on the recognition by each power that it could no longer expand with impunity in Europe, save perhaps in the Balkans, which were still ruled, albeit ever less effectively, by the Ottoman sultan.

Outside Europe the situation was different. On the one hand there were territories like India, already pre-empted by Britain, as we have seen, where foreign peoples could be subjected to European control and their countries opened up to European trade. China, Japan, the Malay Peninsula, and other Far Eastern lands were still independent, and still virtually closed to European penetration. These were opened up in the nineteenth century, and many of them were subjected to European rule.

On the other hand there were still a few virtually unpopulated temperate countries where European settlement might prosper, as it had prospered in North America. By the beginning of the nineteenth century, the two leading territories of this type had already been discovered and their settlement undertaken. Both fell to Britain, the one power venturesome enough to undertake the necessary pioneer work and strong enough to keep interfering foreigners away while they performed their task. Australia, at first used merely as a penal colony, had only a few primitive aborigines, who presented no bar to British expansionism. New Zealand had to contend with the Maoris, a Polynesian people of high culture and social development, whom the British immigrants after a period of fairly cordial relations were compelled for economic reasons to fight in two destructive wars. Neither colony permitted free immigration of non-

British peoples, and both prohibited the entry of Asians. Both achieved self-governing status with little friction, and both are now independent nations of the Commonwealth.

The type of imperialism represented by the settlement of Australia and New Zealand was, however, the last of its kind. The imperialism of the nineteenth century was concerned with other objectives than the discovery of new lands for settlement.

MOTIVES FOR EXPANSION

Economic Motives. The Industrial Revolution, which spread to all the countries of Western Europe during the century, had need for ever expanding markets and sources of raw materials. Such markets were greatest in the already partly industrialized nations of the West, though there were heavily populated areas such as China and India where additional markets could be developed despite the low standard of living of the populations. Much more important than the need for markets was the need for raw materials, some of which could be found only in tropical countries. In these countries the supply of raw materials was uncertain, far too uncertain to justify the investment of much capital in the home industries engaged in processing them. Yet there was an assured market for such products if the source of supply could be controlled.

It was certainly possible for individual traders and relatively small commercial enterprises to buy such products as the natives were prepared to produce and sell without acquiring physical control of the territory; and there was considerable profit in such enterprises, since the European products traded for the tropical materials were of little value in comparison with them. But sometimes much money had to be invested in such aids to commerce as railroads and waterways; and the supply of produce was so irregular that it could not be certain whether these investments would be profitable. It was therefore not unnatural that the European nation which had the power to take the territory by force should ultimately have decided to do so, thus protecting its investments and regularizing the sources of supply. It could always argue with justice that if it did not do so, some other European nation would. Thus the flag followed trade—not, as a rule, vice versa, in spite of the widespread belief to the contrary.

Other Motives. Probably the second most important reason for the revival of imperialism was the competition for national prestige. All the Western nations were engaged in asserting their superiority over other nations in all the ways open to them. The possession of an overseas empire was one such source of prestige, irrespective of whether the empire was commercially profitable or not. Neither the French nor the German empire was ever profitable to the mother country, and the Italian empire was a constant drain on home resources. Governments could obtain funds from their peoples most easily when national prestige was at stake, and patriotic motives could be stressed.

In some European countries, especially Britain and the United States, militant Christianity was strongly in evidence in the nineteenth century. Much of Africa was first explored by Christian missionaries who believed that it was their duty to convert the heathen Africans. Missionaries likewise penetrated into China and the Far East. When they met with difficulties from the natives, who were often spurred on by local religious leaders, their home governments, for reasons of prestige as well as humanity, were compelled to rescue them. Even so, it was the missionaries who took the lead in trying to protect the natives from exploitation by the commercial companies and made efforts to persuade their governments to assume responsibility themselves for the territories, rather than to clothe the commercial interests with powers that properly belonged to government.

THE FAR EAST

The opening up of China is an example of the manner in which commercial interests forced the hand of their governments. China in the early nineteenth century was still an isolated area, uninterested in trading or having any relations with the West. Successive diplomatic missions were unable to make any headway with the emperor, who insisted that Western barbarians should perform the same symbolic prostrations in his presence as his own subjects. China, in his view, was in reality the ruler of the whole world, even though the world did not acknowledge the fact. Its emissaries should therefore give a formal recognition to this sovereignty. The most that he was willing to do was to let foreign merchants have a special concession in Canton.

The economic truth at the time was that the Chinese empire was virtually self-sufficient and that the Westerners had no export products available for which it was worth while for the Chinese emperor to relax his restrictions. But the Westerners desired Chinese tea, for which there was a great unsatisfied demand in their countries. The British East India Company, which enjoyed a monopoly of British trade in the Far East, as well as in India, at last hit upon an export which was acceptable to many Chinese and which permitted huge profits both to the Company and to the Chinese middlemen. This was opium, a product forbidden by the emperor, but grown extensively, and cheaply, in India. For a long time the trade was winked at under the cover of legitimate trade, and opium exports increased to such an extent that the emperor took personal cognizance of it. He sent a special commissioner to Canton in 1839 with full powers to discipline the foreign merchants and destroy the opium.

Though Commissioner Lin was able to carry out his mandate at first, various incidents followed which seemed to justify British armed intervention. In the so-called Opium Wars, the British, aided later by other European forces, compelled the emperor to open his country to Western penetration and concede full rights and "extraterritoriality" to the Europeans in a specified number of treaty ports. Thereafter the emperors decided that it was best for them to attempt to modernize their country, especially the military establishment. But the attempts brought on rebellion from their own subjects, who had no use for "foreign devils," thus compelling the emperor to call on the West for aid. The aid was given at a price. Eventually the Western powers began to carve out for themselves spheres of influence which virtually destroyed the country's integrity and independence.

In 1894, Japan, which had been opened up to trade by American initiative in the 1850's, joined in the free-for-all, and though she was severely called to task by the Westerners and made to disgorge some of her gains, she was able to keep a substantial portion. The United States did not take official part in the competition but insisted that she and all other nations should have equal commercial rights in China, even though these rights had been extracted forcibly by the European imperialists. Likewise, according to this open-door policy insisted on by the United States, no nation was permitted to levy higher duties on the goods of foreigners than on their own. In 1898 the United States won a huge Far Eastern colony from Spain, with whom she had gone to war, largely over Cuba. In the peace settlement that followed she insisted on the outright cession of the Philippine Islands, thereby becoming a Far Eastern power. The French expanded into Indo-China, which they eventually subjected to their rule; the British moved into Burma and Malaya. Only Siam (Thailand) remained independent in this area, though even she was compelled to relinquish to Britain and France some of the lands over which she claimed control.

Meanwhile Japan had adopted the policy of reform on Western lines as the only way to preserve her integrity. She learned Western methods and changed her form of government, military organization, and bureaucracy largely in imitation of imperial Germany, whereas she built her navy according to British models. The result was that she won a war with China in 1894–1895, and another with a major European power, Russia, in 1904–1905. She was then accepted as a near-equal by the West, and the British entered into a naval alliance with her, which bore fruit in the Japanese participation on the Allied side in the First World War.

AFRICA

The Partition of Sub-Saharan Africa. Ever since the late fifteenth century the Portuguese had been ensconced on the east and west coasts of Africa, but they had penetrated little into the hinterlands of their colonies. Until the nineteenth century the slave trade was the economic mainstay of these colonies, the Portuguese making themselves responsible for the assembling of the slaves, usually supplied by African chiefs, and selling them to other European capitalists who transported them to the Americas, mostly to North America and Brazil. In 1807 the British abolished the slave trade in their territories and in 1833 emancipated all their slaves. Thereafter, they used their navy and their influence to put an end to the trade. The Portuguese resisted for a period, then accepted the inevitable but continued to use forced labor in their own colonies. It was not until the twentieth century that they were able to provide Angola and Mozambique (Portuguese East and West Africa) with an alternative economy of any substance; even now these are the poorest and least developed of any African colonies. During the expanding imperialism of the late nineteenth century, as a small power it was as much as Portugal could do to keep possession of her colonies. At one time she tried to join Angola and Mozambique by cutting a swath of Portuguese territory from west to east. But she was easily frozen out by the British and was glad to sign an agreement in 1891 permitting her to keep what she had. If it had not been for the rivalry between the greater European powers and their inability to agree on a fair division of spoils she would certainly have lost them.

The British at the beginning of the nineteenth century possessed South Africa, recently taken from the Dutch, and a few small terri-

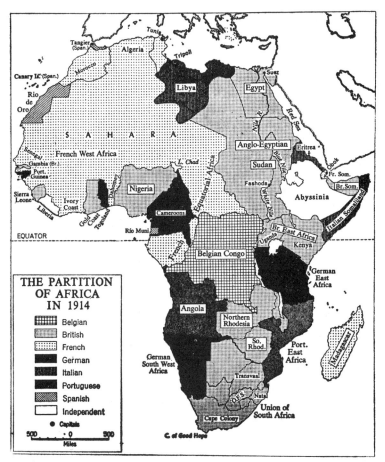

Map by Vincent Kotschar. From Stewart C. Easton, *Western Heritage* (New York: Holt, Rinehart & Winston, Inc., 1961). By permission of the publisher.

tories elsewhere to which she added little until the later years of the century. In South Africa she was faced by the fact that the bulk of the population was of Dutch descent. Having developed a congenial way of life, they wanted no interference from their new rulers, nor had they any intention of abandoning their slaveholding economy. In the 1830's a considerable number of these Boers, as the British called them, trekked into the interior of the country, where they came in contact with the African Bantus, who were slowly moving southward. They defeated and enslaved such of these Africans as they could and established their rule over the remainder, though for several decades they themselves continued under British rule. Meanwhile the British expanded to the east into Natal. When diamonds, and later gold, were discovered in the Boer territories, British and other miners flocked into the country, disturbing the patriarchal way of life of the Boers.

This influx exacerbated the differences between the Boers and the British who ruled from Capetown. The Boers proclaimed their independence and organized two republics which for a time were recognized by the British. But the situation could not last. President Kruger of Transvaal insisted on keeping the British immigrants from any share in the political life of their adopted country and imposed strict regulations which they found intolerable. Cecil Rhodes, for a time prime minister of Cape Colony, meanwhile had won concessions from the Matabele to the north of the South African colony, and wished to bring the whole of Africa south of the Zambesi under complete British rule. His policies and an abortive raid carried out by one of his friends (Jameson Raid, 1895) brought on a final war with the Boers, in which the latter, despite heroic resistance, were defeated. Lenient terms were granted, but the Boer republics were annexed.

In 1910 an experiment was attempted which persisted until 1961. The Union of South Africa was formed, in which Boer and Englishman would have equal rights, and the Union became a self-governing country in the British Empire. But the Boers (Afrikaners) remained a majority of the white population, and ultimately used the political institutions that they had been granted to convert the state into a republic, dominated by themselves (1961). The native Africans outnumber the whites by more than three to one, but as yet have been unable to escape in any essential respect from their servitude.

The journeys of the missionary and explorer, David Livingstone, in the middle of the nineteenth century were the signal for a great scramble among all the European powers for possession of African lands whose very existence he made known fully to the Western world for the first time. The British won the lion's share of the population, the French the greatest amount of land, most of it arid and barren. In every territory some wars were fought with the Africans, but the Europeans never had any serious difficulty in wining them, as soon as they were willing to devote the necessary men and resources to the task. The Belgian king, Leopold II, formed a great commercial company, dominated by himself, to exploit a huge territory in Central Africa. By agreement with the other powers in 1885 he was permitted to keep his conquests provided that an open-door trade policy was accepted for the whole Congo basin. But his methods of exploitation were such that he was subjected to outraged criticism from all quarters. When he died in 1908 he left his personal empire to the Belgian state, which quietly and gradually reversed most of his policies during its rule of fifty-two years.

The Germans were the last on the African scene, since Bismarck had originally preferred to let the French spend their resources on imperial ventures in the hope that they would cease to find the loss of Alsace and Lorraine so intolerable, and he did not wish to compete with them. But when Kaiser William II inherited the German throne and showed himself anxious to build German prestige by acquiring colonies, Bismarck had to agree and accept the gift of colonies offered to him by German agents, who had for a long time been hardly less active than those of other nations. The result was that the Germans won the large territory of German East Africa, now Tanganyika; two West Coast territories, the Cameroons and Togoland; and German South West Africa. After the First World War these were mandated to Britain and France, while a small and overpopulated sector went to Belgium under the name of Ruanda-Urundi. Britain in turn handed over German South West Africa to the Union of South Africa. By the end of the century all Sub-Saharan Africa had been divided among the European powers except the small and independent state of Liberia, founded as a refuge for freed slaves in the early part of the century. By the time of the First World War only Abyssinia (Ethiopia) and Liberia remained independent on the whole continent.

Consequences of the Partition for the Africans. The effect of the partition on African development varied in the different countries. The tribal structure of African society which had survived for centuries was severely shaken by European occupation, probably in most areas beyond the possibility of reconstitution even if the attempt were now to be made. All the European colonial powers exploited their territories economically—which was to be expected, since the major purpose of the partition was to enable the metropolitan power to obtain African produce and sell it after they had processed it, in the countries that could afford to pay for it. The British insisted that the colonies should pay for all the costs involved in their administration, including the salaries of expatriate colonial officials. The French attempted the same policy, but their colonies proved to be too poor to pay their way, and the metropolitan French made up regular budget deficits. The Belgian Congo was the richest of the territories, but the wealth was mostly in the form of minerals; and though on the whole the economic development of the Congo was greater than that of any other colony, the Belgians also took out proportionately greater profits themselves. The Portuguese, always short of capital, and unwilling to accept much foreign investment, developed their colonies least.

The British, French, and Belgians, as a result of their policies, left a considerable infrastructure of railroads, waterways, roads, and other permanent improvements to their colonies at independence; and the British and French left a small number of educated men who had been initiated into the mysteries of European political and cultural life. The Belgians left their colony at independence in 1960 very ill-provided with educated and professional men, though there were considerable numbers of business men and skilled workers. The Portuguese did not encourage education, but a few thousand Africans were granted Portuguese citizenship and were accepted as in theory equal to their rulers. Many of these men, however, left Africa permanently for Portugal and have not been encouraged to return. It remains to be seen whether the veneer of Western culture acquired by African leaders will be sufficient to enable them to bring their independent countries fully within the fold of Western civilization, or whether the vast majority of the people who know little of Western civilization and have known the Europeans only as their masters, will reabsorb their Westernized leaders and develop their own civilization in their own way—a way which may be totally different from that laid out for them by their erstwhile masters.

North Africa. North Africa, being much closer to Europe, and in some places directly across the Mediterranean from a colonial power, was coveted by the expanding Europeans; and it was found more difficult to reconcile the interests of the different European powers in this area than it was in Sub-Saharan Africa, where none save the

Portuguese had any prior commitments, and where there was enough for all. At the beginning of the nineteenth century, the Ottoman Empire was the formal overlord of all the North African coastal areas from Egypt to Algeria, but the degree of vassalage depended upon circumstances, and the Turks were rarely able to command obedience from the semi-independent rulers. Only Morocco was actually independent, even in theory. The French began to move into Algeria in 1830 and subjugated the country in the course of the next fifty years. In 1881 they edged out the less powerful Italians, who were intriguing to take Tunisia. The Italians were encouraged to seek satisfaction elsewhere; but all they could win were two desert areas in the Horn of Africa. They were badly defeated in 1896 at the Battle of Adowa by the Abyssinian emperor Menelik, advised and assisted by the French. As some compensation in 1911 they took Tripolitania from the rapidly decaying Ottoman Empire.

Only Morocco in northwestern Africa produced a serious crisis in the relations between the European powers. France, as the ruler of Algeria and Tunisia, was anxious to round off her territories in North Africa. She had already relinquished her rights in Egypt to Britain, and Britain made no difficulties for her in Morocco. After the signing in 1904 of the Entente Cordiale, which brought to an end friction between Britain and France throughout Africa and aligned the two countries on the same side in European matters for the first time in two-and-a-half centuries, Britain in fact gave active diplomatic support to the French. But Kaiser William II believed that Germany's interests should also be taken into consideration and that Morocco was not simply a matter for arrangement between Britain and France. At least he insisted upon an open-door policy. But in the Algeciras Conference of 1906 the kaiser lacked diplomatic support and gave way to French insistence. Then France proceeded to go much further toward subjecting the country to her control than had been agreed to, bringing on a new Moroccan crisis in 1911, when the Germans sent a gunboat to Agadir to force some concessions by threatening war. Eventually France agreed to give the kaiser some of her Sub-Saharan territory and the crisis was over. The next year the French forced the sultan of Morocco to accept a French protectorate, thus giving France the largest of the European North African empires.

In the early nineteenth century an Albanian officer in Turkish employ in Egypt named Mohammed (or Mehemet) Ali made himself virtually independent of his master and conquered most of the Sudan to the south. He and his successors still acknowledged their Ottoman suzerains and ruled in their name; but the Turks had in fact little to say in their province during the century. The great enterprise of the century was the Suez Canal, which now appeared technically feasible but would obviously require huge amounts of capital; and the European capitalists were quite unwilling to let the Egyptians have full control of the canal as long as their own money was at stake. At last the French gained the concession and built the canal, with capital provided by private interests. Soon after the canal had been built the Egyptian khedive Ismail, in desperate straits for money, put his own shares on the market. Disraeli, then British prime minister, bought them on behalf of the British government, thus making it the largest shareholder in the canal. Ismail accepted at the same time the right of the shareholders to supervise Egyptian finances.

This control, however, caused much unrest in Egypt, and there were several anti-European incidents. At first the British and French intervened together. But the French soon withdrew from the venture, leaving the British to do as they wished. The result was that a protectorate was imposed upon the country by the British, who paid the sultan of Turkey for allowing them to be the protectors, satisfied the creditors, and reorganized the entire administration of the country. Sudan was lost to a Muslim religious leader known as the Mahdi, who kept both Britain and Egypt out of the country for thirteen years (1885–1898). Eventually it was reconquered and the whole of Egypt was efficiently ruled by the British until after the First World War. Then they restored Egyptian sovereignty under a monarch and a parliamentary government, but retained various rights by treaty until after the Second World War.

Thus in the second half of the nineteenth century the European powers parceled out the globe among them. Where they did not rule they divided the various countries into spheres of influence, regulated among themselves by formal treaties and informal agreements. There was almost no part of the world that was not in some manner subjected to the dominating influence of one or the other of the European powers, or of the United States, itself an earlier offshoot of Western civilization. But the Europeans lived among themselves in a condition that amounted to almost an armed truce. War had not actually broken out between them on any colonial question. Whether the conflict of interests would have ultimately brought on an intra-European war must forever remain an academic question— for, as all the world knows, the oft-postponed war did break out in 1914 on an internal issue; and though the actual devolution of the European empires did not begin until the Second World War, it can now be seen that European expansion had reached its apogee in 1914, and from that date it would know only a decline, at first gradual, and then, in our own day, precipitate.

CHAPTER XX

THE BREAKDOWN OF INTERNATIONAL CONCORD (1871–1914)

From what has been said in previous chapters it will be recognized that the word concord in the title of this chapter is more than a little ironical. In fact, the interests of all national states invariably came into conflict. Indeed, it may be argued that this is the necessary nature of the national state, whose very existence is predicated upon its separateness from other nations. International relations have always been marked by power politics, and it is difficult for us to imagine any conditions in the future when this will not be so. It may be possible to reduce tensions between the various nation states and to establish a power system under which, from prudential reasons, neither great nor small powers will dare to disturb the peace. But such a condition can arise only when the balance is so carefully adjusted that the statesmen of all nations recognize the dictates of prudence. Even then accident or misunderstanding may touch off a war that nobody desires, and all hope to avoid. In essence this is what happened in 1914.

THE EUROPEAN ALLIANCE SYSTEM

The advent of Germany to the status of a great power, the greatest, indeed, on the continent of Europe, introduced a new factor into the international system which had, of course, to be taken into consideration in all the European chancelleries. The taking of Alsace and Lorraine from France in 1871 made that country anxious for both "revenge" and restitution. France was unwilling to accept her new status; not all the colonies that she could win with the encouragement of Bismarck could ever compensate for the loss of her two important provinces, both of which were of great value in an industrial age. When Germany herself, after the middle of the 1880's ceased to regard French colonial expansion as permissible and began to covet colonies for herself, even this alternative outlet for French energies was no longer easily available. Thus, France was what may be called a "dissatisfied" power, and at all time there were large numbers of Frenchmen who were anxious for a new war with Germany which would have a different result from that of 1870–1871.

Bismarck was very well aware of the aspirations of France; but when he was dismissed from office by the new kaiser, William II, in 1890, German policy was no longer so much concerned with French susceptibilities. Imperial Germany, feeling herself strong enough to cope with any armies the French could bring against her, did not even make any serious efforts to prevent them from building an alliance system which would counterbalance her own power. Bismarck, on the other hand, had been anxious to keep tsarist Russia and Austria on his own side and to isolate France, even helping to keep her at enmity with Britain over colonial matters. But Britain came to recognize in the early 1900's that it was not advisable to play Germany's game by remaining on bad terms with France. German policy, as directed by the kaiser and a series of chancellors who were of his mind, appeared to her to be much more dangerous than French colonial expansionism. In addition, Germany was her most active trade competitor and was pushing her out of export markets which she had long held; whereas French exports, mainly of luxuries, were not, as a rule, competitive with her own. So after a long period of delicate feeling out of one another, the pro-British French statesman, Delcassé, was able to persuade the British to form the Entente Cordiale of 1904. Even so, the British and French were still not full-fledged allies, nor had they entered into a binding agreement even on the eve of the First World War. The British had for too long been unwilling to enter into foreign "entanglements" to be willing to forego their freedom to throw their weight against any power who seemed more dangerous at the moment. It was the German invasion of Belgium, the maintenance of whose neutrality was a constant of British policy, that eventually brought her into the war by the side of the French.

Bismarck's alliance with Austria and Italy (Triple Alliance), signed as early as 1882, survived until the war, though it became increasingly clear that Italy could not be relied upon, especially if Britain were in the war on the opposite side. His policy of alliance with Russia came to an end with his dismissal, the last treaty (Reinsurance Treaty of 1887) lapsing in 1890. The French took advantage of the resulting coolness between Germany and Russia to press for a treaty, which came to fruition in 1894. The numerous difficulties between Russia and Britain, concerned mainly with the rights of the two nations in the borderland of India, especially Afghanistan, were ironed out in 1907. The line-up of the nations was thereafter unchanged until the war. On the side of what came to be called the Central Powers were Germany and Austria, with Italy as a doubtful third; on the "Allied" side were France and Russia, with Britain as a probable third.

<h3 style="text-align:center">THE BALKAN POWDER KEG</h3>

The crisis which led to the war, however, arose in the Balkans, which had been disturbed all through the nineteenth century. The Ottoman Empire in Europe was obviously disintegrating. First one state and then another won its autonomy and eventually independence, beginning with Greece in 1831. Except for Serbia, all the new nations accepted German princes as their kings. The European powers naturally could not look on idly while Turkey was broken up; for if Russia were to inherit the major portion, and especially if she were to win Constantinople itself, then the balance of power would be seriously upset and such an eventuality would not be tolerated by any of her rival nations. But Austria was the most directly concerned, as the ruler of various Slavic minorities, all of which were restive under her rule. The Slavic states in the Balkans all engaged in Pan-Slavic propaganda, which found a sympathetic response not only among the minorities in the Austrian Empire but in Russia, the greatest of the Slavic states. Relations between Austria and Russia were constantly embittered by the Balkan situation; and the instability of the new Balkan states, whose boundaries were of course extremely fluid, was a standing invitation to intervention. The European private manufacturers of armaments also found in the Balkans a satisfactory market for their products, which was not helpful to the cause of peace.

The Austrians objected most of all to the new state of Serbia, which was the most clamorous in its Pan-Slavic propaganda, and for many years a feeling had been building up in the Austrian chancellery that sooner or later she would have to be taught a lesson. There was no question in Austrian minds but that a local war would be quickly settled in Austrian favor. The danger was that such intervention would lead to a world war, bringing all the European alliances into automatic operation. Some Austrian statesmen, however, believed that the only permanent solution would be for Austria

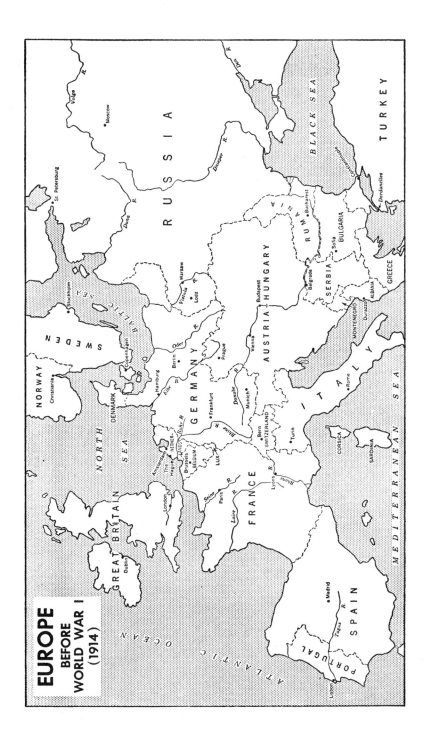

EUROPE
BEFORE
WORLD WAR I
(1914)

to expand her own empire and annex some of the lands now being pried loose from Turkey, thus winning the preponderating influence in all the other new states. In 1908 she did annex Bosnia and Herzegovina, which infuriated the Balkan states of Serbia and Montenegro that had regarded these territories as part of their area for expansion, and offended deeply both Turkey and Russia. The Turks were pacified the following year, but Russia continued hostile. Two Balkan wars in the succeeding years, in both of which Turkey participated, continued to make the Balkans the "powder keg" of Europe. Though both were concluded by treaties, nothing had yet been permanently settled.

THE MURDER AT SERAJEVO AND ITS CONSEQUENCES

The final crisis was brought on by the murder of the Austrian archduke Francis Ferdinand and his wife at Serajevo in the newly annexed but far from pacified Austrian province of Bosnia (June 28, 1914). It was clear that some Serbs in high positions were privy to the murder, which was carried out by a terrorist organization known as the Black Hand. The Austrians therefore despatched an ultimatum to Serbia. Faced with the immediate danger of a war which they could not hope to win if it were confined to their country, the Serbs accepted almost all the severe terms of the ultimatum. But over the last, which would have meant virtual subjection to Austria, they temporized. The Austrians chose to regard this as a refusal and declared war (July 28).

There ensued a frantic effort to avoid a general war. Germany had given Austria assurances which the latter regarded as a "blank check." France renewed her assurances to Russia. Russia decided on mobilization, a long process in that vast country and deemed necessary by her military leaders. The kaiser succeeded in persuading the Russian tsar to withdraw his orders, recognizing that Germany could not permit mobilization on her borders and would have to declare war if the order were not countermanded. But it was in fact too late. The tsar could not reverse the troop movements, and Germany sent him an ultimatum. The French, in answer to an inquiry, informed the Germans that they would have to be guided by their own interests, and proceeded to mobilize; the Germans followed suit as soon as they received the news. Meanwhile Britain had been refused German assurance that the neutrality of Belgium would be respected. All the powers therefore had to recognize that their efforts had been in vain, though the Germans made one more effort on August 1 to persuade the British to let them deal with Russia alone and to keep France neutral.

At seven P.M. on August 1, Germany, having received no reply to her ultimatum to Russia, declared war. Two days later she declared war on France and invaded Belgium. The British honored their agreement on Belgian neutrality (the famous "scrap of paper") and declared war on Germany on August 4, while Austria declared war on Russia on August 6.

Thus began the First World War, in which nations everywhere lined up, almost all against the Central Powers. Turkey and Bulgaria were the only major acquisitions on the German side (November, 1914 and October, 1915 respectively), while Japan, Italy, and the United States joined the Allies (August, 1914; May, 1915; and April, 1917).

CHAPTER XXI

THE WAR AND THE PEACE

The First World War proved to be incomparably the most destructive war known as yet in the annals of history. This was in part the result of the greater capacity for destruction available to modern nations and in part the result of the extensive nature of the operations. Moreover, medical science and nursing service, though much improved in recent decades, were not able to prevent great numbers of casualties from succumbing to their wounds—men whose lives would have been saved in the Second World War. Like the Second World War, it was fought without any clear idea of what kind of peace was to be imposed when it was over; and relatively little attention was given by the governments of the warring nations to the problem as long as hostilities were in progress. The national prestige of each nation was so heavily involved and the peoples so identified with their own national war efforts that there was never much chance for a negotiated peace on the basis of anything but total victory. The eighteenth-century concept of a war fought for recognizable and limited objectives had disappeared, apparently forever; and it became the major task of the nations that assembled at Versailles in 1919 to try to devise measures to prevent future wars altogether. The destructiveness of war was now so evident that a civilized humanity could no longer permit them. This much was understood, but there was little evidence of any fundamental thinking on the kind of conditions that should be striven for in Europe and the world, which would make peaceful coexistence acceptable and desirable to all the nations affected by the peace treaty. On the contrary, the treaty created more nations than ever, each with its own national pride and national interests; and the security provisions provided, ineffectively enough, merely for collective sanctions against breakers of the international peace, rather than for adjustment of the underlying conditions which led to national dissatisfaction with the new order that the treaty imposed.

THE PROGRESS OF THE WAR

The Germans, as usual, were better prepared for war than the French. As in 1870, they began a drive on Paris, but this time were stopped when they reached the river Marne. Although in 1918 they made a few gains beyond this point in their last final assault before their collapse, the Western front was virtually a stalemate for four years. Both sides dug in and engaged in trench warfare, broken only by massive and costly assaults on the enemy positions. The British, able to provide only a small expeditionary force at the beginning, threw waves of fresh troops into the fray from time to time, especially for the extraordinarily destructive Battle of the Somme in 1916. The stalemate in the West made large strategic moves available only in the East, and in minor theaters of war elsewhere. The Germans and Austrians first had to hold off the Russian offensive. This was achieved without any great difficulty before the end of 1914. Thereafter the Russians were almost always on the defensive and lost Poland, Lithuania, and Courland to the Germans.

In 1915 the British decided upon an expedition to the Straits of the Dardanelles at the south end of the Sea of Marmora, in the hope of saving the Balkans from the Central Powers, as well as engaging Turkey directly. If it had succeeded and Turkey had been knocked out of the war, the Allies would have been in a position to relieve the pressure on Russia and could have attacked the Central Powers from the southeast. As a strategic concept it had much to recommend it, but there was difference of opinion among the Allies as to its value, and too few forces were sent to make the move effective. After a slow start the Turks fought back strongly, Greece persisted in staying neutral, while Bulgaria joined the Central Powers, thus adding her weight to the attack on Serbia, which the Austrians had not been able to push to a successful conclusion. Now the Austrians, Bulgars, and Germans, led by a German commander, launched an overwhelming attack against the little country, taking over the whole territory, while the Allies who had landed troops at the Greek port of Saloníki, which they occupied, were unable to provide much aid. These latter troops stayed until the end of the war, but the Dardanelles expedition was called off in October, 1915.

In the next year the Rumanians, encouraged by a few Russian victories, entered the war on the Allied side but were rapidly overwhelmed by Austro-German-Bulgar armies. The Italians entered the war against Austria in 1915, following the signature of a secret treaty granting them some major territorial gains at Austrian expense but did not declare war on Germany until 1916. Even then they were unable to achieve much against either Germany or Austria. Late in 1917 they were overwhelmingly defeated by German and Austrian forces at Caporetto, a defeat from which they did not recover until almost the end of the war.

By the end of 1916 the Central Powers had had much the best of the exchanges by land but had made little progress toward defeating their major enemies, Britain and France. Early in the war they had begun to use submarines against Allied shipping. Then, finding that ineffective, since neutral shipping could take food and supplies to Britain, they began to extend their operations against neutral shipping too. This brought a stern warning to Germany from the United States, especially after the sinking without warning of the passenger vessel, the *Lusitania,* in 1915. Thereafter the Germans modified their submarine attacks. But their surface navy did not prove very useful to them. Armed cruisers did some damage to Allied shipping in the early part of the war; however, the main fleet, large though it was, was no match for the much larger British navy. It destroyed more British ships than it lost in the Battle of Jutland in 1916, but it was not able to escape from the Baltic, and was penned up relatively immobile for most of the war—although occasional ships escaped the blockade and bombarded the English east coast without any noticeable effect on the war.

The submarines, on the contrary, were enjoying a remarkable success—so great, indeed, that Germans began to take seriously the possibility of bringing Britain to her knees through the submarine blockade. She therefore took the decision in January, 1917, to renew unrestricted submarine warfare. When the United States was informed of this decision, diplomatic relations with Germany were at once severed; and as soon as the first United States ships were sunk, war was declared. The submarines continued to wreak great havoc for a few months more; but when the British adopted an effective answer in the convoy system, their losses declined, and they sank more German submarines. The Americans were now in the war; and the Germans recognized that they would have to strike quickly at the Allies before American land troops could be trained.

The Central Powers had their last major success when the Russian armies in late 1916 suffered tremendous casualties in an abortive offensive. This was followed in 1917 by a mutiny of the Russian troops, the abdication of the tsar, and the formation of a provisional government. This government wished to continue the war; but the troops, among whom revolutionaries of all stripes had been sowing "defeatism," were war weary, and the new government could not make its authority accepted. After the Bolshevik Revolution in October, 1917, there was never any chance of a serious renewed war effort. The Bolsheviks finally accepted extremely unfavorable terms in the Treaty of Brest-Litovsk (March, 1918) in order to win time for the completion of the revolution.

With Russia out of the war, the Germans could now turn their full attack on the West. They mounted a major offensive in April, 1918, which made some gains. But the American troops were present now in enough numbers to turn the tide. Under a unified command (Marshal Foch) the Allies fought back and began to advance. When the Germans had been driven back to their own borders, the kaiser abdicated, and the civilian leaders sued for an armistice on the basis of Fourteen Points put forward by President Woodrow Wilson. The Allies, however, imposed their own terms, which the Germans were obliged to accept. The armistice went into effect on November 11, 1918.

THE PEACE SETTLEMENT

The Fourteen Points consisted of a number of general propositions which were hard to convert into actuality and a number of more specific objectives, such as the reconstitution of Poland and the restoration of the kingdom of Belgium. The last point, the one most dear to President Wilson's heart, contained the plan for a League of Nations "to afford mutual guarantees of political independence and territorial integrity to great and small states alike." It was hoped that this provision would give meaning to the first point of "open covenants, openly arrived at" (no secret treaties), since future treaties would be registered with the League.

Wilson fought hard at Versailles for his Fourteen Points, which in the main were accepted as the basis for the peace terms. The peacemakers, with the exception of Wilson, were indeed somewhat lukewarm on the question of the League of Nations, but accepted it at Wilson's insistence. It had already been agreed that new nations would be created, and that the Austrian minorities, in particular would be permitted to have their own states. The question at issue therefore was which of the minorities would become the bases for their own states and which would join together to form larger and more viable states. In theory the new principle of "self-determination" should be applied; but if applied too rigidly, no state would have a chance of success in a world bristling with tariffs, in which each new country would try to create a national economy of its own, as well as all the expensive trappings of nationhood. Ultimately two large new states were created, Czechoslovakia and Yugoslavia, while the new Poland was a large nation with access to the sea through a corridor which cut off East Prussia from the rest of Germany. Rumania was greatly enlarged. Turkey in Europe was confined to Constantinople and a small hinterland, Austria was reduced to a small German-speaking state, and Hungary lost much territory in favor of Rumania. Italy was given the Austrian Tyrol and increased territory on the Adriatic. Four new independent nations, Finland, Estonia, Latvia, and Lithuania were carved out of western Russia.

It need hardly be added that the problem of minorities was not solved by these arrangements. All the new states had minorities under their control, which most of the governments treated with indifferent wisdom, and even in the new creation of Yugoslavia the different ethnic groups within the country quarreled constantly with one another. Czechoslovakia was less plagued by disunity than was Yugoslavia, but even there the less civilized Slovaks resented the domination of the Bohemian Czechs, who had long filled an important place in European culture. Lithuania and Poland quarreled over the possession of Vilna, which both claimed.

Germany, though she did not lose very much territory, was compelled to agree to the payment of an astronomical sum in reparations and to admit to the guilt of having caused the war. She also had to submit to an army of occupation, to the permanent demilitarization of the Rhineland, and to total disarmament. The Socialist government which had come to power in the new German Republic was compelled to sign the treaty, since the country remained under blockade until it was signed. All Germans regarded it as a dictated peace, inequitable, and not to be lived up to except under compulsion. When the reparations were scaled down in 1924 after a ruinous inflation and the invasion of the Ruhr by the French and Belgians to ensure their payment, a few responsible German ministers, especially Gustav Stresemann, tried to win their fellow Germans to the idea that they could be restored to their rightful position in Europe

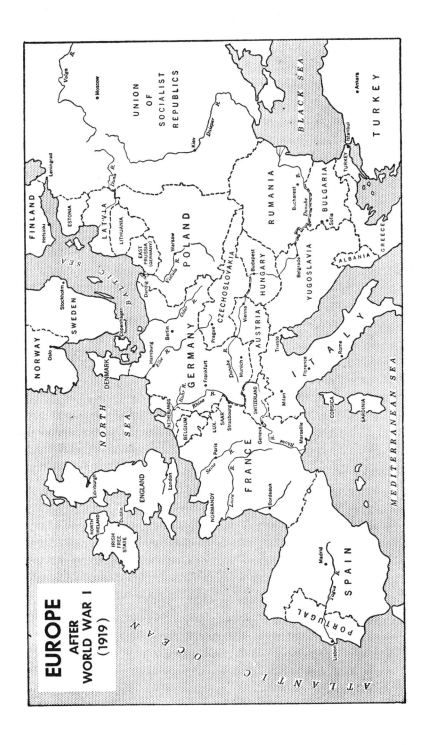

EUROPE
AFTER
WORLD WAR I
(1919)

only by accepting the treaty and co-operating with the victors. Though the policy was attempted for a few years, and Germany entered the League of Nations, subsequent events proved that the treaty still rankled. When Hitler proceeded to scrap its provisions by unilateral action he became a hero to his people, and thereafter they followed him, even into a new war which was almost all of Germany's own making.

Thus the "Long Armistice" began, a brief period in the history of Europe, marked by the efforts of the new nations to establish themselves securely and by the corresponding efforts of Germany to restore the position taken from her by the war and the peace—and by the attempts of the new League of Nations to police the settlement with fewer and less assured means than those available to the victorious powers at the Congress of Vienna in 1815.

CHAPTER XXII

THE LONG ARMISTICE

The era of the Long Armistice between the World Wars falls naturally into two periods, with 1929 as the dividing line. Up to the Great Depression which began in that year, Europe seemed to be slowly struggling back to its feet. There had been an era of prosperity, especially in the United States. Britain and France had recovered in most respects from the war. Germany appeared to be on the way to taking her place once more in respectable European society. Though Italy had been taken over by a dictator, Mussolini in 1929 seemed on the whole an improvement on the corrupt democracy that had preceded his rise to power; the extent of his tyranny was not widely known, and he did not show signs of wishing to expand his power beyond Italy. The new states had set up democratic institutions which functioned with varying degrees of effec tiveness; most of their boundary problems had been settled, if not to the satisfaction of all parties. Of these new states, only Lithuania had already submitted to the absolute rule of a dictator, though strong personalities such as Marshal Pilsudski of Poland, who had won his office by a coup d'état, in fact dominated their countries, while retaining some parliamentary forms. Soviet Russia was still struggling through her revolution, and it was widely believed that it could not succeed. But she was effectively quarantined from the rest of Europe, which troubled little about her. The League of Nations had settled down to its work and had had some success in settling a few minor problems that might have caused difficulty. The League was to a large degree dominated by France, who had built a new system of alliances designed to ensure that Germany would never again feel herself able to break the peace with any chance of success.

Then the Great Depression struck all the European countries and the United States, with repercussions that were political as well as economic. It paved the way for the rise of Adolf Hitler to power in Germany, and the imitation of his apparently successful totalitarianism in every new state except Czechoslovakia and Finland. Even France was not unaffected, though totalitarianism was not imposed until after her defeat by Germany in 1940. Britain and the other older democracies survived without political upheaval, as did the British dominions and the United States. But none of the countries had fully recovered its economic strength by the outbreak of the Second World War.

THE RUSSIAN COMMUNIST STATE

The Revolution of 1905. Reference has already been made to the fact that Tsar Nicholas II granted his country a constitution in 1905. This event was the direct result of the failure of the Russian armies during the recent war with Japan. For many years a revolutionary impetus had been building up against the tsarist government. Three left-wing revolutionary groups had been organized, together with a number of more moderate parties. The revolutionary groups, the Bolsheviks, Mensheviks, and Social Revolutionaries (the latter mostly composed of peasants) all wished to overthrow the government, having little confidence in mere constitutional reform; the other, more moderate, political parties were anxious for Russia to follow the same path as the other European nations.

The revolution in 1905 began with a march of workers led by a priest. When the procession was fired upon by the tsarist troops, a wave of strikes began which was supported by the moderates as well as by the extremists. The tsar gave way and agreed to set up a duma with a liberal franchise. But the Duma brought into office by the election was strongly antitsarist, as was the second, called less than a year later. The tsar then changed the basis of the representation and the franchise, thus ensuring a conservative government, which under Peter Stolypin attempted a program of reform, especially in the countryside. After Stolypin's murder in 1911 the reform program was slowed down, and Russia entered the war with a conservative parliament and much power still remaining in the hands of the tsar.

The Bolshevik Revolution. In March, 1917, as already noted, the tsar was compelled to abdicate by a mutiny of his troops, accompanied by strikes in the capital (formerly St. Petersburg, now Petrograd). The Duma then set up a Provisional Government to carry on the war and arrange for a permanent constitution. The Provisional Government was generally moderate in complexion with only one socialist member, Alexander Kerensky, who was far from being a revolutionary. But in the few months of its rule it was not able to establish its authority, especially in the face of disobedience by the Petrograd Soviet, dominated by the revolutionary groups, who were still at odds among themselves but saw victory in sight. They were of no mind to support a bourgeois government led by the moderates. The Soviet became more radical after the return from exile of the Bolshevik leaders, Lenin and Trotsky. The latter attempted a coup in Petrograd in July which was a failure; Lenin went into exile in Finland and Trotsky was imprisoned. One result of the attempt, however, was the resignation of the titular head of the Provisional Government and his replacement by Kerensky.

This brought on a military counterrevolution led by General Kornilov, who had no intention of obeying a socialist prime minister and planned to destroy the Provisional Government and the Soviet by military means. The move was a total failure since most of the troops refused to follow the general, while the workers refused to transport him to Petrograd. But Kerensky was now dependent on his left-wing support. Trotsky was released and Lenin shortly afterward returned, both with their prestige as activists greatly enhanced, so that their Bolshevik party for the first time was able to win a majority of the Petrograd Soviet. This was the signal for a Bolshevik coup which this time was successful and Lenin assumed the leadership of the government. When the voting for the constituent assembly called by the Provisional Government took place, the Bolsheviks found themselves outnumbered nearly two to one by the Social Revolutionaries. They therefore dispersed the assembly by force before it had transacted any business, thereby driving many of the more moderate revolutionaries into opposition.

By the end of 1917 the Bolsheviks were clearly only a small minority in the country. But they had the most determined leaders and an organized police force (Cheka) devoted to stamping out all counterrevolutionary activity. They were also in the long run favored by attempts at intervention by foreign powers. The various counterrevolutionary forces that enrolled armies to overthrow the Bolshevik government were never able to agree on their objectives, and seldom enjoyed much local support; whereas the Bolshevik army (Red Army) organized by Trotsky could claim to be defending Russian soil as well as the Revolution. In the end the Red Army became an effective force and drove the foreigners out of the country, even managing by the end of 1918 to retake the Ukraine, which had been established as a German-dominated independent state under the treaty of Brest-Litovsk. Another war with the Poles in 1920 confirmed the Russians in their possession. The independence of Latvia, Lithuania, Estonia, and Finland, however, was recognized by the Bolsheviks and they remained independent until the Second World War.

The Early Years of the Soviet Union. During the first years of the revolution the Bolsheviks instituted a system known as War Communism which was little but a collection of policies designed for the major purpose of seeing that enough supplies were forthcoming to enable the government to carry on and win its wars. Factories initially were run by the workers through their committees; later when these proved unable to ensure production, by government officials. In 1921 Lenin instituted what was called the New Economic Policy, which permitted a certain amount of private enterprise. Under this system the economy partly recovered from the devastation of the previous years, thus permitting Lenin's successor, Joseph Stalin, to undertake a new phase of the revolution.

The Institution of State Socialism. Stalin abandoned the aim of immediate world revolution, which had been the original objective of the Bolsheviks, in favor of "socialism in one country." To achieve this aim he decided that the country must be industrialized by whatever means were available to the government and against any opposition. At the same time private agriculture must be collectivized, either through compulsory co-operatives (collective farms) or state enterprise (state farms). All private landholding was to be abolished, and the richer peasants made to conform or face "liquidation." Thus the first Five Year Plan which established targets of production to be attained began in Ocobter, 1928; ever since that time there has been a plan in operation. The production quotas under each plan have to be fulfilled by the responsible officials on pain of serious penalties, penalties which the regime has not hesitated to enforce.

The immediate result of these measures was a serious famine, especially in the Ukraine, and serious resistance from the richer farmers who refused to be collectivized. But over the years the system was established, and it has changed little in essentials to this day, while a new generation of Russians has grown up which has known no other system than what is still called Communism but has turned in practice to one more properly entitled State Socialism.

The Soviet System of Government. The Russian state is a Union of Republics, each with its own governmental forms, and its official name is the Union of Soviet Socialist Republics (U.S.S.R.). It is not a federal government; the central apparatus in Moscow, the new capital, sets all majority policy for the constituent republics. The Soviet government has in practice always been a dictatorship exercised by the General Secretary of the Communist party (the name replaced the Bolshevik party in 1918) through his control of the party mechanism. The way to promotion in the U.S.S.R. is through the Communist party, which is organized at the local level in cells; and the majority of those who rise in the service of the Russian state begin party life in the cell and gradually ascend in the party hierarchy. The major policy-making body in the state is the Politburo, now called the Presidium, which is chosen by the Central Committee of the Party and in theory is responsible to it. There is also a state apparatus made up of two houses, which together make up the Supreme Soviet. These bodies choose a Council of Ministers headed by a prime minister. The members of the lower house are elected by universal suffrage, in accordance with the constitution of 1936 under which the Soviet Union operates. The government is therefore democratic enough in form, but in substance there is no democracy, since all representatives must be either members of the Communist party or approved by it. The Party, in fact, though it has been kept a small elite body in the country, therefore dominates the state.

Foreign Policy. The Soviet Union played little part in European affairs until the advent of Hitler to power in Germany. Then Stalin began to appreciate the danger of continued isolation in the face of such a formidable and vocally anti-Communist nation. When Germany left the League of Nations in 1933, the Soviet Union entered (1934), with Maxim Litvinov as foreign minister, thereby beginning a policy of co-operation with the West. In 1936 and succeeding years Stalin purged a number of old revolutionaries and army officers, accusing them all of treasonable co-operation with foreign powers, an accusation which the West found it impossible to credit. But the whole process added to the general distrust of the Soviet government in the West. It was never believed that the Soviet Union would take any active part in the League's program of "collective security," and she was not consulted over the partition of Czechoslovakia, carried out with the consent of Britain and France in 1938. When

Germany continued to make advances, Stalin decided that the policy of attempted co-operation with the West had been a failure. While he carried out desultory negotiations with the British and French, he entered into conversations with Hitler looking toward a nonaggression pact in the event of war between Russia and the West. The pact was finally signed in August, 1939. Less than two weeks later Hitler invaded Poland, and the Soviet Union by agreement was permitted to occupy the eastern part of the country.

ITALIAN FASCISM

The Rise of Mussolini to Supreme Power. By 1922 Italy had already established a dictatorship, largely as the result of postwar conditions. Ever since unification in 1870 stable governments had been the exception in Italy, in part owing to the multiplicity of parties. The party in office usually had to buy support from the minority parties, not by programs that appealed to them but by more tangible rewards; few had any belief in the honesty of the elections. The consequence was a widespread disillusionment with the democratic process and a readiness for any change that might result in more stable and effective government, whatever the price to be paid for it. When Italy received far fewer benefits than she had anticipated for being on the winning side during the war, and when the postwar government showed little sign of being any better than previous ones, the general discontent in the country was such that many people were willing to follow a leader who seemed to know what he wanted and had the necessary determination to force his way to power. The fact that he had little or no program of reforms to put into execution when he had won the power escaped the attention of most Italians.

By the end of 1921, Benito Mussolini, formerly a socialist and pacifist but later a convinced supporter of the war, had already organized groups of "Fascist" toughs whose main activity was breaking up the rival gangs of left-wing and Communist groups. This won him the support of many leaders in industry who believed, as it turned out correctly enough, that once in office he would favor their interests above those of the organized workers who inclined to the left. In the general elections of 1921 Mussolini's Fascist party was still unable to win many seats; but he nevertheless began to demand that he be made prime minister. When the government tried to suppress the Fascist gangs, King Victor Emmanuel II refused to grant it the necessary authority, but preferred to accept Mussolini. The latter staged a so-called "March on Rome" in October, 1922 (a march in which few used any other than public means of transportation). Three days later the king sent for Mussolini, who had remained discreetly in Milan, and made him prime minister, thus granting him full control of the executive. Parliament was intimidated into accepting him and granting him dictatorial powers for a year, and thereby signed its own death warrant. In due course Mussolini made enough alterations in the parliamentary and electoral structure to enable him to control all legislation.

Thus the regime of Mussolini was always legal, resting upon the support of the king and a packed parliament. The real ruler was, however, the Fascist party, completely under the control of its leader and founder. The Fascist Grand Council, made up of loyal party members recruited from local cells but appointed by Mussolini, was an advisory body with no real powers. The party controlled all governmental appointments. Overt opposition within Italy was scarce and easily suppressed by the Fascist public and secret police. Mussolini ruled from 1922 until the invasion of Italy in 1943 without any serious and concerted opposition within his country.

Italy in the 1930's. The achievements of the era were disappointingly small for such a long era of undisputed dictatorship, though Il Duce, as he was called, "made the trains run on time" and was responsible for a few spectacular and expensive public works. Labor unrest was controlled and manufacturers were protected, at the price of cutting the party in on their profits. There was no incentive to produce, and Italy enjoyed few benefits from the short era of general prosperity in the 1930's. The Depression, however, hit Italy as hard as any other country, since her exports were for the most part unessential. Only remittances from Italian emigrants abroad enabled the economy to survive as well as it did. In the 1930's Mussolini's only answer to the Depression was to build up his armies and engage in an imperialist venture in Ethiopia. Until the conquest of Ethiopia in 1936 Italy was generally hostile to the designs of Hitler's Germany, although Mussolini was flattered by the German fuehrer's imitation of his methods. When the League of Nations, however, imposed some economic sanctions on Italy, and he found himself diplomatically isolated in Europe, his answer was the alliance with Germany, known as the Axis, followed by the Anti-Comintern Pact directed against Communist Russia, in which

Japan was the third partner. Once the alliance with Germany became an accomplished fact, Mussolini quickly lost the initiative to his stronger German partner and could hope for nothing but a share in the spoils. The country was dragged into the war in 1940 on the German side as soon as intervention appeared likely to be profitable; the regime was destroyed, however, only by the Allied invasion. Thereafter Mussolini himself, rescued by the Germans from an Allied prison, was the titular ruler of a puppet regime in northern Italy until he was captured and executed by Italian resistance fighters in 1945.

TOTALITARIAN GERMANY

The Failure of the Weimar Republic. The Weimar Republic of Germany, set up on the abdication of the kaiser in 1918, was a regime dogged by misfortune rather than one necessarily doomed to failure as a result of its own incompetence. The Germans, as noted earlier, were not prepared to accept the Treaty of Versailles as a freely negotiated peace by which they were morally bound. Many of them were unaware of the extent of their defeat, since their country had never been invaded, and they regarded the reparations as an intolerable imposition. In 1922–1923 when their richest industrial area was occupied by the French and Belgians for the purpose of forcing them to pay the reparations, a ruinous and uncontrolled inflation followed, which the German government did little to prevent, even though it could probably have achieved little. In 1924 when the Dawes Plan scaled down the reparations, there was a quick economic recovery. Loans from the United States enabled payment of reparations and aided the modernization of German industry. Even so, the prosperity was brittle, and the new export markets won by the German industrialists could not be relied upon, since it was clear that they would be lost if ever there were a prolonged period of economic warfare between the industrial nations.

Until 1929 the German government recognized their dependence upon reasonably friendly relations with the West, but the policy had little support at home. The German mood continued to be one of national frustration. The middle class, which had lost almost all its property and investments in the inflation, lacked self-confidence, and the officer class which had been so strong in imperial Germany nursed a bitterness against the regime which by agreeing to the disarmament of the country, had left it without the only means of honorable employment for which it was fitted. An agreement with Communist Russia by which some officers were trained abroad and gave technical assistance to the Russians was little compensation for the loss of prestige and employment from which this class continued to suffer.

The Rise of Adolf Hitler. When the Depression hit the country in 1929 the Germans began to make demands for another scaling down of reparations, which was quickly agreed to in the Young Plan, accepted by the Germans in a referendum late in 1929. Unemployment began to mount, and President Hindenburg, a successful wartime general, turned to a government of the Right, led by Heinrich Bruening, in preference to the customary left-wing governments which alone had been able to command parliamentary majorities in the past. This government was unable to secure majorities, but was maintained in office by the president under an emergency clause in the constitution. Successive elections in the following years marked the rise of the National Socialist (Nazi) party, led by Adolf Hitler, and of the Communists. Neither of these parties was willing to cooperate with the governments headed by other parties, thus further preventing truly parliamentary government. Hitler had attempted a coup d'état as early as 1923, and spent the next years in prison. When he was released, he and his party made little headway until the Depression.

The years of right-wing government were occupied by both Nazis and Communists in organizing irregular bands of paramilitary forces, in which the former held a distinct advantage since they were financed by leading industrialists, as were the Fascists in Italy. As unemployment rose, so did Hitler's electoral majority; and though the very last elections before Hitler became chancellor in 1933 showed a slight decrease, the Nazi party became by far the largest in Germany. Ultimately Hindenburg, after failing with two governments which ruled entirely by decree, bowed to the inevitable and Hitler became chancellor in January, 1933, backed by a party of industrialists as well as by his own.

A fire which destroyed the Reichstag (parliament) building was used by Hitler as an excuse to outlaw the Communist party, and within a few months he had established himself in a position of supremacy. When Hindenburg died in 1934 Hitler assumed the p.:esidency, and the office was in fact abolished. On this occasion and from time to time thereafter, he held plebiscites to approve his policies; all of course gave him huge majorities.

German Expansion under Hitler. During the following years Hitler denounced one by one the restrictive clauses of the Treaty of Versailles, and was able to do so with impunity. The only really dangerous moment before 1938 was when he marched his army into the demilitarized Rhineland in March, 1936. At this point Franco-British intervention could certainly have stopped the fuehrer but, though many French leaders desired it, the British had no intention of fighting to maintain what remained of the Treaty. The previous year they had signed a naval treaty with Hitler which bound the Germans not to build more than 35 per cent of British tonnage, and this satisfied their immediate interests. The French were not willing to move alone. From 1936 onward the Germans engaged in all-out rearmament which partially solved their unemployment problem and paid for it by a planned program of economic self-subsistence and mobilization of national resources—"guns instead of butter." From this year also they could rely on the benevolent neutrality of Italy.

In 1934 an effort to stage a Nazi revolution in Austria failed, largely owing to the opposition of Italy. In 1938 the Austrian chancellor was compelled by threat of force to permit his country to be annexed. Immediately afterward Hitler began a campaign in Czechoslovakia by which he hoped to take over the country with the aid of the German-speaking minority in the Sudetenland. The British and French were at last seriously alarmed, but in the end they decided that the only policy was to "appease" Hitler and let him have his way. At the Munich conference of September 29, it was agreed that he could have the Sudetenland, but the rest of the country would be protected by an international guarantee. The Czechs felt themselves unable to fight alone, and the Russian offer of aid was not taken seriously. In spite of the guarantee, Hitler took over the whole country in March, 1939.

The British and French then offered unilateral guarantees to Poland, obviously the next country up for partitioning, and entered into belated conversations with the Soviet Union. But Hitler negotiated separately with the Russians, as noted earlier, and paid no attention to the Franco-British alliance with Poland. On September 1, 1939, Hitler invaded Poland. Two days later

Britain and France declared war on Germany, thus beginning the Second World War.

THE MAJOR DEMOCRACIES DURING THE LONG ARMISTICE

Britain. Britain had emerged from the war in an economic position far different from that of prewar days. Though she had survived the war with her political institutions intact and her country undamaged, she had lost her economic supremacy forever, as well as the flower of her young manhood, many of her potential postwar leaders having been killed, especially during the three years of voluntary enlistment when the ablest and most patriotic young men flocked to the colors. During the war Britain had been compelled to dispose of a large percentage of her investments abroad, and she had lent extensively to her allies. She had herself contracted a huge debt to the United States. Though France owed her money and she was entitled to her share of German reparations, she could look for no return from these sources, since she soon negotiated an agreement that she would accept from France and Germany only what she was required to pay to the United States. This left the sale of her investments, used to finance her war effort, as a permanent and irrecoverable loss. She was thus compelled to increase her income from the sale of goods and services abroad if she were to balance her international accounts.

This proved to be an impossible task. The United States was a new and powerful economic competitor, her own industrial plant was rapidly becoming obsolete, and capital was lacking for industrial development. Her coal mines were a wasting asset, with high costs, and unable to compete in export markets with the cheaper coal from such countries as Poland and the United States. During the war, India, formerly her largest export market for textiles, had learned to produce most of her own supplies. Thus during the entire interwar period Britain was in a state of near-depression, and some industries, such as coal mining, never emerged from it. This sluggishness of the economy lies behind much of Britain's political weakness during the period. She was being compelled to adjust herself to a position in world affairs commensurate with her new economic status; and above all she was anxious to avoid even the possibility of being compelled once again to fight a world war.

After a period of relative prosperity in some industries, Britain was hit hard by the Great Depression, and by the expense of her social security program initiated before the war by the Asquith Liberal government. Health and unemployment insurance were now compulsory, but both could be financed only by workers with a steady income. Between 1929 and 1931, when a Labor government happened to be in office, the number of unemployed increased catastrophically; but the government did not care to cut the unemployment benefits, even though the insurance fund was bankrupt, preferring to extend assistance by direct government grants. Finally the Labor cabinet split on the issue, and a "National" coalition government came into power. By a program of deflation and austerity it restored the country's finances but was unable to bring about full recovery from the Depression. This National government, dominated by Conservatives, faced with the dynamism of Nazi Germany, could devise no policy save reliance upon the "collective security" of the League of Nations, hoping that Hitler's appetite for expansion could be appeased without damage to any vital British interests.

The policy was probably doomed from the beginning, having regard to the character of Nazi Germany; but as late as the Munich Conference of September, 1938, Prime Minister Neville Chamberlain believed he had won, as he promised his people, "peace in our time." Not until the complete absorption of Czechoslovakia in March, 1939, did he recognize his failure and attempt, almost too late, to compensate for it.

France. France had of course suffered more physical damage from the war than Britain and had suffered an appalling number of casualties, which with her low birth rate she was unable to make good. She was able, however, in a great burst of energy to repair the physical damage, as she had done in 1871. But the effort cost her dearly, especially since she was for some years unable to obtain any reparations from Germany. Faced by a growing inflation, she entrusted the government to an orthodox financier, Raymond Poincaré, who devaluated the franc and thereafter restored financial stability. However, once Poincaré's term of government was over, the usual party politics and unstable governments plagued the country; no coalitions could be devised which enjoyed secure parliamentary support until this was achieved, very briefly, in 1936. Even so, for several years France weathered the Great Depression better than Britain. She had not engaged in any major program of industrialization, and was not so dependent upon exports. She remained primarily an agricultural country, and her exports were mainly of agricultural products and handcraft luxuries.

When the full force of the Depression finally did hit France, she was unable to effect any recovery. Moreover, after the rise of Hitler, parliamentary government was threatened both from the right and the left, as in Germany. But Fascist groups attempting to exploit antigovernmental riots in 1934 met with a different response than that in Germany. The Communists who had been demanding a revolution and the end of parliamentary government, decided to throw in their lot with the other left-wing parties, and institute long overdue social reforms. Thus came into being the Popular Front government of 1936, led by the Socialist Léon Blum. This government enacted the reforms, including social security and the shorter working week. But the country's economic apparatus was too far run down to permit these measures without ruinous inflation, feared by most classes. Moreover, the industrialists opposed the reforms by every available means. Blum lost some of his more moderate supporters in the Chamber of Deputies, and was compelled to resign. His successors repealed some of the reforms, and the government was finally granted power to draft the workers. The result in the last years before the war was an almost constant government by emergency decree and a prolonged and serious class struggle which prevented France from playing any active part in the restraining of Hitler. The measures taken were virtually confined to the construction of a great system of fortresses on the borders of Germany, known as the Maginot Line—a suitable symbol for the generally negative attitude taken toward all reform, as well as toward the expansionism of Hitler.

The United States. The United States after the war failed to recognize the economic responsibilities of a creditor government to whom all the Allied governments were in debt. She raised her tariffs frequently, culminating in the Hawley-Smoot tariff of 1930; and she would not release the hard-pressed European governments from their obligations to meet their war debts, even when Germany refused to pay reparations. Thus the dollar was always a scarce currency. Though the United States was a large exporter of goods which the world for a period could not do without, the means for payment were not available to the Europeans. The United States exporters were thus compelled to sell on credit, largely by pouring money in the form of loans into the most favored European countries, especially Germany, who was thereby enabled to modernize her industrial equipment, as we have noted, as well as to pay her reparations.

An orgy of speculation in the stock market in the 1920's at last led in 1929 to a crash, which brought on the Great Depression. The United States virtually ceased to buy abroad and to lend to foreign governments and enterprises, while capital already invested returned to America as fast as possible. The chain reaction from the beginning was rapidly felt in the United States and abroad. When President Franklin D. Roosevelt assumed office in early 1933, he instituted a program that he called the New Deal, which for the first time brought social security to America; and he tried to "prime the pump" by using tax money to finance a number of much-needed public improvements and restore confidence in the economy. Meanwhile Congress was soured by the refusal of foreign governments to honor their financial obligations, an attitude toward Europe shared by most Americans, who were disillusioned by the results of the war and had been deeply shocked by the role apparently played by their own armament manufacturers, as well as by their huge profits. Congress in the 1930's therefore adopted a policy of attempted isolation, reflected in a number of Neutrality Acts. Since the Senate had refused to ratify the Treaty of Versailles, the United States was not in the League of Nations; and though she was prepared to co-operate on occasions when she felt her interests threatened, in general the European powers paid little attention to her. The United States sponsored a Peace Pact signed in 1928, which had no teeth in it and was a virtually meaningless gesture; she tried to persuade the League to take some action in Manchuria when Japan invaded that country in 1931; she took part in a prolonged Disarmament Conference held in Geneva which could naturally come to no agreement in the face of the evident German intention to rearm; and she was largely responsible for the failure of the World Economic Conference in 1933 called by the League, when President Roosevelt refused to consider the stabilization of currencies—though even without the American refusal it is doubtful if this would have been achieved. She also agreed not to intervene in the Spanish Civil War. During the remainder of the 1930's the United States became increasingly disillusioned with the policies of her former allies, but gave no positive leadership, contenting herself with exhortations and offers to play the honest broker in the event anyone was willing to discuss the obvious dangers to the peace of the world presented by the international situation.

THE LEAGUE OF NATIONS

The League of Nations, without the United States, fell in the 1920's largely under the domination of France, who was determined to see that Germany should never again be in the position to threaten the peace of Europe. To this end she concluded alliances with nations that had most to lose from German aggression and with Soviet Russia. These nations as a rule then backed her in the League, which dutifully registered the treaties; but most other countries which had not signed formal alliances with France regarded this treaty system as, in French eyes, little less than a substitute for the League itself.

The League was successful in solving a number of minor problems, but in 1931 had to contend with an obvious aggression by a major power, Japan. The result was the dispatch of the Lytton fact-finding commission, which concluded after a long period of study that Japan had indeed aggressed. The only result, however, was the withdrawal of Japan from the League. When Italy invaded Ethiopia in 1935 the British and French preferred to work for a compromise, as in pre-League days, under which the Ethiopians would have made some concessions but retained at least a part of their country. However, the League and British public opinion were of a different mind. The National government in Britain bowed to the storm and thereafter took the lead in imposing economic sanctions on Italy. It was, however, found impossible to obtain agreement on the imposition of the crucial sanction on oil, and Italy went ahead with her conquest, thereafter allying herself with Germany.

THE SPANISH CIVIL WAR

Only two months after the capture of the Ethiopian capital a civil war erupted in Spain, which had been a republic only since 1931. The first republican government was to the left of center and attempted some essential reforms, including curbing the power and reducing the property of the Catholic Church. But this government after only two years had to face elections which it lost by a heavy margin. The new right-wing governments attempted to set back the reform, with the result that the country was beset by strikes, including a very serious insurrection of the miners in the province of Asturias, which was put down with great severity. In 1936 the left-wing parties, formed, as in France, into a Popular Front, won a decisive victory in the elections. This was the signal for the organization of a conspiracy in Spanish Morocco led by army leaders determined to overthrow the government. There followed three years of bitter civil war, during which General Franco, aided by German and Italian volunteers and supplies, wore down the resistance of the government, which was able to rely on no secure foreign aid except some trickles from the Soviet Union and a number of independent volunteers, some recruited by the Communist parties in the various European countries. All the European nations, including Germany and Italy, agreed not to intervene in the conflict; but the agreement was honored only by the Western democracies. Thus the totalitarian states were able once more to take advantage of the will-to-peace of the democracies, and Spain has been under the totalitarian rule of General Franco ever since.

THE WORLD ON THE EVE OF THE WAR

After the conclusion of the Munich Conference of 1938, Hitler was at the summit of his real power. Britain and France had permitted him to extend his territories without fighting; and there seemed no reason to believe that a limit had been reached to their formidable powers of endurance, at least as long as concessions were made at the expense of other nations. The United States, sheathed in splendid isolation, was apparently equally prepared to let Hitler have his way. When Hitler proclaimed that he had "no further territorial demands," all were ready to believe him. A British statesman even offered it as his opinion that the world was entering upon a new "golden age of peace."

It is impossible to say what might have happened if Hitler had refrained from armed intervention and continued to make the demands coupled with threats that had served him so well in the past. He did not of course cease to make these threats and demands, as, for example, when he suggested a redistribution of colonial territories; but he had evidently decided that he was now strong enough to win a war, and this was what he really wanted—if for nothing else, as a revenge for the defeat of 1918. When he instructed his generals to take the rest of Czechoslovakia in March, 1939, it should have been clear to him that a rupture of such a recent international agreement could not be tolerated by the other parties to it. Even if Chamberlain had been willing to appease him further, as he was not, British public opinion would not have followed him. Thereafter it was only a question of trying to win as many allies as possible and preparing the people for war.

Both tasks were performed indifferently by the French and British governments, which had been so long accustomed to the thought that war was unthinkable that it was difficult to change their attitude overnight. The result was that when Germany at last invaded Poland in September, 1939, she had an overwhelming preponderance of power, except on the sea, and won a series of victories that did not cease until in the summer of 1941 she invaded Russia. The resources of Russia, and later of the United States, who aided the Allies in many ways before her actual entry into the war (sale of overage destroyers, the Lend Lease Act, etc.) and was obviously "neutral in favor of" the Allies, were required to shatter Hitler's dream of conquest. But it is well to remember, as German foreign office documents have now shown, that if Britain and France, or even France alone, had acted when Hitler marched into the Rhineland in 1936, the fuehrer would have been overthrown by his own army, and perhaps the world would have been spared the Second World War within a single generation.

CHAPTER XXIII

THE SECOND GLOBAL WAR AND ITS CONSEQUENCES

The Second World War was fought on so many fronts that it is impossible to recount them all in this book. The first phase involved the swift German conquest of Poland, followed, after an interval of six months, often known as the "phony" war, during which little military action was taken, by an attack on Norway and Denmark, the conquest of France, and the relative immobilization of Britain after the failure of the Germans to force her out of the war by bombardment from the air. This phase of the war, completed in 1941 with the German conquest of Yugoslavia and Greece, was won decisively by the Germans, who then organized what they called "Fortress Europe." The whole continent of Europe outside Russia was then either Axis-controlled or neutral.

The second phase began with the invasion of Russia in June, 1941. Though the Germans made advances deep into Russia, they attained none of their main objectives. The turning point came at the Battle of Stalingrad, which lasted from August, 1942 to February, 1943. Thereafter the Russians gradually pushed back the Germans until in 1945 they were able to invade Germany herself and complete their victory. Yet a third theater of war was the South Pacific, which was almost exclusively an affair of Japan and the United States. Japan began the attack in December, 1941, by bombing Pearl Harbor in the Hawaiian Islands and followed it up by the conquest of the British, French, Dutch, and United States possessions in the Far East. The United States had to fight back slowly from this initial reverse, but in time the greater resources available to her wore down the irreplaceable navy and air force of Japan; and by "island-hopping" the Americans drove the Japanese troops from their fortified positions in their empire. In preference to invading the Japanese home islands, they dropped two of the newly invented "atomic" bombs on Hiroshima and

Nagasaki and thereby compelled the Japanese to accept an unconditional surrender.

Meanwhile, the Germans, who had declared war against the United States immediately after Pearl Harbor, were hard put to it to defend their European Fortress against the combined troops of the British and the United States, aided by other fighting men who had escaped from the Continent and by troops from the British dominions. The Western Allies began the assault in 1942 by winning North Africa, from which center they invaded southern Italy. The Italian government capitulated, but the Germans stopped further advances by taking over the defense of northern and central Italy. Not until 1944 were the Allies able to mount a further major attack on the Continent. But the attack, when it came, was strong enough to push back the Germans from France, Holland, and Belgium in 1944. In 1945 Germany was invaded from the west, the attack synchronizing with the final Russian advance from the east. Hitler committed suicide at the end of April, 1945, and a few days later the Germans agreed to unconditional surrender.

THE COLD WAR

Disagreement on War Aims. The Soviet Union in the first years of the war was determined to improve her own security position and win as much for herself as she could from the fluid situation in Europe brought on by German aggression. She hoped—and apparently Stalin, at least, always expected—to be able to avoid war with Germany but did what she could to prepare herself for the eventuality. She quickly compelled the small Baltic republics to grant her military bases and occupied them during the German attack on France in 1940. When Finland refused her demands she invaded that country late in 1939—incidentally being expelled from the League of Nations for this aggression—and imposed peace terms early in 1940. Nevertheless, Hitler decided to invade Russia, and she was involved willy-nilly in the war on the Allied side. Britain at once accepted her as an ally and sent what help and supplies she could, as did the United States, since the Soviet Union was brought quickly within the scope of the Lend Lease Act. Relations, however, between the Soviet Union and the Western powers were never cordial, and in conferences held during the later years of the war Stalin always accused the Western world of allowing Russia to bear a disproportionate share of the human losses and demanded an early invasion of the Continent before the West believed itself to be ready. The West, in turn, was unable to persuade Stalin to renounce her nonaggression treaty with Japan and invade Japanese-held China until the war was almost over.

In spite of the many grounds for distrust between the uneasy allies, there was little thought given in the West to the future shape of Europe, although British Prime Minister Churchill from time to time urged its consideration on President Roosevelt. For example, the decision as to whether the Americans or Russians should be the first to enter Berlin was made without full consideration of its political consequences. At the Yalta Conference while Germany was collapsing and her defeat imminent, Stalin put forward certain incompletely spelled out demands which were accepted by the West in the belief that the Russians were mainly interested in ensuring their own future security—whereas Stalin intended in fact to make use of his victory to expand the area of Europe under Soviet control, thereby spreading Communism. If the Soviet intentions had been understood in advance, the negotiations would certainly have followed a different course—even though by the time of Yalta the Russian position in Eastern Europe and Germany was so strong that it probably could not have been weakened without an open quarrel, and perhaps even actual hostilities, between the erstwhile allies. The Russians could have been frozen out of areas not yet under their control; and the Western position in the following years might have been improved thereby.

The Soviet Satellite System. The territorial settlements, some of them still not yet sanctified by formal peace treaties, were made almost entirely at the expense of Germany. The Polish frontier was moved westward to within a short distance of Berlin, while Russia annexed the areas she had ruled during the war. The Baltic states remained a part of the Soviet Union. Czechoslovakia was restored as an independent nation, and the Balkan states remained much as they had been in the interwar period. Though the West stuck out for democratic regimes in Poland and elsewhere, intrigues by Russian and Polish Communists soon reduced Poland to a Russian satellite, with a Communist form of government. In Czechoslovakia, which enjoyed a brief period of independence under a democratically elected Communist prime minister, a *coup d'état* by the Communists was carried out in 1948, as a result of which she

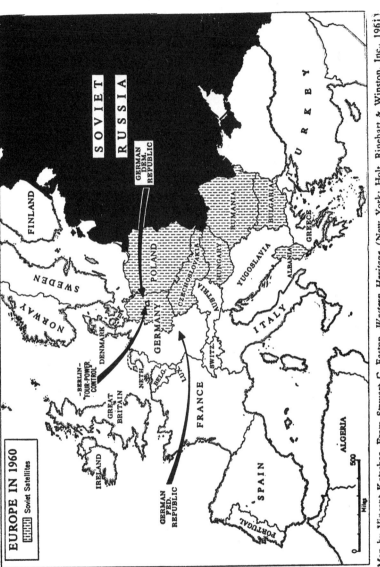

EUROPE IN 1960
▦ Soviet Satellites

SOVIET RUSSIA

GERMAN DEM. REPUBLIC

FINLAND

NORWAY

SWEDEN

DENMARK

IRELAND

GREAT BRITAIN

NETH.

BELG.

LUX.

—BERLIN—
FOUR-POWER CONTROL

GERMANY

POLAND

CZECHOSLOVAKIA

AUSTRIA

HUNGARY

RUMANIA

YUGOSLAVIA

BULGARIA

ALBANIA

GREECE

TURKEY

ITALY

SWITZ.

FRANCE

GERMAN FED. REPUBLIC

SPAIN

PORTUGAL

ALGERIA

0   500
Miles

Map by Vincent Kotschar. From Stewart C. Easton, *Western Heritage* (New York: Holt, Rinehart & Winston, Inc., 1961)
By permission of the publisher.

became a Soviet satellite. Hungary followed substantially the same path. The Balkan states with the exception of Greece became Communist, but Yugoslavia left the Soviet orbit in 1948, though remaining Communist.

This was the limit of Soviet expansion; and it is noteworthy that all the countries that moved into the Soviet orbit were those where the Soviet Union had enough military power available and in reserve to make resistance to her wishes futile. In Greece a Communist movement to overthrow the government was finally driven back with British and American aid. Thus the world has been faced with an alteration in the balance of power which has so far proved permanent. There are only two really first-rank powers, the United States and the Soviet Union, the latter ringed by "satellite" regimes, which have organized their countries along lines approved and inspired by her. In between are the Western European democracies, almost all in alliance with the United States in the North Atlantic Treaty Organization (NATO), all of which have undergone a remarkable economic recovery.

Between these two areas stretched the no man's land of Germany, which after the war was placed under four-power control (United States, Britain, France, and the Soviet Union). The larger area under the Western powers was consolidated into the Federal Republic of Germany in 1949 and moved into the Western orbit. A few months later East Germany, under Russian control, was proclaimed the German Democratic Republic with a Communist government. Only Berlin, the former capital of Germany, remains under four-power occupation, an enclave within East Germany which has hitherto remained impervious to all Soviet designs and efforts to destroy it. A blockade instituted by the Russians in 1948 was broken by an airlift of supplies organized by the United States, with such serious consequences for Russian prestige that it was abandoned; no move on a similar scale has been attempted since.

Competitive Co-existence. The result of the postwar recrudescence of Russian imperialism was to leave relations between the Soviet Union and the West at all times unfriendly. This condition has been with some accuracy described as the cold war. It can hardly be disputed that the foreign policy of the Western powers and the United States in the postwar period has been very largely dictated by the ever present fear of further expansion by the Soviet Union. Much attention has even been given to the possibility of internal subversion of the Western nations by Communist parties and by individual Communists working clandestinely to overthrow democratic governments. No such movement as yet has come within measurable distance of success, in spite of the existence of large Communist parties in many European countries.

On the more positive side the United States learned from the failure of her interwar policies that her position as a creditor nation must be taken more seriously than after the First World War. In 1947 she launched a large-scale plan for providing the European countries with the financial and technical means to rehabilitate their economies (the Marshall Plan); this was an unqualified success. Every year she has expended several billion dollars in aid to foreign countries, including in recent times underdeveloped nations, among them, former European colonies. But after the Korean War (1950–1953) a marked change took place in American thinking and policies. The intervention of Chinese "volunteers" during the war led to an unremittingly hostile attitude toward Communist China, who was regarded as at least as much a threat to United States interests as was the Soviet Union. China was successfully kept out of the United Nations, in which she had been "branded" as an aggressor for her part in the Korean War, and she has not yet been diplomatically recognized by the United States. Feeling that she was under constant threat from the expansionism both of the Soviet Union and of Communist China, the United States began to rely increasingly on military alliances. It was always far easier to obtain authorization from Congress for foreign military than economic aid; and aid of both kinds was more usually granted to countries which seemed likely to be bulwarks of defense against the encroaching Communists.

After the Second World War the United States possessed a monopoly of the atomic bomb and was in a position to threaten to use it without fear of retaliation. This fact spurred the Russians to devote a disproportionate amount of their scientific personnel and equipment to producing a similar weapon. They succeeded in 1949. Meanwhile, the United States succeeded in devising a much more lethal weapon, the hydrogen bomb. In due course the Russians imitated this feat. Thereafter both countries engaged in the competition to perfect means of delivering these new weapons. For several years it has been a matter of common knowledge that each has enough bombs to destroy the other, thus evening the balance of power in a manner never possible in earlier epochs of history. This "balance of terror" led to efforts, especially by the United States, to develop a "graduated deterrent" which in the event of war would save a nation from having to launch a massive nuclear attack, thus subjecting herself to a similar attack in return. When in 1962 the Russians installed missiles capable of carrying nuclear warheads from their newly acquired satellite in Cuba to the eastern United States, President Kennedy, in a series of carefully calculated moves, made it clear to Soviet Premier Khrushchev that this threat could not be tolerated and compelled him to withdraw the missiles. The first serious effort to halt the arms race met with success in August, 1963, when a limited test-ban treaty was signed and ratified. All the signatories (which included all the more important nations except China and France, both engaged in developing their own nuclear weapons) undertook not to make any further nuclear tests in the atmosphere. Thereafter relations between the United States and the Soviet Union continued to improve—although in 1965 stepped-up American military intervention in Vietnam elicited strong protests from the Soviet Union.

The Communist Revolution in China. In this history of the Western world most developments in the Far East have hitherto been left unrecorded. An exception, however, was made in Chapter XIX, when we considered the impact of Western civilization on China and other Oriental countries. In the postwar period some of the long-term results of this impact have become apparent, and they deserve some consideration here since they are likely to affect the West for a long time to come. The Chinese revolution which began in 1911 with the overthrow of the Manchu dynasty entered a new phase after the Second World War. The Chinese Republic had some achievements to its credit in the 1920's, but from 1931 onward it was involved in a war with Japan which taxed all its resources; few reforms could be put into operation until the war was over. When peace was achieved with the defeat of Japan by the Western powers in 1945, there was already in existence a native Communist movement in the northwest of the country, led by Mao Tse-tung. This movement grew to considerable proportions in the immediate postwar years, and resulted in a civil war, at the end of which the Chinese Republican regime led by Chiang Kai-shek was driven out by the Communists. It found refuge in the island of Formosa, ceded to the Allies by Japan after the war. The entire mainland was organized as a "People's Republic" by Mao Tse-tung, while the Republic of China continued to exist on Formosa, still recognized by the United States and some other countries as the government of China. Stalin for a long time looked askance at the Communist regime on his borders as a possible ideological competitor. Not until 1947 did he give it any substantial aid. When the new Communist government was installed in 1949, he entered into an alliance with it which did not, however, call for automatic military aid in case of attack. Until 1958 the Soviet Union extended various credits to China, who could obtain them from no other source. These credits, however, were mostly on a short-term basis, and China had to begin repaying them long before she was in a position to do so without hardship. Many other areas of friction developed between the two nations, whose interests clashed in so many fields. Not least was Mao Tse-tung's claim to be the world's leading Communist spokesman after the death of Stalin. He criticized Premier Khrushchev severely for his willingness to accept co-existence with "imperialism," and in recent years China has attempted to compete with the Soviet Union for the allegiance of neutral states and former colonies. Some time ago the Soviet Union ceased to grant or renew any credits or give any military aid to China. It is doubtful whether the two nations can now even be considered allies—although both as champions of Communism and of "anti-imperialism" can be relied upon whenever opportunity arises to engage in verbal opposition along similar lines to the Western democracies.

The Korean War and Its Consequences. In spite of her economic weakness, ever since 1949 China has obviously been a power to be reckoned with as she has not been since the fall of the Manchus. Her huge population, now under a unified government, makes it possible for her to engage in conventional warfare with almost unlimited reserves of manpower, and in 1965 she exploded her first nuclear device. This potential was demonstrated in the Korean War (1950–1953) when China drove American forces back from her borders and thus saved the North Korean Communist government from accepting any dimunition of its territory. It has never been proved that either China or the Soviet Union was aware in advance of the proposed invasion of South Korea by North Korea and its Soviet-trained army in June, 1950. The Soviet Union, in particular, can hardly have been aware of North

Korean intentions since she remained absent from the meetings of the Security Council which authorized United Nations (mainly American) intervention. She was absent from all meetings of the Security Council at that time, since she objected to the presence at its deliberations of Nationalist China instead of the recently organized People's Republic of China. But she could easily have returned and cast a veto, thus leaving the onus of intervention entirely upon American shoulders, without any United Nations shield.

However this may be, when the United Nations forces, led by General MacArthur, after a weak start, had succeeded in rolling up almost the whole of North Korea in a counterattack and approached the Chinese border, the Chinese government issued a strong warning. This was disregarded by the General, who did not take it seriously. Nevertheless, when his troops reached the river Yalu, Chinese "volunteers" intervened in force and drove back the United Nations troops. For a period they even controlled the Korean capital of Seoul. The result was a stalemate and prolonged peace talks which eventually produced a peace unsatisfactory to the West, on the basis of a continued division of Korea. Thereafter the Chinese took an ever more active part in Far Eastern politics and subjected to their complete control all the borderlands of the former Manchu empire, including Tibet. Chiang Kai-shek had never, even at the height of his power, been able to restore these lands to their ancient allegiance. Lastly the Chinese laid claim to various territories in the high Himalayas which had been included by the British within the Indian boundaries at a time when they controlled India. The Chinese built a strategic road in lands claimed by India and in 1962 engaged in hostilities with India in this area. They won a complete victory against the unprepared Indians but made no effort to pursue their advantage beyond securing undisturbed possession of the lands they had claimed.

THE DEVOLUTION OF THE WESTERN EMPIRES

The Far East. The other development of crucial importance that has been in process ever since the Second World War has been the achievement of independent status by the former colonies of the Western powers. The Philippines, already promised independence by the United States before the war, achieved it immediately after the war. Britain granted independence to India, Burma, and Ceylon soon afterward. The peoples of the former Dutch East Indies had to fight the Dutch who returned after the wartime Japanese occupation; but the Dutch were compelled to concede independence to the United States of Indonesia in 1949. The French returned to Indo-China, but were never able to establish a secure hold on their former colony, in face of the opposition of a Communist leader, Ho Chi Minh. A desultory war was carried on for many years, during the later stages of which Ho Chi Minh received some support from China. In 1954 an uneasy peace was concluded on the basis of a partition of the country between the Communist (Viet Minh) North, supported by China and the Soviet Union, and South Vietnam, supported by aid from the United States, France, and other Western powers. The remainder of the colony was divided into two independent kingdoms, Laos and Cambodia.

Cambodia has retained her independence and accepted the friendship offered by China in preference to military and economic support from the United States. Laos and Vietnam, however, have continued to be unstable and divided between Communists and non-Communists. Since 1954 the United States has constituted herself the champion and protector of the latter.

In Laos a *modus vivendi* was agreed to by which the Communists (known as the Pathet Lao) virtually control the sector of the country which borders on North Vietnam, from whose Communist government they receive technical and military support. The central government of Laos exercises only nominal authority over the Pathet Lao, and its leader, Prince Souvanna Phouma, exercises such power as he does by virtue of American support.

In Vietnam, divided as it was by the Geneva Agreements, the north continued to be ruled by Ho Chi Minh and his Communists. For nine years following the agreements power in South Vietnam was exercised by an aristocrat named Ngo Dinh Diem and his family. This regime was backed by the United States, who virtually took the place of France in this area as its protector. By agreement with the United States Diem refused to permit the holding of the elections which according to the terms of the Agreement were supposed to unify Vietnam in 1956. Thereafter revolts against the Diem regime became more frequent, and in 1959 there began a full-scale rebellion, led by a group calling itself the National Liberation Front, which included Communists and non-Communists

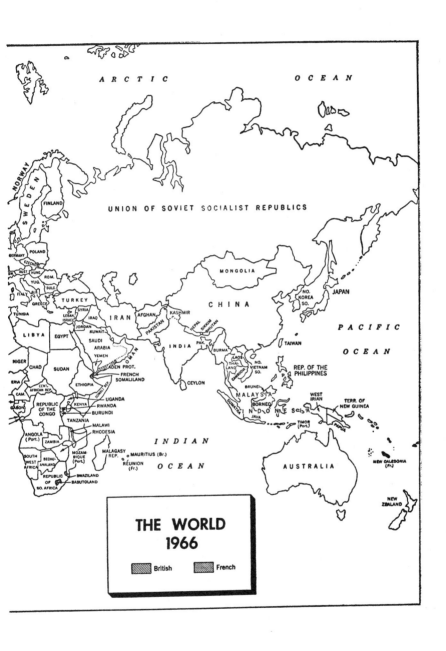

ARCTIC OCEAN

UNION OF SOVIET SOCIALIST REPUBLICS

NORWAY

SWEDEN

FINLAND

GERMANY

POLAND

CZECH.

SW.

AUST. HUNG. ROM.

ITALY YUG. BULG.

ALB.

GREECE

TUNISIA

TURKEY

SYRIA

LEBAN.

ISRAEL

IRAQ

IRAN

AFGHAN.

KASHMIR

JORDAN

KUWAIT

PAKISTAN

NEPAL

SIKKIM

BHUTAN

MONGOLIA

CHINA

NO. KOREA

SO.

JAPAN

LIBYA

EGYPT

SAUDI ARABIA

YEMEN

OMAN

ADEN PROT.

FRENCH SOMALILAND

PAK.

INDIA

BURMA

TAIWAN

PACIFIC

OCEAN

NIGER

CHAD

SUDAN

ETHIOPIA

LAOS

THAI-

LAND

CAMBODIA

NO.

VIETNAM

SO.

REP. OF THE

PHILIPPINES

ERIA

CAM.

CENT.

AFRICAN REP.

SOMALI REP.

CEYLON

GABON

REPUBLIC

OF THE

CONGO

UGANDA

KENYA

RWANDA

BURUNDI

TANZANIA

MALAWI

RHODESIA

BRUNEI

MALAYSIA

SUMATRA

BORNEO

I N D O N E S I A

JAVA

WEST IRIAN

TERR. OF

NEW GUINEA

PAPUA

ANGOLA

(Port.)

ZAMBIA

MOZAM-

BIQUE

(Port.)

MALAGASY

REP.

MAURITIUS (Br.)

RÉUNION

(Fr.)

INDIAN

TIMOR

(Port.)

SOUTH

WEST

AFRICA

BECHU-

ANALAND

SWAZILAND

REPUBLIC

OF

SO. AFRICA

BASUTOLAND

OCEAN

AUSTRALIA

NEW CALEDONIA

(Fr.)

NEW

ZEALAND

THE WORLD
1966

British   French

but which obviously had the moral support of Communist North Vietnam. For several years the rebellion made slow headway, with homemade arms and arms of American origin captured from the South. Recently there has been more evidence of the importation of arms manufactured in Communist countries, including China.

The guerrilla armies of the NLF (usually known in the West as the Viet Cong) eventually proved too strong to be withstood by the American-trained South Vietnamese armies, even though the latter had all the arms they could use and greatly outnumbered the guerrillas. Diem was murdered in 1963, and no stable government has yet taken the place of his. Elections have not been held, and various attempts to create an acceptable civilian government have failed. At present a military junta is exercising governmental authority. Early in 1965, when the Viet Cong controlled between three quarters and four fifths of South Vietnam's territory, President Johnson ordered the bombing of North Vietnam, a policy which was expected to persuade Ho Chi Minh to enter into negotiations. However, Ho Chi Minh insisted that he did not control the Viet Cong but that it was an indigenous movement directed against the South Vietnamese government and that its sole purpose was to unify the country—as had been promised in 1956. When the bombings did not have the desired effect, President Johnson concluded that his only recourse was to send in many more American troops and to commit them to ground warfare on a large scale. Obviously the "escalation" of the war is a dangerous policy, even though it may be the only one open to him. As yet neither the Russians nor the Chinese have intervened except with supplies and equipment. Both have showed extreme caution in the face of American military might. But it is not easy for either to accept the calamitous loss of prestige that would be involved in deserting their fellow Communists in the East. It may be that the time is nearing when fruitful negotiations can be held—even though no such prospects are as yet visible on the horizon.

After the Second World War the British returned to Malaya and re-established their control. After a brief attempt to rule in the old prewar manner, they decided to prepare the country for eventual independence under a parliamentary form of government. During the period of preparation, Communist terrorist groups, mostly composed of Malayan-Chinese, attempted to overthrow the government; but the Malays fully supported the British in their efforts, and eventually put an end to the rebellion. The independent nation of Malaya was proclaimed in August, 1957, and Singapore was granted the special status of autonomous state in 1959, under a left-wing government, with Britain retaining some safeguards. On August 31, 1963, a new Federation of Malaysia came into existence. It included not only Malaya and Singapore but also two territories (North Borneo and Sarawak) in the north of the island of Borneo, the rest of which belonged to Indonesia. The latter objected to this new Federation on the ground that it was a neo-colonialist project of the British, who were trying to maintain their influence in the Far East by military means (they had a treaty with Malaysia and kept a large military and naval base on the island of Singapore). Indonesia therefore refused to recognize the new state, and when Malaysia was chosen as a member of the United Nations Security Council in 1964, she left the United Nations altogether (the first nation to do so). Relations between Malaysia and Indonesia remain bitterly hostile, and Indonesia has conducted some armed raids on the Malayan coast and infiltrated troops into the Malaysian sectors of Borneo. In August, 1965, Singapore, which had its own difficulties with the mainland territory of Malaya to the north (Singapore was controlled by men of Chinese ancestry, whereas the rest of the Malay Peninsula was controlled by the Malays), seceded from the Federation of Malaysia and became an independent state.

Of the other small British colonies in the Far East only Hong Kong remains, by permission of the Chinese government, which finds it useful for numerous purposes, not least as a listening post in the Western world. It is still extremely prosperous, even though it is indefensible.

Africa. In the late 1950's Africa began to move rapidly toward independence. In the 1940's little progress was made, but beginning with the Gold Coast (Ghana) in 1957, there was a continuous procession of new states, few with viable economies and almost all still linked closely with the mother country in economic matters. None of the countries had more than a small minority of educated persons at the time of independence. But the force of nationalist ideology was so strong and the Africans made life so difficult for their masters that it was considered better to grant independence than to delay it so long that all good will would be lost.

The largest and richest colony, the Belgian Congo, indeed was so little prepared for independence that it was not until 1965, after almost five years of chronic instability—marked by an army mutiny and United Nations intervention on a grand scale, as well as by the secession of its richest province, Katanga—that its first constitution since independence was written and accepted. The country was ruled by a central government, whose prime minister was the Katangan leader Moise Tshombe. In 1965, following a widespread rebellion, Tshombe was deposed by President Kasavuvu. Soon afterward Kasavuvu was ousted by General Joseph Mobutu, who suspended the constitution.

Only in the countries where there were substantial bodies of European settlers was there a prolonged struggle for independence. In these countries the Europeans, accustomed either to ruling the country (as in Southern Rhodesia) or having it ruled by the metropolitan power as in Kenya), were extremely reluctant to hand over power to their former servants, whom they were used to regard as little better than savages. Nevertheless, all the British colonies except Southern Rhodesia (now called simply Rhodesia, in view of the independence of the former Northern Rhodesia under the new name of Zambia) achieved their independence. Rhodesia's white minority, determined to maintain power, in November, 1965, unilaterally declared the country's independence rather than hand over any more power to the Africans. The British, joined by most of the United Nations, thereupon inaugurated economic sanctions against the rebels. Portugal has been faced with rebellions in both her African "overseas provinces," Angola and Mozambique, the former's still not entirely suppressed and the latter's as yet in its early stages. She has instituted some reforms but has shown no signs of willingness to concede political power to her Africans. The former Union of South Africa, since 1961, the Republic of South Africa, left the Commonwealth rather than modify her policy of *apartheid* (separateness of the races). She has set aside for "Bantustans" a very small part of the country where the Africans can live on their own reservations under elected governments of their own choice. One such reservation, the Transkei, has already come into existence. But the white South Africans are determined to keep the rest of the country completely under their own control and to maintain the subjection of the Africans by the most severe laws in operation in any civilized country. From time to time the United Nations has given consideration to the condition of the

Africans in South Africa and in its dependent territory, the former German South West Africa (still a League of Nations mandate, since South Africa has refused to convert it into a United Nations trust territory). However, no plan for imposing sanctions on the country has yet been accepted by the major Western powers. They continue to trade profitably with the Republic, which in turn is enjoying the greatest era of prosperity in its history.

THE UNITED NATIONS

Organization—Security Council and General Assembly. Lastly, mention should be made of the organization upon whose shoulders rests much of the responsibility for settling the inevitable disputes in a world made up now of more than one hundred, at least nominally, sovereign states, each attempting to administer a national economy and each entitled as a nation to run its own foreign policy. Scarcely a dozen of these nations wield any real power in the world, but each has a vote in the United Nations General Assembly and in all its committees.

When the founding nations met at San Francisco in 1945 to organize an international body to replace the defunct League of Nations, it was at once clear that the major powers were not prepared to abate any of their national sovereignty; nor were they ready to allow other nations with less power to have any say in the determining of their national policies. As always, these continued to be decided on the basis of national interests. To give effect to this determination on the part of the major powers, all questions concerning international security were to be decided only by the Security Council, on which five powers, United States, the Soviet Union, Britain, France, and China, were to have permanent seats. For action to be taken by the Security Council, all the permanent members had to be in agreement and none vote against the proposal. This meant in effect that the permanent members had a veto on all actions taken by the Security Council—and it was intended at that time that the General Assembly, in which all members were equal and there was no veto, should be entitled only to discuss matters brought to it by the Security Council, as well as other subjects not involving international security. Substantive resolutions required a two-thirds vote in the General Assembly.

The Soviet Union for many years found, as might have been expected, that she was constantly in disagreement with her fellow permanent members; and she cast numerous vetoes. It therefore began to seem to the Western powers that the Security Council would become incapable of taking any effective action for want of agreement between the two hostile blocs. At the initiative of United States Secretary of State Dean Acheson, the General Assembly then passed by far more than the necessary majority a resolution known as the Uniting for Peace Resolution, according to which, if the Security Council did not take action, the General Assembly might recommend action—though of course it did not have the power to put it into effect without the Security Council. The result of this resolution, which has been used on several occasions, has indeed been to bypass the veto and to increase the power and influence of the General Assembly, and especially of those small powers whose votes are always necessary to make up a two-thirds majority. Thus the curious and anomalous situation now prevails that a great deal of attention is necessarily paid to the views of those powers which have least actual responsibility and ability to maintain the peace; and much energy is spent in trying to line up majorities for the different resolutions favored by the Great Powers (but seldom introduced by them). Nevertheless, out of this fluid and developing situation in the United Nations it is a fact that world opinion has found a means of expressing itself—even though doubts must still be harbored as to whether their opinion necessarily reflects the greatest collective wisdom available to the world.

Successes and Failures. The achievements of the United Nations in its sixteen years of existence are far from negligible. It sponsored the new state of Israel, and it brought an uneasy armistice to the Arab-Israeli war that followed. It still polices the armistice since no final peace has been agreed upon, and the Arab states refuse to recognize the existence of Israel. It cast its halo over the Korean War, which was at the time regarded as a test of United Nations determination to resist aggression. Its influence was probably crucial in 1956 when Israel, France, and Britain invaded Egypt and found the United States and the Soviet Union for once united against them in the United Nations. At all events they retired without victory, and the United Nations again policed the armistice. In 1960 the United Nations was appealed to by the newly independent government of the Congo to expel the Belgians who had returned to the country to protect their nationals, threatened by a mutiny of the

Congolese army—and no doubt also to see that their heavy investment in the country was not altogether lost in the ensuing anarchy.
The Security Council was able to exercise enough pressure upon
Belgium, a small power, to compel their evacuation. But the mandate given to Dag Hammarskjöld, the secretary-general (later
killed in an airplane accident while on a peace mission in Africa),
was probably too great for any man to fulfill with the resources at
his disposal. Moreover opinion was so seriously divided in the
Security Council, and in the General Assembly was so overwhelmingly anticolonial, that any sanctions taken by the secretary general
were certain to be misinterpreted by one side or the other. Secretary U Thant, who succeeded Hammarskjöld, took even more
forceful action to reunite the country, from which (as already noted)
the province of Katanga had seceded. The United Nations troops,
with logistical aid from the United States, invaded the province,
and Moise Tshombe, its leader, went into exile (whence he eventually returned to become premier of the united country). The Soviet
Union and France objected to the use of United Nations forces for
this purpose, and have to this day refused to pay for the operations.

On the other hand, the United Nations was unable to achieve any
results when the Russians proceeded to stamp out a rebellion against
the Hungarian government in 1956, even though Hungary was
nominally an independent state. It has been unable to persuade or
coerce the Union of South Africa to hand over her mandated territory of South West Africa to the trusteeship of the United Nations,
as did all the other powers who held the League of Nations man-
dates. It was not able to take any action in either Algeria or Portuguese Africa, which were regarded by their rulers as part of the
metropolitan territory and not as colonies; it could take no action
in Cyprus when the Cypriotes engaged in a terrorist rebellion against
the British. It has not been demonstrated that any United Nations
trust territories achieved their independence any earlier than they
would have done had they been ordinary colonies—though it is
possible that United Nations pressure did aid in the general independence movement in Africa.

There are areas outside the arena of international politics where
the United Nations, like the League of Nations before it, has achieved
excellent results. The various specialized agencies have done much
to aid in the improvement of world health and sanitation, the care

of children, and similar social services; it has also organized much technical aid to the underdeveloped countries. These successes are beyond dispute, and they have undoubtedly helped to encourage international co-operation in limited spheres where politics and the cold war do not intrude.

Summary: The Value of the United Nations. In summary, therefore, it may be said that the United Nations has justified itself as an organization where men and women from all nations can get together and express their opinions and the policies of their governments and can learn those of others. If its real power remains that of the major cold war opponents, and all the rest is illusion, it is also true that at the present time when the power of the two opposing blocs is so evenly balanced, and each is hesitant to use force openly, world opinion as expressed in the United Nations has probably had some deterrent effect on nations that might otherwise have used force. But it remains true that when a major nation believes that its vital, as distinct from its peripheral, interest is involved—as the Russians in Hungary in 1956 and the United States in Cuba in 1961 and in Vietnam and the Dominican Republic in 1965—it will adopt its own policies as it sees fit, without giving more than passing consideration to the opinions of the lesser countries represented in the United Nations. The United Nations also has had no discernible influence on the arms race between the major powers.

But if the United Nations did not exist, the world would be deprived of its forum for discussion of differences. It is the only true supranational organization, and as such it remains the depository of the world's hopes for a saner future in which there will be a truly peaceful coexistence among nations. The world of 1966 is not a world of peace and it is far from a sane world. What we have now is a heavily armed truce, during which each side probes constantly into the weaknesses of the other, attempting to exploit each advantage of its own and each weakness of its opponents. Over all these efforts looms the danger of a thermonuclear war, which no one desires but which neither side refrains from threatening, and which all know may yet explode, whatever the United Nations may do or not do. Thus, if there is an air of unreality over its deliberations, this is not its fault, but the fault of its major component nations, and in some instances of its minor nations who try to exploit the situation for their own apparent immediate gain. The world has never been more dangerously poised on the brink of disaster in all its history than it is in this year of 1966. If the United Nations with all its imperfections can help in relieving its tensions, it will have been worth every cent that it cost; without it the future would unquestionably appear even more bleak than it does.

CHAPTER XXIV

CONCLUSION—THE WORLD IN THE 1960'S

In the last chapter the political picture of the world as it appears in 1966 was presented in a summary. In this brief concluding chapter the world in the 1960's is discussed more from the point of view of the realities which underlie the political divisions and will survive them as problems to be solved even if universal peace and disarmament were to be accepted by every nation capable of making war. In this area the promise is so great that it is often impossible for thinking men to restrain their impatience at the backwardness of the world's political and social structures which so patently hinder its fulfillment, even though they too may be unable to agree on the particular kind of political and social changes which are desirable. The promise is held out by the still continuing Industrial Revolution, already discussed in Chapter XVIII, and by the scientific advances of the last two centuries, to which we have not yet devoted our attention. Obviously not all of these can be recorded here. What will be attempted is only a summary of the kind of achievement and research that has been carried out and is still in progress, together with the hope that it holds for the future of the planet.

THE PROMISE OF SCIENCE

The nineteenth century saw a spectacular advance in chemistry, dating from the crucial late eighteenth-century experiments of Lavoisier, who was the first to isolate oxygen. During the following centuries the chemical structure of all known compounds was investigated and the periodic table of elements compiled. In the nineteenth and twentieth centuries the atomic structure of matter was verified and a general picture of the subatomic particles obtained, which is still in the process of being filled in by physicists. Above all, a method of scientific investigation was formulated which is far more rigorous than anything that was imagined by Newton, though it was he and Galileo who first introduced it to the Western world. The scientist now knows how he must proceed, the type of mathematics to be used in each kind of investigation; and his fellow scientists in all parts of the world understand his procedures. None of the discoveries has been confined to one nation. Even though some nations have tried to keep part of their knowledge secret, especially if it is deemed to have possible military application, the fact is that scientific knowledge is so widely dispersed and so easily available to those capable of understanding it that, with the proper training and facilities, scientists of all nations are capable of quickly repeating the experiments made by other nationals and coming to the same conclusions. A scientific world fraternity has therefore come into being, whose members are united with one another more closely in their knowledge and interests than with nonscientists, even of their own nation. This is *objective* and *verifiable* knowledge open to all men and transcending all the particularisms of nationality.

Since this science and the engineering based upon it have shown such spectacular practical results in the creation of new products and, in general, in making the utmost use of the materials provided by nature, all those men and women who have come within the orbit of that Western civilization that gave birth to this science wish to share in the plenty this has made possible. There is no scientific or technical reason why they should not so share. What stands in the way is the political and social structure of the world.

The problem of disease is as old as history. Western man in the nineteenth and twentieth centuries has for the first time learned to control some of these diseases. Biological science has contributed much to human knowledge of the mechanism of disease, the greatest pioneer being Louis Pasteur, the nineteenth-century French chemist, who was the first to formulate clearly the bacterial origin of many communicable diseases and to verify his hypotheses by controlled experimentation. Once the mechanism for the transmission of the disease was understood, the next step was to attack it at the source. Thus the anopheles mosquito (malaria), the tsetse fly (sleeping sickness), the flea (bubonic plague), and other insects and microscopic organisms were attacked in their own habitats, and gradually the diseases carried by them have been brought under control. With the aid of the vaccination process, which consists in essence in giving the human being a slight touch of the disease, thereby bringing the protective mechanisms in his body into play, certain other diseases due to viruses have likewise become preventable. Moreover, the pharmaceutical industry has engaged in constant research to produce better drugs capable of slowing down the multiplication and action of bacteria to enable the human organism to survive until its own vitality is able to bring about recovery. The result has been a great increase of life expectancy, especially in the Western nations, where hospitals, doctors, and public sanitation have been available.

This increase, however, has not been confined to the richer Western nations. The knowledge has been spread abroad to every land in the world, in part through the agency of the United Nations, and in almost all there has been a call for medical missionaries from the West. Since many of the more serious epidemics were especially virulent in tropical countries, where conditions favored them, Western medicine has had often spectacular results in the lowering of infant and maternal mortality and in the prevention of communicable diseases. Though the surface has only been scratched, and the possibilities are almost infinite, it is enough to say here that modern medicine holds out very great promise for the betterment of mankind, as does also the related science of nutrition, which has made the world conscious of the importance of eating the right kind of foods for the maintenance of health.

It is nevertheless clear that the advance of medicine is bound to produce an immense number of social problems. In a poor nation which lacks technical knowledge and is perhaps short of actual physical resources, the increase of population resulting from the use of Western medicine cannot be regarded with equanimity. How are all the new mouths to be fed and the new hands provided with work? How can a new nation transform its ancient social structure based on subsistence agriculture and a high death rate? If epidemics do not kill off the population, how are the survivors to be cared for? Even in the West the problem is still awaiting solution. The great increase in the number of aged, and the preference in Western countries for employing only the youthful and able-bodied, have made it difficult for these older men and women to find a way of spending their declining years in dignity and reasonable comfort.

Science moves inexorably forward. Scientists do not know the solutions to the problems they raise; they merely work, and the result of their work is cast adrift in the world, for the world to use or misuse as best it can. Its march cannot be hindered; there can be no moratorium on discovery and invention. But nevertheless it poses a challenge to Western civilization and to the world which has been influenced by it; and this challenge must someday be met by what Arnold Toynbee has called a "creative response." The promise is there, and it is for the human beings in the world to decide if it is to be fulfilled or not.

THE HAVES AND THE HAVE NOTS

The Western world, led by the United States, and the Eastern bloc, led by the Soviet Union, each has its set of answers, neither of them certainly the last word to be said on the subject. In between are the so-called uncommitted nations, determinedly neutral and unwilling to accept dictation from either party in the global struggle, but willing to take whatever seems useful that is offered by either. These nations may be generally characterized as "have-nots," those in most need of assistance of all kinds from all quarters. There is also another class of have-not nations which have attached themselves to one or the other of the two alliances, no doubt in most cases because they believe they can obtain more from their "side" by committing themselves than by remaining neutral, and sometimes because they have no alternative. The leaders of both alliances are engaged in a war of propaganda; both attempt in their own ways to hawk their ideological wares to peoples usually utterly uninterested in such commodities. Each side is firmly committed to the notion that its "way of life" is superior to that of the other, but neither is prepared to allow the issue to be decided solely by free choice, uninfluenced by the major powers. On the contrary, it regards the entry of any uncommitted nation into the camp of the other as little short of a national disaster and does everything it can to prevent it. Each engages in competition for prestige and approval, with the prize the allegiance, as it hopes, of one or another of the neutrals. The United States and the Soviet Union are currently engaged in a "race" to the moon, a project which is enormously expensive and of no discernible economic value except insofar as profits accrue to the industries involved—though conceivably some military advantages may incidentally be derived from the venture. Of course, for prestige and cold war purposes it must be a race, and not a co-operative human enterprise. It cannot be carried out slowly over a few decades lest one side steal a march on the other and get there first.

WESTERN CIVILIZATION—A BALANCE SHEET

The Western world has produced the most materially successful of all civilizations in world history. From its very inception it has held before itself wider horizons than any other; its dynamism has been unquestionable, its thirst for expansion insatiable. It has, quite possibly, in the process brought more misery to more human beings in the course of its career than any other; but at the same time it has almost put an end to human slavery in its own realms, and it has impressed upon its own conscience the indignity involved in the subjection of one human being by another. It has exalted human dignity by coming to the conclusion that all human beings as individuals have certain rights of which no government may deprive them, and by devising forms of government under which individual citizens may play their part in their own governing. Lastly, it has made possible the abolition of human poverty in the widest sense of that word.

It is an impressive achievement, but its promise remains far less than half fulfilled. If Western civilization is to be the last of the separate civilizations that history is to know, if the fruits of that civilization are to become the permanent heritage of mankind, so that hereafter there will be one world civilization and numerous ethnic and national cultures, each contributing to the whole, then it is indeed time for Western man to take stock of the world he has made thus far—and see how far short it falls yet of what it may and could become, and begin to train his imagination and frame his ambitions accordingly.

KEY DATES IN WESTERN HISTORY

B.C.

THE PREHISTORIC AGE

ca. 500,000	Java Man and Peking Man
ca. 150,000	Neanderthal Man
ca. 50,000	*Homo sapiens* (Cro-Magnon Man, etc.)
ca. 8000–5500	Mesolithic Age
ca. 5500	**Neolithic Revolution in Near East**

THE ANCIENT NEAR EAST

ca. 3000–2200	Old Kingdom of Egypt
ca 3000	Bronze Age in Sumer and Crete
ca. 2000–1792	Middle Kingdom of Egypt
ca. 1800	Hammurabi Code
ca. 1800	Hyksos invasions of Egypt
ca. 1580	Reconquest of Egypt by Theban princes
1468	Conquests of Thutmose III
ca. 1377–1360	Religious Revolution of Akhenaton
1296	Battle of Kadesh between Hittites and Egyptians
ca. 1260	Exodus of Hebrews from Egypt (?)
ca. 1004–965	Reign of King David in Israel
910–606	**Assyrian Empire**
760–700	Greek colonization of Sicily and southern Italy
753	Traditional date of founding of Rome
721	Fall of Samaria to Assyrians

THE GREEK AND ROMAN REPUBLICS

621	Constitution of Draco in Athens
606–509	Etruscan rule in Rome
594	Reforms of Solon in Athens
586	Fall of Jerusalem to Nebuchadnezzar
549	Cyrus becomes king of Persia
538	Return of Jews to Jerusalem
509	**Beginning of Roman Republic**
508	**Constitution of Cleisthenes in Athens**
494	First secession of plebs in Rome
490–479	Persian invasions of Greece

401

457–429	Ascendancy of Pericles in Athens
449	Twelve Tables in Rome
431–404	**Peloponnesian War**
338	Victory of Philip of Macedon at Chaeronea
336–323	Reign of Alexander the Great
327–290	Samnite Wars in Italy
301	Final division of Alexander's kingdom
281–272	Roman Wars with Pyrrhus
264–241	First Punic War
218–201	**Second Punic War**
167	Revolt of Maccabees against Antiochus IV of Syria
146	Macedonia becomes Roman province
66–62	Conquest and reorganization of Asia by Pompey
60	First Triumvirate
58–51	Conquest of Gaul by Caesar
44	Murder of Caesar
43	Second Triumvirate
31	**Battle of Actium—beginning of reign of Augustus**

A.D.

THE ROMAN EMPIRE

14	Death of Augustus
33 (30?)	**Crucifixion of Jesus Christ**
69–96	Vespasian and the Flavian dynasty
96–180	The "Good Emperors"
235–284	"Barrack" emperors
284–305	Reign of Diocletian
312	Constantine becomes emperor of West
313	**Edict of Milan**
325	Council of Nicaea
330	Foundation of Constantinople
340–348	Conversion of Goths to Arian Christianity
ca. 400	Honorius removes Roman capital to Ravenna
451	Battle of Chalons—partial defeat of Attila the Hun
476	**Odoacer deposes last Roman emperor—"Fall of Rome"**

THE EARLY MIDDLE AGES

| 481 | Clovis founds Merovingian kingdom |
| 535–554 | Reconquest of Italy by Justinian |

590–604	Pontificate of Gregory I, the Great
622	**Flight of Mahomet from Mecca (Hegira)**
622–630	Persian Wars of Heraclius
635–715	Era of Muslim conquests
664	Synod of Whitby
726	Beginning of Iconoclastic Controversy
732	**Battle of Tours—victory of Charles Martel over Muslims**
756	Donation of Pepin
768–814	Reign of Charlemagne
843	**Treaty of Verdun**
871–900	Alfred the Great of England
962	**Restoration of Empire under Otto I**
987	Foundation of French monarchy (Hugh Capet)
1018	Bulgaria incorporated into Byzantine Empire
1066	Norman Conquest of England
1077	**Henry IV does penance at Canossa**
1095	First Crusade proclaimed
1122	**Concordat of Worms**
1183	Treaty of Constance between Frederick Barbarossa and Lombard League
1189–1192	Third Crusade

THE LATER MIDDLE AGES

1198–1216	Pontificate of Innocent III
1204	Latin conquest of Constantinople (Fourth Crusade)
1215	**Magna Carta**
1220–1250	Reign of Frederick II
1236	Capture of Cordova by Christians
1268	Execution of last Hohenstaufen
1273	Rudolf of Hapsburg becomes Holy Roman Emperor
1295	Model Parliament of Edward I
1302	Summoning of States-General by Philip IV
1305–1376	**"Babylonian Captivity" of the papacy**
1337–1453	Hundred Years' War
1378–1417	Great Schism
1414–1418	Council of Constance
1453	**Fall of Constantinople to Turks**
1455–1485	Wars of the Roses
1469	Union of crowns of Aragon and Castile
1492	**Discovery of America by Columbus**

THE EARLY MODERN EPOCH

1497–1499	Voyage of Vasco da Gama to India
1517	**Ninety-five Theses of Martin Luther**
1519–1521	Conquest of Mexico by Cortes
1519–1522	First circumnavigation of world by **Magellan and** crew
1545–1563	**Council of Trent**
1555	Religious Peace of Augsburg
1581	Independence of Dutch Republic
1598	Edict of Nantes
1613	Beginning of Romanov dynasty in Russia
1618–1648	**Thirty Years' War**
1648	Peace of Westphalia
1649	Execution of Charles I of England
1683	Last siege of Vienna by Turks
1688–1689	**Glorious Revolution in England**
1689–1725	Reign of Peter the Great
1700–1721	Great Northern War
1701–1714	War of the Spanish Succession
1713	**Peace of Utrecht**
1740–1748	War of Austrian Succession
1756–1763	Seven Years' War
1772	First Partition of Poland
1775–1783	**American War of Independence**
1787	**American Constitution**

FROM THE FRENCH REVOLUTION TO THE FIRST WORLD WAR

1789	**Beginning of French Revolution**
1794	Fall of Robespierre
1804	Napoleon becomes emperor of French
1814–1815	**Congress of Vienna**
1830	July Revolution in France (revolutions in Belgium and Poland)
1832	First Reform Bill in England
1839–1840	First Opium War in China
1846–1848	United States-Mexican War
1848	**Year of Revolutions**
1853–1854	Visit of Commodore Perry to Japan
1859	Franco-Italian War with Austria
1861–1865	**United States Civil War**
1861	Emancipation of Russian serfs
1866	Austro-Prussian War

1867	British North America Act (Dominion of Canada)
1869	Opening of Suez Canal
1870–1871	**Franco-Prussian War**
1870	Unification of Italy
1871	Unification of Germany
1875	Beginning of French Third Republic
1882	British occupation of Egypt
1899–1902	Boer War
1904	Entente Cordiale between Britain and France
1904–1905	Russo-Japanese War
1908	Austrian annexation of Bosnia and Herzegovina
1914 (June)	**Murder of Archduke Francis Ferdinand**
1914 (July-August)	**Beginning of the First World War**

THE FIRST WORLD WAR AND THE LONG ARMISTICE

1917 (April)	United States declaration of War with Germany
1917 (November)	**Bolshevik Revolution in Russia**
1918 (March)	Treaty of Brest-Litovsk
1918 (November)	Armistice between Allies and Central Powers
1919 (June)	**Treaty of Versailles**
1920 (January)	Beginning of League of Nations
1920 (March)	Final rejection of Versailles treaty by United States Senate
1921–1927	New Economic Policy in Russia
1922 (October)	**Mussolini's "March on Rome"**
1923 (January)	Franco-Belgian invasion of Ruhr
1923 (November)	Hitler "Beer-Hall Putsch"
1925	Treaties of Locarno
1928	First Five Year Plan in Russia
1929	Stock-market crash in United States
1930–1935	**Great Depression**
1931	Statute of Westminster (complete independence of British dominions)
1931 (September)	Japanese invasion of Manchuria
1933 (January)	**Hitler becomes chancellor of Germany**
1933 (January)	Franklin Roosevelt becomes United States President
1935 (October)	Italian invasion of Ethiopia
1936 (July)	Beginning of Spanish Civil War
1936 (October)	Rome-Berlin Axis
1938 (March)	German Annexation of Austria
1938 (September)	Pact of Munich

| 1939 (March) | German occupation of Czechoslovakia |
| 1939 (August) | **Nonaggression agreement between Russia and Germany** |

THE SECOND WORLD WAR AND ITS AFTERMATH

1939 (September)	German invasion of Poland
1939 (November)– 1940 (March)	Russo-Finnish War
1940 (April)	German invasion of Norway
1940 (May)	German invasion of Holland and Belgium
1940 (June)	German occupation of Paris
1941 (June)	German invasion of Russia
1941 (December)	Japanese attack on Pearl Harbor
1942 (August)	Beginning of siege of Stalingrad by Germans
1942 (November)	Landing of United States forces in North Africa
1943 (September)	Surrender of Italy
1944 (June)	**Allied invasion of Normandy**
1944 (July)	Expulsion of Germans from Russia
1944 (August)	Liberation of Paris
1944 (October)	Decisive naval victory by United States over Japan
1945 (February)	Conference of Yalta
1945 (May)	**Unconditional surrender of Germany**
1945 (August 6)	**Atomic bomb dropped on Hiroshima**
1945 (August 14)	**Unconditional surrender of Japan**
1945 (October)	Establishment of United Nations
1947 (March)	Announcement of Truman Doctrine
1947 (June)	Announcement of Marshall Plan
1948 (February)	Communist coup in Czechoslovakia
1949 (April)	**Signing of North Atlantic Treaty (NATO)**
1949 (May)	Proclamation of basic law for Federal Republic of Germany
1949 (October)	Proclamation of People's Republic of China
1950 (June)	**Beginning of Korean War**
1950 (November)	Uniting for Peace Resolution passed by United Nations General Assembly
1953 (March)	Death of Stalin
1954 (October)	Signing of Western European Union treaty
1956 (October)	Invasion of Sinai peninsula by Israelis
1956 (November)	Hungarian revolt crushed by Russians
1957 (October)	Launching of "Sputnik" by Russians
1958 (January)	Beginning of European Common Market

1958 (May)	French army coup in Algeria—government of de Gaulle
1958 (September)	Referendum on French constitution–formation of French Community
1959 (January)	Castro takes over Cuban government
1960 (June)	Independence of Belgian Congo
1960 (July)	United States institutes economic sanctions against Cuba
1960 (July)	Security Council authorizes United Nations force in Congo
1960 (November)	**Election of John F. Kennedy as United States president**
1961 (April)	Abortive invasion of Cuba by Cuban exiles
1961 (August)	Erection of wall between East and West Berlin
1961 (August)	Resumption of nuclear testing by Soviet Union
1962 (January)	Expulsion of Cuba from Organization of American States
1962 (July)	Independence of Algeria
1962 (September)	Netherlands abandons control of West Irian (Netherlands New Guinea)
1962 (October)	Confrontation of United States and Soviet Union over missiles in Cuba
1962 (Oct.-Nov.)	Frontier war in Himalayas between India and China
1962 (November)	Victory of de Gaulle party in French parliamentary elections
1963 (January)	French veto of Britain's entry into European Common Market
1963 (April)	Formation of coalition government in Congo, marking formal end to secession of Katanga
1963 (April)	Encyclical *Pacem in Terris* issued by Pope John XXIII
1963 (August)	**Limited test-ban treaty signed**
1963 (October)	Adenauer retires from chancellorship of West Germany
1963 (November)	**Assassination of John F. Kennedy; succession of Lyndon B. Johnson as United States president**
1964 (October)	First explosion of atomic weapon by Communist China
1964 (October)	Fall of Khrushchev from power in the Soviet Union

1964 (November)   Election of President Johnson by decisive majority for a full four-year term
1965 (February)   United States begins bombing of North Vietnam
1965 (April)   Intervention of United States in Dominican Republic
1965 (August)   Secession of Singapore from Malaysia
1966 (February)   De Gaulle announces intention of withdrawing French troops from NATO command
1966 (December)   Coalition government of Christian and Social Democrats in West Germany; Kurt Kiesinger, chancellor
1967 (June)   Arab-Israeli war

INDEX